THE DEMATERIALISATION OF KARL MARX

Foundations of Modern Literary Theory

The Dematerialisation of Karl Marx

Literature and Marxist Theory

Leonard Jackson

Longman
London and New York

Longman Group UK Limited,
Longman House, Burnt Mill,
Harlow, Essex CM20 2JE, England
and Associated Companies throughout the world.

Published in the United States of America
by Longman Publishing, New York

First published 1994

ISBN 0 582 066549 CSD
ISBN 0 582 066557 PPR

British Library Cataloguing-in-Publication Data

A catalogue record for this book is
available from the British Library

Library of Congress Cataloging-in-Publication Data
Jackson, Leonard, 1934–
    The dematerialisation of Karl Marx: literature and Marxist theory/Leonard
Jackson.
        p. cm. --(Foundations of modern literary theory)
    Includes bibliographical references and index.
    ISBN 0-582-06654-9. --ISBN 0-582-06655-7 (pbk.)
    1. Marxist criticism. I. Title. II. Series.
PN98.C6J27 1994
801'.95--dc20   93-39201
                                                               CIP

Set by 7 in Bembo
Produced by Longman Singapore Publishers (Pte) Ltd.
Printed in Singapore

Contents

Acknowledgements

I am immensely grateful to Ian Birchall for reading an earlier version of this book; his incisive comments and his deep knowledge of the whole Marxist tradition helped me to rethink and reshape the book, though I am sure that he will disagree with my final position as much as he always has with every intermediate one. I feel in fact that I am a lifelong pupil of his, though one who has never quite managed to graduate into being a Marxist. I am also grateful to Irving Dworetzsky for commenting on some sections, and to my students on OM25, OM325, EL381, and EL385-6, etc. As always, my main debt is to my wife and colleague, Eleanor Jackson. The defects of the book I put in all by myself.

The Publishers are grateful to Routledge for permission to reproduce an extract from 'The Contemporary Relevance of Hegel' from *Language, Mind and Value* by J.N. Findlay (Allen & Unwin, 1963).

To

LJ   IMJ

EJ

Introduction
A Defence of Economic
Materialism

This book is a hostile account of the politics of modern literary theory, which I regard as revolutionary fantasy. But it is also a defence, by a non-Marxist, of one of the main principles of Marxism. I argue that literary theorists and critics, influenced by their own marginal position in the economy, have abandoned the one element of Marxism which has explanatory value: the principle that human culture and cultural history are mainly determined by their economic basis. Marxist economics is false; Marxist regimes were disgusting; but economic materialism is true. But by one road or another – either direct regression to Hegel or, more recently, by doomed attempts to unite Marxism with post-structuralism – critics have returned Marxist theory to the modern equivalent of a Hegelian or left-Hegelian problematic: to speculations about the relationship between society and subjectivity, and about the possibilities of putting an end to class, race, or gender oppression by operating at the level of ideological representations. Meanwhile it has been left to Conservative politicians to exercise power by operating on the economy first,[1] and getting round to the curriculum a decade or more later. Marxists, and others on the radical left, have lost the class war by turning into idealists; Conservatives have won it by operating on strict materialist principles.

Literary theory has been the intellectually dominant and creative form of discourse about literature in Britain from the 1970s to the present, replacing literary criticism in that role. It is not very satisfactory as theory: not, at least, if you think of it in comparison with theories in physics or genetics or generative linguistics. It doesn't, that is, explain anything or have any useful technical applications. But nobody can doubt that it is intensely political, and politically radical. It has consistently proclaimed its own political status; many theorists have supported the essentially totalitarian position that every discourse is political, either in what it says or what it suppresses; there is no neutral space for aesthetic or ethical questions. Moreover, theory aims at revolutionary changes both in consciousness and in society. In this context the most unlikely figures – a text-analysing anti-metaphysician like Jacques Derrida, an authoritarian psychoanalyst like Jacques Lacan, or an idealist Nietzschean historian of ideas like Michel Foucault – have had credentials as revolutionaries; and plenty of people in the world's English departments are still beavering away at the necessary tasks of destroying theoretical humanism and undermining Western rationality, without quite realising the absurdity of the enterprise.

The place of Marxism in this intellectual milieu is a peculiar one. The dominance of radical literary theory has coincided, roughly, with the decline of the last phase of Western Marxism.[2] Western Marxism is itself a rather special form of Marxism, specially attractive to what Mannheim called 'marginal intellectuals' – like literary critics and philosophers – and characterised by a weakening of the central Marxist principle of economic determination, and a return to Hegel.[3] You cannot really understand how an economic theory like Marxism can have given rise to so much work on subjectivity, consciousness, art and culture unless you go back to its intellectual origins in the idealist tradition of philosophy, and in particular in Kant and Hegel, where these issues are properly worked out.

In this book, I have given two chapters to the roots of idealism, and the dialectic of Hegel, and am conscious of them not being enough. Kant and Hegel lived on inside Marxism, and were constantly being called on to supplement its deficiencies, until Marxism itself died. They also set out philosophical issues which later non-Marxist theorists, like most of the post-structuralists, are still reworking. Indeed there is a sense – set out, before post-structuralism was invented, by that great Hegelian, Findlay – in which Hegel *was* a post-structuralist. So also, on the account given by Marx and Engels, were the left-wing Hegelians whom Marx and Engels repudiated. I mean that there are real and important analogies between post-structuralism and these earlier idealist positions (also held by marginal intellectuals), and that any attempt to reconcile Marxist and post-structuralist themes was bound to recreate either a Hegelian or a left-Hegelian problematic in disguise.

The mature Marx was neither a Hegelian nor a post-structuralist. He was a realist and materialist, who had consciously rejected philosophy for science. He was fully conscious of the difficulties of carrying out the determinist programme of nineteenth-century science in the social realm, which is why he retained a materialist version of the Hegelian dialectic. In the twentieth century there are other ways of avoiding these difficulties: modern science, which includes quantum mechanics and chaos theory, takes a less deterministic view of prediction, and the social sciences need to be rethought to take account of this. What Marx never did was to adopt the more or less consciously anti-scientific view of many 'Western

Marxists' – which I find in Lukács, in Gramsci, in Bakhtin, and in many other favourites of modern theorists.

The beginning of what might be called the 'theory period' of modern British literary discourse showed a great flowering of rather scholastic Marxist theory, nominally scientific and anti-Hegelian, and under the sign of the French philosopher Althusser; however, it still contained squidgy dollops of Hegelianism channelled into it through the work of Lacan; and it was the Lacanian element, the theory of the construction of the human subject in ideology, which prospered. In the 1980s, this version of 'scientific Marxism' rapidly collapsed, though Lacan remained. Althusser was succeeded in active influence on the left by anti-Marxists like Foucault. Many radical positions remained, which had some connections with Marxism. It is very hard to hold any left-wing position which does not have **some** resonance with some part of the Marxist tradition. But the central intellectual interest of Marxism – which is the interest in political economy, in the influence of the forces and relations of production on the development of society as a whole – largely disappeared from literary theory. So also did the interest in literary history, which is rarely nowadays presented as an interesting theoretical problem. Classical Marxism, with its theory of epochal social transformation, makes even Aeschylus and Milton relevant to present-day politics. Post-Marxist cultural studies often finds difficulty in seeing the political relevance of any writings earlier than the nineteenth century,[4] and sometimes in any writings earlier than the present moment.

In defiance of this consensus I want to assert that there is one principle at the heart of classical Marxism which is clearly true; which has great explanatory value in cultural theory and in cultural history; and which should be retained, even if all the rest of Marxist theory is abandoned. It is the founding principle of historical materialism: that the political, legal and other structures of society, and its ideology (metaphorically making up the superstructure of society) are partially determined by the forces and relations of production (metaphorically, the base of society). If the relations of production (for example, private property rights or, as recently in Eastern Europe and the Soviet Union, control by the Communist Party) come into conflict with, and begin to restrict the forces of production (e.g. make it impossible to produce goods or food), the former will be more or less rapidly transformed. This transformation will be followed by a more or less rapid transformation of the superstructure. Whatever has happened to the credibility of the rest of Marxism, this principle at least has not been put in question by the recent revolutions in the old Soviet Union and the Eastern bloc; on the contrary, this principle explains those revolutions.

The advantage of a principle of this kind to literary and cultural analysis is its explanatory value. Literary and cultural phenomena may be partially explained in terms of the underlying economic realities which help to cause them. Cultural change can be partially explained in terms of underlying economic change. The whole cultural history of mankind can be partially explained in terms of underlying economic developments. Nobody, of course, has ever supposed that economic factors provide a complete explanation for superstructural phenomena; still less, that the superstructure can be reduced to the economic base. This is a causal, not a reductive theory. Similarly one is not entitled to say that a poem is a force or relation of production in disguise. On the contrary, it is the formal product of a partially autonomous human activity. One is, however, entitled to say that a poem expresses some conflict among the forces and relations of production, at a particular point in history, in disguised form; and in certain circumstances that is one of the profoundest things that can be said about a poem. What Marxism shows here is how art can embody and make conscious in disguised form some of the deepest conflicts in a society: namely, the hidden economic conflicts. It is these conflicts which are the motor of historical change; therefore, the history of literature is also a window onto the economic history of mankind. Only such a history can enable us to understand the full significance of political and cultural conflicts in the present.

Some Marxist criticism is good; some is bad; but until recently pretty well all of it was based on the principle just summarised. The same principle of interpretation has also been widely applied by Marxist and non-Marxist historians. This principle, which Marvin Harris calls **cultural materialism**, has been very successfully applied in cultural anthropology as well. Many of what Harris calls the riddles of culture – why India had sacred cows; the relation between protein deficiency, war and male chauvinism in band-level societies; the conversion of sacrificial into non-sacrificial religions – can be solved by this economistic approach,[5] and contribute to a general cultural history of mankind, which is not limited to the high cultural traditions of economically advanced countries.

The fundamentally idealist nature of radical literary theory in the last thirty years is shown by the fact that it is precisely cultural materialism in this sense which has been most thoroughly rejected. The word 'materialism' has been retained; but it is used by Raymond Williams and a host of lesser figures to express the obvious and trivial facts that all cultural phenomena have material vehicles, exist in social institutions, and are the products of human practices. It did not need Marx to tell us this; and the emphasis is inconsistent with his mature work. This idealist and regressive transformation of the notion of materialism is a part of the long and zig-zag march of Western Marxism back to left-Hegelianism.

There is at present a school of literary criticism that calls itself **cultural materialist**, though it is diametrically opposed to the anthropological kind. It descends from the work of Williams, who was a culturalist to begin with, and only permitted himself to come to terms with Marxism when he had examined the Western variety carefully and found it free from economism. He did not reconcile the two: he merely rebaptised his own culturalism as cultural materialism. Its main theoretical endeavour, as its present followers will readily inform you, is 'to get away from the base-superstructure metaphor'. This is something that a real economic materialist like Marx would not want to do.

It is interesting to compare the powerful claim of the traditional economistic Marxist, that great works of literature reveal deep objective economic conflicts, which one may be able to act on, with the much weaker claim of the modern cultural materialist that substantial texts may be read as revealing ideological splits that we may be able to talk about. 'Substantial texts are in principle likely to be written across ideological faultlines because that is the most interesting kind of writing; they may well not be susceptible to any decisive reading. Their cultural power was partly in their indeterminacy – they spoke to and facilitated debate' (Alan Sinfield 1992, p. 235).

The last stage in the decay of Marxist literary theory came nearly twenty years ago, when younger theorists began to argue that Marxists should not employ the category of literature at all.[6] This is now a fairly orthodox position on the left: that the concept of a category of works supposed to have special literary merit is itself part of bourgeois ideology. It is a revolutionary act (and perhaps nowadays the only one conveniently available to the English teacher) to overthrow the literary canon and install popular fiction, however supportive of capitalism the stereotypes of this fiction may be. Certainly this is a revolution against the autarchy of F.R. Leavis, which must be of considerable importance to those who have not noticed that F.R. Leavis is dead.

But it is also a revolution against the entire tradition of Marxist aesthetics, from Marx and Engels themselves through Lukács and Gramsci, down to Goldmann and Althusser. A common assumption of this tradition is that works of literature are cognitive instruments which give insights into the contradictions of society and the trajectory of history; and that to provide such insights is a literary merit. Marx thought Balzac, a reactionary writer who uncovered the nature of capitalism, far more important than any purely propagandist socialist could be. The tendency of the recent left has been to reject the very possibility that works of literature can give such insights; such insights are the work of the critic, which may be done just as well on soap opera as on Tolstoy.

The ultimate revolution is thus the revolt of the academics against being oppressed by great writers, especially writers of the past; and in favour of studying very minor ones, especially contemporaries. As revolutions go, this has many advantages. Writers are fairly easy to attack; most of them are dead; the rest are usually very poor, and have much lower prestige than academics do. Teaching dull students how to understand major works from past civilisations can be quite difficult; one has to introduce them to history and explain obscure cultural references to Achilles or Jesus Christ; and at the end of the day the politics of traditional masterpieces is invariably wrong: they are aristocratic, sexist, racist, Christian, imperialist, or worse; and, in the absence of an epochal theory of cultural change, to teach the masterpieces appears to endorse the politics.

No modern critic, concerned for his political correctness, can afford to emulate the tolerant broad-mindedness of Karl Marx; nor needs to show Marx's historical culture, nor his interest in the literature of antiquity. The fundamental reason for this is that modern critics do not believe in the existence of underlying economic contradictions, which great literature can uncover, and which can bring about epochal changes in society. Their politics is the politics of superstructures. Their political criticism is therefore the criticism of surfaces. Some post-structuralist theory offers a very high-level rationalisation of this position: that surfaces are all; there is no deep structure. This leads to a delusion of impotence. Some post-structuralist theory argues that history is not a real process that has happened in the past, and created us, but a story constructed in the present, that we write, and can rewrite if we choose. This leads to a delusion of omnipotence.

I have myself no faith in a socialist transformation of society and think that a liberal democracy is probably the best that can be achieved; though not one in which there are more than three million unemployed, and homeless people are begging and dying on the streets of London in winter. I follow Marx in believing that there are real underlying economic structures of society, which determine the political, legal and ideological possibilities of each period; that it is in conflicts within these economic structures that the dynamic of history is to be found; that one of the things works of literature can do is to respond to those conflicts, and make us aware of them; and that the depth and importance of the underlying economic contradictions it exposes, and the epochal nature of the historical change that it indicates, has always been one of the reasons for calling a work great, though it may not always have been a conscious reason.

It is for the critic drawing on the tradition of Marxism – the modern version of which is anthropological cultural materialism – to point out the underlying economic causes of cultural phenomena; and to offer interpretations of cultural work in economic terms, rather than staying within the closed circuit of ideological representations. This function is just as important as it ever was if we are to understand and control our own future.

NOTES

1. It died.
2. Merquior 1986, *Western Marxism.*
3. Lichtheim 1971, *From Marx to Hegel.*
4. Consider the blankness shown by Eagleton in confronting Marx's views on Greek tragedy – Eagleton 1983, p. 12.
5. Harris 1975; 1978; 1980.
6. Bennett 1979.

PART ONE

The politics of literary criticism

CHAPTER ONE

Literary Criticism as Political Reaction

Scholarship, Criticism and Theory in the Twentieth Century

SUMMARY

When Marxism hit the English departments, they went theoretical; literary criticism had been so anti-theoretical, and so conservative, that political and academic radicalism seemed to go hand in hand. Yet there is nothing new or intrinsically radical about theory. All three of the main discourses of literature – **scholarship**, **criticism** and **theory** – go back to ancient Greece,[1] and have had many different political orientations in the course of history. In Britain and the United States, scholarship was displaced by literary criticism as the intellectually dominant academic discipline in English in the 1930s; it was a progressive move. In the same way literary criticism was displaced by literary theory in the 1970s. Each displacement left a furious and despairing old guard of academics, and an intolerably smug new wave.

These academic revolutions were accompanied by, and partly driven by, a politics of academic fantasy, in which literature teachers negotiated a shifting and unstable relationship of mutual rejection with the whole twentieth-century world. This politics swung with gestural extremism from the monarchism of T.S. Eliot – aligning him with the court of Charles I and Archbishop Laud – to the Maoism of the 1970s' revolutionaries – aligning them with urban guerrillas. From this arises the illusion that criticism – actually an apolitical mode of self-cultivation – is inherently reactionary, while theory is inherently new and radical.

Few, if any, critics or theorists have been vulgar enough to admit an admiration for the valuable developments of the twentieth century – modern science and technology, or bourgeois popular democracy. This is presumably because both of these tend to marginalise literary critics and theorists, and cast doubt on their usefulness. The violent and unreasonable politics of literary academics, and their extraordinary global metaphysical claims, stem from this marginality. Their politics have been self-defeating. The reactionary élitism of the later Leavisites went along with Labour victories; the triumphal left-radicalism of the theorists foreshadowed Conservative hegemony and the collapse of socialism. It is useful to ask what we can learn from this.

1   LITERARY THEORY AND SOCIAL REVOLUTION

Everybody agrees that recent literary theory has a political agenda. It aims to destroy the class system, patriarchy, imperialism and the bases of the Western metaphysics that supports all three. In the course of doing this, it will probably make the distinctive category of Literature redundant, which old-fashioned critics may regret. But as consolation for this, its methods of rhetorical and narrative analysis will be applicable to the whole of intellectual culture, or **ideology** as it is more properly called: to mathematics and science no less than popular television shows; and this will help to bring about a cultural, and in due course a political, social and economic, revolution. So runs yesterday's radicalism. In what was till a very short time ago the unwithstandable future of the intellectual left, the literary and cultural theorist was to be philosopher-king.

Actually, literary theory was more ambitious than that: it also aimed to change the nature of human subjectivity, or at least our concept of it. It aimed to establish, or at least to recognise, a 'decentred subject' which is really a set of effects of textuality. This contrasts with the unified subject of bourgeois humanism which claims to be the source of experience and values and actually, according to the left, is the principal support of individualist and capitalist ideology. It is really impossible to overstate the claims of modern literary theory; this is the most ambitious discourse since Hegel's system of philosophy was constructed.[2]

Literary theory, in the forms still most common in Britain at the time of writing, is then the most radical branch of intellectual socialism; it is perhaps the only branch which continues to grow. This may be because it is the branch furthest away from its material roots in the working classes, and it may be because it is a branch that has not yet discovered that its tree has been cut down. But literary theory in this political form has only been with us since the 1960s, and has only been the academically dominant practice since the 1980s. Many of those who practise it have hardly realised either their victory or their defeat.

Their victory is an academic one. They occupy chairs and external examinerships; they have provided the very terms in which we now discuss literature; and books labelled 'literary theory' occupy whole sections of university and left bookshops. But they often conceive themselves still to be fighting for a space for their subject, at a time when they are rulers of all academic space.

Their defeat is a global and popular one. It seems as if at the present time there is no large body of people in the entire world that feels inspired by the socialist project, though there are plenty who are inspired by nationalism or fundamentalist religions. Socialism belongs only to marginalised intellectuals, and traditional Marxism belongs nowhere. Very few literary intellectuals admit that they deserve any blame for this.

2   THE REVOLUTION IN CRITICISM OF THE 1930s

When literary criticism is considered by such doughty fighting persons as theorists, it is often seen through a furiously partisan haze. For the left, literary criticism was an inherently reactionary discourse, concerned with evaluating books from a subjective point of view, while remaining unaware of the class basis for that particular subjectivity. It set up hierarchies and canons of literature which are now among the strongest ideological supports for the most reactionary aspects of our society. As a discipline, the theoretical left now believe, literary criticism was self-uncomprehending, and often deliberately mystificatory. It had no theoretical basis, was empiricist in method and was properly superseded by literary theory. How valid are these charges?

Thirty years before the dawn of radical theory, literary criticism too had been a revolutionary discipline that had to fight for its place in the academy and was associated with the emergence of a slightly new sub-class. I.A. Richards and F.R. Leavis, in the late 1920s and 1930s, were not simply practising a well-accepted discipline in a challenging new way. They were fighting for the right of professional literary criticism to exist at all in an institutional domain ruled not by critics but by historical scholars and gentleman connoisseurs. The same battle was fought in the United States, also in the 1930s, and was the background to the emergence of the 'New Critics'. The great institutional days of literary criticism in Britain and America were perhaps from the 1940s to the 1960s, when it had achieved some institutional security, but not lost its creative and personally transforming power.

A similar war broke out in France in the 1960s, where a representative encounter was that between the scholar Raymond Picard and the critic Roland Barthes.[3] In France – at once belated and avant-garde – the critical and the theoretical revolutions were conjoined; the critic Barthes was influenced by the philosopher Derrida. Given that battles like this had all been fought out in Britain and America thirty years before, one might have expected young English critics to dismiss them as rather old stuff. However, literary politics, like the fashion business, works in cycles; many young women discovered the miniskirt in the 1980s. Young English critics seized upon Barthes and others for help in attacking an established Leavisite literary critical orthodoxy in the name of a new leftist literary theory. Not for the first or last time, Paris found itself not only thirty years behind, but also ten years ahead of Anglo-America. (The Barthes–Derrida circle eventually managed to put over the long-dead and entirely obsolete linguist Saussure as the very latest thing, in the homeland of Chomsky.)

All literary theorists agree that Barthes trounced his opponent. But then, since modern literary theory descends partly from the work of Barthes, they would, wouldn't they? One shouldn't lightly accept this without (a) reading Picard's book and (b) asking oneself whose view of Racine one actually believes. Barthes' triumph was one of style and timeliness, not scholarly argument; and just so had been the triumph of the Anglo-American critics over their scholarly opponents, thirty years before.

The most violent and polemical, and perhaps the most famous, of the critical revolutionaries of the 1930s was F.R. Leavis. Modern students who see Leavis as the very archetype of academic authority have to be reminded that his whole life was shaped as a passionate rebellion against that authority; that is, against the historical scholars and second-rate literary connoisseurs of the 1930s, seen by him as occupying positions of academic and social power and having no critical ability at all. For him the whole literary establishment was a monstrous gang, which had to be fought by any effective means. In 1933 an indignant reviewer thought him a Communist;[4] and indeed he did then advocate, as inevitable and desirable in the long term, some form of economic communism. It is ironic that by the end of the 1960s, revolting students saw him as a

Fascist, or at least as a pillar of the English establishment. One might say that like the literary theorists of recent times but with more personal reason, the Leavis of the 1960s never grasped that he had won, and was now the government.

We must change the metaphor slightly, since Leavis never actually got the Cambridge chair he deserved, and to that extent was **not** the government; he never achieved institutional power. But he established a new canon of serious literature which is still very largely in place, and set the orthodox critical approach to it. Yet even at the end of his life, Dr Leavis could hardly bring himself to believe that he was the Pope, though he had been successfully distributing anathemas and encyclicals for upwards of forty years, and had hundreds of thousands of followers.[5] For the heretics of Theory, however, who found disciples of his in every English department, it was, and still is, Leavis's authority which was the main one to be overthrown, and the sacredness of the books he had canonised which had to be destroyed.

The twentieth-century victory of criticism over scholarship is not to be identified with the biography of one man. It was, like the later victory of literary theory over criticism, a set of intellectual battles accompanying a deeper underlying social change. And it was international; or at least, Anglo-American. W.K. Wimsatt records one notable moment from the American history:

> Back in the mid-1930s, Professor R.S. Crane of Chicago had a conversion, from straight, neutral history of literature and ideas to literary criticism. His essay, 'History versus Criticism in the University Study of Literature', in the *English Journal*, October 1935, was for its date a revolutionary document, a signal victory for criticism. It drew a line between history and criticism with convincing clarity, though perhaps so severely as to have helped to raise some later needless embarrassment between academic critics and their colleagues.
>
> (Wimsatt 1954, p.41)

Wimsatt points out the source of the embarrassment in a footnote: Crane believed 'a large part of literary historical studies not only non-critical but not even ancillary to criticism' (which would come to imply, in the light of the emerging critical orthodoxy in American education, that these studies were educationally useless and had a doubtful right to exist). This of course was explosive stuff, since the justification of academic jobs depended upon it; but it was no more than Richards and Leavis had been suggesting in England, and Leavis put the point with far more brutality.

What then was the nature of this new and extraordinarily privileged form of discourse, which its followers came to see as one of the great intellectual achievements of the twentieth century, fully comparable in intellectual stature with anything in natural science or philosophy; which an astonishingly wide range of intellectuals in the 1950s and 1960s actually read; and which Leavis claimed should be the proper centre of the modern university? I am not happy with any of the accounts the modern left give: they miss both the deep personal meaning and the ultimate social absurdity.[6]

3   THE ENGLISH STUDENT OF THE 1950s

The literary criticism of the 1950s was, at best, a peculiarly honest and self-analytical version of the pursuit of personal truth. The ideal critic (who might very well be an undergraduate under instruction) was, or aspired to be, the ideal reader. He[7] knew the major works of literature; had done his homework on the period and the language, and understood all the allusions; he had of course read every word of the text under discussion. On the other hand he had read, and needed to read, much less of other people's criticism than the good student of today. The reason for that was that to read other people's responses might very well interfere with the authenticity of his own. For the next stage in his work, and in a sense the only stage that really mattered, was something that required, not an elaboration of concepts, but a stripping away of defences. It was a direct confrontation of the naked self with a masterpiece. But it was also a public confrontation. The deepest and most subtle feelings that were aroused were to be made available for a delicate analysis in a language of literary appreciation; and, under the protection of that language, for public and explicit discussion.

That training in emotional honesty was available for purposes outside literature as well. It transferred directly to personal friendship – even, on occasion, to emotional honesty between rivals or enemies. It amounted to a critical awareness of the range of one's own possible feelings: to a complex self-knowledge. A literature student gained a knowledge of the complexities of the self and its emotions that made the engineer or scientist – even, perhaps particularly, the academic sociologist or psychologist – seem crude and un-self-aware.

The sad thing was, it was also a training in conformism; in emotional dependence; in literary snobbery; in political apathy; and in self-deceit.

The pressure for emotional conformity arose because of the requirement that literary feeling should, ultimately, be accounted for; that it should be justifiable as the direct response to some identifiable aspect of a text; and the assumption that any qualified and sensitive reader who was not actually despicable or wicked would be likely to respond emotionally in the same way.

Since actual readers differ from each other, in these circumstances there is bound to be a covert war about the legitimacy of feelings. If the consensus is that certain feelings – those evoked by Shelley, say – are immature and self-indulgent, there is considerable pressure on anyone aspiring to be a good critic to suppress these feelings: either to repress them and become unconscious of them, or to cultivate a split in his own critical personality, expelling some of his spontaneous feelings into an immature self that perhaps likes worse than Shelley – science fiction, detective stories, or romances – and retaining as approved parts of an official critical self what were originally much milder feelings of critical approval for Pope and Henry James. A great deal of emotional energy must now go into maintaining this artificial critical self, and trying to grow out of one's own authentic responsiveness.

I am describing a nightmare. The conformism of the upwardly mobile is in any period an internal nightmare and an external comedy. The modern theorist is often in just as bad a position, spending much of his time reading theory that he is supposed to find illuminating, though in fact he doesn't understand it, and that for the very good reason that in fact it doesn't make sense;[8] compelled in his critical discourses to make continual gestures of solidarity towards groups with which he has no common interests or values; and to make radical gestures towards a political revolution that he perfectly well knows is not coming and that he would not want if it did come. But the inauthenticities of the present do not excuse or wipe away those of the past.

4   THE POLITICS OF LITERARY CRITICISM

It was not easy then to attribute a politics to literary criticism. If you had asked a literary critic what his personal politics were, he could have given a straightforward answer. Mine, for example, when I started literature teaching, were moderate socialist: that is to say I voted for the Labour Party under Harold Wilson, and approved retrospectively of the work of the Labour government of 1945. If you had asked me what the politics of literary criticism were, I could have given no answer at all; it would have been like asking about the politics of chemistry or arithmetic. Literary criticism as such had no politics: though some people said that it had a very strong morality. But this official apoliticality hid some serious contradictions in critical practice, which rested on underlying contradictions in the critic's social role.

Any critic then would write with respectful attention to T.S. Eliot, and in dialogue with the positions of F.R. Leavis. But it is impossible to do this without at some moments, and for professional purposes only, accepting a distinctive politics of the extreme right. It is easy to present this in caricature, since sometimes the right-wing positions took a comic form. Thus T.S. Eliot said openly that he was Royalist in politics; analysis shows that the king he was supporting was Charles I.[9]

More important than these personal absurdities was a general pressure towards an idealisation of the past, in which early seventeenth-century English society was presented as having a spiritually healthy culture, from which later humanistic thought is a disastrous decline. Here again the idealisation I am concerned with begins with T.S. Eliot, with his theory of 'the dissociation of sensibility', briefly presented in his essay 'The Metaphysical Poets' (1921): before the fall, thought and feeling were united, in a single sensibility and a single image; after it, poets like Milton and Dryden thought and felt in separate fits and starts. This view was taken up not only by Leavis but by a vast orthodoxy of critics who came to find astonishing virtues in the reign of the Tudors and early Stuarts; with honourable exceptions like Empson, who described Renaissance monarchies as thoroughgoing police states. Leavis and others (following Blake, Lawrence, etc.) added a second and steeper fall at the time of the industrial revolution, and indicated that it was extremely difficult to build a high civilisation on any basis but an agricultural society.[10]

But the most deeply political feature of literary criticism was precisely its apparent refusal of politics: a refusal to recognise the relevance of the handling of political issues to the question of literary merit, even when dealing with overtly political writers like Shakespeare, Milton, Bunyan, Swift, Blake, Shelley, or Conrad. We can see this most clearly in the work of Dr Leavis, which suggested this list of authors, but it was very widespread; a quite different type of critic, C.S. Lewis, would refuse to discuss the political allegory in Book V of *The Faerie Queene*.[11] The result of this is that the trained literary critic, not despite but because of his training, failed to respond to the full force of some texts − like Swift's *Modest Proposal* − when that force was a political one; and failed to condemn horrors like Spenser's conception of justice, enforced in Ireland by the rack.[12]

The marks of reactionary politics (which are not necessarily present in any one critic, but are a feature of the whole discursive formation of literary criticism) are then a fundamental, root and branch condemnation of the culture of present-day industrial society; the idealisation of past, pre-industrial societies; and the refusal to admit into literary critical discourse essentially political questions of any period. The exclusion was in fact slightly broader than that: critical discourse was defined in relation to a definite 'literary' use of language that admitted general ideas only when they were transformed into literature. It thus became impossible to point out, within literary criticism, that Shakespeare had more reactionary views than Milton; though one could say, quite falsely, that Shakespeare transformed his views into poetry and Milton did not. The same point would apply to, say, Henry James and Bernard Shaw. One could point out that James translated all the ideas he employed into art, while Shaw did not; but not that James's politics were reactionary and mystificatory, while Shaw's were not.

These political contradictions in critical practice resulted from contradictions in the social role of literary élites. The literary critic, in Leavis's phrase, was the ideal reader. He had to be intelligent enough to understand the text in front of him. That meant, given the complexity of many English texts, he had to be supremely intelligent. He had to be well-informed enough to grasp its allusions. That might require formidable scholarship. He had to be sensitive enough to respond emotionally to the work; but balanced and critical enough to hold it at a distance and judge. That required personal maturity. He had to be alive enough to the social movement of his time to see the significance of the work. That required an awareness of social process that probably made any particular political commitment seem rather shallow. As a literary critic, one was detached from, and in quality of analysis superior to, all known parties. Everybody agreed that the greatest political poem in the English language was Marvell's poem on Cromwell, with its beautifully ironic balance, and its tribute to the dignity of Charles I at his execution. By comparison Shelley's *Ode to the West Wind* seemed to us vacuous; and I don't think it would have occurred to us that it was a political poem at all, still less that it might be the anthem of a party one might wish to join.

These humanly superior and rather God-like creatures, the trained literary critics, could find an appropriate outlet for their abilities teaching liberal studies in the technical colleges; this had its spiritual advantages over writing advertising slogans for Unilever or Hedley, though the money was not so good. Otherwise there was journalism (my option), or school-teaching, or getting some very different training for a career in accountancy or the law. In short, things were as they are now: English degrees, whether dominated by an orthodoxy of scholarship, of criticism, or of theory, are of the most marginal relevance to serious work in modern society. People with English degrees are marginal people with no marketable skills except as English teachers; they are only slightly better off than sociologists. This is a cardinal external fact about the discipline which has to be taken into account in assessing its internal development; indeed, it is possible to argue that much of the internal development is simply a reaction to this external fact. Scholars, critics and revolutionaries have succeeded one another in their dominance of English literary discourse; and this is because English Literature has not mattered to the economy in three successive ways.

5   THE SUCCESSION OF THE BLOODY KINGS

We can think, without too much implausibility, of academic literary study in the twentieth century as a succession by bloody violence of three different discursive forms: literary history and scholarship; literary criticism of the type described above; and left-wing literary theory. It is easy to trivialise wars of this kind: the scholar's fury is a traditional subject of comedy, and I won't always resist the temptation to talk of paper-knives dripping with blood. But there were real reasons for fury. Each of these discourses has the curious property of trivialising what is most deeply important in the practice of its predecessor, and, even worse, of setting up the merest tyros of the new school as judge and jury over the deepest things produced by the old one.

Consider the contempt with which literary critics treated distinguished scholars. The literary critic of the 1930s pronounced himself sole judge of the critical relevance of anything the scholar might produce. The critic's reading of a poem was truth and immediacy; the scholar's information was relevant to that reading only if the critic said so. Naturally the scholars protested that they had themselves been reading literature for many years: what did a new critic have apart from a plentiful lack of historical information, to grant him superior discrimination?

All that he seemed to have was a set of new tastes and new critical dogmas that justified him in rejecting some of the best writing in our literature, and some of the most productive critical approaches of the immediate past. Swinburne, Shelley and even Milton were found wanting. Thackeray and (for some critics) Dickens disappeared from the list of great novelists. And not only academic literary history, but political history, social history save as inferred from works of literature, and even at times the history of ideas were seen as irrelevances. Marxist interpretations appeared as not merely irrelevances, but as wild ideological distortions. Author-psychology and even character analysis fell into discredit as critical methods, and hence the new science of psychoanalysis seemed irrelevant or discreditable. One of the greatest academic critics of Shakespeare, A.C. Bradley, who relied almost exclusively on a sophisticated form of character analysis, became a non-person, and remains so to this day: he is used exclusively to warn students about the kind of essay they should not write. The standards of literary form changed too. The archetype of all literature became the metaphysical poem – though this had previously been regarded as a minor and rather eccentric form. Shakespearean play and Victorian novel alike had to be reread as unified dramatic poem. The greatest of them survived this ordeal very well: works that did not were relegated to a minor league. A very good phrase to describe any real work of literature was to be found in the title of a book by Wimsatt (1954): *The Verbal Icon*. This captures both the intense concentration on the individual work, and the danger that the work of literature would become, literally, a fetish. But that is not a danger Wimsatt and the new critics saw.

The obvious danger of this approach – that of treating each work in formalist isolation – was sometimes mitigated by a strong concern for a unified literary tradition, and a willingness to make quite daring inferences from that literary tradition to the underlying social order of the past. Such inferences could be used – and were used by Dr Leavis – in the fight against Marxist criticism. In this way he produced an alternative to the Marxist account of history: his potent myth of the organic society and its decline, which was actually a pure projection from particular readings of a particular selection of texts.

When literary theory came along, some of these dogmas survived; though with startlingly new, and often allegedly Marxist reasons given for them. Character-analysis and author-psychology were as unacceptable as before, but the reason now was that they showed a humanist belief in the unitary human subject; this was something that became politically unacceptable, when Marxists of the 1970s had to adopt 'theoretical anti-humanism'. The history of ideas returned to favour – but in the form of paranoid Foucauldian romances about the past. Other dogmas changed. Artistic unity was no longer a requirement, perhaps not even a recommendation, for a work of art – symptomatic cracks and contradictions being of far more critical interest. All this showed the popularity of current French intellectual fashions.[13]

But the most frightening change was that the unchallengeable basis of literary criticism itself – the truth and immediacy of critical responses – was rejected as both metaphysically and politically suspect. Subjective responses were seen as an effect of ideology; and the crudest student readers could place them in terms of whatever happened to be the current political line. The more sophisticated theorists could combine an attack upon the metaphysics of immediacy derived from Derrida, with one on the autonomy of the ego derived from Lacan, place them in the framework of a new linguistic idealism derived from a complete misrepresentation of the linguistics of de Saussure, and call the whole thing Marxism, in the name of Althusser.[14] Under such heavy guns, few literary critics had the armour to survive.

Naturally the critics protested that they had a politics of their own, often much more rational and subtle than the new revolutionary formulae; but had never confused political judgements with critical ones. All protests were in vain; they merely served to confirm that the critics were prisoners of an ideology they could not even perceive, and were not theorists enough to analyse. Nor did the obvious relativist argument have much effect – namely that one had quite as good grounds for believing in the literary merits of Shakespeare as one had for believing in the theoretical truth of the system of Marx or even Althusser.

The agony of the superseded scholar in the first half of the twentieth century was thus replaced by the agony of the outdated critic in the second half; and neither could really understand what had happened to him.

All this is overdrawn; I am being too schematic in talking of a simple temporal succession of discrete and opposed groups. Real literature departments have always contained scholars, critics and theorists, not always of the political left; and the categories have never in fact been mutually exclusive. C.S. Lewis is an obvious example of a major scholar in literary history, politically to the right, who was also an important critic and theorist. He made mediaeval allegory and Spenser available, as living literary experience, to a whole generation of readers, though he was quite incompetent in handling modernist literature, and much despised by some critics as a result.[15] (Leavis despised him; so probably did Eliot; Empson did not.)

And in present-day literature departments, it is never possible to infer from the fact that someone is a distinguished mediaevalist that they haven't a strong interest in narrative theory, some interesting views on the work of Virginia Woolf, and long-standing membership of the Socialist Workers' Party. The sharp opposition I have drawn between scholar, critic and radical theorist belongs rather to the world of stereotypes than realities; yet the stereotypes are themselves real, and have affected syllabuses, academic policies and personal relations. There really are (if I am to believe some former students of mine) institutions where the literature teachers and the theorists belong to different departments and different generations; won't speak to each other; and wouldn't understand each other if they did.

And it really is true that there have been three phases of orthodoxy in English teaching, even if at any one time a student is likely to be conscious both of an old orthodoxy and a new one. I was perfectly conscious of the war between scholarship and criticism as a student in Oxford in 1954: it was when Cambridge had hired the scholar C.S. Lewis away from us, to counteract the dreadful influence of the critic F.R. Leavis.

6   SOCIAL CRITICISM, MODERNISM AND THE NEW LEFT

There is a great deal of difference in the way in which the three phases of orthodoxy in English teaching have taken the social and economic irrelevance of their subject into account. Often, the scholars of the early part of the century were satisfied with the society they lived in – if only it would stop changing! – and with the standards they had inherited for judging literature and art (by which, unfortunately, much modernist art and literature – like the work of Picasso, Stravinsky, Eliot, Joyce and Woolf – was unintelligible rubbish). Other scholars less satisfied with the twentieth century ignored the modern world completely, and made an imaginative life in the past: the age of Shakespeare, for example, or the middle ages. Only too grateful to have the opportunity to continue their research, whether in poorly paid academic jobs or in the leisure sometimes afforded by non-academic occupations and sometimes by private incomes, they buried themselves in the past they were excavating.

The critics, on the other hand, had taken the full implications of the modern movement in literature and the arts: they saw that not only was it necessary to react to Eliot and Lawrence and Kafka and Joyce, but that all earlier literature had to be evaluated in the light of that reaction; one had to judge, as one had to live, in a modern world, even if one found its tendencies profoundly depressing. The critics were thus marked by the dignified seriousness with which they faced up to social disintegration, alienation and anomie, and their refusal of escapism and romantic fantasy; while historical scholars such as C.S. Lewis looked like escapist romantics.

The point is, that this is the period in which the two complementary tendencies in literature that appealed to the bourgeoisie and were therefore within the critical capacity of the scholars – the movements we call romanticism and realism – had been replaced, at the highest level of art, by modernism: that is, by an art in which formal experimentation is used to express the futility of ordinary bourgeois aims and interests.

This sense of futility, or alienation, was certainly a real social phenomenon, though there were questions that could be asked about its extent and its cause. Was it the alienation of a limited group of humanist intellectuals from the predominantly scientific, technological and utilitarian preoccupations of their society? Or, as some Marxists argued, the alienation from the proletariat of the fruits of its own labour, which towered up over it as an alien and oppressive reality? Or the alienation of Man, in a technologico–Benthamite society, from nature and from historical culture? Literary criticism, taking modernist works seriously but not accepting Marxist explanations, clearly implied the last view: Leavis, and writers in *Scrutiny*, often made it explicit.

Supported by this great sense of tradition that they had found or constructed, and by a reactionary politics far more subtle and profound[16] than many of the blimpish scholars who had preceded them, the critics could face up to their society and criticise it. Those at least who were strongly affected by literary modernism found themselves with a superb critique of the emptiness, self-destructiveness, and futility of the modern world, which had been articulated by some of the greatest literary masters: by Conrad, by Eliot, by Lawrence, by Kafka. All it needed was interpretation. The critic, marginalised by society, could offer a profounder criticism of it than the engineers and businessmen who actually made it work. He could do this by transmitting the profundity of other men. He succeeded to the position of the priest, at least in the sense that he could comment on the world in the light of sacred scriptures. The English teacher in school, with his Lawrence in hand and his Leavisite interpretation of it, was genuinely offering a religious education (see A.S. Byatt, 1978, *The Virgin in the Garden*, for a vivid novelistic picture set in the early 1950s). The liberal studies lecturer, actually teaching young recruits to the world of business and technology which he criticised, was perhaps more like an army chaplain.

But of course neither of them could change the society they worked in; nor would they have thought it remotely realistic to expect to make such changes. The focus was, therefore, on changing individuals: opening horizons, making possible personal development. The notion of bringing about radical social change was to be the special province of the **radical literary theorist**. The latter took account quite consciously of Marx's thesis on Feuerbach: 'The philosophers have interpreted the world in various ways: the point is to change it.'

These radical literary theorists were made available, from the 1960s on, by the rise of a New Left within a newly developing marginal intelligentsia: a sort of Polytechnic intelligentsia. The literary critique of society could thus be replaced by a radical political critique no longer based on élitist cultural assumptions, and aiming to change society, not merely lament it. However, the inherent limitations of the social base of this new left critique soon showed through. By the circumstance of its origin in philosophy, sociology and literary theory, and its place in the academy, the radical political critique became essentially more élitist than the literary critique it replaced.

There had always been a serious problem for Marxist critics in accommodating themselves to modernism. Bourgeois art was at least potentially a universal art, available to the working classes. Modernism was an élite art, often built upon reactionary assumptions about the world. Marxist thinkers like Georg Lukács and Christopher Caudwell found themselves condemning it. It was a cultural necessity for the New Left to make a critical accommodation to modernism; otherwise nobody would have taken New Left accounts of literature seriously. Literary criticism was, in its most creative phase, essentially a way of adapting to literary modernism; and had the élitism of literary modernism built into it. By the time the New Left had developed theoretical reasons for admiring Joyce and Kafka, new theory was as élitist as literary criticism had ever been.

Nevertheless, from the early 1970s, and armed with an understanding of *Ulysses* as a revolution of the word, a cabal of lecturers set out to change the world in the radical ways listed in the first paragraph of this chapter. Unfortunately, after twenty years we have to say: *Si monumentum requiris, circumspice.*[17] The success of their efforts can be measured by the number of elections in a row lost by the British Labour Party and the American Democrats to parties on their right. Left-wing theorists seem to have had no influence on practical politics save possibly to help left-wing militants alienate voters, split the Labour Party and ensure the triumph of reaction; and now even what seemed to be the inalienable achievements of the 1945 British Labour government are being destroyed. There is of course no suggestion that literary theorists are specially responsible for this; but they share the failure of the New Left as a whole.

The New Left had been gripped by a profound vision of social change (or possibly a superficial and silly vision), and thought that it could remodel society and consciousness, and as a natural but incidental consequence, art. In a sense the very basis of its appeal was romantic fantasy: its birth was surrounded by student riots and their motto was that the imagination was now taking power. The problem for leftist theory now is, what does it do when the most solid intellectual basis for its theory of social change – Marxism – seems to have collapsed, and the fantasy and wish-fulfilment elements are exposed?

NOTES

1. Scholarly enquiries were held to establish the correct text of Homer in sixth-century Greece; though the great age of scholarship was Alexandrian. Poems were discussed in seminars by the Sophists in the fifth century; a critical analysis of a poem is given, attributed to Socrates, in Plato's *Protagoras*, a dialogue which shows literary criticism being replaced as a moral discipline by philosophy. (Nothing is new!) The first major theorists of literature are Plato and Aristotle.

2. For the abolition of literature as a category: see Bennett 1979; Eagleton 1983. For the theory of the subject see Easthope 1988. For the transformation of literary studies into cultural studies see Easthope 1991. For the global ambitions of literary theory see Danto 1989. For the radical leftism of the dominant school of literary theory it would be misleading to give particular references; we are dealing not with a rainstorm but a climate. See Methuen, New Accents series, *passim*; Routledge, most of their recent books on the subject; the Essex Conferences on the Sociology of Literature, etc. For further discussion see Chapter 9, this volume.

3. Raymond Picard 1956, *La Carrière de Jean Racine* (Scholarly and authoritative account; gained him chair of French literature at the Sorbonne.) Roland Barthes 1963, *Sur Racine*. Very personal interpretation. Barthes 1964, 'Les Deux Critiques' – essay contrasting interpretative or new criticism and traditional or university criticism – in *Essais Critiques*, 1964. Picard 1965, *Nouvelle Critique ou Nouvelle Imposture* – attack on this new French critical movement. Barthes 1966, *Critique et Vérité* – partly a reply to Picard, partly an attempt to move to 'higher' questions like what kind of language a critic should use, and what kind of knowledge he can be said to have. (A Picardian would call this evasion.) All these details, and more, can be found in Barthes 1966, *Criticism and Truth*, trans. Katrine Pilcher Keuneman with a foreword by Philip Thody.
Cf. Jackson 1991, *The Poverty of Structuralism* for further discussion of Barthes.

4. 'Let me say, then, that I agree with the Marxist to the extent of believing some form of economic communism to be inevitable and desirable, in the sense that it is to this that a power-economy of its nature points, and only by a deliberate and intelligent working toward it can civilisation be saved from disaster. (The question is, communism of what kind? Is the machine – or power – to triumph or to be triumphed over, to be the dictator or the servant of human ends?)' F.R. Leavis, Restatements for Critics, *Scrutiny* vol. I, no. 4. The critic was Arthur Calder Marshall 1933: see F.R. Leavis 1974, *Letters in Criticism*, p. 28.

5. Williams 1979, *Politics and Letters*: 'One must remember that by this time, although Leavis still thought of himself as an outsider in his last years, he had completely won. I mean if you talked to anyone about the English novel, including people who were hostile to Leavis, they were in fact reproducing his sense of the shape of its history.'

6. Far the best I have seen is Ian Hunter: 'Aesthetics and Cultural Studies', in Grossberg, Nelson and Treichler 1992; he speaks of 'individuals

problematising themselves as potential subjects of aesthetic experience'. But this applies to the Schillerian aesthetic attitude; it doesn't fit Leavis's strenuous moral commitment.

I would myself see interesting parallels to the discourses of Wittgensteinian philosophical analysis, and of psychoanalysis. All three are moral therapies, that remake the human subject. Cf. Jackson, forthcoming, *Making Freud Unscientific.*

7. Or she. There was nothing specially masculine about this work. But one needs a singular pronoun. It was a very singular process.

8. See Jackson 1991, *The Poverty of Structuralism*, for an attempt to discriminate between the elements of post-structualist theory that do, and those that do not, make sense.

9. See particularly the two essays on Milton in Eliot 1957. Other claims – that he was a Catholic and a classicist, and was looking for a principle of order and authority outside the individual – are in the context of European Fascism altogether less funny. (Though Lawrence said that this classiosity was bunkum and cowardice.) Cf. Eliot: 'The Function of Criticism' in Eliot 1932.

10. For example, F.R. Leavis, 'Under which King, Bezonian?' *Scrutiny*, Dec. 1932. But it is a common refrain.

11. C.S. Lewis, 1936, *The Allegory of Love*, p. 321.

12. Lewis is better than his own theory here – he does condemn the Irish policy Spenser was associated with, and agrees that Spenser's imagination was corrupted by it. But he still assumes that the historical allegory is irrelevant to the poetic value of the poem.

13. Cf. Jackson 1991 and this volume, Chapters 8 and 9.

14. Coward and Ellis 1977; Rée 1979; Easthope 1980.

15. The description of Lewis (1936, *The Allegory of Love*, OUP; 1961, *An Experiment in Criticism*, CUP) as a literary theorist will surprise some people, but can easily be justified in terms of the theoretical issues he raised and the hypotheses he put forward. The young Lewis nearly became an academic philosopher; had he done so, he would probably have been that twentieth-century rarity, an English Hegelian.

He was also a fine writer of children's fantasy and science fiction; a great celebrity as a religious apologist: and has become an unofficial saint among some American Christians. These qualities have done him no good at all with the left.

16. 'Profound' here means profoundly mystificatory. A profound book is one in touch with something – in the unconscious or at the level of basic economic contradictions, say – that is deeply hidden. Some books fetch these things out to the light. Henry James, say, in his treatment of social issues, covers up the underlying contradictions of his society so that it is very difficult to see them; whereas Dickens exposes them.

17. This famous epigraph on Sir Christopher Wren: 'If you want a monument, look about you' stands in St Paul's Cathedral. The New Left stand in the ghost of an imaginary cathedral of socialism, through whose non-existent walls can be seen the real monuments of capitalism stretching away all over the world – punctuated only by the wreckage of what was 'real existing socialism' and the guerrilla camps of nationalism and religious fundamentalism.

A more modest motto might be 'Some of this is my fault.' For example, if New Left thinking hadn't helped split the British Labour Party, Mrs Thatcher would never have achieved power. Anyone on the radical left now (including feminists) ought to be asking anxiously: 'Are my hopes for radical change actually self-indulgent fantasy, like the revolutionary slogans of the 1970s? Will I have to say in twenty years: "Some of this growth of reaction is my fault"?'

BOOKS

I.A. Richards 1924 *Principles of Literary Criticism.*
1929 *Practical Criticism: a Study of Literary Judgement.*
William Empson 1930 *Seven Types of Ambiguity.*
T.S. Eliot 1932 *Selected Essays.*
F.R. Leavis 1936 *Revaluation.*
1948 *The Great Tradition.*
1952 *The Common Pursuit.*
1975 *The Living Principle: 'English' as a Discipline of Thought.*
F.R. Leavis (ed.) 1968 *A Selection from Scrutiny* (2 Vols).
René Wellek and **Austin Warren** 1949 *Theory of Literature.*
W.K. Wimsatt 1954 *The Verbal Icon: Studies in the Meaning of Poetry.*
George Watson 1962 *The Literary Critics.*
David Lodge 1972 *Twentieth-Century Literary Criticism.*
1988 *Modern Criticism and Theory.*
A.S. Byatt 1978 *The Virgin in the Garden.*
Terry Eagleton 1983 *Literary Theory: an Introduction.*
Leonard Jackson 1991 *The Poverty of Structuralism.*
Anthony Easthope 1991 *Literary into Cultural Studies.*

PART TWO

The foundations of Marxist theory

CHAPTER TWO

The Mental Basis of Reality

Idealism and the Human Subject

SUMMARY

The central question of this book is why so many intellectuals, in a remote and non-economic field like literary theory, went Marxist. One possible answer is the intellectual merit of the Marxist tradition itself. This could seem surprising only to those who identify Marxism with a narrow economic determinism and a highly politicised attitude to literature. If we take the Marxist tradition back to its idealist origins in the work of Kant and Hegel we shall find that Marxism offered a profound redefinition of our ideas about human subjectivity, human culture and the nature of history. It is these issues over which theorists have been arguing in the last thirty years.

The battle between idealism and materialism, which preoccupied all Marxist thinkers from Marx himself to Althusser, goes back at least to Plato in the fifth century BC, as does the question of the comparative validity of the analytical and dialectical method. The concept which anti-humanist theorists have spent thirty years or more attacking, that of a universal human rationality, which is a part of a universal human nature, was given its philosophical definition by Kant; and it is with modern forms of Kantianism – logical, biological and social, in the work of, say, Lévi-Strauss and Chomsky – that Marxists have recently needed to contend.

Is there, as Kant believed, a universal human nature, giving rise to a universal conception of literature and culture? Or is 'human nature', as Hegel's dialectic suggested, something historically constructed, which changes with time? Is human nature and the culture that seems to express it something based on universal properties of human biology, or even of reason itself? Or is it, as Marx proposed, merely the side-effect of a system of social relations, ultimately, perhaps, determined by the features of the current mode of production? Is the nature that we feel to be ours, and all the values that seem to rest upon it (taste in books and literature, taste in people, love or hatred for war) merely, as the vulgar Marxists claimed, our class-consciousness, playing out underlying conflicts with other classes in a disguised, ideological form so that we do not recognise them?

1   THE ROOTS OF IDEALISM

Marxist materialism is a strongly realist philosophy and, as I shall argue, is perfectly right to be so. Nevertheless, one of its greatest strengths is that it is also an inverted form of idealism. It draws, therefore, as ordinary mechanical materialism does not, on an age-old tradition of sophisticated thought about human culture and human subjectivity. The tradition began with Plato, and reached its highest point of sophistication in the work of Kant and of Hegel, before Marx turned it upside down, and summarised and encapsulated it in his own work. It there became the hidden basis of all subsequent theories of ideology; and it tends to re-emerge whenever intellectuals start to concentrate on ideological questions at the expense of underlying material ones. Modern theories of discourse are a revival of this tradition; they are Hegelian and even Platonic without recognising it.

1.1   Mathematics and experiment in the investigation of reality

Idealism is not coterminous with philosophy, though its roots go very deep. Philosophy began, along with natural science, as speculation about the ultimate nature of the world; and we can pick out several major techniques that were developed for making that speculation more controllable and precise. Among the earliest of these techniques was **mathematical modelling**, which is at least as early as Pythagoras. Another was **systematic observation and experiment**, which was well established by the time of Aristotle, but presumably dates from much earlier, since it is continuous with, on the one hand, Babylonian and Egyptian astronomy, and on the other, mercantile and artisanal traditions of practical enquiry and invention. These two techniques are, to this day, the basis for modern natural science.

On a naive interpretation, these techniques are taken to give direct information about reality. I would myself accept this interpretation – subject, of course, to the standard reservation that all theories are conjectural and uncertain and that all observations are made initially within the framework of existing theories.[1] On this view, we have no certain knowledge about reality; we can only make hypotheses and try to test them. But these hypotheses are not fictions. They are guesses about the nature of reality. They assume, in their very form, that there is a reality which is logically prior to our conjectures about it.

Many sophisticated thinkers, and I suppose all literary theorists, will find this claim metaphysical and naive. The argument against it runs as follows: since by hypothesis our only access to reality is by conjecture (or thinking – or ideas – or discourse – or signification) it is the conjectures (thoughts, ideas, discourses, signifiers) that are real, and what they produce is only a construct, a fiction, a useful model. To borrow Derrida's terminology: we cannot escape from the play of signifiers; there is no transcendental signified. This is the account which classical Marxism would reject – and which I would reject – as idealist. The main objection to it – which I suppose many theorists would regard as a merit – is that it blurs the distinction between reality and fiction, and between hypothesis and fiction.[2]

When we put forward a scientific theory that explains certain phenomena by postulating the existence of some entity like a chromosome, or some process like chemical combination, we are in my view – and, more important, that of almost all working scientists, though not necessarily philosophers of science – claiming that chromosomes exist, and chemical combination happens. Scientific theories keep changing, of course; so we must reckon with the possibility that we are mistaken in making these claims. But the claims themselves, however provisional, are existence claims; and natural science is therefore an ontology, though not necessarily a complete ontology, and always a provisional one.

I do not think it is a coherent position to say that our theories only concern models. The existence of a model can affect what happens in a model universe; but it is hard to see how it can affect what happens in the real universe. And it is a proposition as well established as any that if we act on entities postulated by scientific theories, we can affect the real universe. We can base a manufacturing industry on certain processes of chemical combination; we can affect inheritance by manipulating genes.

Indeed, if it is taken seriously, the claim that making a model, or operating on a model entity, can affect the real universe is more like a piece of sympathetic magic than it is like science. Most people who make a claim like this really mean something different. They mean that their model electron is a model of a real electron, incorporating all that we know about it at the moment, and thus enabling us to predict some of the effects that operating on real electrons will have. But this account restores the ontological claims of the theory. To make a model of an electron is to make claims about the properties of real electrons.

1.2   Two further intellectual methods: logic and dialectic

I spoke of several techniques for making speculation about ultimate reality both more controllable and more precise, and mentioned two: mathematical modelling, and systematic observation and experiment, which are the bases of natural science. There are two more that were pretty fully developed by Socrates and Plato. They are more self-reflexive and critical than the first two, and in the modern sense, more philosophical; though I am not suggesting, of course, that they play no part in a fully-developed natural science. The first is a consideration of the nature of valid argument. It is the area of theory pioneered by Socrates, and developed into a mature system by Aristotle. It corresponds squarely to modern **logic**, though this has received a stupendous technical development in the formal logic of the twentieth century. It is now fully integrated with mathematics; and it has a full-scale modern technology based on it: computing.

Logic and mathematics do not provide a set procedure for making discoveries. Science has no set discovery procedures, though it keeps finding useful lines of enquiry. There are no rules for making hypotheses. The function of logic and mathematics is to work out precisely what the consequences of a hypothesis are, so that it can be tested.

The second technique – which is to be found described in detail, in a very anti-scientific context in Plato's *Republic* (530–34b) – is a procedure which, in modern terms, is intended to clarify ideas that are found to be unclear. Plato calls this **dialectic**. In Plato's early Socratic dialogues, dialectic is simply a method of clarifying concepts through argument. A definition of some concept is advanced; Socrates, or another partner in the dialogue, offers a counter-example, to show that that definition will not hold; an alternative definition is put forward; and the dialogue proceeds until consensus is reached on some adequate definition, or failure to agree, is acknowledged. Some version of dialectic appears in many idealist systems, though it is not idealist in itself. It becomes idealist only when it is used, as in Plato's later work, to construct an ideal version of the world, which is then claimed to be the real world. We can usefully contrast the valid negative, or Socratic dialectic with the more dubious constructive, or Platonic dialectic, even though they come from the same author.

1.3   Idealism and the Platonic dialectic

In this book I use the word **idealist** to characterise those philosophies which hold that the world is wholly constructed in thought, or in discourse, or as meaning, and **realist** to characterise those which hold that some entities exist independently of any thoughts we may have about them or descriptions we may give of them. Idealist philosophies tend to use dialectical arguments not merely to clarify concepts but in an extended way to establish the substantive nature of the real world.

All idealist philosophies rest on a very ancient philosophical claim which also underlies science. There is a tradition, certainly pre-Socratic and probably pre-Greek, to the effect that the world of appearance(s) is illusory, and that the real world has a quite different character. For example, the world of appearances might be supposed to be **many**; and the real world, **one**. It is often very difficult to grasp what a claim of this kind means; and Plato quite properly used dialectic to clarify such claims.

However, even when such claims are clear, there is a serious problem about empirically verifying them. A claim of this kind cannot be checked by examining the contents of experience because, by hypothesis, the contents of experience will consist only of appearances. All we can do is ask questions about what underlying realities we can legitimately infer from these appearances. An inevitable result of this approach is that it seems as if our sole guarantee that experience gives us access to a real world is an **epistemological** theory – that is, a theory about what knowledge is reliable, and what knowledge is not. Philosophy thus goes down the epistemological road; it begins to treat claims about knowledge as philosophically more fundamental than claims about existence.

One reason that this seems to be a plausible strategy is that there are two areas – logic and mathematics – in which pure argument appears to provide knowledge about the world. It greatly impressed Plato – and should still impress us now – that we can be certain of the truth of a geometrical theorem without needing to make any empirical observations, and that our knowledge will not be contaminated by the errors and inadequacies of these observations. Plato hoped to develop the dialectic to give similarly certain knowledge in other areas.

Unfortunately it turns out that logic and mathematics are the only instruments that give certain knowledge; and that they give us knowledge only about abstract objects like pure numbers, or about the possible structures of real objects like garden sheds, or about the necessary consequences of the assumptions we make about hypothetical objects, like electrons. Apart from this, for our knowledge of the real world we have to make do with guesswork (conjecture, hypothesis) checked against observation and experiment; and it can never be completely checked. We can thus never have certain knowledge in empirical science, or practical affairs. Plato could not have known this.

It seemed to Plato, and has seemed to innumerable idealist philosophers since that time, that the objects of which we can have certain knowledge, by the eye of the mind, can be said to have a superior reality to those about which we merely have opinions. A startling way of putting this is to say that there is a world of ideal objects, or **forms**, which are apparent to the intellect alone and not the senses, and of which everyday objects like tables and chairs are mere copies. This is Plato's 'theory of forms'.

The opposite view – naive realism – would be that tables and chairs exist blockishly and contingently in the world just as they seem to exist; and the ideal table is a concept which exists in our heads, or as an entry in a dictionary, merely for classificatory purposes. The objects would continue to exist even if we had no concepts of them (though no doubt we needed the concepts to make these items of furniture in the first place). But natural objects like mountains or stars would exist even if human beings didn't.

Plato's mature ontology seems to me a little like that of a modern mathematical physicist. It claims ultimate reality for certain quasi-mathematical forms and a kind of secondary reality for objects of appearance in so far as they partake in these forms. He never worked out the details satisfactorily, but took the discussion to a remarkable depth (in the *Parmenides*, *Theaetetus*, etc.). But his fundamental method of enquiry is very unlike that of modern science, and very close to that adopted, twenty-two centuries later, by Hegel. It is the method of dialectic. It begins with the destructive analysis of ordinary concepts:

'Then dialectic alone', I said, 'proceeds in this way, by destroying the hypotheses, right up to the first principle itself in order to establish it. Finding the eye of the mind embedded in an absolute bog of mud it gently draws it out and leads it upwards, using the studies we have discussed as helpers and assistants.'

(*Republic*, 533c–d)

(These 'studies we have discussed' are practical studies or mathematical ones.) Dialectic is now given an ontological interpretation:

'And you give the name dialectic to the process of grasping the explanation of the nature and reality of each thing? And you agree that anyone who cannot give an explanation both to himself and to another has, to the extent that he cannot, failed to understand the thing in question?' 'What else could I say?' he replied.

(trans. Gwynneth Matthews 1972) Ibid., 534b

Plato has thus turned dialectic – basically a process for reaching agreement on the analysis of concepts – into a process for the generation of descriptions of the nature and reality of objects – that is, an ontology. The steps from this to the Hegelian dialectic, so far as I understand it, seem to me quite small; though it took both Kant and Hegel to take them.

2   THE IDEALS OF REASON

2.1 *Science and the sceptics: Descartes, Berkeley, Hume and Newton*

In a sense the modern world has repeated the philosophical development of the ancient one. First came new developments – the new astronomy, the work of the Royal Society – in mathematical modelling and empirical enquiry; then philosophical enquiry into the nature of knowledge and the nature of language. The sceptical idealism of Descartes proceeds from an epistemological question: what is there whose existence I cannot possibly doubt? His immediate answer is: I cannot doubt that I am thinking; therefore I cannot doubt that I exist. The 'I' therefore becomes the name of a substance which is certainly known to exist; while what the 'I' is thinking about is only inferentially known to exist. An **epistemological** question has led to an **ontological** theory that privileges the mind over the material world. All later idealism stems from this Cartesian move.

The first fruit of this theory is in fact dualism, in which mental substances are set over against physical ones. The second fruit is perhaps Bishop Berkeley's idealism, which unifies the world again by reducing it all to ideas; and seems to deny the reality of an unexperienced world. (If nobody is thinking about the world, it doesn't exist.) The third is Hume's scepticism.

Hume denies that we have any evidence either for the existence of a continuing mind, or for the existence of continuing bodies, or for anything beyond the bare flux of experience. One consequence of this approach is that the world seen by philosophy is a very different place from that seen by science. For science offered, in Newtonian theory, not only an acknowledgement of the existence of continuing bodies, but a detailed prediction of some aspects of their behaviour – for example, of the orbits of the planets – without limit of time. But Hume's point is that the propositions of science, like those of common-sense theories of continuity, rest upon a tacit principle of induction according to which we can extrapolate from observed regularities to unobserved ones. Yet the principle of induction itself rests on faith; we cannot prove it logically; and we cannot infer it from experience without assuming it in the first place.[3]

Hume's philosophy, while irrefutable, was impossible to believe, not merely for the philosopher himself when off-duty and in cheerful mood, but for any working scientist who took his own presuppositions seriously. Natural science offered, and still offers, ever more specific mathematical predictions about the world, while supporting them with an ever increasing variety of empirical data. But the empiricist philosophy associated with natural science entirely failed, and in this form still fails,[4] to support the content of science. The greatest of the empiricists, Hume, had destroyed the principle of induction that was supposed to support the entire scientific edifice. On his arguments, there was no principled basis for providing any reliable predictions about the world; we couldn't even deduce that the sun would rise tomorrow. It was in response to that sceptical challenge that Kant's arguments were produced.

2.2 The transcendental idealism of Kant

The special type of argument that Kant employs has become known as transcendental argument. The basic assumption that he makes is that he does not have to justify the sciences, or the moral law, or aesthetic judgement, or our insight into functionality and purpose; but to explain how we can possibly come by them. He therefore attempts to reason backwards, from the knowledge that in his view we undoubtedly have, to the implicit presuppositions that, combined with experience, enable us to have it. These presuppositions, or preconceptions, or forms of intuition, or *a priori* truths he places in the mind itself.

We might note immediately that this is not in the least an outdated position. A version of it is adopted by Lévi-Straussian structuralists; another version by Chomsky and cognitive scientists. It is also Kant who provides the classical account of that **liberal humanism** which most cultural theorists of the last thirty years have spent their time attacking. Liberal humanism assumes that there is a human subjectivity prior to all historical and social conditions which determines a set of cognitive, ethical and aesthetic principles. What these principles are is discussed in Kant's three great *Critiques*: *The Critique of Pure Reason*, which deals with knowledge, *The Critique of Practical Reason*, which deals with principles of action (ethical principles) and *The Critique of Judgement*, which deals with aesthetic judgements and with teleology.

The best summary I know of Kant's central argument, in *The Critique of Pure Reason*, comes from the idealist David Ritchie (1893). 'If knowledge be altogether dependent on sensation, knowledge is impossible. But knowledge is possible, because the sciences exist. Therefore knowledge is not altogether dependent on sensation.' (p. 10). This argument depends on the older view that scientific knowledge is a form of certainty, not merely conjecture.

As Ritchie points out, what this non-sensational element is must be discovered by taking the different stages and kinds of knowledge separately. One can be a Kantian without believing that Kant is right at every step – or in any step – of his specific analysis. The essential point is, however, that part of the phenomenal reality we know is constituted by the mind that knows.

Some paradoxical results follow.

(a) The reality we experience is a construct; we have no access to objects as they are in themselves; metaphysics (that is, an account of the world as it is in itself, or of the nature of God or the ultimate reality of the world) is impossible, though because of the way our minds are, we can't help trying.

(b) We have access only to the intuitions (raw experiences?) that objects cause in us; but by applying our inbuilt conceptual machinery to these intuitions, we manufacture an objective world, with all the properties required by science – including that of existing in Euclidean space and in time, and apparently being entirely determinist; and this world is not an illusion.

(c) It is a peculiarity of such a world (actually a peculiarity of the framework of Newtonian science, which Kant accepted) that though it is actually constructed by a mind, it is wholly mechanical, and allows no room for human freedom of action! On the other hand, the mind which is uncovered by transcendental reasoning is free, but is not in the empirical world at all.

These positions leave Kant perched upon a philosophical knife-edge from which it is very easy to fall off. If you reject the notion of unknowable things-in-themselves as unintelligible, then you fall off into idealism, along with Hegel and also with modern relativists who often trace their ancestry to Nietzsche or to Husserl: for you, the mind constructs the world and it makes no sense to talk of a world existing independently of any point of view. If you reject the transcendental step, you fall into mechanical materialism: for you, the mind passively records a life that proceeds deterministically without its intervention. Marx tackled this problem in the *Theses on Feuerbach*.

It is the second of Kant's great critiques, *The Critique of Practical Reason*, which offers the major transcendental argument that the human mind, at least, is free. 'Practical' here means moral; Kant accepts that that we can make moral judgements of human actions; and points out that the presupposition of any judgement that an action is right or wrong is that it is voluntary. People must be free to decide, or it would not make sense to praise or blame them for what they do. Hence people cannot be mechanically determined, like robots or computers. On the other hand Kant does not hold that people act randomly, for no reason at all, or could be praised for doing so if they did.

For Kant, autonomous human action is action which flows not from external causes or even natural inclination but from reasons, deriving from general ethical principles. Freedom is thus identified – in a curious and very unromantic fashion – with acting for good reason rather than acting on either external causation or inner impulse. In Roger Scruton's version (1982): 'every rational being must so act as if he were by his maxims a legislating member of the universal kingdom of ends'. All this emerges from considering the necessary presuppositions for our moral judgements.

A materialist would learn from Marx to argue that behind this very abstract moral ideal is a socio-political one: that of a republic in which every citizen is a legislating member of the governing body of the state. This socio-political ideal, in turn, is the political programme of a definite class – the bourgeoisie – in Prussian society. It is worth pointing out that this is the class not merely of rich merchants, but of public officials: Kant himself, as a professor, was a public official. There is in fact something very civil-servantish in Kant's morality: there is the concern to make policy universal and fair, detach it from the personal interests of the official who administers it, and so forth.

In the next generation of philosophy, Hegel made this connection in a very sharp way. He suggested that the state bureaucracy was actually the universal class that gave a historical embodiment to universal reason, which could otherwise have no political existence. It was left for Marx to point out that this class embodied a very strong bourgeois class interest; and to claim the role of universal class for the proletariat. This is how the extraordinary metaphysical notion of a universal class got itself into the Marxist tradition, which it has haunted ever since.

2.3   Philosophical, psychological and social Kantianism

Kant's fundamental position is that the categories of the mind, which produce the structure of the world we live in, etc., are the categories of a universal rationality which any entity that experiences the world at all must possess. It is easy to reject this view, for all concepts except perhaps those of logic and mathematics. But it is a peculiarity of the Kantian arguments that, when rejected at this philosophically abstract level, they return at an empirical one, as arguments either about empirical psychology or about empirical sociology and intellectual history.

For Professor Strawson in *The Bounds of Sense*, psychologising was merely a bad habit that Kant fell into when presenting his arguments. It is not just that he continually uses the language of an obsolete faculty psychology. It would be just as bad if he used a modern psychological theory. The arguments of Kant are supposed to set the limits of empiricism, and so cannot be based on any empirical properties. But if we reject Kant's position as philosophy, it remains as psychology; or perhaps as sociology. The point is, there are still basic concepts in terms of which – empirically – we are found to think. Where did we get them from? Are they built into our psychology, and to be seen ultimately as effects of human biology: inherited categories? Or are they sociological in origin – acquired during socialisation, developed in some culture in the course of its intellectual history, and perhaps the effect of some aspect of social or economic structure?

2.3.1 *Psychological Kantianism*   Geometers no longer accept that space is necessarily Euclidean, or that it is necessarily separate from time. But human beings still spontaneously think that way. Why? Is it for an empiricist reason – that our local portion of space–time easily cuts up that way, and so we learn that way of analysing it? Or is it, as Kant thought, that the specifications of Euclidean space are built into our minds; but not, as Kant thought, because any mind has to be like that; rather because in the course of natural selection, Euclidean space has been built into our brains?

Or consider how we learn human languages. According to Chomsky, we have the basic pattern set up in our brains before we ever do learn them. Chomsky explicitly rejects empiricist learning theory, and says he is a Cartesian; but he is really more like a Kantian. He claims, in effect, that we have a pre-existing set of unconscious linguistic concepts available to interpret as language whatever words and phrases we happen to hear spoken around us. As small children we use these concepts (called 'linguistic universals') to build up a systematic unconscious description (a 'grammar') of the particular language being spoken.

Lévi-Strauss has given a similar description – though much less detailed and much less empirically based – of the underlying mental basis of all social life. The structures of all actual societies appear to be materialisations of deep underlying mental structures. Lévi-Straussian structuralism has thus thrown a new light on Kantian philosophy – or perhaps it would be better to say that, on analysis, the underlying philosophy of Lévi-Straussian structuralism seems to be a Kantian one; everything develops out of structures innately present in the human mind. Lévi-Strauss himself has accepted the description of his project as 'Kantianism without the transcendental subject'. (See next sub-section; and Jackson 1991, *The Poverty of Structuralism*, Chapter 3.)

2.3.2 *Sociological Kantianism* The third possible source for the basic categories we think in – beside transcendental reason and human biology – is the basic norms of the social group. If transcendental reason gives us philosophical Kantianism, and the notion of innate mental structures gives us psychological Kantianism, then the notion of hypostatised sociological categories gives us a sociological Kantianism. This is the position taken by some Marxists – for example, Lucien Goldmann (1948) – and not only Marxists; for example, Israel Knox (1936) accepts it as a possibility.

It seems obvious that many of our ethical and aesthetic categories are reflections of aspects of our societies. It seems less likely that the forms of society are relevant to our general concept of space or our childhood preconceptions about the grammatical form of sentences. In sociological Kantianism, the universal principles of reason and judgement that Kant relies upon become simply the accepted norms of our own culture, or as Marxists would have it, of our own ideology.

It is on this assumption that some on the modern left think themselves justified in offering a critique of 'Western rationality', and some feminists talk, absurdly, of 'masculine logic'. The assumption in both cases is that what are usually offered as transcendental principles to guide all thought are actually no more than local social norms, and could in principle be replaced by other norms. In some cases this can clearly be done. A category like 'home' would probably be unintelligible to a hunting–gathering nomad, and it is also true that he would have no home, in the sense in which a village-dweller has a home. But no human group is without a language or a system of family relationships, and the basis of these is biological, though the variations in their form are cultural. And standard logical principles – e.g. CKCpqpq – are universally valid and would remain so, even if there were nobody in the world to whom they were intelligible, or indeed, even if the world were barren, and had never carried life or intelligence of any kind.[5]

One of the main functions of sociological Kantianism is to explain why it is that our ethical and aesthetic judgements take on an air of naturalness and necessity. A moral law is a social norm, but it is one that has become a part of the self-identity of the subject. An aesthetic principle is a social norm; but again, it is one that has become part of the self-identity of the subject. That is the source of the intrinsic necessity and objectivity that these laws are felt to have. They are constitutive principles of the moral and the aesthetic for that subject. That is why people can have such immensely strong convictions on moral and aesthetic matters. What they feel is right, or find attractive, has been taken from society and is thus known to be outside the self; but has become the very foundation of the self that is judging or being attracted; and is, therefore, also the personal expression of that self.

At this point an important qualification arises. *A priori* truths of the third category are true only while society remains static. History alters them. With that observation, Kantianism terminates; and Hegelianism begins.[6]

NOTES

1. K. Popper 1963, *Conjectures and Refutations: the Growth of Scientific Knowledge.*
2. See Chapter 10 for further discussion.
3. One form of the principle is that, if something has happened often in the past, it will happen often in the future. The only basis for believing this is past experience; and the only basis for reasoning from past experience is the principle of induction itself!
4. In my view Karl Popper (1959; 1963; 1972) has provided a satisfactory alternative basis for empiricism in the principle of conjecture mentioned earlier. On his view we never do know that the sun will rise tomorrow. All empirical claims have the status of temporary conjectures, held till they are refuted (i.e. till they cease to work). I think the sun will rise tomorrow because I think the earth is spinning on its axis and can't easily be stopped; an earlier thinker might have thought the sun was being carried round the earth by an angel, who had a duty not to stop. Both of these are good bases for prediction.
5. The formula CKCpqpq in standard Polish logical notation means 'If a proposition "p implies q" is true, and the proposition "p" is true then the proposition "q" is true.' This composite proposition is an analytic truth and a tautology; it is true in all possible worlds, but makes no substantive claims about any of them.

6. This is rather a schematic division. The historical Kant was well aware of the existence of history; and the historical Hegel did not think that every concept was subject to historical change. But the essential point remains.

BOOKS

Plato Fourth century BC *Republic.*
 Theaetetus.
 Protagoras.
 Parmenides.
 Plato's Epistemology and Related Logical Problems (Selections by Gwynneth Matthews 1972).
René Descartes (ed. Anscombe and Geach) *Philosophical Writings* (OU, 1970).
Immanuel Kant 1781 *Critique of Pure Reason.*
 1788 *Critique of Practical Reason.*
 1790 *Critique of Judgement.*
G. Hegel 1807 *The Phenomenology of Mind.*
Noam Chomsky 1966 *Cartesian Linguistics.*
Mahaffy and **Bernard** 1889 *Kant's Critical Philosophy for English Readers.*
Israel Knox 1936 *The Aesthetic Theories of Kant, Hegel, and Schopenhauer.*
Ernst Cassirer 1945 *Rousseau Kant Goethe: Two essays.*
Lucien Goldmann 1948 *Introduction à la philosophie de Kant.*
P.F. Strawson 1966 *The Bounds of Sense: An Essay on Kant's Critique of Pure Reason.*
Roger Scruton 1982 *Kant.*
Leonard Jackson 1991 *The Poverty of Structuralism.*

CHAPTER THREE

A Complete Bourgeois Ideology

The Philosophy of Hegel

SUMMARY

G.W.F. Hegel is the great philosopher of the progressive development of human thought – of the principle that new ideas and cultural forms are built by taking up the old ones, and at once encapsulating and transcending them in new forms. For him, cultural tradition is an active, developing human Mind or Spirit, which realises itself in history in the form of nations, cultures and institutions. Marxist materialists, however, call this the development of ideology, and see it as a reflex of material developments.

Hegel's philosophical system is actually a superb example of a complete ideology. The whole of human history is presented as leading triumphantly up to Hegel's present system of ideas. All human knowledge is woven together in a fashion which provides a metaphysical justification for the existing order of things – political, religious, social and artistic. A special method of reasoning is provided – the dialectic – which makes it 'possible to prove that that history, and that order, are necessary properties of the world.

Engels sharply distinguished between Hegel's system, which he thought profoundly reactionary, and his method, which both he and Marx thought potentially revolutionary, because it depended on the incessant overthrowing of established concepts. (Modern deconstructionists take the same view of their procedures.) When Marx inverted the system, and modified the dialectic to cover class conflict rather than conceptual opposition, he turned ideology into the historical product, rather than the foundation of society. The foundation of society became an economic one. Hegel's system remained as an inexhaustible quarry from which theories of ideology can be taken.

Neither Hegel's system, nor his method, can sensibly be defended nowadays. But he has lived again in the works of those who have rejected him – Marx, Kierkegaard, Russell . . . – and has lived again and again in the Hegelian Marxisms of the twentieth century. It is more surprising to note that the relationship between structuralism and post-structuralism can be mapped directly onto the relationship between Kant and Hegel: Lévi-Straussian structuralism is a Kantian enterprise; and post-structuralism is the Hegelian dialectic with an ironic and destructive twist.

1   THE HEGELIAN SYSTEM

The German idealist philosophers who followed Kant rejected as self-contradictory a Kantian notion which is also the fundamental principle of philosophical realism: that there can be things-in-themselves which are distinct from any idea we have of them. In doing this, they made possible the construction of purely idealist systems of thought. In these, to lay out the contents of human knowledge is exactly the same thing as to lay out the real contents of the world; and to show the logical connections between parts of human knowledge is to show the logical necessity of the structure of the world. The greatest of these systems was that of Hegel, which is set out most fully in his *Encyclopaedia of the Philosophical Sciences* (1817, 1830), and it dominated philosophy up to the time of Marx.

In this system, the most general category is the **Idea**, which covers all reality: it thus corresponds to the overall principle of idealism itself, of reality as an objective system of ideas. The Idea can be broken down into three lesser categories: the Idea-in-itself, or the **Logical Idea** or logic; the Idea-outside-itself, or **Nature**, or science, and, encapsulating and reconciling these two opposed conceptions, the Idea-in-and-for-itself, or **Mind**,[1] or the human sciences. It will be seen that in modern terms these correspond roughly to logic and mathematics, to the natural sciences, and to the human sciences, morality, literature, etc. We still work roughly within this intellectual framework, and I am sure Hegel was right in thinking that it is imposed on us by the nature of things.

The Logical Idea is a very general category – Hegel himself compared it with the thoughts of God prior to the creation of any finite being –

which breaks down into subcategories eventually covering all the standard concepts of metaphysics and logic. These include, at the most basic level of metaphysics, the categories of being, nothing and becoming; and at the most basic level of logic, various types of judgement and syllogistic argument.

Nature covers the whole of what we would call the natural sciences, though they are not viewed in a very scientific way. It stretches from the most general concepts of space, time and motion down to animal and vegetable organisms.

Mind covers not just what we nowadays think of as psychology, but all the sciences of man. Its first subdivision, Subjective Mind, covers everything from the soul and consciousness down to sense-perception and thinking. Its second subdivision, Objective Mind, covers everything that goes to make up society – including, for example, the family, civil society and the state. Civil society, in turn, will include the system of wants (economics), the system of justice, and the police and corporations. Hegel goes into astonishing detail: another topic covered under Objective Mind is contract law! The third subcategorisation of Mind is Absolute Mind, which covers Art, Religion and Philosophy. All the historical schools of art and literature are to be found in here, and all the religions too. But the absolute religion is Christianity, and absolute knowledge belongs to philosophy.

On the face of it, what Hegel is offering is a pure classification system; a kind of topic-based library catalogue of all the books ever to be written. But there is more to it than that, because he also offers a special mode of reasoning, **the dialectic**, for getting from one category to another. If you start at the most basic category of metaphysics (being – it occupies the bottom right-hand corner of the system when it is laid out as a chart), there are dialectical arguments to take you from one category to another, and up to the supercategories that cover them, until you have reached absolute knowledge and delineated every aspect of the Idea. This is the nearest Hegel's system gets to a vision of God.

The essential process in Hegel's dialectic is one of reconciling, yet at the same time preserving contradictions. He undertakes to show that even a very simple category, like being, is inwardly contradictory. If you say of something simply that it is, without saying what it is, you are in effect saying nothing about it; the category **being** is identical with the category **nothing**. But this is a contradiction: how can reality be at once being and nothing? Only by being in a state of movement from one to the other: by **becoming**. (Some people find arguments like this compelling; others find them empty plays on words.) A similar argument takes us to a category at a higher level. If we say that X is something in particular, we are saying that it is not other things. So **determinate being** reconciles and preserves the contradiction of being and negation.

I discuss the dubious validity of arguments like this in the next section. If they are valid, in the end the whole Hegelian category system will be shown to be dialectically necessary. Since the categories are supposed to be, not the arbitrary inventions of a librarian, but the categories of reality itself, we will have shown that the current state of reality itself is dialectically necessary, including not only the pure categories of logic and nature, but many reassuringly familiar features of social reality, such as private property.

This is what is meant by calling Hegel's system an 'ideological' system in the modern sense. It doesn't just present the whole of current human knowledge and say 'this is the best account we can currently give of the nature of the world'. What it does is to incorporate the whole of human knowledge in an extended demonstration that the state of the world is on the whole necessary and right. As Hegel put it in *Philosophy of Right and Law* (1821), 'What is actual is rational; what is rational is actual.' This is the highest principle of conservative philosophy (to look at everything that exists, and try to find a rationale for it); though as we shall see in the next chapter, it can also be used by radicals (if a law is not rational, does it have a right to exist?).

Things are complex enough when we look at Hegel's philosophy statically, as a dialectical encyclopaedia; they get worse when you consider that the whole system is also supposed to correspond to the development of consciousness, and also to the development of cultural categories in the course of human history. A key work here is the early work, *The Phenomenology of Mind* (1807). This is mainly organised round the categories of a developing consciousness – from simple perception to self-consciousness, and so on. But it does not hesitate to use historical categories like the master–slave relationship as explanations for the development of psychological categories like self-consciousness.

The idea that we can only recognise ourselves as conscious beings in the mirror of some other consciousness is not implausible in itself; in recent times, it is one of the foundations of the thought of Jacques Lacan, to mention only one psychologist. Hegel's point, however, is that for primitive man, this leads to war! We fight and kill other people to make them recognise us. But of course they do not recognise us in any very satisfactory way when they are dead. So we let them live as slaves. The master lets the slave live so that there is someone to appreciate him as master. But the slave has the better of the transaction. He has a master to recognise as an example of a free consciousness; but the poor master only has a slave, recognition from whom hardly counts. Moreover, the master is now cut off from the real physical world, since it is the slave who works upon that, and develops his own potentialities while doing so. So all the developmental possibilities are now on the slave's side.

This is obviously myth, not history; and it is the foundation of other myths, like the Marxist myth of the world-saving proletariat. Beckett has great fun with it in the relationship of Pozzo and Lucky (*Waiting for Godot*). But in Hegel this movement between psychological or metaphysical principles and history is normal. For him, the Greek city state is humanity's attempt to realise a principle of universality; but its parochial nature contradicts that. The revolutionary state is humanity's attempt to realise absolute freedom, but destroys it, because it dissolves the articulations of society – the class system, for example – without which freedom cannot exist. One can see a real history beneath these judgements, though it is a highly tendentious one.

'Mind' – the human spirit – is thought by Hegel to develop in history, just as consciousness develops in the individual, by overcoming contradictions of this kind; and human history is essentially the history of this developing mind. In arguments like this the question of whether one is in historical time, or psychological time, or no time at all becomes impossible to answer.

We thus have the dialectical development of ideas presented as a psychic biography of the human spirit, from its primitive origins to its grasp of absolute knowledge round about Hegel's own time and largely by means of Hegel's own system. The episodes of this biography are formed by the historical succession of human cultures. Each one is destroyed by its own cultural contradictions and gives way to the next. Marxism was to take up this notion of historical contradictions which lead to social change, and try to give it a materialist sense, replacing logical contradiction with fundamental economic conflict. But the picture Hegel gives us is that of a world-spirit engaged in a continuous argument with itself, where each stage of the argument – each resolution of an earlier contradiction – produces a new stage of development.

2   THE HEGELIAN METHOD

It was the Hegelian method, not the system, that was admired by Marx and Engels; and a version of that method, the dialectic, remained central to Marxist theory from the 1840s to the 1960s. Yet it was always densely obscure, and difficult to explain or defend to non-Marxists, including some Hegelian philosophers. Some of the problems are those of adaptation; but some derive from problems in Hegel's own work.

2.1   Does the dialectic exist?

The crucial question about the Hegelian dialectic is whether it exists at all. Hegel presents it, as Plato had presented his dialectic millennia before, as a method, comparable to mathematics, or empirical reasoning, but if anything more powerful: a special method which is a reflection of the special contents of philosophy. In the following extract from the *Science of Logic*, I give Hegel's own account of his method, interspersed with some comments that explain what I understand by it, or what sense I can make of it; otherwise, quotation is continuous:

> The essential point of view is, that we have to do, altogether, with a new concept of philosophical method. As I have elsewhere recalled [*The Phenomenology of Mind*, Hegel 1807] Philosophy, since it is to be Ordered Knowledge, cannot borrow its Method from a subordinate science, such as Mathematics, any more than it can rest satisfied with categorical assertions of pure intuition [as mathematicians do], or use reasonings based on external reflection [as empirical scientists do]. But it is the nature of the content [presumably the world as a whole, philosophically analysed] and that alone which lives and stirs in philosophic cognition, while it is this very reflection of the content which itself originates and determines the nature of philosophy.

Hegel formulates his method in terms of two Kantian notions: the Understanding, which creates the objective world by applying concepts to intuitions – it 'makes determinations' – and the Reason, which works upward from the concepts employed by the Understanding to general conceptual principles. But this last makes a negative, critical step before it can make a positive, constructive one:

> Understanding makes determinations and maintains them. Reason is negative and dialectical because it dissolves into nothing the determinations of the Understanding; Reason is positive because it is the source of the Universal in which the particular is comprehended.

Kant had written of a dialectical use of reason (which he thought vain) to establish knowledge beyond experience, but Hegel disagrees:

> Just as Understanding is commonly held to be something separate from Reason regarded generally, so dialectical Reason is held to be something separate from positive Reason.

Hegel now introduces his own master category, that of mind or spirit, to reconcile understanding and reason. The notion of mind as negation has resonances through philosophy right down to Sartre, to go no later.

> But in its real truth Reason is Mind – Mind which is higher than either Reason which understands, or Understanding which reasons. Mind is the negative, it is that which constitutes the quality alike of dialectical Reason and of Understanding;

Here follows Hegel's succinct account of the fundamental logic with which 'mind' operates; it takes a simple and general concept and produces a more specific and determinate one. (A concept of the understanding so produced is what, on Kantian principles, will combine with intuitions to produce phenomena – elements of the objective world.) So far, any non-Hegelian might agree: it is the function of the mind to produce specific and determinate concepts with which to grasp the world. But for Hegel this is done by the power of the negative: you get to more specific concepts by negating simple ones:

> it [Mind] negates the simple and thus posits that determinate distinction which is the work of Understanding,

At the same time 'mind' moves upward to higher and more comprehensive concepts, which become (I suppose) the simple concepts of the next stage; at least, this is my interpretation of the difficult words that follow:

> and just as truly it resolves this distinction, and is thus dialectical. Yet it does not abide in the negation which thus results, but is *therein just as much positive*, – thus it has thereby established the first Simple, but so that the Simple is also a Universal which is in itself concrete;

Thus we arrive at the very puzzling notion of the concrete universal, which continues to play its part more than a century later in Hegelian versions of Marxism – in the aesthetic theories of Lukács, for example:

> under this universal a given particular is not subsumed; but in that determination, and in the solution thereof, the particular has also been coincidentally determined.

This logical, or para-logical process of the construction of **concrete universals** is inherent in the concepts themselves; but it produces, or rather, is, the movement of mind which gives absolute knowledge and determines the content of knowledge too:

> This movement of Mind, which in its simplicity gives itself its determinateness and hence self-equality, and which thus is the immanent development of the Notion – this movement is the Absolute Method of knowledge, and at the

same time the immanent soul of the Content of knowledge. – It is, I maintain, along this path of self-construction alone that Philosophy can become objective and demonstrated science.

(Preface, *Science of Logic*, Hegel 1812)

The key word here is **self-construction**. Knowledge is not a reflection of some pre-existing and contingent reality: knowledge (and reality) are built up as a demonstrable system by mind in its functioning.

2.2   Critics of the dialectic: Marx, Russell, Popper, Findlay

This then is Hegel's dialectical method, in his own words. To many philosophers and logicians it has seemed illogical; and I agree with them. But other philosophers have thought it a valid method. It was common in nineteenth-century expositions, though not modern ones, to set it out almost in diagrammatic form, as Thesis; Antithesis; Synthesis. At a serious level, Bertrand Russell's friend and mentor, the philosopher McTaggart, produced a version of Hegel's method so rigorous that it enabled him to show that a considerable part of Hegel's content should be left out as inconsistent with it. Even in the very first argument, in which 'being' and its complement 'nothing' are encapsulated in the higher concept 'becoming', McTaggart showed that the notion of 'becoming' ought not to include a temporal element, but should be a purely logical 'transition to being determinate'.

Hegel's most powerful critic, Karl Marx, also agreed on the importance of the dialectical method – once it had been purged of its idealism and made materialist. Not that he expected everybody to admire it: it was, he said, 'a scandal to the bourgeoisie' because it kept on breaking down concepts in a revolutionary way. And from Marx's time to the present, his followers have made it the very hallmark of bourgeois inadequacy to think 'undialectically'. It is not often clear what this means. Sometimes it seems to mean 'thinking too precisely and in fixed concepts'; and sometimes it just seems to mean 'I disagree with your results but cannot fault your logic.'

One of the greatest of Marxist philosophers, Georg Lukács (*The Young Hegel*, 1938, reprinted 1966), speaks of dialectic as 'a method which bourgeois interpreters of the *Phenomenology* have never been able to comprehend' and accuses one commentator, Haym, of 'incapacity' – for suggesting that in this work history and psychology rather interfere with each other. Lesser Marxist thinkers have often used the word 'dialectic' as a club with which to hit anybody who deviates from the current party line.

At any rate it is clear that there has been a wide range of opinion that puts a high value on the dialectic. But not everybody agrees. A large number of philosophers, who attach little value to Hegel, think that the dialectic is actually a logically unsound method of argument; and that the whole of Hegel's philosophy is based on crude logical mistakes. More worryingly, other philosophers, who greatly admire him and have devoted their lives to studying his work, have concluded that there is no such method as the dialectic at all. It is a piece of charlatanism, or an illusion. How can this be?

Hegel's *Logic* is baffling; and it has the strange quality of being more baffling to those who have a profound knowledge of logic than to those who do not know very much about it. I am thinking, for example, of Bertrand Russell. Russell came to the conclusion (Russell 1946) that the whole imposing edifice was founded on a mistake: that of confusing qualities and relational properties. I am not sure that he is right; I am not sure of anything where Hegel is concerned. But nobody has ever been better qualified to make this judgement than Russell: one of the three or four men who can be said to have founded modern formal logic, co-author of *Principia Mathematica*.

Russell also dismissed Hegel's curious conflation of logic and metaphysics with human history. This he hardly considered serious enough to offer serious arguments against; mere irony would do: 'World history, in fact, has advanced through the categories, from Pure Being in China (of which Hegel knew nothing except that it was) . . .' (Russell 1946, p. 762).

It is customary among social scientists and Marxists to dismiss Russell's view as mere incomprehension, not worth taking seriously. But this really will not do. Early in his life, under McTaggart's influence, Russell became a Hegelian, and remained so for two or three years (Russell 1967, p. 63). He went on to study the foundations of mathematics and logic – and to lay new foundations. In the course of this work he had to introduce 'a new mathematical technique, by which regions [like the properties of infinite sets, or of negation] formerly abandoned to the vaguenesses of philosophers were conquered for the precision of exact formulae' (p. 145).

So the fact is that when Russell rejected the dialectic, because of the unsoundness of the logical arguments within it, he knew exactly what he was doing, and had good grounds for doing it. By Russell's standards – the standards he had to adopt to produce his work at all, and the standards all modern formal logicians accept, the system of *Principia Mathematica* is a genuine system and holds together logically; that of Hegel does not hold together logically and is secured by obscure rhetoric.

There is a sophisticated Marxist/Hegelian response to this point. It is that the production of formal systems is itself a product of bourgeois rationality, and to be understood in dialectical terms (cf. Lukács 1966). But this doesn't make Hegel's logic any better. There is also the unsophisticated response that bourgeois thinkers just can't understand the dialectic, so there. But it is hard to see the libertarian aristocrat Russell as a bourgeois apologist, or paid lackey of the capitalist system, unless one sees every articulate critic of Marx or Hegel as such.

A more plausible example of a philosopher who 'doesn't understand what he's attacking' is Karl Popper; and I have no intention of defending *The Open Society and Its Enemies*. But (given the extreme obscurity of Hegel's formulations) Popper's account of dialectic in *Conjectures and Refutations* (1963), seems not totally unfair as a possible, though admittedly adverse, summary.

However, as I have said, we don't need to turn to avowed anti-Hegelians to doubt the dialectic. J.N. Findlay – a Hegelian so committed that he could find Hegel's treatment of science 'brilliant' – in one of the more thorough treatments there has been (*Hegel – a Re-examination*, 1958) concluded that there was no definite dialectical method, and Hegel's method often masks the true nature of his thought. Walter Kaufmann (*Hegel: Reinterpretation, Texts and Commentary*, 1965) went further. *The Phenomenology* is merely a 'logic of passion'. Hegel throws himself into one philosophical position after another, exhausting each in turn. Ivan Soll, Kaufmann's student, caps this by arguing that the *Logic* is merely a 'logic of passion' (Soll 1969). Charles Taylor (*Hegel*, 1975) says 'In fact the PhG (*Phenomenology of Mind*) is more impressive and persuasive as interpretation of certain passages of political and religious history than it is as argument.' With friends like these, the dialectic needs no enemies.

2.3   Rescuing the dialectic

One is bound to ask, then, can we rescue the dialectic? I think in fact that we can, and we should, as a valuable instrument in a number of areas including literary theory. But the way to start is with a bold counter-attack, delivered by J.N. Findlay in the very area of mathematical logic in which the principal weaknesses of the dialectic would seem to lie.

For Findlay retracted his view that there was no definite dialectical method. One year after his book was published, in a paper called 'The Contemporary Relevance of Hegel' (*Language, Mind and Value*, Findlay 1963) he gave an account of the dialectical method in the following terms:

I should say that the basic characteristic of the dialectical method is that it always involves higher-order comment on a thought position previously achieved. What one does in dialectic is first to operate at a given level of thought, to accept its basic assumptions, and to go to the limit in its terms, and then to proceed to stand outside of it, to become conscious of it, to become clear as to what it really has achieved, and how far these achievements do or do not square with its actual professions. In dialectic one sees what can be said about a certain thought-position that one cannot actually say in it. And the sort of comment made in dialectic is not a comment on the correctness or truth of what is said in a certain manner or in terms of certain concepts, but a comment on the adequacy or logical satisfactoriness of the conceptual approaches one has been employing. In dialectic one criticises one's mode of conceiving things, rather than the actual matter of fact that one has conceived . . . . What Hegel does is in fact extraordinarily like what is done in modern syntactics or semantics or similar formal studies, when we pass from discourse in a language to discourse about that language, when we make a language an object-language for a metalanguage. It includes, of course, the further willingness to make what is brought out in this manner itself part of a widened object-language, but this is likewise something regularly done in many metalinguistic exercises. What is further important to realise is that such metalinguistic dialectical comment always involves the possible emergence of definite novelties of principle, things not formally entailed by what one has done at the lower level. Sometimes these novelties are slight, mere reaffirmations or endorsements or particularly stressed versions of what one had previously thought: sometimes, however, they involve an ironical swing-over to what is totally contrary, the assertion about X of something which is just the opposite of what X itself intends or asserts, as when we assert from a higher level the complete nullity of a distinction which a lower level vehemently makes; sometimes again they involve the making clear of a conceptual inadequacy, and the concealed need for some sense-making, saving complement. Sometimes, still more remarkably, they involve a reversal of perspective which turns a problem into an explanation: we come to see in certain very difficult contrasts and oppositions the 'very nature' of something which requires just these contrasts and oppositions and so renders them acceptable.

With great panache, Findlay goes on to suggest Cantor's theory of transfinite numbers, and Gödel's theorem concerning undecidable sentences, as cases in point. These are very impressive examples; much more impressive, actually, than the Hegelian triad of being, nothing, and becoming, to which he goes on.

My own feeling is that Findlay has, at great cost, made his case. He has established that there is a legitimate dialectical method in philosophy: but a linguistic and logical method alone. This dialectic – which is sound – says nothing about such Hegelian topics as the development of consciousness through contradiction, and still less about the actual content of being. So far as it is a valid method, it is less than fully Hegelian; and it wasn't Hegel who practised it in its valid form. So far as it is Hegelian, that is to say, idealist and ontological, it isn't strictly valid.

2.4   Hegel as post-structuralist

All the same, Findlay produces some quite marvellous examples of the 'dialectical swing-over in the history of philosophy', which make the Hegelian method seem both fruitful and central, whatever one thinks of the Hegelian system:

> Descartes's Cogito which turns universal first-order doubt into absolute higher-level certainty, Anselm's similar transformation of the God doubted by the fool into a being that even the philosopher cannot doubt, Hume's ironic claim that the hideous pantheism of Spinoza was in fact indistinguishable from a belief in an underlying substantial soul, Wittgenstein's solipsism which by eliminating the possibility of talking about another person's experiences ends by making it impossible to speak of one's own, etc., etc. We perform similar dialectical moves when we recognise concreteness to be an extraordinarily abstract notion, the idea of beauty to be profoundly unbeautiful in its non-sensuous remoteness, the militancy of the 'free-world' to be in danger of becoming tyrannical, the null-class or class devoid of members to be itself a perfectly good member of a class of higher order, the absence of the *doux printemps d'autrefois* to be itself lamentably present, the wonderful abstractness and gratuitous purity of a behaviourist theory to testify unwittingly and unwillingly to the existence of what can never be fully evinced in behaviour, etc., etc.

At this point the relevance of Findlay's reconstructed dialectic to our modern concerns becomes unmistakable. Say no more (one is inclined to say), all is now plain. Hegel was a post-structuralist.

But Findlay (who was of course writing before post-structuralism was invented) has a caution to offer:

> [Dialectic] is a method in which step 2 is a true and inevitable and sometimes ironic comment on what has been present at step 1, step 3 a true and inevitable comment on what has been present at step 2, and so on. If at any stage in this proceeding, a step is not the true and inevitable comment on what went before, wrung from it by reflection, then the step in question is not valid. Hegel's dialectic is not an amusing or boring parlour game of setting up arbitrary oppositions and then arbitrarily 'overcoming' them. The emergence of the oppositions and their overcoming must be the inevitable fruit of reflection on what the notions are, if it is to be valid at all: it must, as Hegel says, be the *Erfahrung*, the experience of the previous phase, or, more radically, it must simply be what is involved in the conscious view that the previous phase has gone before, much as, on a plausible analysis of time, the content of the present simply is the pastness of whatever has gone before it.
>
> (Findlay 1963, pp. 219–22)

Can one take seriously this thesis of the relationship of post-structuralism to the dialectic? Obviously no formal proof is possible. The dialectic is at best an exceedingly ill-defined method; post-structuralism is a chaotic and consciously ironic intellectual movement. The terms of the argument are too vague for precise arguments to bite on them. And, however negative his methods, Hegel is concerned with the construction of a totalising system; Derrida, for example, with unsettling existing systems by shaking their foundations. In this respect, as we shall see in the next chapter, it is the Left-Hegelians who resemble the post-structuralists.

But I think there are three theses worth defending.

The first is, as I have suggested, that the underlying philosophy of the structuralist programme was, and had to be, Kantian;[2] the post-structuralist development of it corresponds to the Hegelian critique of Kant, in the way in which it attempts to break down fixed, pre-existing conceptual categories.

The second is, that there is a rational core to all forms of post-structuralism, which is this: that if one takes any totalising intellectual system, and takes the small details, or the voices, which are systematically excluded from it, one can invariably subvert the whole system. This rational core seems to me to be an aspect of the negative side of the Hegelian dialectic – though to be fair one might equally describe it as the Socratic dialectic, which is the negative or non-constructive side of Platonic dialectic. We have here a fairly general method of critical philosophy.

The third is, that post-structuralism has produced, and of its nature can produce, no totalising system. Its parts, however, tend to occupy, in a curiously skewed way, the intellectual territory once occupied by the whole Hegelian system. Lacan on consciousness, Derrida and a distorted Saussureanism providing the Logic, Foucault offering an idealist reinterpretation of history; even Althusser, with his desperate attempt to deny Hegel and set Marx back on his feet, ending up with what I shall describe as an idealism of discourse, and a theory of the subject, that are essentially left-Hegelian.

But that requires another chapter. In the meantime, a more pressing intellectual question awaits us. How can a system and a method, as abstract, as conceptual, and ultimately as conservative in its outcome as this, have been converted into a materialist theory of history, underlying a programme for revolution? For that two steps needed to be taken: the step into left-wing Hegelian philosophy, and the step out of philosophy altogether, into a new theory of history, and a critique of bourgeois economics.

NOTES

1. *Geist* – can legitimately be translated either 'Mind' or 'Spirit'. The former emphasises the insistent rationalism of Hegel's approach; the latter shows how far it is a substitute for a religion.
2. This argument is fully developed in Jackson 1991, *The Poverty of Structuralism*.

BOOKS

G. Hegel 1807 *The Phenomenology of Mind*.

1953 *The Philosophy of Hegel* (ed. Carl Friedrich).

1817, 1830 *Encyclopaedia of the Philosophical Sciences*.

1971 *Hegel's Philosophy of Mind* (ed. Findlay and Miller).

David Ritchie 1893 *Darwin and Hegel, with other philosophical studies*.

J. McTaggart Ellis McTaggart 1910 *A Commentary on Hegel's Logic*.

W.T. Stace 1923 *The Philosophy of Hegel: A Systematic Exposition*.

J.N. Findlay 1958 *Hegel – a Re-examination*.

1963 *Language, Mind and Value*.

Walter Kaufmann 1965 *Hegel: Reinterpretation, Texts and Commentary*.

Ivan Soll 1969 *An Introduction to Hegel's Metaphysics*.

Charles Taylor 1975 *Hegel*.

CHAPTER FOUR

Hegelian Marxism

Alienation, the Dialectic and Socialist Science

SUMMARY

This chapter offers an account of Marx's early left-Hegelianism, which has
been more influential on Western Marxism – and hence on literary theory
– than his mature economic science. It also considers the problem of
moving from an idealist philosophical system, whether intended to
provide a rationale or a critique of the existing social order, to a putative
science of society, intended as a basis for overthrowing the existing order,
and establishing scientific socialism. I take as main text for discussion the
Theses on Feuerbach – the brief unpublished early notes which Engels later
retrieved. In their very brevity, incompleteness, and suggestiveness, these
probably represent Marx at his most philosophically profound, though
there is surely no excuse for taking them as defining Marxism.

As we shall see in later chapters, Western Marxists returned to the early
Marx because they wanted, not a science of society, but a critical
philosophy; and literary theorists have tended to follow them. I would like
to have a materialist science of society, though I doubt if Marxism is it;
and use the *Theses* to raise again the question of whether it is possible.
Faced with the difficulties posed by nineteenth-century determinist
concepts of science, Marx evolved the materialist dialectic: an adaptation
of Hegel's dialectic which obviously will not work. Modern physics, and
the mathematics of chaos theory, which extends far beyond physics,
suggest different terms for this problem: a theory of society which is fully
materialist and economically reductive, but neither dialectical nor
determinist. There is an odd parallel here with Marx's early thesis on
Democritus.

1   THE THREE SOURCES OF MARXISM

Marxism was constructed out of German idealist philosophy, French and English utopian socialism, and Anglo-Scottish political economy. The last was essentially an ideology of current capitalism, but was projected as timeless economic truth. Each of these had to be transformed. Political economy had to be shown as a historical product, that could change in the future. Idealist philosophy had to be turned into a materialist science of history and society. This science had to become the basis, not of projected socialist utopias, but of a scientific socialism, with a practical programme for the revolutionary transformation of society. I deal here with the philosophical problems that Marx faced, rather than the political and economic ones, though of course they all interconnect.

2   THE LEFT-HEGELIANS

2.1   *Hegel as conceptual revolutionary*

Marx began as a follower of Hegel – a junior member of a coterie of left-wing Hegelians who aspired to change society by making a philosophical critique of it. If one thinks that society is based on human ideas, this is not an unreasonable project; nor is Hegel an absurd master to choose, so far as intellectual method is concerned. If concepts were all that mattered, he would be the most revolutionary of philosophers. He is never satisfied with a concept; he tests it to destruction, negates it, sublates it under a higher, more comprehensive concept;[1] then starts the whole process over and over again. He is the philosopher of perpetual conceptual revolution. Politically it is another matter. There is a central principle in his philosophy which does not change, and which can have malign political effects. It is the principle that reason will embody itself in the world; it cannot be stopped; we can see its working in actual history; and if we can't, that is because it isn't really reason. In the phrase previously quoted from the beginning of the *Philosophy of Right and Law.* 'What is actual is rational; what is rational is actual.'

Such a principle as this is double-edged. It could lead to radical conclusions: to a condemnation as in some sense non–actual or unreal of those aspects of the Prussian state which were manifestly irrational. But it was more likely to lead to conservative conclusions: to the view that since the state was, after all, actual, there must be some rationality in it, even if that did not obviously appear. In these circumstances, philosophy, however radical its handling of concepts, becomes simply a means of justification for the status quo.

That is what Hegel's mature political philosophy became. The young Hegel, as Lukács[2] pointed out, was very radical. The old Hegel was a distinguished pillar of the Prussian state. More to the point, his mature philosophy expounded the meaning of that state. And the meaning of the state is no less than the ethical idea!

To see what this means, it is necessary to toil again, for a little, through the labyrinths of Hegel's fantastic system. For Hegel the human soul and consciousness belong to the subjective aspects of mind or spirit; and they need to be objectified in the world as objective aspects of spirit – that is, human institutions – before we can pass on to the final realm of absolute spirit. Institutions like property, contract and the criminal law are thus much more metaphysically dignified than one supposed: they are the objectification of the human spirit. Thus the category of **property** arises directly from the fact that human beings are persons, not to be used as means towards an end, and things are not persons, and may be appropriated. As Stace puts it (1923, p. 383): 'It is not merely property, but *private* property, which is here shown to be a necessity of reason. For the right of property springs from and inheres in the *single* individual person. Hegel is therefore opposed to schemes for the abolition of property.'

Private property therefore ceases to be a mere economic matter, and acquires an extraordinary metaphysical grandeur, as a necessity of reason itself.

These institutions belong to an area of abstract right: of what is right independently of individual conscious experience. Their partial negation – non-abstract right as it were, or the ordinary individual moral life – is what we think of as morality: purpose, intention and well-being, goodness and wickedness. It is the synthesis of these two – of abstract right and moral experience – that is the field of social ethics. At the heart of social ethics we find the institution of the family. (It is, after all, there that property rights and personal feeling combine.) When we pass beyond the limits of the family, we move to the larger, non-family relationships that make up civil society. And the higher synthesis of these family and non-family relationships is the state. Thus the state is the highest embodiment of the ethical idea; and on this basis we can even work out what constitution it ought to have. (Constitutional monarchy with a strong executive and a legislature and the people kept well under control.) This time, metaphysics has arrived at a justification in terms of dialectical reason of a reformed Prussian monarchy.

It is possible to make this a little more palatable by explaining that it isn't necessarily the actual empirical Prussian state that Hegel lived in that has that meaning; it is more the ideal state, the rational state. And it embodies the ethical idea through standing not for any particular interest but above all interests. And there is even a radical political hope implicitly built in, of the following kind: if the official philosophy of the state says that this autocratic monarchy is the incarnation of the ethical idea, perhaps it will become so. (Perhaps, even, the king will adopt a proper constitution.) Even so, this is clearly a philosophy to make democrats sick at heart. And in fact few liberal philosophies have ever succeeded in being as right-wing as Hegel's *Philosophy of Right and Law*. At one point in this document he manages to put part of the blame on the slave for the ethical shortcomings of slavery. (Because the slave doesn't actually kill himself rather than be a slave.)

Yet there were several cracks in this philosophy that the young left-wing Hegelians could exploit. Some concerned questions of substantive belief. Hegel had interpreted religion as a step on the way to the absolute knowledge, or knowledge of the absolute, conferred by philosophy. Turn that round, and one has an attack on the truth of religion, which becomes a mere partial understanding, in picturesque terms, of the truths that philosophy alone discloses. Hence no Hegelian could be a fundamentalist religious believer. The young Left-Hegelians did their best work in making religion incredible.

Other cracks radiate from the fundamental principle that only the rational is the real. Once accept this, and every powerful argument that an existing practice is irrational, becomes a powerful argument that it is, in some sense unreal; and nothing would be lost by abolishing it. Both church and court could be pushed towards unreality by the dialectic of the Left-Hegelians.

Until recently, one might have thought it impossible to believe that a political institution would collapse simply because it had come to seem irrational and therefore unreal. But the recent collapse of the Communist parties in Eastern Europe looked very like that. They collapsed because they had come to seem, in the light of their own ideological premises, hopelessly irrational; nobody believed in them any more. However, in their case, there was also the question of economic collapse to be considered: the base went before the superstructure did. The German state of Marx's early days, like the Soviet state under Stalin, or modern capitalism, was made of sterner stuff. It could not be talked out of existence by a few philosophical dissidents.

In *The German Ideology*, Marx and Engels left an unforgettable verdict on the Left-Hegelian philosophical movement:

As we hear from the German ideologists, Germany has in the last few years gone through an unparalleled revolution. The decomposition of the Hegelian philosophy, which began with Strauss, has developed into a universal ferment into which all the 'powers of the past' are swept. In the general chaos mighty empires have arisen only to meet with immediate doom, heroes have emerged momentarily only to be hurled back into obscurity by bolder and stronger rivals. It was a revolution beside which the French Revolution was child's play, a world struggle beside which the struggles of the Diadochi appear insignificant. Principles ousted one another, heroes of the mind overthrew each other with unheard-of rapidity, and in the three years 1842–45 more of the past was swept away in Germany than at other times in three centuries.

All this is supposed to have taken place in the realm of pure thought.

(p. 27)

It is in these terms that Marx and Engels sardonically dismiss the achievements of an intellectual left to which they themselves had up to that point belonged. If their view is correct, Left-Hegelianism was not in the least like the powerful dissidence that brought down Communism in the 1980s. In its pretentiousness and its political ineffectuality, there is rather a parallel with the intellectual left in the West from the 1960s on.

Consider the gigantic revolution of Derrida, who makes tremble the entire metaphysical enclosure of Western thought. Or that of Deleuze and Guattari, who replace the ideal of Oedipalised, socialised man by the ideal of the unsocialised schizophrenic. Or the work of Foucault, who makes truth a mere product of power and finds power everywhere. Who has not felt the metaphysical ground tremble beneath his imagined feet as he has read the post-structuralists? Or consider (with all reverence) the triumphant revolution in our conceptions of women wrought by the feminists. Do not these things constitute a revolution which makes the failed French revolution of 1968 look like child's play?

And we cannot dismiss these modern revolutions, in the way that Marx and Engels dismissed theirs, by saying that they took place in the realm of pure thought. They did not. As any modern materialist will tell you, they took place in the wholly material realm of discourse. That makes a lot of difference.

If I am right in my general argument, this strange parallelism between the Left-Hegelianism of the 1830s and 1840s, and the post-structuralism of the 1970s and 1980s, is much more than a casual resemblance. The move from structuralism to post-structuralism is an exact parallel to the move from Kant to Hegel. Structuralism, as Lévi-Strauss acknowledged, is based on the Kantian idea of discovering pre-given mental structures that control experience. And – thinking strictly of forms of argument, for the moment – whatever is valid in the various forms of post-structuralism is fully contained in the extended concept of the Hegelian dialectic, described by Findlay. (I would myself go a stage further, and argue that whatever is valid in post-structuralism is also present in the Socratic dialectic, and can be defined as the application of *reductio ad absurdum* arguments to our concepts.)

Furthermore, at the social level, like causes produce like effects. Both the Left-Hegelians and the post-structuralists were economically and politically marginalised intellectuals, with a literary and philosophical background; the ideology they produced is fully explicable in these terms. There is even a standard Marxist theorisation. The process of production of a philosophy that matches the 'possible consciousness' of a group like this is theorised in Goldmann's 'genetic structuralism' – see Chapter 7. In the life-history of Marxism, the way out was the same as the way in. Marxism died, as it was born, in the departments of what *The German Ideology* called critical criticism; and it died of idealism.

2.2   Alienation, the intellectuals and the proletariat

Most of German philosophical criticism (Marx and Engels say all of it) was confined to attacks on religious conceptions. The most important of these – it provides the core of the concept of **alienation**, and is very important for the theory of **ideology** – was Feuerbach's early work *The Essence of Christianity*. This argues that men's beliefs about God are a mystified version of intuited truths about themselves. Men become conscious of themselves, in fact, by becoming conscious of objects (this is an essentially Hegelian position). The object in which they affirm their full human nature is God: on him they project their own powers and attributes, raised to infinity. Religion, treating God as real and man as derivative, is actually treating the properties of man as real and man as a mere attribute. Logically, it is inverting the relationship between subject and predicate.

Marx took up this methodological point in 1843–4 in his powerful critique of the idealist doctrine of the state found in Hegel's *Philosophy of Right and Law* 1843–4.[3] Hegel, he argued, was throughout inverting subject and predicate. That is, when Hegel finds that some material element of society falls under some concept he argues that **the concept has found itself a material embodiment** in that element of society. Marx's thoroughgoing dismantling of this ideas-first approach is the first step on his road to historical materialism. But he remains deeply marked by it; and by the Hegelian argument from contradiction. One of the most important substantive elements of Marxism, central to all its forms down to the present day, was actually derived by Marx from a purely philosophical argument, employing Hegelian dialectic. This element is the notion that the fundamental revolutionary class is the proletariat.

Hegel recognises that there are many antagonist classes and institutions with their own special interests. In accordance with his principle of finding a real embodiment of any important general principle, he looks for something to embody the interests of the state as a whole: he finds this in the class of officials – in real life, the Prussian bureaucracy – who have no interests of their own apart from the interests of the whole state. In his 'Critique of Hegel's Doctrine of the State', Marx has no difficulty in demolishing this claim, and does so at inordinate length. In his Introduction to his 'Critique of Hegel's Philosophy of Right', published in 1844 in the *Deutsche–Französiche Jahrbücher*, and beginning with a Feuerbachian critique of religion, Marx looks for a new class which shall carry the burden of German emancipation. He finds this in a class totally alienated from the state and from society:

> in the formation of a class with *radical chains*, a class of civil society which is not a class of civil society, an estate which is the dissolution of all estates, a sphere which has a universal character by its universal suffering . . . which cannot emancipate itself without emancipating itself from all other spheres of society, and thereby emancipating all other spheres of society . . .
>
> By heralding the *dissolution of the hereto existing world order* the proletariat merely proclaims *the secret of its own existence*, for it is the *actual* dissolution of that world order. By demanding the *negation of private property* the proletariat merely raises to the rank of a *principle of society* what society has raised to the rank of *its* principle, what is already incorporated in *it* as the negative result of society without its own participation.[4]

By the standards of science, or indeed of most philosophy, these are very bad arguments; indeed, they are nothing more than literary conceits, in a vein of philosophical sarcasm that Marx was to continue all his life, and that finds a characteristic expression in, for example, *The Eighteenth Brumaire of Louis Bonaparte*. But they are not bad as Hegelian arguments. If it is all right for Hegel to find the principle of the state embodied in the bureaucracy, it is all right for Marx to find the principle of the revolution embodied in the proletariat.

In his book *Modern Tragedy* Raymond Williams finds something in this passage far deeper than the 'philosophical sarcasm' I have suggested. He sees it as an essentially tragic vision of revolution – of revolution as 'the inevitable working through of a deep and tragic disorder, to which we can respond in varying ways but which will, in any case, in one way or another, work its way through our world, as a consequence of any of our actions'.[5] This seems to me one of the finest things that has been said in modern times, either of revolution or of tragedy. If left-wing literary critics generally operated at this level of seriousness, one would wish to be of their number.

I am afraid that the main attraction of the proletariat for intellectuals comes from a slightly different source: romantic identification. Many intellectuals, from well before Marx's time to the present day, have felt thoroughly alienated from the characteristic concerns of bourgeois society, which can reasonably be described (and, in *Capital*, were to be in very precise terms described) as making a **fetish** of **commodities**. This feeling of **alienation** underlies a great deal of romantic and modernist art. In art, however, it is presented as a feeling: *angst* or existential anxiety perhaps. Its underlying socio-economic causes, assuming it has them, are not necessarily known to the artist, and it is often seen as the inevitable and universal condition of humanity. The young Marx, the young Lukács and the young college lecturer in the later twentieth century are equally likely to feel this way; it is a reasonable feeling to have. The question is, what is its cause?

Hegel had described the whole of history as a dialectical process of growth in which mind alienated or objectified itself into the world, in the form of social institutions, for example, and then resumed the new objects into itself by constructing a higher sense out of their very contradictions; we have seen how this happens with private property, the family and the state. Absolute mind was the terminus of this whole process: thought thinking about itself, the subject identical with the object, the meaning of the whole luminously present in the existence of the whole. This mystical vision of identity was produced by dialectical reason, but made real by reason working within history. **Alienation** or objectification is an essential step on the way, but mind alienates its own substance only to resume it at a higher level.

Marx, brilliantly or confusingly, identified both forms of **alienation** with the condition of the proletariat, which sells its labour (alienating its own creative substance) to make commodities to be sold rather than objects to be used for its own creative purposes. In doing this it builds up capital for others, and its own labour thus takes on the form of an alien power that oppresses it. The proletariat would resume that creative substance into itself only by a process of political and economic revolution that brought it control of capital (its own congealed labour) again. Such a revolution would abolish alienation, along with more material evils like poverty, war and the state – the early Marx thought it would even abolish the division of labour as well.

Given this myth to work upon, for ever afterwards, bourgeois intellectuals could call upon their own feelings of alienation and project them into the entirely different situation of the working class. Their feelings, and indeed their intellectual principles, often blinded them to the views of actual proletarians. The son of a banker, like Georg Lukács, hating the bourgeoisie himself, could hardly be expected to notice that many of the working class wanted nothing so much as to become bourgeois, and could easily identify with the very interests he was alienated from. But if he did notice he didn't care; what mattered was the consciousness that could be **imputed** to them: namely, that of a class self-consciously taking control of society and its own destinies, and so overcoming alienation.

The doctrine of the proletariat as the destined revolutionary class became the central political doctrine of the whole Marxist movement, and remains so, for some, down to the present day. Thus, for Lukács, in the 1920s, the proletariat was uniquely privileged epistemologically: only it could see the truth about society; the bourgeoisie was self-blinded. Of course, individual proletarians were not privileged in this way: it was imputed consciousness that mattered; if you wanted to know what the consciousness of the proletariat was, you asked the party. Lukács was too extreme on this point even for Lenin; but Lenin's principle of the centrally disciplined party ensured that it was party workers and not proletarians who eventually decided what the proletariat wanted.

For Marxists, after the revolution, the proletariat was entitled to hold a dictatorship over society, until counter-revolution had been quelled and communism brought about. Of course, in practice, when a form of socialism was installed throughout Eastern Europe, this dictatorship was exercised by the Communist Party; with results that we all know. A privileged class of bureaucrats ruled despotically and inefficiently in the proletarian name, until all the economies collapsed and there were popular revolutions against the party.

But why was the proletariat given this theoretical significance in the first place? One is entitled to ask: 'Did our whole revolutionary faith rest on a set of literary paradoxes, constructed by marginalised intellectuals to protect their own self-esteem? Or did the later, materialist Marx find some better arguments?' In fact, by the time of *The Communist Manifesto*, in 1848, better arguments had been found. One such argument was the prediction, on purely economic grounds, that the proletariat would continue to increase in numbers, while the bourgeoisie would shrink in numbers as big capitalists gobbled up little ones. Meanwhile, the operations of industry itself would discipline the proletariat and create industrial armies. In the end (so the story went) the victory of the proletariat would be inevitable. And, unlike other revolutions in which one ruling class replaced another but continued to oppress the classes below, the proletarian revolution would leave no classes below it to oppress. Hence oppression would end.

This prediction is materialist and non-paradoxical, and successfully hides the Hegelian dialectic and the theory of alienation from which it originally sprang. It turned out, however, to be quite false, both in the short term and the long. The 1848 revolutions failed. Bourgeois society managed to spread its capital around till it could not be confiscated (much of modern industry in capitalist states is owned by financial institutions like pension funds);[6] the proletariat decreased as a proportion of the population; and where there were socialist revolutions, they merely installed new bureaucratic ruling classes which were never less than oppressive and sometimes became genocidal. Predictive failure as comprehensive as this casts some doubt on the scientific basis of the predictions. To assess this we need to consider the new Marxist social science.

3.   THE *THESES ON FEUERBACH*

Sometime between 1842 and 1848 Karl Marx invented a new science: that is, he transformed a system of philosophy and a set of philosophical controversies into a putative science of history and society, which was later given the name **historical materialism**. He did this at a time when he had quite enough personal and political problems to solve; he had to change countries twice, make his own contribution to an international wave of revolutions, and begin life-long exile in England. These biographical matters do not concern this book. He also had to face a number of specifically philosophical issues, and to take positions on these, which have influenced the tradition of Marxism down to the present day, and without which the application of Marxist theory to cultural questions cannot be understood. A full history of the early development of Marx's thought would have to cover a range of major texts: the *Economic and Philosophical Manuscripts of 1844; The Holy Family* (1845); *The German Ideology* (1845–46); *The Poverty of Philosophy* (1846–47). I shall concentrate on something much smaller than that: a fairly close reading of some of the *Theses on Feuerbach*.

There is a superb review article on this period, *Ludwig Feuerbach and the End of Classical German Philosophy*, written by Engels in 1888, five years after Marx's death. For many years it was taken as the definitive account of the way in which Marxist materialism evolved out of the Feuerbachian kind; and it probably deserves this position. To this article Engels appended a set of eleven brief notes that he had dug from an old notebook of Marx, dated 1845. These notes were not intended for publication; they do not offer considered opinions; they have an urgent dogmatism as of someone beset by philosophical problems that he did not want and very much wanted to get out of the way. Yet it is not too much to say that they have become one main source for a whole set of Marxist philosophies, sometimes referred to as 'Western Marxism' or, not quite equivalently, 'humanist Marxism';[7] I call them Hegelian Marxism. These stand as an alternative to the central philosophical tradition of official Communism, the tradition which descends from Engels, and was often called **dialectical materialism**. The *Theses on Feuerbach* are now usually published separately; a hundred people in the West now read them for every one who reads Engels's article. I think this is a pity.

Despite their brevity, the *Theses* offer a sketch of a whole new philosophy, distinct both from the German idealisms that had preceded it, and from enlightenment materialism. This philosophy offers a new account of materialism, determinism and human freedom; of human nature as a product of social relations rather than as a pre-given essence; of the human ability to change circumstances in changing itself; and of the unity of theory and practice.

3.1 Materialism, determinism and human freedom

The most difficult intellectual problem in laying the foundations for a materialist science of society, which could be the basis of a scientific socialism, was the determinist nature of nineteenth-century natural science. There is a difficult logical problem facing anyone who tries to construct a materialist theory of politics and history. The eighteenth-century materialism which Feuerbach and his contemporaries inherited was based on a Newtonian conception of science. Suppose we conceive the world as an array of particles interacting according to known mathematical laws. As the eighteenth-century scientist Laplace argued, given the present state of the world and the mathematical laws governing it, we can in principle calculate its exact state for any other point in time, past or future.[8]

But in that case, the future is as fixed as the past. The scientific laws that govern the whole world govern also the operations of the human body. The mind can exist, if at all, only as a passive instrument of observation that watches the world happen. (This is what Marx called 'contemplative materialism'.) If the material world is all there is, and the material world is like that, then human freewill is a nonsense, and both political action and human history are meaningless illusions.

Idealism, by contrast, sees the mind as something active in making the reality that it perceives, and capable of making decisions about actions which affect both the social and material world. Now it is clear that people actually do make such decisions, and make them on the basis of reality as it appears to them. They do not automatically and unconsciously respond in the manner of a clockwork robot. They do not even automatically but consciously respond to material stimuli, in the manner of a clockwork robot with a ghostly observer attached somewhere or other.[9] They actually think and decide to do things. There appears therefore to be a prima-facie case for the idealist position rather than the materialist one.

It might be thought that the problem here is merely an inadequate conception of science. Writing in 1888, Engels pointed out that for the contemporaries of Feuerbach, modern chemistry and biology did not exist. Nowadays, he said, we conceive the physical world as a world of processes rather than things; and we see the biological world as an evolving one. Does this let us off the hook? Not really. It is still the case that late nineteenth-century science looked for causal explanations and was deterministic in character. A completed nineteenth-century chemistry and biology might look unimaginably different from the billiards-ball determinism of the eighteenth century; but it would still be expected to give a full causal account of the behaviour of the world – including the human beings in it. And such an account would still render the notion of human decisions, or human political action, meaningless.

An alternative tactic is to argue that, in Marxism, materialism means something quite different from its ordinary meaning in scientific philosophy (often qualified as 'mechanical materialism'). Engels for example claimed that there was a dialectic of nature, which described dialectical processes occurring in the material world itself; and the laws of this dialectic formed the framework for science. Thus a grain of barley when it germinates ceases to exist as grain and becomes plant, the negation of the grain; from the plant we get seeds, which are '**the negation of the negation**'. Water, placed on a burner, heats up steadily; at a certain point it boils. This abrupt change of state illustrates '**the transformation of quantity into quality**'.[10] From considerations like this developed the framework of 'dialectical materialism', which was philosophical orthodoxy for most of the world's Marxists through most of the twentieth century. It is not clear that this either makes sense or makes voluntary human action comprehensible. I discuss a rather specialised later version of it in Chapter 6, in the section on Caudwell.

Marx in 1845 offers the sketch of an alternative conception of materialism:

The chief defect of all existing materialism (that of Feuerbach included) is that the thing, reality, sensuousness, is conceived only in the form of the *object* or of *contemplation*, but not as *sensuous human activity*, *practice*, not subjectively. Hence, in contradistinction to materialism, the *active* side was developed abstractly by idealism – which of course does not know real, sensuous activity as such. Feuerbach wants sensuous objects, really distinct from thought objects, but he does not conceive human activity itself as *objective* activity . . .

(Thesis I – compare also Thesis V)

As with most of the *Theses*, this can be interpreted in several different ways. It could be merely the reasonable claim that materialism has to account for human activity. Or it could be the claim that materialism should be reconceived as the study of the subjective side of objective human activities. That would be radical indeed; it would bring Marx much closer to Heidegger, and would constitute a complete break between Marxist 'materialism' and ordinary materialism. Later theses take us further on this road:

The highest point reached by contemplative materialism, that is, materialism which does not comprehend sensuousness as practical activity, is the contemplation of single individuals and of civil society.

(Thesis IX; see also Thesis X)

It will be seen from this that there is a very clear sense in which the materialism of the early Marx is not traditional materialism at all; one might call it a mysticism of sensuous social practices. It is easy to see why the *Theses* have appealed so strongly to Hegelian Marxists, humanist Marxists, existentialists, encounter-group therapists and such like, who were repelled by the dogmatic materialism of orthodox Marxism. It is worth reiterating, then, that the *Theses* are only unpublished notes by the young Marx. There are still traces of this approach in many of the later unpublished works: in particular the *Grundrisse* of 1857. But when we look at the mature claims of the published works – the 1859 *Preface*, or *Capital* – we find a very different sort of materialism: primarily economic, but compatible with Darwinian naturalism.

3.2 Human nature as a product of society

In the theses, Marx makes a radical break with traditional materialism in his conception of human nature. The traditional view (it goes back to classical Greece, as do most of these debates) is that man has an essential nature – non-Marxist materialists like me would say a biological nature – and on top of this, a second nature is formed in him by the society in which he grows up and lives. This way of thinking is not politically innocent. There is a long tradition in social philosophy of postulating some essential human nature, deducing from it the kind of society that is natural for man; and then drawing political conclusions.

We find this in Hobbes, who made the desire for power the centre of human nature, and deduced that the natural state of man was a state of war, each man against each other man; 'and the life of man, solitary, poor, nasty, brutish, and short'.[11] From this assumption Hobbes concluded that we need an absolute sovereign to protect us from each other. We find it in Locke, who argued that in a state of nature men are in a state of perfect equality and perfect freedom to order and dispose of their possessions and persons (interesting that they should have possessions in a state of nature!). Locke concludes that we all have a natural right to restrain those who commit wrongs (like taking our property away). We may voluntarily give up this right by entering a society; and delegate our natural powers for a longer or shorter period to some governmental body.[12]

We find this in Rousseau, who makes his original principles those of self-preservation and empathy with other human beings.[13] We find it in the twentieth century in Freud, who early on makes his pair of principles self-preservation and sexuality; and later combines self-preservation with sexuality (as *eros*), and opposes them to a combination of aggression and the drive towards death (later sometimes called *thanatos*).[14] All these thinkers base social doctrines on assumptions about primary, pre-social instincts. Sometimes like Hobbes and Freud they argue that society must be used to restrain these instincts; sometimes like Rousseau, or the Utopian Socialist Fourier,[15] that it must be used to help fulfil them. But the appeal to instinct is common and in my view rational; the claim that human beings have no biological nature, or that this is irrelevant to social philosophy, seems, prima facie, absurd.

Marx found this appeal to instinct in many of his sources; in Fourier no less than Feuerbach; and even in Adam Smith he could read that man had an innate tendency to truck or barter.[16] On this view complex social institutions like religion express the essence of human nature; even the market under capitalism expresses the essence of human nature: a point which is frequently made by the right today. Marx rejected this mode of arguing, and tipped the balance far in the opposite direction. What we think of as human nature, he argued, is actually the set of social relations; the 'individual' human being is always a product of society:

Feuerbach resolves the religious essence into the *human* essence. But the human essence is no abstraction inherent in each single individual. In its reality it is the ensemble of the social relations . . . .

(Thesis VI)

Feuerbach, consequently, does not see that the 'religious sentiment' is itself a social product, and that the abstract individual whom he analyses belongs to a particular form of society.

(Thesis VII)

This anti-individualist position has become central, not just to the Marxist tradition, but to the whole tradition of sociological enquiry. Later followers of either tradition have not hesitated to adopt this doctrine in extreme and absurd forms: 'There is **no such thing** as human nature', they argue, as if innate biological capacities did not enter into the matter; as if you could socialise a chimpanzee and make a university vice-chancellor out of it.[17]

3.3   Changing circumstances and changing the self

In Marx's terms, the alternative to an idealist theory of society is a materialist one. But as we have seen, nineteenth-century materialist theories are also determinist ones; and determinism leads to worrying logical paradoxes when it is applied to human actions. Suppose we say that human culture is determined by material factors, by the environment; and if you improve the environment, you will improve the culture. The question arises: does it make sense to say 'we have power to improve the environment' if the culture that includes the decision to improve the environment is a more or less passive consequence of the environment? One might as well say 'The environment has power to improve the environment.' What we really need, of course, is the conception of a creative human response to the environment. That is, the conception that people respond to material reality in their own unexpected and unpredictable ways. But is this conception compatible with materialism or Marxism? (It would, after all, be perfectly acceptable to Dr Leavis, and is what Dr Leavis sees as the **difference** between his own position and Marxism.)[18]

In his third thesis, Marx took up this question from a political rather than a logical point of view:

The materialist doctrine concerning the changing of circumstances and upbringing forgets that circumstances are changed by men, and

that it is essential to educate the educator himself. This doctrine must, therefore, divide society into two parts, one of which is superior to society.

This is surely a very acute point. Anyone who says 'we can raise people's standards by improving their conditions' is tacitly supposing that there is a 'we' superior to the people concerned, with power to change their conditions. On such an assumption rests the whole theory of élites, on which Leavis, for example, relied for his theory of the university.

The coincidence of the changing of circumstances and of human activity or self-changing can be conceived and rationally understood only as revolutionary practice.

Here we have a rational conception of the often puzzling Marxist thesis of the identity of theory and practice. As men change their circumstances, so they change their consciousness, and understand their circumstances in a new way. But one must ask, why revolutionary practice? Logically, any practice will do; it only needs to be revolutionary if the changes to be made are very great. The philosophical point, which comes from Hegel, is that human beings change their own subjectivity by changing the world of objects. To speak of revolutionary practice only is unnecessarily limiting; this seems to be a political point placed in a philosophical argument in which it doesn't belong. However, it must be recognised that the whole activity of philosophy in this time was conceived as political; and Marx is already consciously attempting to provide a philosophy of revolution.

Theses like the above have been very attractive to Western humanist Marxists, who fundamentally want to get away from materialism and the notion of a science of society. Combined with the theses about practice, they have led to the Western tradition in which Marxism is regarded as a philosophy of praxis. Perhaps the most famous exponent of this was the Italian Communist leader Antonio Gramsci. In the *Prison Notebooks* he always refers to Marxism as the Philosophy of Praxis.[19] Part of Gramsci's reason, admittedly, was to disguise his meaning from any Fascists who might read what he had written. But it was also a matter of philosophical conviction. He was as hostile to the 'vulgar materialism' of Plekhanov as to the idealism of Croce; he saw the notion of 'inevitable stages of history' as inviting political passivity. He strongly attacked the orthodox handbook of Soviet Marxism, by Bukharin, which employed a dialectical materialist framework, for its philosophical crudity.[20]

Praxis often appears as an epistemological category; thus Georg Lukács (1923) argues that for the proletariat, theory and practice coincide as it comes to know the world in the process of transforming it. (It is not clear why they should coincide. It is perfectly possible to transform the world by accident without in the least knowing what you are doing.) It could, however, be an ontological category. On this view we would have to say that social practices are ultimate realities; the world of science is built up out of them. An electron is a disguised human practice.

If this is the case, Marxism is not a materialist, but an idealist system: for it, actions and practices are real, but matter is constructed in the mind, or in discourse. Some people have tried to maintain the materialism of Marxism by labelling practices 'material practices'. But if human practices are reckoned material, and matter, as conceived by current science, is not, we have changed our notion of materialism in a far-reaching way. The approach here is utterly different from Marx's approach in his second preface to *Capital*. This is actually compatible with orthodox brain–mind materialism, where mind is merely the natural functioning of the brain, and ideas are a reflection of the world, translated into forms of thought. The later Marx's thought was in intention scientific, even if it faced formidable scientific difficulties. Western Marxism was often not scientific even in intention. The point is discussed in Chapter 7.

3.4 *Marxism as theory and practice*

Marx's main concern in the *Theses*, as in his later, published works, is a practical, revolutionary one; but he still manages to say more interesting things than he ever managed later on about purely philosophical problems like the grounds of knowledge, and the relationship between knowledge and practice. A whole group of theses touch on these. Marx shows the desperate impatience with these problems of a man anxious to get on and construct his theories before the deluge comes:

> **The question whether objective truth can be attributed to human thinking is not a question of theory but is a practical question. Man must prove the truth, i.e. the reality and power, the this-sidedness of his thinking in practice. The dispute over the reality or non-reality of thinking that is isolated from practice is a purely scholastic question.**
>
> (Thesis II – see also Thesis VIII)

There is an ambiguity here. This might be a philistine claim that theories do not matter, or it might merely be the claim that the truth of theories has to be tested in practice – a point on which Marxists are in agreement with pragmatists and empiricists. The famous last thesis is even more impatient:

> **The philosophers have only interpreted the world, in various ways; the point is, to change it**.
>
> (Thesis XI)

These theses have often been abstracted from their original context. Marx was confronted with philosophies of activist conservative idealism, which recognised the active nature of the mind in constructing its world, but did not wish to change the actual social world; and philosophies of contemplative radical materialism, which described how a passive mind observed and was affected by an existing material world, but logically could not explain how that mind could ever act to change the world. What he was trying to do was to make materialism active and practical – to show how human beings could be conceived in material terms, and yet seen as active in the world and able to change it. If these theses are abstracted from their context and given a wholly general application, they become a charter for intellectual philistinism of the worst kind: advice not to think, but to agitate, or even advice that party advantage determines what is true.

Marx in his mature phase at least cannot have believed this. He must have believed that in order to change the world it is sometimes necessary to understand it. Why else should he have written *Capital*? The entire purpose of his enquiry was to understand capitalism in order to change it. Of course this will also involve changing working-class consciousness of capitalism – making capitalism seem like something that can be changed, rather than an unchallengeable horizon of human effort. In the twentieth century, Western Marxists came to lay great stress on this side of the dialectic, making Marxism much more voluntaristic and idealist. But writing *Capital* involved years of ordinary scientific research, looking at statistics and factory inspectors' reports. This approach presupposes that capitalism is real and can be studied objectively; and that consciousness can be changed by rational arguments based on facts.

An alternative, and far more rational, interpretation is to say that Marx is only arguing a special case of the position that **the only possible test of our theories is to construct practices on the basis of those theories and see if those practices work**. In chemistry and physics this would be merely a description of ordinary experimental method! This interpretation of Marx has always been violently rejected by the young anti-scientific activists of Western Marxism – starting with Lukács in *History and Class Consciousness*. But it has three advantages. First of all the claim is true. If this is what Marx meant he was obviously right and non-Marxist materialists can enter into dialogue with him. Second, it is the interpretation Engels adopted in the work cited above: and Engels, Marx's lifelong collaborator, was in the best position of any human being to know. Finally, the claim is practical: it leads to non-fanatical politicians who hold their theories provisionally, and will revise them in the light of practice, and to theoreticians who try to provide theories which work. This is a very practical sense of the Marxist slogan 'the unity of theory and practice'; though it is as likely to lead to reform as revolution, and might lead one to abandon Marxism altogether, if Marxism turns out not to work.

4 NON-DETERMINIST SCIENCE: MARXISM, MATERIALISM AND CHAOS THEORY

It is possible that the progress of twentieth-century science has changed the terms of our problem in a way in which the progress of nineteenth-century physical science did not. This is not merely the familiar epistemological point that we regard scientific theories as conjectural and temporary nowadays. There is also a fundamental sense in which twentieth-century science is no longer determinist, and does not claim to offer exact predictions of the future, even conjecturally, even in principle. This arises from the conjunction of two developments in science, one in the early twentieth century, and one in the last twenty years. The first is quantum theory; the second, chaos theory. The two together have odd implications for Marxist theory, and indeed for the social sciences in general.

In the early twentieth century it was discovered that very small particles have individually unpredictable behaviour. This does not mean that there are no scientific theories that apply to them. The theory of quantum electrodynamics, which offers statistical predictions about the behaviour of aggregates of particles like electrons and photons, is the most mathematically precise empirical scientific theory ever devised.[21] But all it is possible to say about the combinations, collisions, decays, and re-creations of individual particles is what the probabilities are. This destroys the Laplace model of a determinist universe.

From the beginning there have been people ready to suggest that the uncertainties of quantum effects in the brain make some sort of logical space for freewill. Marxists (from Marx onwards)[22] have always disliked this particular defence of freewill. Caudwell (1939, *The Crisis in Physics*, p. 232) is particularly vituperative: 'Jeans, Eddington, and even Schrödinger, all share this desire to prove that modern science permits freewill. There is no stratagem too mean for this unconscious bourgeois illusion to use to buttress itself . . .' But even for the non-committed, this theory has always seemed a non-starter on purely physical grounds. On the scale of fundamental particles, the brain is an enormous system; chemistry and biology appear to be governed throughout by the statistical effects which can be calculated with such enormous precision, rather than by the uncertainties affecting individual electrons.

The recent development of chaos theory may have changed the picture. Chaos theory is a branch of pure mathematics which investigates the behaviour of complex interacting systems. Most scientific research into the real world has assumed that small changes in the initial state of any system will produce only small changes in the final state. Consider an open door: push it hard, and it will slam; push it softly, and it will swing gently to. Chaos theory shows that there are many systems which do not behave like this. A very small disturbance may cause only a very small change of state. But an equally small disturbance following that may produce an enormous change of state. It may produce a sudden switch, from a stable state to a chaotic and unpredictably variable one. (A classical dialectical materialist would say that chaos theory is a precise mathematical formulation of one of the laws of dialectics: that small quantitative changes may add up to produce sudden qualitative change.)

A moment's reflection will show that there have always been simple real world systems that behave like this. Take a stretched rubber band and pull on it a little more: it stretches a little more. Pull on it a little more still, and it snaps. The tap half turned on runs smoothly; wholly turned on it sputters chaotically all over the place. More worrying for us than either of these examples is the familiar folk-anecdote that shows that human **history** has always been supposed to be like that:

> For want of a nail, the shoe was lost . . .
> For want of a shoe, the horse was lost . . .
> For want of a horse, no message came . . .
> For want of the message, the battle was lost . . .
> Through loss of the battle, the kingdom was lost . . .
> And all for want of a horse-shoe nail.

History, this story implies, is an essentially chaotic system in which tiny initial contingencies are amplified without limit; and you cannot have a predictive science of it.

There are many common systems of everyday life which appear to show chaotic behaviour. The best known is the weather. Scientifically speaking, the world's weather system is very well understood. That is, all the equations of fluid dynamics and so forth that affect it are known. Furthermore, our weather stations can supply us with a great deal of data;

and our supercomputers can make calculations of enormous complexity in real time. For all that, weather predictions for more than a few days ahead rapidly get out of phase with reality. Tiny variations in the present state of the weather are rapidly amplified to enormous dimensions. It has now become a standard image to say that the flapping of a butterfly's wings in Britain may, a month later, produce a hurricane in the Gulf of Mexico.

There are two systems of great importance to any form of materialism, and in particular Marxist materialism, which probably display chaotic behaviour of this kind. The first is the human brain. It seems very likely that the human brain, viewed simply as a material system without any regard for the human significance of what it does, is just the kind of complex system that can amplify quantum uncertainties up to the point where they become uncertainties in gross behaviour.

There is in a sense nothing particularly surprising about this; at an experimental level, it has been known for years. Any physicist who observes a track in a cloud chamber has amplified a quantum effect up to the point where it influences gross behaviour. (A fundamental particle decays – that is an effect at the quantum level. It throws off a particle that makes a track in the cloud chamber – that is a gross physical effect. The physicist takes a photograph and makes a note of the event. That is a really gross effect in the physical world.) What chaos theory suggests, however, is that the brain might possibly be working in this way all the time. It makes plausible the old suggestion that quantum uncertainties make the brain, simply as a physical system, essentially non-deterministic. But if that is the case, is its behaviour constrainable by other laws – laws of thought, laws of logic, etc.? Does this make sense within materialism of any kind?[23]

It may seem, incidentally, that these issues are very unlike anything Marx could have known about, or would have concerned himself with. Quantum theory, after all, comes eighty years after the *Theses on Feuerbach*. But this is not so. Taken on a sufficiently large scale, the history of ideas repeats itself. Two thousand years and more before Marx, a determinist atomic theory – that of Democritus – was superseded by one with non-determinist elements incorporated – that of Epicurus. The explicit purpose of the non-determinist elements was to make room for human freewill. And Marx's very first academic work was a thesis on the natural philosophy of Democritus and Epicurus, written five years before the *Theses on Feuerbach*.[24] He would probably take a keen interest in the modern continuation of this debate.

The second system that almost certainly shows chaotic behaviour is the social system. I am not talking here of historical contingencies like battles. Consider some moderately well-defined sub-part of the system, like an economy, as represented in a macroeconomic model. Such a model will have the form of a set of equations, like the equations that define the model used to predict the weather, and economic data that supply the values of the variables in those equations. It seems clear that any model that comes near to representing even a single national economy will be so complex and so interconnected that it will display chaotic features: very slight initial variations in inputs may produce gigantic final effects. If that is so, such large systems are essentially unpredictable. This may seem to be a rather abstract defect of the model employed; but it almost certainly reflects the underlying properties of the real economy modelled.

If this is correct, there is a good mathematical basis for the standard Marxist denunciation of 'the chaos of the market'. Markets really do produce chaotic and unpredictable behaviour, and this really does make it impossible for any individual to predict the course of an economy, and act rationally within it. It doesn't however follow that the usual Marxist answer – a planned economy arranged to satisfy human needs – will work any better. Rational planning is possible only where prediction is possible. Where predictions are false, planning based on them can make things worse than they would be if one reacted in a quick *ad hoc* way without an overall plan. It is entirely unclear that there is any form of modern economy where the type of prediction that would be needed for overall planning can be made. The actual record of centralised planned economies (human needs cannot be identified or satisfied; the people starve, are poor in consumer goods, and are poisoned by industrial wastes) is abysmally worse than that of non-centralised unplanned ones; and this at least is something one could have predicted.

From the point of view of the Marxist enterprise, of building a materialist science of history and economics which will enable us to take control of our own lives and make our own history, modern scientific developments offer both a gain and a loss. Ordinary, non-dialectical materialism, in the light of twentieth-century science, no longer entails a brain–mind determinism, and may allow space for freewill and politics. For Marxism, that is a gain. But the same light makes the possibilities of rational economic planning look very much less convincing. That is a distinct loss.

NOTES

1. 'To sublate' – technical philosophical translation of Hegel's word *aufheben*. A concept found to be contradictory is raised to a higher level of discourse in which the contradiction is annulled while its significance is preserved. See Findlay's account of the dialectic (quoted in my Chapter 3) for the only sense that has ever been made of this curious process.
2. Georg Lukács 1954, *The Young Hegel*.
3. Karl Marx 1840–59, *Early Writings*. 'Critique of Hegel's Doctrine of the State' 1843, pp. 57–198; 'A Contribution to the Critique of Hegel's Philosophy of Right and Law: Introduction' 1843–4, pp. 243–57.
4. Karl Marx 1840–59, *Early Writings*. 'A Contribution to the Critique of Hegel's Philosophy of Right: Introduction', p. 256.
5. Raymond Williams 1966, *Modern Tragedy*.
6. These are not always independent. At his death in 1991, it was discovered that the capitalist Robert Maxwell had stolen the pension funds of Mirror Group Newspapers. It is a matter of opinion whether Maxwell was an untypical nineteeth-century robber baron, or a type whose existence reveals the essential nature of most capitalists now. Who does control the pension funds that own so much of modern industry? Is Dickens's *Little Dorrit* still the relevant text to consult? (See next chapter.)
7. Anderson 1976; Merquior 1986, pp. 7, 227.
8. P.S. Laplace 1796, *Essay on the System of the World*; 1799–1825, *Celestial Mechanics*. *See* Charles Singer 1959, *A Short History of Scientific Ideas to 1900*, pp. 311–12, for a brief account of Laplace's work.
9. G. Ryle 1949, *The Concept of Mind*.
10. Friedrich Engels 1877, *Anti-Duhring*, Chapters 12, 13; see also Engels 1940, *Dialectics of Nature*.
11. Thomas Hobbes 1651, *Leviathan* part I, Chapter 13.
12. John Locke 1960, *Two Treatises on Government*.
13. Jean-Jacques Rousseau 1754, *Discourse on Inequality*.
14. Sigmund Freud 1929, *Civilisation and its Discontents*.
15. Charles Fourier 1972.
16. Adam Smith 1776, *The Wealth of Nations*.
17. See Norman Geras 1983, for a refutation of these extreme positions.
18. F.R. Leavis 1952, 'Literature and Society' in *The Common Pursuit*, p. 152.
19. This name referred in Italy to a rather left-Hegelian tendency, introduced by Antonio Labriola, and followed by the anti-materialist Rodolfo Mondolfo and the Italian translator of the *Theses*, Giovanni Gentile. Gramsci was also influenced by, though he opposed, the idealist philosopher Benedetto Croce. See Gramsci 1971, *Selections from the Prison Notebooks*: Introduction by Hoare and Nowell-Smith, pp. xxi–xxv; pp. 386ff.
20. Antonio Gramsci 1971, pp. 419ff.
21. Richard Feynman 1985.
22. See below; and next footnote.
23. For a deep, if taxing treatment of these questions, involving the mathematical concept of computability, see Penrose 1989, *The Emperor's New Mind*.
24. For discussion, see George Thomson 1955, *The First Philosophers*.

BOOKS

Karl Marx 1843–44 *A Contribution to the Critique of Hegel's Philosophy of Right: Introduction.*
1844 *Economic and Philosophical Manuscripts.*
1844 *Critique of Hegel's Doctrine of the State.*
1845 *Theses on Feuerbach.*
all from *Early Writings*, ed. L. Colletti (Penguin 1975).
Karl Marx and **Friedrich Engels** 1846 *The German Ideology.*
1848 *The Communist Manifesto.*
Friedrich Engels 1888 *Ludwig Feuerbach and the End of Classical German Philosophy.*
Sidney Hook 1936 *From Hegel to Marx.*
George Lichtheim 1963 *From Marx to Hegel.*
István Meszáros 1970 *Marx's Theory of Alienation.*
Leszek Kolakowski 1978 *Main Currents of Marxism* (3 vols).
Christopher Caudwell 1939 *The Crisis in Physics.*
Richard Feynman 1985 *QED: The Strange Theory of Light and Matter.*
James Gleick 1987 *Chaos.*

CHAPTER FIVE
Scientific Marxism

Marxist Theories of History, Society, Revolution and Value

SUMMARY

Marxism in its mature form consists of three elements: a materialist interpretation of history and politics; a critique of capitalist political economy; and a commitment to socialist revolution. These elements are to be found in all Marx's own work from *The Communist Manifesto* of 1848, or even earlier, to the posthumous volumes of *Capital*. Like thousands before me, I use as a basic text for discussion the 1859 *Preface* to his first major mature economic work, *A Contribution to the Critique of Political Economy*. This is a programmatic statement which Marx published himself and endorsed again in the second edition of *Capital*; it has very high authority.

The *Preface* is taken as the source of Marx's general framework for historical, political and economic analysis, which later became known as **historical materialism**, and which is, in my view, his main contribution to human thought. I give a brief commentary on this to bring out what Marx meant, to defend his position **as** reductive economism and **against** charges of crude economic determinism, and to bring out its implications for the sphere of ideology and culture. The obvious meaning of his words is in my view often diametrically opposed to what modern sophisticated Marxists and post-Marxists, influenced by such different figures as Althusser, Foucault, Derrida, etc., have claimed. I consider some of their arguments later in this book.

Since Marxism stands or falls by its economic rather than its literary claims, I have also discussed some elementary problems of Marxist economics: they concern the labour theory of value and the concept of surplus value. But I conclude with an account of *Capital* as a influential work of European literature rather than economic science, which has had its effect by constructing a heroic legend of the proletariat.

1   HISTORICAL MATERIALISM

The clearest and most convincing statement ever made about the materialist conception of history is that by Marx himself, in his *Preface* of 1859 to *A Contribution to the Critique of Political Economy*. This offers an account of his whole method and procedure as developed up to 1859. Marx refers to the passage again as a reliable summary of his method in an afterword to the second edition of *Capital* in 1873. The *Preface* therefore has the highest possible authority as a statement of Marx's lifelong position. In this respect it is quite unlike the *Theses on Feuerbach*, which as early notes not intended for publication carry no authority at all, except as evidence of one stage in Marx's private thinking.

The *Preface* is a masterpiece of clarity and intellectual power; but it is very concise. In this it resembles nothing so much as one of those computer applications which is distributed on a single floppy disk, and expands on installation. One puts the disk in: file upon file springs into existence and installs itself on the hard disk of the machine, megabytes of data; until finally one is in a whole new computing environment and can perform tasks that were quite impossible before. Just so with the *Preface*. One clause establishes a new science of society; a second gives it an empirical basis. A few sentences set out the structure of all human history; another few sentences take us to the end (or possibly to a new beginning) of time. In one sentence, every superficial aspect of human society is placed on its fundamental determinative or constraining basis. The nature of art and literature is expounded in two words.[1]

The whole of this section is a commentary on the key passage of the *Preface* – about half of one of Marx's long paragraphs. Marx's words are in bold type, and quotation is continuous. Although I have inevitably made some interpretations, none of them is intended to be tendentious. This passage, and this section, is a simple summary of what I take Marxism to be. These must be the most frequently quoted words from Marx, except perhaps for the lines from *The Communist Manifesto*: 'All history is the history of class struggle' and 'Workers of the world, unite; you have nothing to lose but your chains'; and they have far more authority.

1.1   Social structure

In the social production of their existence,

i.e. in working to produce food, clothing, etc., and (on my interpretation of these words) in raising children,[2]

men inevitably enter into definite relations

e.g. working for a master or indeed (if you take account of the fact that Marxism has a theory of the family as well) entering marriage

which are independent of their will,

– though they might be able to choose this master or that, or whether to marry or not, they do not individually invent the institutions of work or marriage, but find them in existence, and if they ignore them, they have to pay a price. It is this passage which justifies the claim that Marxism postulates the existence of an objective structure of society, consisting of definite relations independent of the wills of the members of society who enter those relations. There is, therefore, a Marxist sociology.

namely relations of production appropriate to a given stage in the development of their material forces of production.

We now get the central empirical claim of Marxism: that the objective structures of society are actually economic relations of production. This is the claim that sets Marxism apart from other forms of sociology or structural anthropology, which don't see economic structures as more basic than other structures. 'Western Marxism' often abandons this empirical claim.

It is worth giving an example of how economic structuring might work. Consider a 'hydraulic society' like ancient Egypt, where the harvest was dependent on irrigation agriculture: work in canals and fields provides the main **forces of production**. The land was theoretically owned by a king who was also a god, and administered through his priests: these were the **relations of production**. These correspond to the forces of production in the following sense: at that time there was no other social structure in which the peasants could have been induced to cooperate in opening the canals at the right time of year, since they could not have understood or been sufficiently influenced by the technical necessities of irrigation agriculture.

The 'material forces of production' here include hand-tools, canals, and perhaps – this is never quite clear – the limited technical knowledge available of how to use these to irrigate fields. One can see that the exact role of technical knowledge is something of a problem for a materialist theory of history. Tools are useless without concepts; but if you take that point too seriously you might as well go back to Hegel and make ideas the driving force of history.

The totality of these relations of production constitutes the economic structure of society,

– For Marx, the economic structure includes relations of production but not forces of production, though what is later called the 'base' of society often includes both. In Egypt, the economic structure includes the king–priest–peasant structure for controlling the canals, but not the canals themselves; in the ancient world, the master–slave structure but not the physical estates, the slaves that work on them, or their tools; in feudal society, the relationship of holding an estate from a feudal lord, upon promise of military service, but again not the estate itself; in modern society, the structure of bourgeoisie owning factories and proletariat working in them, but not the factories themselves. Crudely, these relations of production are relations of effective ownership – the question is: who controls the productive resources of the society?

the real foundation, on which arises a legal and political superstructure

– this is the famous metaphor of 'base and superstructure' which is often interpreted as implying that there is a determining causal relationship, such that for any given economic base, there is one and only one political and legal superstructure that is possible. The history of the world is thus a succession of modes of production, each of which brings with it appropriate legal and political forms. This interpretation cannot possibly be true, however; for Marxism is a movement of political struggle; and struggle is only possible if there are alternatives to struggle for.

In fact the connection between base and superstructure is not causal but functional. The 'superstructure' of laws and political procedures exists essentially to secure the existing property or production relations. This is not necessarily the way lawyers and politicians will describe the matter. They may, like Hegel, give all sorts of idealist reasons for existing laws and institutions. But if property and production relations are threatened, they will protect them by changing laws or institutions. If they fail to do this, the economic structure of society will collapse. It is clear that while this possibility exerts a very strong pressure, it falls short of determining just what the laws and political institutions will be. Law and politics are a human response to economic constraints, not a mechanical consequence of them. Marxists would call the relationship 'dialectical'.

It is not clear whether Marx would concede that some laws – e.g.

against murder – and some political arrangements – e.g. those that secure against arbitrary government by an individual – have a partially non-economic character, and are desirable in themselves. Probably not. And even a non-Marxist might concede that there are no legal and political absolutes – there are stages of history in which homicides have to be handled by blood-feud, and stages in which government naturally devolves to a tyrannical warlord. But the strong claim that every feature of law and politics is a response to economic pressures seems utopian – it implies that after the revolution there will be no crime or personal oppression.

and to which correspond definite forms of social consciousness. The mode of production of material life conditions the general process of social, political, and intellectual life. It is not the consciousness of men that determines their existence [as Hegel had suggested]**, but their social existence that determines their consciousness.**

– It is obvious that the peasant's relation to the Pharaoh-God, and, still more, the peasant's understanding of himself in relation to the Pharaoh-God, are conditioned by the necessities of irrigation agriculture in ways of which both the peasant and the Pharaoh are quite unaware. In particular they will have a false, religious understanding of the class relationships of the society, and fail to understand the technical basis of those relationships. And the same goes for ancient [classical] and feudal societies, and of course, for our own. This view – that our very consciousness is determined in ways unknown to us by the economy in general, and by our class position within it – is the profoundest insight of Marxism, and the foundation of all Marxist cultural theory.

The question is, how far is it true. Modern relativists often want to see our whole understanding of the world as something socially conditioned, rather than as a reflection of objective realities. This undermines all truth-claims – those of science and those of common observation as well. But in our example it is clear that not everything that the ordinary Egyptian understood about his society was false. There is no suggestion that he thought canals were mountains, or that food could be regularly produced without labour. He did think that various animals were sacred, and that his king was a god. It is tempting to make a division in his consciousness between those aspects of the world which he truly understood, and those in which he was the prisoner of a false consciousness, or an ideology. This ideology – in particular, the ordinary Egyptian's understanding of the king and priest aspects of the social structure – does not reflect the truth; it reflects concealed economic necessities of the society. In the same way we would expect mediaeval or modern men to have some degree of false consciousness about the economic aspects of their own society.

One is bound to ask, does this go for Marx as well? Or does the historical materialist, uniquely, understand the underlying economic realities of his society? The answer to this is yes, he uniquely does. Marx was not a relativist about historical materialism: he thought it was true. Marx would have agreed with Althusser in differentiating science from ideology, and believing his own work to be part of science. One does not need to argue from this that everything that is not science is ideology; nor that there is a part of consciousness, namely science, which is not conditioned by social existence at all and floats free from society. But a claim that the detailed structure of science is determined directly by social existence, and has no independent truth-value, would be impossible to defend, and would undermine Marxism itself.

1.2   Social change

Marx now turns to social change; and at this point, I think, he begins to model his general theory very closely on the course of a particular historical event: the French Revolution of 1789.

> **At a certain stage of development, the material productive forces of society come into conflict with the existing relations of production or – this merely expresses the same thing in legal terms – with the property relations within the framework of which they have operated hitherto. From forms of development of the productive forces these relations turn into their fetters.**

We think here of nascent manufacturing industry and bourgeois development, held back by the crazy feudal patchwork of the French *ancien régime*, which couldn't even finance itself; and it all seems very convincing. In this case, however, some of the advance guard of the revolution were actually pretty conscious of their fetters. Does the same pattern hold elsewhere? Well, there is the English Civil War, which can certainly be read in this way; though at the time many thought that was about religion. However, perhaps it does not matter so much what men thought they were fighting about:

> **The changes in the economic foundation lead sooner or later to the transformation of the whole immense superstructure. In studying such transformations it is always necessary to distinguish between the material transformation of the economic conditions of production,**

which can be determined with the precision of natural science, and the legal, political, religious, artistic, or philosophic – in short ideological forms in which men become conscious of this conflict and fight it out.

It is clear that for Marx the economic historian does understand what the lawyers, politicians, priests, artists and philosophers are deceived about. It is interesting that art – including, presumably, literature – is flatly described as an ideological form in which men become conscious of economic conflicts and fight them out. A whole school of interpretation is founded upon that assumption; and I personally believe it to be the most valuable point Marxism has to make about literature and the arts.

It is, however, still a deeply ambiguous claim. Does Marx believe that art and literature have no autonomy or intrinsic form of their own, but are merely one way among many of disguising the class struggle? There have been plenty of Marxist critics in every generation to argue this. Or does he mean that they do have a relative autonomy, but the class struggle enters deeply into them in an ideological disguise? Most of the personal remarks about literature of both Marx and Engels suggest that they would have held the latter, more limited view; as usual, many modern leftists are to the left of the founders of Marxism on this point.

But the point about ideological disguise is not of course confined to art; it is quite general:

Just as one does not judge an individual by what he thinks about himself, so one cannot judge such a period of transformation by its consciousness, but, on the contrary, this consciousness must be explained from the contradictions of material life, from the conflict existing between the social forces of production and the relations of production.

'Social forces' is new; before, we heard of 'material forces'. Presumably the conflict referred to is between, for example, the collective character of work in factories, and the individualist character of the private ownership of factories. Somehow, it is on the basis of a contradiction like this that one must explain early nineteenth-century politics and, say, the Romantic movement in literature.

It is interesting to ask how far this principle stretches. Does it only apply to the interpretation of revolutionary periods? Modern bourgeois historians are in fact quite equal to the task of explaining most historical developments in economic terms. If that is all there is to the materialist conception of history, then in some bourgeois quarters – not all – the materialist conception of history has won the day; Hegelian idealism has been beaten off without trace; it is difficult enough to preserve just so much idealism as is contained in the principle that, if, for example, we are writing the history of a science, we should pay attention to the scientific arguments in it, as well as to the supposed economic determinants of scientific development.

What distinguishes Marxist historiography from the bourgeois kind is a special stress on revolutions, and a prophetic certainty about their course:

> **No social order is ever destroyed before all the productive forces for which it is sufficient have been developed, and new superior relations of production never replace older ones before the material conditions for their existence have matured within the framework of the old society. Mankind thus inevitably sets itself only such tasks as it is able to solve, since close examination will always show that the problem itself arises only when the material conditions for its solution are already present or at least in course of formation.**

Marx had some arguments for this view, at least in relation to his hoped-for proletarian revolution; the claim can be defended. But it does sound more like an article of revolutionary faith than a historical law. Marx is, I think, cheering himself up after the failure of the revolutions of 1848, and settling in for a longer haul. When 'Mankind' arrives on the scene, and starts 'setting itself tasks', we are back, surely, with Hegelian idealism, if only in a metaphor.

Certainly we are back in Hegelian territory with the grand scheme of history that immediately follows. It is a summary of what is set out more fully in *The Communist Manifesto* (and before that, in *The German Ideology*). The very feel of such grand schematisation is Hegelian; so also is the prophecy of an end of inherent conflict, and a solution of the last antagonism – even if Marx speaks of the 'material conditions' for such a solution.

> **In broad outline, the Asiatic, ancient, feudal and modern bourgeois modes of production may be designated as epochs marking progress in the economic development of society. The bourgeois mode of production is the last antagonistic form of the social process of production – antagonistic not in the sense of individual antagonism but of an antagonism that emanates from the individuals' social conditions of existence – but the productive forces developing within bourgeois society create also the material conditions for a solution to this antagonism. The prehistory of human society accordingly closes with this social formation.**

Now this is very grand – as a prophecy of the end of time – but Marx does rather need arguments to put forward as well. And in fact he has such arguments, though he does not rehearse them here. Some of them are familiar from *The Communist Manifesto*. But first, let us consider the obvious questions raised by the prophecy. Why should bourgeois society be the last inherently antagonistic one? Why shouldn't there be a long succession of equally antagonistic ones? Alternatively, why should it end at all?

Marx thinks bourgeois society will end because he thinks he has detected in it the same kind of contradiction that he describes above. The relations of production – capitalist ones – are now acting as fetters on the forces of production; so they will be burst asunder, and everything will change. Specifically there are certain inherent tendencies in capitalism: for the number of capitalists to be steadily reduced (fewer necks to be wrung), while more and more people are thrown into the class of the expropriated, to strengthen the revolution.

This last class, the proletariat, is right at the bottom of the social pyramid. The French Revolution, the English Civil War, were run by classes which still had something to lose, since below them were classes yet to be liberated. Nothing is below the proletariat; so when it liberates itself, it will have to liberate everybody. There will be no fundamental antagonisms left, as a basis for a future class war.

However, the whole filthy business (Marx's words) would no doubt start again, if, as before, there were shortages of goods, and competition for resources. But capitalism has had one merit, and the bourgeoisie one great achievement. They have increased the forces of production more than any other mode of production the world has ever seen. There need be no more shortages, and no more competition for the means of life. It is in that sense that capitalism has provided the means for its own supersession.

Marx's historical arguments, in *The Communist Manifesto* and elsewhere, are in many ways remarkably convincing; but history refused to be convinced. In the long term what became clear was that capitalist crises, of which there have been many, are in no way analogous to the crisis of the French *ancien régime*. It is clear now – though it was not clear even as late as the 1930s – that whatever is wrong with capitalism, it isn't that it places fetters on production; and whatever is right with socialism, it isn't that it facilitates production. Marx's mistake here was the most fundamental error in socialist theory; and world socialism may have just died of it.

In the short term, the revolutions of 1848 had failed; and Marx, in poverty-stricken exile, set himself to find out why. The result of his labours, over many years, was *Capital*. To make any useful comment on that requires at least another section, and perhaps another book: I will confine myself here to some elementary comments on the basis of Marxist economics, the labour theory of value; and to making a point which is badly neglected – that *Capital* is a great literary masterpiece, and articulates an influential heroic myth.

In the years after Marx's death, a theory of the relationship between the economy and the rest of a society was extracted from passages like the one above, and given a systematic – even a diagrammatic – form. This is the theory that any society has an economic base – consisting of the forces and the relations of production – and a political and cultural (or ideological) superstructure. The nature of the political and cultural superstructure is then said to be **determined** by the economic base. This determinist model has often been presented as the Marxist model of culture.

Just how strong this determinism can be, without running into the logical problems of determinism discussed in the previous chapter, is a matter of controversy. If it is complete – that is to say, if every detail of political institutions and cultural forms is determined by the economic base – it severely limits the freewill of both politicians and artists; indeed, it would seem to be pointless to engage in either politics or art, since one's efforts can have no influence whatever. Only economic innovation can actually change anything. This is almost as incompatible with Marxist political activity as with any other kind; though one could, I suppose, make it the basis of a view that one should act only through trade unions and factory organisations.

If one goes one further step and argues that, within the economy, the relations of production are in turn determined by the current state of the forces of production – that the nature of the class system is determined by whether the dominant mode of production is agriculture or factory production, and by what kind of agriculture, and what kind of factory – then one arrives at technological determinism. For the technological determinist, there would be no point even in engaging in class warfare. The only way to change a society would be to smash the machines it uses, or invent new ones. I do not see how a technological determinist could be a Marxist at all.

At the other end of the scale one might argue that political activities, legal forms, and cultural products in general show a very high degree of autonomy; only in fairly indirect ways, and in the last historical instance, are they determined by the economy. Culture is determined by the economy in the last instance, because men cannot produce cultural products if they cannot feed themselves and keep alive. Short of that, it is pretty autonomous; and furthermore, cultural and political activities can actually have an effect on the economy. Propaganda can change the way we think about the economy; a change of government can actually affect the economy itself.

This is a common-sense view which a non-Marxist can easily hold; but there are great Marxist thinkers who have believed something like it. To judge from some of his letters, Engels, at the end of his life, was among their number.[3] The problem with this position is that it seems to throw away the basic Marxist insight. If culture – that is, ideas – can affect the economy, surely we are almost back with Hegel again, and are no longer historical materialists? Engels's sturdy common sense, however decorated with the rhetoric of dialectical materialism, doesn't solve the philosophical problem.

2   *CAPITAL*: THE THEORY OF VALUE IN ECONOMICS

The title of the 1859 book, from whose *Preface* I have been quoting, is *A Contribution to the Critique of Political Economy*. The subtitle of Marx's major work, *Capital* – all volumes – is *A Critique of Political Economy*. Most of Marx's professional life was spent in developing a critique of Anglo-Scottish political economy. Political economy is a genre whose most famous representatives were Adam Smith and David Ricardo; it can be thought of either as an important stage in the development of the science of economics, or as an early ideological defence of capitalism. There is something curiously Left-Hegelian about Marx's enterprise of attacking capitalism as a system by attacking its theoretical apologetics; and presenting as contradictions of capitalism what are often no more than contradictions in classical economic theory.

The first volume of *Capital* was published in 1867. By that time, classical political economy was effectively dead: killed by its own contradictions, but naturally leaving capitalism unharmed. A new science of economics was developing on which many of Marx's arguments failed to bite. It is inevitable that a modern commentator should judge Marx's scientific work as a contribution to economics; but in a sense it is not. Marx's economics and Marshall's economics[4] belong to different disciplines: they talk past each other. Hence, Communists have always been able to assume that Marx demolished the assumptions of bourgeois economics; and bourgeois economists have always been able to refute Marx in a footnote.[5] Serious engagement was almost impossible.

The central and peculiar feature of Marx's economics is that it attempts to explain the capitalist exploitation of labour – on the face of it, a moral and political concept – in strict scientific terms, without calling upon any external moral standard. For this purpose, Marx adopts Ricardo's theory that the sole source of economic value is labour. Capital is not an independent source of value in its own right. It must therefore be derived from the extraction of surplus-value from the labourer. He may well be paid according to his own value (which in economic terms will be the cost of producing him – that is, of supporting him and his family). But he produces greater value than that; and the capitalist pockets the difference. This theory has considerable importance, as on it must rest much of the Marxist claim to provide a strictly scientific socialism. But it has crippling weaknesses.

2.1   The labour theory of value

The ultimate basis of the labour theory of value, for Marx, is probably a philosophical one derived from Hegel: the conception that he had in his earlier writings – such as the *Economic and Philosophical Manuscripts of 1844* – of labour as the expression of man's species-being. Human labour in general is here thought of as general human creativity; it is what makes men human. Under capitalism, when men are wage-workers, making things in which they have no particular interest, for the capitalist who pays their wages to sell to people they do not know, man's species-being, his essence, becomes alienated from him. The capitalist gets his capital as an accumulation of the surplus from their labour. So capital is a monstrous creation by the workers which now stands over against the workers; they made it, and it now controls them. Marx abandoned much of the Hegelian terminology of this period; but the essential insight remains. Naturally, Marx is unwilling to abandon this view of labour for the point of view of a later economic science which regards labour simply as a cost of production which it is best, in everybody's interest including that of the worker, to reduce to a minimum.

On Marx's mature view, capitalism is distinguished from earlier modes of production in that goods and services come in the form of commodities which can be bought and sold. In looking at economic value we must distinguish between the **use-value** of commodities and their **exchange-value**; it is the latter which Marx seems to consider as the economic value in the proper sense, and this exchange value is determined by the congealed human labour which the goods contain. This value may be either installed in the goods by the labour of those who make them, or transferred from the congealed human labour contained in the capital goods (machinery, etc.) used to make them. These capital goods in turn got their value from earlier human labour; one may have to go a long way back, but all value comes from human labour in the end.

This value is not the same as the price of the goods; settling the precise relation between values and prices is a scientific problem. But values are certainly what underlie relative prices; they are what are scientifically important, and it is values which Marx discusses in *Capital*, volume I. Making the transition from the scientifically fundamental concept of values, to the observable features of relative prices, is known in the literature as the 'transformation problem'; and Marx thought he had solved it. An account of his solution can be found in *Capital*, volume III (p. 154 onward): most economists think it won't work.

There is an obvious objection to the view that the value of a commodity (that is, something made in order to be sold) is determined by the amount of labour embodied in it. It is, that on this view a commodity made by an incompetent workman, who takes twice as long, will have twice the value of one made by a competent workman. Marx is briskly sarcastic with this objection, dismissing it as obvious that what confers value is not the actual labour time, but the socially necessary labour time. Halve that (by inventing a new machine, say) and you automatically halve the value of each commodity, including those made by the old methods.

The trouble with this correction is that it gives away the main intuitive argument for the labour theory of value. One can see how, in a metaphysical sense, real labour might confer real value on whatever it shapes. If Picasso changes the shape of a piece of old iron, we will value it just because he has laboured on it (though we shall not be very interested in the amount of time he took). And one can see how, in a traditional society, there might be both a customary price for a job and a customary labour time for performing it. But socially necessary labour in a market society is a mathematical abstraction. One can't see intuitively how that can convey value to anything. And one can't easily, using Marx's own tools, determine what precisely the quantity of socially necessary labour is in any one case.

What is even more awkward is that one can determine this quantity fairly easily, using the tools of the bourgeois economics developed during Marx's lifetime, and dismissed by Marx and most Marxists as apologetics. One uses what is called a 'marginalist' argument.

Consider a market in which there are many people who might be able to produce a particular commodity; but because of differences of skill and equipment, some of them can do so with less labour than others. If the price for the commodity is high, then even the slow and expensive producers will be able to make it at a small profit; and the efficient ones will make a considerable profit. Each increase of price will therefore bring fresh producers into the market.

But what is made must be sold; consider a market in which there are many potential purchasers with very different incomes. If the price for the commodity is low, then even the poorest will be able to buy some; the richest will be able to buy a great deal. Every fall in price will increase the amount of the commodity that can be sold.

In this situation there will be one, and only one, price at which everything that is made can be sold.

This is the price which is:

(a)   just high enough to cover the costs of the last unit made by the highest-cost, least efficient producer (if it didn't cover those costs he would stop making the commodity);

(b)   just low enough to be bought by the poorest purchaser who can manage to buy (if it wasn't that low he wouldn't buy it).

We can call this the price fixed by the interaction of supply and demand. Notice that this price is fixed without direct use of the labour theory of value.

We could, if we wished, call the labour expended by that last, least efficient producer the socially necessary labour for that commodity. And we could, on the basis of that, calculate the price of the commodity. But it would be quite redundant; we derived the labour cost from the price in the first place. On this approach, the 'transformation problem' is a wholly unnecessary one; and the labour theory of value is entirely redundant.

2.2   Labour, labour-power and the theory of surplus value

The labour theory of value was not Marx's own; he took it from Ricardo. Marx's innovation was to use that theory to explain how it was that capitalists, who appear to be buying the labour of their workforce at its fair market value (or why should the workers continue to sell it?) nevertheless make a lot more out of this labour than the labourers do.

The obvious answer to this is of course that the capitalist is bringing something of his own to the situation, namely, his capital; and capital (especially in the form of machines) makes labour much more productive. However, according to the labour theory of value, only labour produces value; and this applies as much to the value of the machines as to anything else. Labour must have given the value to the machines which they then confer on commodities. Where in the whole circuit can the capitalist extract the surplus labour that makes up his capital?

Marx's answer is that the capitalist buys from the labourer not labour, valued in terms of what it can produce, but the worker's power to labour, valued in terms of what that power cost to produce – that is, in terms of the food, drink, shelter, etc. that the labourer needed in order to develop and preserve his powers. Labour-power has a value, just like any other commodity; according to the labour theory of value this will be the labour necessary to produce the labour-power in question. What the capitalist buys is a week of somebody's labour-power, and he pays for it at its true value – the goods necessary to produce it (that is, to maintain the labourer and his family for a week). But the expenditure of labour-power for a week produces a week's labour and embodies this as value in the commodities the labourer has produced. The value of these might well be enough to support two labourers for a week. The capitalist pockets the difference. Marx calls this surplus labour.

It will be seen that the chief feature of this theory is that it makes no quantitative predictions at all. The actual amount of surplus labour will depend wholly upon negotiation between capitalist and worker on such matters as the length of the working week. The outcome of that negotiation will depend wholly upon the industrial strength of the two parties. If many workers, in a non-unionised industry, confront a few well-organised capitalists, the settlement will be bad for them. They may well accept near-starvation wages if the alternative is actual starvation. If, on the other hand, a strongly-unionised, highly skilled workforce confronts a few highly competitive capitalists, as happened until recently in the newspaper industry, they may well force individual capitalists to hand over their whole capital, for the privilege of running their own business for a few years, until they have no more capital and are forced to sell out. In this case 'surplus labour' is a negative quantity.

Quantitative predictions can be made in this case too by a version of the marginal analysis employed before. All that is necessary is to consider labour – not, NOT labour-power – as a commodity whose price is determined by the market. Its price is the price which the last capitalist is prepared to pay, and the union (or the last worker) is prepared to accept, for the last unit of labour to be agreed upon. (A higher price would produce more labour, but no available capitalist will afford it; a lower price would attract more capitalists, but no available worker will work for it.)

Of course behind this purely commercial negotiation lurk real material relationships, economic, political and even military. Starving workers, collapsing newspapers, hostile governments, police cordons, and even guns, may play a part. But it will be seen that in this equilibrium, however arrived at, the distinction between labour and labour-power plays absolutely no part at all.

2.3   Marxism and the metaphysics of value

A concept, or a distinction, that is central to a philosophical system but
has no empirical content at all, is often called metaphysical. The Marxist
concept of value as embodied labour, the distinction between labour and
labour-power, and perhaps even the concept of surplus-value, seem to
play this metaphysical part within Marxism.

At first sight, the distinction between labour and labour-power seems
to make most empirical sense. One can imagine a capitalist buying half an
hour's labour from one man – specifying precisely what he should do for
that half hour – and half an hour's labour-power from another – leaving
what the man should do to be determined later. But this is not the
distinction Marx needs; it has no empirical implications for prices or for
surplus labour.

The distinction he needs is between half an hour of labour, and the
labour needed to produce that half an hour of labour (that is, the labour
needed to support that labourer and his family for half an hour). And this
distinction is needed solely to provide a basis for the notion of surplus
labour; which in turn is needed to give a precise-sounding scientific basis
for the essentially political notion of exploitation.

But it does no more than give scientific form to the crude intuition
that labourers ought to get the whole product of their labours; anything
that goes to a capitalist is stolen. It doesn't offer any way to calculate
prices, or profits, or other quantitative economic variables.

That is not to deny that Marx has plenty of discussion of technical
economic matters like these. The four volumes of *Capital*[6] are full of it.
But the quantitative parts of the discussion have little to do with the
underlying metaphysic of value. As we have seen in the example above,
we don't find the price of a commodity determined by whatever labour is
socially necessary to make it; we find the quantity of labour that is socially
necessary determined by a calculation from the price; and the price is
determined at the margin by supply and demand.

It is also not to deny the point that we need more fundamental
concepts than those used in marginal analysis if we are to explain
economic phenomena rather than merely describe them. But a concept
like utility (often derided as metaphysical) is far more satisfactory than the
Marxist concept of value for this purpose. Utility is an abstraction from
use-value; it is deemed to accrue whenever we get pleasure or satisfy our
wants. When we do something we don't want to do, it provides a
negative utility – thus, most labour has a negative utility, though the
rewards for it have a positive utility. We exchange things, or exchange

labour for things, in order to maximise utility. Such a theory as this offers far better explanations of economic phenomena, including those concerning labour, than the labour theory of value.

Neither theoretical concept is politically neutral. Inevitably, an economics centred upon the theoretical concept of utility goes along with a politics centred on the consumer. Work, and the worker, become means to a utilitarian end; and this is unacceptable to Marxists, at the deepest level, because they identify with the active but suffering worker, and not with the satisfied consumer, even when these are the same empirical person. Behind Marxist economics is the vision of man remaking himself through labour. Behind utilitarian economics is the vision of the fallen Adam having to work if he wishes to eat.

It may be that this is ultimately what is responsible for the immense attraction Marxist economics has had for Western intellectuals in the twentieth century. The notion of work as a creative outlet is central to the self-conception of the intellectual. The notion of work as an unfortunate but necessary cost of the efficient production of consumer goods is by comparison revolting – particularly if, like most Western intellectuals, you don't attach the highest human value to motor cars and video recorders. But if the Eastern European experience is anything to go by, the Marxists are wrong. A polity centred on the worker appears to produce a whole society of the poor, the apathetic and the bored. A polity centred on the consumer means that at least some of the jobs are interesting (even the job of designing the cars and the video recorders, though not the production line work); and most people find their lives enriched by at least some of the products, even if intellectuals don't.[7]

3 *CAPITAL* AS NINETEENTH-CENTURY ENGLISH LITERATURE

There is a common critical trick nowadays of rereading scientific works as if they were literary texts. Freud, for example, is more often than not read in this way, and Darwin has been occasionally read so. In general I am not in favour of this practice: it rests on a false metaphysic of general textuality, and a blatant imperialism of the literary critic, who is unable to respond to scientific works on their own terms, and insists on taking them on his. But there is a special case for treating *Capital* in this way. It is a work which, from the time it was published to the present day, has totally failed to convince any specialist in the science it deals with who was not already, on other grounds, a believer. Yet it has produced passionate – even religious – conviction in millions of non-economists. I want to suggest that this is because of its literary qualities – the way in which it manages to capture the most profound suffering of the nineteenth century – that of the industrial working classes – and to articulate the most potent myth of redemption – that of proletarian revolution – while presenting that suffering and that myth within the framework of a fictional but convincing science: the theory of economics which became the basis of 'scientific socialism'.

The case I am going to argue – and it is only at first sight that it will seem preposterous – is that a number of the works of Marx, including very obviously *The Communist Manifesto*, and less obviously, *Capital*, function as a nineteenth-century equivalent of that dead literary form, the epic poem. An epic poem is a historical poem – though it is not quite sufficient to say, with Ezra Pound, that it is just a poem with history in it. The function of the great epics has been to create a narrative in which generations to come can understand themselves, their own origins, their tribal history, and their deepest social values. *The Iliad* articulates the relationship of the classical Greeks of the fifth century, not merely to legendary ancestors but, through fragments preserved in the poem, to the actual empires of the Mycenean bronze age; and at the same time expresses, in the quarrel between Achilles and Agamemnon, the central historical contradiction of classical Greek society: its universal culture and its fissiparous politics. *The Aeneid* articulates not merely a legend of the Roman past, but the imperial mission of the whole of Rome's future; and it articulates metaphorically, in the conflict between Aeneas's duty and his love for the Carthaginian Dido, some of the brutal contradictions in that civilising mission – the historical Rome actually destroyed Carthage. Both are poems men have learned at school and then lived lives of action by.

The epic poem has been dead since Milton's day; and as Pound remarked, the true English epic is in Shakespeare's historical plays rather than in *Paradise Lost*. Pound's own *Cantos* don't seem to me to provide a valid continuation of the epic tradition, though there is history in them, and legend, and polemical economics looking slightly surprised to find itself in such surroundings. And it is only part of the truth to say that the novel has taken over. The novel is often a profoundly unhistorical form, providing a superb realisation of contemporary society, but projecting it as though existing conditions were eternal, and there was no public history. (The novel, one might say, is a bourgeois form; and to deny history is part of its purpose.) There are of course great exceptions, like *War and Peace*, and smaller ones like the works of Scott. It is also true that, on a suitable critical reading, all novels are historical ones. But then the narrative shape of history is being derived by the critic from some other source – perhaps from Marx – and brought to them from outside.

Functionally, in Victorian society, the true successor to the epic poem was to be found neither in poetry nor even in the prose novel, but in history. The man of the early nineteenth century got his picture of past civilisation not from any novel, but from Gibbon's *Decline and Fall of the Roman Empire*. In Victorian times, the histories of Macaulay and Carlyle, and more sober histories like that of John Richard Green, sold as widely as any novel. It is these which, in a cultivated urban society, play the ancient part of the epic in giving a shape to historical recollection and defining national identity. There is a precedent for this already in classical times. The histories of Herodotus and Thucydides are conscious successors to epic poetry (as Cornford showed in *Thucydides Mythistoricus*) designed to commemorate heroic deeds. Such histories often have heroes; Carlyle, indeed, offered an explicit cult of heroes and hero-worship; but the most important hero is never a particular Greek statesman, Roman emperor, or English king. It is a collective subject: the Athenians, civilisation, or, as in Green, the English People.[8] History offers the heroic deeds of a collective subject.

It is clear that *The Communist Manifesto* offers a history of just this kind, in which the collective subjects are classes. It is a short epic of the heroic deeds of the bourgeoisie, a collective hero who swaggers across history, transforming the earth; and finally gets his collective neck wrung by the hands of a glorious Shelleyan phantom: the proletariat. This needs no argument; what of *Capital* ?

The specific genre to which *Capital* belongs, political economy, is the genre of which the representative classics are Adam Smith, *An Inquiry into the Nature and Causes of The Wealth of Nations*, and David Ricardo, *On the Principles of Political Economy and Taxation*. Political economy was not a narrow, technical genre, as economics later became. In creating social self-awareness, it ranked with history, as part of the broad genre of social and political analysis to which people like Macaulay, Carlyle and Mill contributed. By comparison with Marx, however, the work of Macaulay and of Carlyle sinks into insignificance. Carlyle in particular stands out as a vaporous rhetorician whose voluminous work contains not one intellectually defensible analysis of a complex idea, and not one single precise description of anything. To find English work of the same merciless denunciatory force as Marx we must look outside the nineteenth century at the works of Swift: in one place only (*A Modest Proposal*) does Swift match Marx in intensity: his terrible metaphor (that the English landlords having eaten up all the wealth of Ireland, they should solve its problems finally by eating all the Irish children) gathers half its force from the real condition of Ireland. But of course Swift does not have Marx's philosophical or scientific understanding of the evils he is denouncing.

It is possible to argue that *Capital* is the greatest work of English literature in the nineteenth century. There is a rather trivial objection to this classification: it was written in German by a German. What qualifies it as English is that it was written in England; that its genre, political economy, was an Anglo-Scottish one; and that the whole of its illustrative material – a great part of the work – consists of descriptions of English social conditions. What qualifies it as literature is, first, the extraordinary sickening vividness of these descriptions. It in no way limits the praise due to Marx that most of these are not his own writings, but selections from the reports of the English factory inspectors. He made the selections, and gave them an overall historical meaning, within a profound theory of history. The descriptions of English factory practice, in the original reports – the child of seven who spends sixteen hours a day at a machine (his father has to kneel down and feed him, for he cannot leave it!); the children under thirteen in the phosphorus match industry, dying of phossy jaw; the journeyman bakers who work in temperatures of 90 degrees from 11pm to 7pm the following day, with only the shortest periods of rest – are merely horrifying. In the context of Marx's theory of capital they acquire a representative quality, and a sombre, tragic inevitability, as we see how the dynamics of capitalism could not but produce practices as horrible as these.

The one major masterpiece of the nineteenth century to be set with *Capital* is Darwin's *Origin of Species*. The literary effect here is quite different. The prose is clear, precise and sober. The arguments are wholly scientific. What is humanly important is going on in the background. The Christian religion is being quietly dismantled. Teleological thinking about nature is coming to seem irrational. Man is being placed fairly with the animals, as available to scientific knowledge as a horse or a volcano, and with no more transcendence in him than either.

Marx greatly admired Darwin and (with some semblance of truth) saw himself as the Darwin of the social sciences. I would half accept that view, if we confine it to an estimate of the importance of the materialist interpretation of history. But in truth *Capital* is not at its strongest as a scientific work. The difference in the effects of each work, within its own science, was very marked. The *Origin of Species* immediately transformed the science of biology – one might say, transformed the collector's science of natural history into the explanatory science of biology. Every competent geologist and natural historian alive recognised its importance, whether they agreed with it or not. All current biology descends from it, and accepts most of its positions.

By comparison, the publication of *Capital* coincided with a decisive shift away from the fundamental theory on which it was built, the labour theory of value. No economist who was not a political follower of Marx has ever accepted his particular version of this theory, with its elaboration into theories of surplus value and exploitation. Most professed Marxists now reject this theory. It has never been made to work, technically, in the sense of predicting (say) prices correctly. Its defenders have to give metaphysical or ethical grounds for sticking to it. Mainstream economics ignores the work of Marx. We are left with the paradox of a great work of literature whose tragic force partly depends on its being built upon an entirely spurious science.

The comparison with the novel is both necessary and difficult to make. Novels create the illusion of a social world; but it is an illusion even when it is carried out with the majestic command of George Eliot in *Middlemarch*, and it would make no sense to analyse her imaginary world with the same intellectual tools that are appropriate for professedly historical and scientific works. Most of the features for which people read novels – in particular, characterisation and plot – are obviously absent from *Capital*. But Marx presents what the novels fail to present – the true position of the most important class in that society, the working class; he offers the most imaginatively convincing account – I am not sure it is the true account – of the most important conflict in that society, between capitalists and workers. After reading Marx, one sees the greatest nineteenth-century novels as novels that suppress these central social issues.[9]

Something has to be allowed here for the limitations on the genre imposed by the susceptibilities of its public. Dickens is far more forthright about some social issues in his journalism than in any of his novels, and *Capital* is more easily compared with Dickens's journalism. (Maybe we should re-evaluate the relative merits of Dickens's novels and his journalism; perhaps our students would prefer the latter!) But the real difference is one of emotional seriousness. I happen to have been rereading *Capital* at the same time as *Our Mutual Friend*. To move from Marx to Dickens was rather like moving from Tolstoy to Dickens: that is, it was rather like moving from major art to minor – in the sense that one felt one was moving from reality to a lukewarm bath of sentimentality (Lizzie Hexam, Jenny Wren, the Boffins) stirred up by rather patronising comic turns (the Boffins again, Podsnap, Wegg and his taxidermist crony). What is lacking in the novel here is an adult seriousness of feeling that can cross class barriers. But the comparison with Dickens is not always in Marx's favour.

It is a curious paradox. When we read *Capital*, our feelings tell us: here is a great masterpiece, far greater, because far more serious, than anything by a novelist like Dickens. Yet Dickens, in *Little Dorrit*, is a better scientist than Marx. The controlling metaphor of that book, if we extract it, runs: A commercial society is a debtor's prison; the more you are in debt in such a society, the higher is your rank in it. That is actually a more serious scientific description of Dickens's society than the labour theory of value. Finance capital is a form of debt, which the financier promises to pay interest on as his profits come in. The more of this kind of debt you can accumulate, the more of society's economic activity you control; but the debts entirely control what activities you can undertake. It is literally true that a capitalist society is analogous to a debtor's prison. (Consider also the case of someone with a large mortgage, unable to change jobs. He too is imprisoned by his wealth, which is a large debt.)

It is possible to salvage the labour theory of value only by a very radical rhetorical move, which those who believe Marx to have been an economist will think worse than scepticism. One can take the theory as a powerful controlling metaphor, fully comparable to controlling metaphors (like that of the debtor's prison) around which Dickens built his later works. What Marx did was to express the central importance of working people in society, the fact that they, and not the ruling classes, are the real builders of civilisation, in the metaphor that labour, and labour alone, has the power of creating value. That metaphor he worked out with extraordinary ingenuity, through the whole extent of *Capital*. It isn't science. But its working out in depth and detail gives an overwhelming rhetorical effect of scientificity. That's why non-economists are convinced.

The industrial revolution is the most important historical event ever to happen in Britain, and the second most important in the history of the world.[10] Not all epic subjects get epics; but this one has. It is *Capital*, which is the *Iliad* of the class war. And before we reject the comparison as absurd, we might notice that *Capital* has at least one property of the major successful epic: it provides the myth that still controls our sense of what is important about the past. We still think of our society as a capitalist one, though it is not self-evident that the functioning of capital is the most important, defining feature of it. (The functioning of science or industry are probably that.) Without Marx, we would perhaps understand the industrial revolution in a quite different way. Certainly, without Marx, we should be unlikely ever to have perceived the proletarian as an epic hero. Yet that is exactly how left-wing intellectuals – Georg Lukács, Edward Thompson, or Raymond Williams, for example – have been seeing him for more than a century now; it underlies an entire school of Marxist historiography and a great deal of leftist criticism.

NOTES

1. The words are **artistic** and **ideological**. Obviously there are several ways of expanding Marx's brief phrases. The obvious interpretation is that art is one of the ideological forms in which men become conscious of conflicts over the control of the forces of production and fight them out. I think this claim is true, and profound; it is part of a position that I call **cultural materialism**. Of course it is a programmatic claim, and doesn't get interesting until you attempt to describe in detail just how class or other conflicts are turned into traditional iconography or literary fictions.

2. Perhaps in these words Marx was thinking of economic activity alone, and not reproductive activity. However, Marxism – from *The Communist Manifesto* to Engels' *The Origin of the Family, Private Property, and the State* – has always incorporated theories of family and clan structure as well. A materialist theory of history that ignored family structures obviously would not work at all. In pre-industrial societies family structures are the principal structures for organising both production and distribution.

3. Engels, letters to Conrad Schmidt 1890, Joseph Bloch 1890, Franz Mehring 1893. In Feuer (ed.) 1959.

4. Alfred Marshall 1890, *Principles of Economics*. Probably the best text from which to learn classical economics; for many years the standard textbook.

5. In the eighth edition of Marshall, 1920 edition, one page out of 700 is devoted to refuting Marx.

6. We can think of *Capital* as an ongoing exposition in five volumes beginning with *A Contribution to the Critique of Political Economy* (1859) as the first, *Capital*, vol. I (1867) as the second; the posthumous works *Capital* vols II and III (ed. Engels) and the posthumous *Theories of Surplus Value* (ed. Kautsky).

7. I wrote originally 'Most people like the products, even if intellectuals don't.' This is impossible to deny; but many Marxists would see this as capitalism conditioning people to like unnecessary products. The statement 'Most people find their lives enriched by at least some of the products' is more challenging. I have in mind for example those who are helped by high-tech medicine and drugs; old people whose lives would be a desert without a television set; busy people who can find an enormous variety of good pure food at a supermarket; families who find work, school and recreational transport in a small car; and so forth. Critics of consumerism should always at least try to imagine the pro-consumerist case.

8. J.R. Green 1874.

9. Interesting that it should be the greatest: a more minor figure like Disraeli can't be criticised in this way.

10. On strictly materialist principles, that is. On the same principles, the most important historical event – though it was actually an extended process and took place before writing was invented – was the agricultural revolution of the neolithic period, by which man was transformed from a rare animal hunting and gathering in small nomadic bands to a common one cultivating crops and tending herds. This process is the origin of many religions, and is celebrated indirectly in every fertility ritual or associated mythological story. See later discussion of cultural materialism in anthropology (Chapter 10).

BOOKS

Karl Marx 1847 *The Poverty of Philosophy*.
   1848 *The Communist Manifesto*.
   1859 *A Contribution to the Critique of Political Economy*.
   1867 *Capital: A Critique of Political Economy* (3 vols).
Friedrich Engels 1888 *Ludwig Feuerbach and the End of Classical German Philosophy* (in *Marx and Engels*, ed. Lewis S. Feuer, 1959).
   1877 *Anti-Duhring*.
   1940 (posthumous) *Dialectics of Nature*.
Alfred Marshall 1890 *Principles of Economics*.
V.I. Lenin 1908 *Materialism and Empirio-Criticism*.
   1930 *The Teachings of Karl Marx*.
G. Plekhanov 1908 *Fundamental Problems of Marxism*.
Louis Althusser 1965 *For Marx*.
Louis Althusser and **Etienne Balibar** 1968 *Reading Capital*.
G.A. Cohen 1978 *Karl Marx's Theory of History*.
M. Harris 1969 *The Rise of Anthropological Theory*.
   1980 *Cultural Materialism*.
Leszek Kolakowski 1978 *Main Currents of Marxism* (3 vols).
Jon Elster 1985 *Making Sense of Marx*.

PART THREE

Marxist theory and literature

CHAPTER SIX

Economistic Marxism and Critical Interpretation

The Case of Landscape and Caudwell's History of Poetry

SUMMARY

I want in this chapter to do something very difficult: namely, to defend a simple and unfashionable economistic and historicist model of Marxist interpretation, based directly on Marx's claim that, in art, the class struggle is worked out at an ideological level. A consequence of this is that works of art can sometimes give us information about underlying class struggle, when it is not apparent to less sophisticated instruments.

In the first section of this chapter I construct a deliberately simplified case study in a very familiar area – English landscape painting – to show how, by the application of Marxist theories of history and ideology, it is possible to find in works of art what amounts to a **political unconscious**:[1] that is, a deep political content of which both audience and creator may be unaware, but which is nonetheless profoundly important for both. This underlying content is an embodiment of some phase in the class struggle.

In the second section some critical objections to this procedure are considered, using an article by Dr Leavis on Jack Lindsay's Marxist interpretation of Bunyan. It is usually thought that *Scrutiny* easily saw off the Marxist challenge in literary criticism in the 1930s; my example suggests the encounter was a draw.

The third section shows how it is possible to rewrite the whole history of English poetry on these lines, using the work of Christopher Caudwell, and to place it within a general philosophical theory – which Caudwell called 'dialectical materialism', though not every dialectical materialist would have approved. Some criticisms of this approach are also offered, but a protest is entered against the way the modern left has dismissed Caudwell.

It will be clear that the style of Marxist interpretation I am admiring is that of intelligent orthodox Communists of the 1930s.[2] The style I am avoiding is that of Althusserians of the 1960s and 1970s. The reason for this is given in Chapter 8: that the underlying philosophy of Althusserianism made no sense.

1   VISIBLE BEAUTY AND THE CLASS STRUGGLE: A STUDY IN LANDSCAPE

1.0   Marxism, humanism and cultural history

Marxism is not a theory of literature or general culture: it is a programme, now looking implausible, for the transformation of society. That programme is indeed based on a theory; but of history and economic relationships. The theory is that the driving force of history is conflict over the control of productive resources: class conflict. Do we need reminding that, for a Marxist, all history is the history of class conflict?[3] It carries on, now hidden, now open; and other aspects of history – wars, politics, legal systems, general culture and high art – are to be interpreted in terms of the underlying class conflicts which are fought out through them.

Marxist theories of culture are usually contrasted with **humanist** ones. The humanist holds that there is a universal human nature, found in all societies, though oppressed in some; art has its significance in its direct appeal to some feature of this human nature. For the humanist, the long tradition of representational art, from the caves of Lascaux twenty millennia ago, through the vivid wall-paintings of early Egypt and Crete, to Renaissance paintings of classical legend, and eighteenth- and nineteenth-century landscapes, is evidence of a massive continuity and uniformity of human nature, taste and talent, and teaches us to know ourselves.

A humanist conception of art as a whole invites us to propose a humanist theory of its nature. The classic example of such a theory is perhaps that of Kant, which as one would expect, works by way of a transcendental deduction, starting with the kinds of aesthetic judgement we actually make ('This landscape is beautiful. That one is sublime.') and moves to establish the presuppositions – the intrinsic properties of the human mind – that make these judgements possible. Kant offers a two-stage theory, about aesthetic judgement of nature, and aesthetic judgement of art; both, he holds, involve our tendency to find purpose in the world. Kant holds that though we cannot necessarily ascribe any actual or definite purpose to nature or to natural objects, the subjective needs of the human faculty of judgement cause us to look for, and perceive, a kind of purposiveness in them.

A beautiful landscape is one that harmonises with this subjective judgmental faculty. A beautiful work of art similarly conveys an **aesthetical idea** (of general purposiveness without any specific purpose). It does not convey any rational idea of purpose; it is the product not of understanding and science but of genius. This 'idealism of purposiveness, in judging the beautiful in nature and art, is the only hypothesis under which critique can explain the possibility of a judgement of taste which demands *a priori* validity for everyone (without grounding on concepts the purposiveness that is represented in the object)' (Kant 1790, p. 196). Kant also has a notion of the sublime: a sublime landscape – like a Swiss mountain – tends to overthrow the faculty of judgement; the feeling of sublimity arises because it awakens our sense of the grandeur of human moral feelings.

There are powerful insights, but also many things to object to in this extraordinary theory. What worries not only the Marxist but virtually any cultural historian is that it finds a sublime, metaphysical and universal reason, grounded in the essential nature of the human mind, to declare the taste of an eighteenth-century gentleman binding on the whole of humanity. The cultural historian does not merely point out that tastes change; but consciously or unconsciously follows Hegel in showing that the relevant aspects of the human mind are constructed anew in every generation, working from what has gone before. Cultural history still has something very general to teach us, something about our common humanity: but what it has to teach us is that our minds, our tastes, our reactions to the world are historically constructed, and develop in time.

The Marxist agrees with the cultural historian here; but adds the specific claim that these changes in the human mind have an economic basis; they are in some sense an aspect of the class war. Our apparently spontaneous tastes are an aspect of ruling-class ideology in each period; and the class war is being fought through them. When I respond to the art of the past, therefore, two class wars are being fought out: that of the former age, and that of my own.

1.1   The English countryside and the class order

When I look at a landscape painting, politics is far from my mind. Here is a beautiful picture of beautiful countryside, I feel: and I am not initially conscious even of applying historically constructed categories. The subject of the painting seems natural to me: what indeed could be more natural than nature? And my feelings seem to be naturally evoked by it. For a naive modern viewer like myself, a direct response to an eighteenth- or nineteenth-century landscape painting is something simple: it requires no theoretical justification or analysis. It is something natural: landscape painting virtually defines what we mean by 'nature'. It is something unpolitical: looking at a landscape painting does not feel like being in the class war, on either side of the barricades. In feeling this way, I have tacitly adopted a humanist theory of art: there are real properties of nature, which appeal to universal features of human nature, by way of this medium. It follows that I might expect anybody who had the leisure to look to respond as I do; and the present popularity of this genre gives some empirical support to my feeling.

If I lower my head to the catalogue I get a rather different view. Landscape painting is not in fact a naive art form. It has always been a heavily theorised genre, and an eighteenth-century amateur could learn a great deal about what to look for, both in general and in detail, from Hutcheson, Cozens, Gilpin, Reynolds, Burke and others.[4] Such discourses are a conspicuous part of governing-class ideology in the period; they have an obvious ideological function in attempting to guide and control the taste of the whole governing class, including, of course, the landowners. Very little of this theory is overtly political, though it is naturally saturated in class assumptions. It is either humanist theory, or technical advice on how to paint.

If I move to the bookshop or the library, I can reach a further level of sophistication. It is many years ago, in adolescence, that my mind was first rapt away by the ideal landscapes of Claude Lorraine. If I consult the work of John Barrell,[5] I can find a superb account of the way that was done: the way my eye was caught, and drawn into infinite and luminous depths of colour, framed by darker buildings, rocks or trees, and separated from me by a great perspective of alternate light and dark countryside. More to the point I find that the eighteenth-century viewers were as entranced as I: they too took from Claude an ideal structure of landscape as a framework in which to view and reorganise the actual structure of the countryside. Poets like Thomson also adopted this point of view. It begins to seem that when I look at a landscape it is not my own spontaneity that is responding, but the cultural history of centuries, and of an entire class with which I did not realise I had so much affiliation. Somehow an eighteenth-century aristocrat's concept of a prospect has grafted itself onto my urban twentieth-century working-class mind.

There is more to it than that. At the beginning, landscape art actually ranked third in the eighteenth-century hierarchy: first came history painting, with its epic significance; then portraiture. There was a fairly elaborate political theory of history painting, to which again Barrell provides a guide.[6] Here I learn of the republic of taste which our theorists began to establish, which is almost an extension of the class order, and in which painting has the clear purpose of promoting civic virtue. And we learn how at the end of the century, under the threat of revolutions, the republic of taste began to separate out from the political republic; by the time of Ruskin, landscape had succeeded history painting as the dominant genre, as painting had come to offer private rather than public satisfactions. To me, history painting seems dull; but then it would, wouldn't it – since my mind is the product of this history.

Barrell's account of this history – very imperfectly summarised here – seems to me difficult to doubt; and I would not describe it as Marxist. The project of describing the developmental history of the political ideologies surrounding painting is at most left-Hegelian; and of course, none the worse for that. Even so, it appears to have aroused immense opposition. The basis of this opposition is that the ideology of landscape painting has been accepted as a truth: that nature is a revelation of authentic value transcending politics. That movement, long ago, into the depths of a Claude was an escape from urban political realities for a working-class boy: *The Daily Telegraph* reader, like me, needs landscape as an escape from politics into nature. What can the Marxist possibly have to say against that? Let me return from the subtle and nuanced account of Barrell to something rather crude.

One thing the Marxist has to contribute is a blunt reminder that most of the nature concerned is private property. One explicit intention of a great deal of the art is to celebrate the position of the landowner. In this sense, the class meaning is blatant and clear. But it would be naive to leave the question there. Many of the pictures in this genre do not directly call the landowner to mind. They can be, and are enjoyed on the assumption that anyone can enter into that landscape, and the viewer in a gallery does not even mentally ask the landowner's permission. Far more viewers think of God as the creator of a landscape than think of the Earl of something or even of the designer Capability Brown.

What the pictures do call to mind is the landscape itself. This is an inescapably referential genre, even when the landscape in a particular picture is an invented one. The viewer is looking through the pictures at a pre-existing reality, which already has a set of meanings. The country is man-made. It is a physically constructed reality, with a socially constructed set of meanings. These meanings are not static; they are in fact modified by the landscape paintings themselves, and the ideal pictures of one generation may even become the model for an actual park in the next. We have to recognise this dialectical interplay between landscape paintings and landscapes, which helps to construct a general cultural concept of nature. But to look for the site of the class war we have to shift our main focus of attention from the paintings to the landscape they paint.

The particular type of English countryside celebrated by this genre of painting is that created in the last phase of aristocratic rule. It is a countryside of great houses, set in private parkland, and surrounded by farms worked by tenant farmers. The great houses are not a pure luxury; they are the physical setting in which the governing class of the country lives, and a great many of the final decisions of that government, both local and national, are taken in those houses. The parks are ornamental landscape, in the service of the landowners and establishing their position; during the eighteenth century, the idea of regular ornamentation was replaced by a cunning simulacrum of unspoilt or natural countryside, often produced by careful and extensive remodelling at enormous expense. The tenanted farms on the other hand existed for agriculture – the economic basis for the entire order of society. At the bottom of the whole society were the landless labourers, who became figures in the landscape.

Most eighteenth-century Englishmen would have denied that a class war was going on. It was seen as the order of nature that men of good family and immense wealth should own the countryside, leasing parts of it for productive purposes to sober god-fearing men of an altogether lower order; while agricultural labourers were miserably poor and sometimes starving. But this order was buttressed by artificial means. Savage laws existed to control all offences against property. The number of offences carrying the death penalty steadily increased throughout the century. These laws – essentially for offences against the governing class – were administered by an amateur magistracy drawn exclusively from that class. In effect, the class order of aristocratic society was maintained by the perpetual threat of death.[7]

It is not reasonable to describe a society such as this as one in which there is no class war. On the contrary, it is a society in which the class war has been fought and won, by the possessing classes; and in which these are now in military occupation of their territory, maintaining their rule by condign punishment of offenders from the non-possessing classes. It is, however, to the interest of such a ruling class to establish its rule as something natural and unchallengeable rather than as something merely military. In all aristocracies, a major part in this is taken by a mystique of birth, and by a characteristic class education. But at a certain stage in the development of aristocracy, a great part also is played by a mystique of security and naturalness.

One mark of the Georgian house and surrounding park is its defencelessness. The park is surrounded by a wall, not a fortification. It is defended by a few outdoor staff, not by a military garrison. It is carefully contrived, in the later eighteenth century, to look like a fertile natural wilderness, on which few human feet (and those all belonging to the family or the staff) have trodden. But nobody tries to take it over and dig in it. It contains grazing deer, which are a very tasty meal for the starving; but nobody thinks of taking them. At the heart of it is an enormous, and quite defenceless house; it has no embrasures for armaments, like a castle, but vast windows out of which to look at the private park: and no riotous crowd ever arrives to break them.

Such peaceful and secure domination is a mark of enormous underlying power. The power is real enough. An eighteenth-century nobleman would sometimes eliminate a whole village in order to secure his peaceful vistas. The village would not rebel. He would have no war on his hands. His victims would go quietly to the new place that he assigned. To the Marxist, that is not a sign that no class war was taking place. It is rather a sign that one side in the class war was possessed of overwhelming strength. With such strength and security, of course, goes peace, in the straightforward sense of absence of worry about losing one's possessions and being overthrown.

In the real world, of course, there were occasional agricultural riots, and across the channel at the end of the century the *ancien régime* was overthrown. But the English countryside – which means essentially the English country house and its appurtenances: the private park, the surrounding farms worked by efficient and cheerfully respectful tenant farmers – was a living symbol of the naturalness and the eternity of the class order. The paintings – including the very greatest of them – are a distillation of that symbolism.

My arguments so far have been schematic and crude, since I am interested in establishing a very crude and shocking case: namely that landscape painting, which seems so natural and unpolitical, is actually a political genre celebrating a crushing aristocratic victory in the class war. The point is an obvious one nowadays, I suppose; but it is still capable of shocking the naive viewer, who sees only beautiful pictures of a beautiful countryside. I am myself just such a naive viewer, in most ways, and it continues to shock me. But are such insights too crude and generalising to make for good criticism of individual artists, or individual pictures?

A good analytical critic of the paintings can in fact provide a very delicate and nuanced account of the ideological development of art in this period. Consider John Barrell's book of 1980, *The Dark Side of the Landscape: the Rural Poor in English Painting 1730–1840*, on Gainsborough, Morland and Constable. In the figures of the poor, Barrell is choosing what both Gainsborough and Constable would have seen as very subordinate elements in landscape composition, and using them successfully to chart an ideological history, in which we emerge from pastoral into a kind of realism: in Gainsborough 'rural labourers cease to be "happy husbandmen" and become "the labouring poor" ' (p. 31). With some Gainsboroughs, placed 'in the context of E.P. Thompson's account of how working-class consciousness was made in the late eighteenth and early nineteenth centuries, we can see them as attempts actively to resist or deny the creation of that consciousness'; and there are cross-references to poetry, in which what had by the early nineteenth century become the politically dangerous sentimentalism of Goldsmith's *Deserted Village* was answered by the repressive Conservative realism of Crabbe's *Parish Register* (p. 73).

1.2 Art and the political unconscious

In such interpretations Marxist theory is called upon in two different ways. The general theory of the 1859 *Preface* tells us that art is one of the ideological spheres in which the class struggle is worked out. It is this theory which justifies us in looking beneath the peaceful surface of the work at an underlying struggle which is not only not represented in it, but is actually explicitly denied. We look at one of these pictures, where, tucked away in a small part of the landscape God made, some contented and industrious labourers are going about their immemorial business, and we say: here is someone who wants us to think that this oppressive class order is something given, immemorial and good. We thus actively turn an implication of the picture into a propagandist statement, and we are entitled to do this because our theory tells us that art has these ideological functions.

We also use Marxist theory in a second way: to determine what specific class struggle the picture actually represents. At the centre of Marxism is its theory of history; and this is not merely a general claim that the class struggle exists, and accounts for all the other struggles: it incorporates a detailed narrative history of the world, seen as a sequence of modes of production in each of which a different type of class struggle has primary importance. This in turn is carried through into a detailed history of the class struggle in the form it took in particular economies, and the way in which that influenced the general structure of the whole society concerned. Our interpretation of an English landscape painting will turn on a specific interpretation of the history not just of English painting but of English land, and what it meant to those who did, and those who did not, own it. Consider the interpretation of eighteenth-century society given in Thompson's *Whigs and Hunters*, for example.

We can say that, generally speaking, a Marxist interpretation of a work of art involves placing the work in its historical context, itself understood in terms of a Marxist narrative of underlying class conflict; and identifying the way in which the underlying class conflict is transformed and represented. This makes the process sound mechanistic and formulaic; but of course I am at the moment working in terms of a stylised formula. In any concrete interpretation, finding the connecting thread between the actual economy, the structure of society, and the prevailing cultural forms can be complex and difficult enough.

What is important about this theory is that it provides us with a Marxist basis for making claims about the significance of works of art. For on the basis of this theory it is possible to view the work not simply as a conscious propagandist exercise, but rather as a way in which, in Marx's words, people become conscious of the class struggle and fight it out. It is true that the disguise here – vicious class repression into peaceful landscape – seems to be a particularly impenetrable one; that it seems in some ways more like becoming **unconscious** of the class struggle than becoming conscious of it. But this is in fact the general case. People become conscious of the underlying contradictions that threaten their society, in the first place, by building elaborate imaginary structures that disguise and deny the threat.

There is an interesting parallel here with Freudian theory. A dream – or a work of art – is a disguised fulfilment of a repressed wish. The emotional power of the dream – often focused on apparently unimportant details – stems in reality from the depths of the conflict which the dream does not allow into consciousness. In the same way, in the realm of society rather than the unconscious mind, the emotional power of a work of art – focused, perhaps, on some non-social feature of a landscape – may depend on an underlying conflict in society which is never explicitly referred to; and which can be recovered only by interpretive analysis backed up by explicit social theory. The Marxist critic is a social psychoanalyst uncovering the political unconscious of a work.

For this reason we are often as fully entitled to draw conclusions from what is absent in a genre of art as we are from what is present. If we find, for example, that a presentation of the English countryside regularly excludes the harsher aspects of the life of labourers, we are entitled to count that as an idealisation of landscape that is part of the political meaning of the genre. This is certainly one of the grounds we can bring for holding that English landscape painting, in its primary political meaning, is an apologia for the governing class of landowners.

1.3   The change of meanings with historical change

I have been talking so far about the art work placed in its own period of history: the products of a late aristocratic society as viewed by aristocrats themselves. Their consciousness of a threat to their own order is here obscurely mediated by paintings which construct that order as natural, peaceful, beautiful and immutable. But it is a notorious fact that these paintings, as living works of art, have outlived the social order in which they were produced. They are as popular now as they have ever been, and command enormous prices from people who are in no sense aristocrats. In the summer of 1991 the Tate Gallery in London housed one of the largest exhibitions of Constable landscapes there has been. In spring 1993 the Royal Academy could safely bank on English watercolours.

What then do pictures of these landscapes mean to a viewer who may live in a later time, and does not come from the aristocratic class? A viewer who may be bourgeois or even working class, and who has no unconscious apprehensions of his lands being rent from him, since he possesses none worth taking? The principles of Marxist interpretation would demand that we place the pictures in their new historical setting, and ask how the new class struggle appropriate to that setting is worked out in them. Three obvious answers stand out.

1.3.1 *An old subjectivity for a new class*   One answer, particularly appropriate for bourgeois viewers near the original time, is that such a viewer is admitted to a small part of the subjectivity of the original owner. He has some access to the beauty and the peace of the original estate, without ever having had the social anxieties. Of itself, this has no political implications; the viewer is not fighting any class war. But of course, he may well come to value the existence of such estates; or at least of the beautiful landscape this social order produced. Such a position at least dampens down any rage he may feel at the oppressiveness of the order. If it turns out that this beauty is actually dependent on the oppression of a large part of the people of the countryside, the viewer may come, in Tom Paine's words about Burke, to pity the plumage and forget the dying bird. He may support oppression for the sake of beauty.

Marxists who have followed some such chain of reasoning as this may therefore feel it is incumbent upon them to reject forms of art – Georgian architecture, both of town and countryside, great parks, landscape painting and aristocratic portraiture, the music of Haydn and Mozart, played in those aristocratic salons – all of which certainly expressed and were entirely dependent on that social system. A conviction that the system was evil and ought to be suppressed may therefore play back into a rejection of the art that the system produced.

On this basis, a whole world of pleasure is sacrificed to a political principle. For although every single one of these artistic forms was developed in intimate relationship with a definite social system, every single one can also be taken over – indeed has been taken over, again and again – for the use of other classes in other social systems. Perhaps the clearest example here is the park, which can become a working-class pleasure simply by being opened to the working class. But the music is pretty class-mobile too. It transferred without difficulty from an aristocratic to a bourgeois ruling class, and then again to the upwardly mobile elements of the working classes. Marxist critics never look quite so insanely puritanical as when they are judging works of art in terms of their class origin, or even in terms of the class structures these works are currently used to support. (As many critics of Shakespeare currently do.)[8]

1.3.2 *New meanings for a new class*   The second answer to our question above is that works produced in one historical situation may take on a new set of meanings in a new historical situation. In a new class structure based on industry and commerce, with a society that is almost entirely urban, the meaning of the country changes completely. It represents human needs which are not satisfied for the urban industrial and commercial worker, whether working class or bourgeois. It represents space, fresh clean air and water, healthy exercise, freedom of movement, congenial work, a sense of life and growth. This, to the urban worker, is what the country is for; along, of course, with good fresh food from contented animals. In the paintings, the meaning of landscape changes too. For the viewer with no understanding of the original society, a new golden society of the past is projected, whose very reason of being is to show what a society would be like in which the contradictions of urban society did not exist or were resolved. Landscape becomes Pastoral again.

Not only Marxists, but sophisticated critics in general have felt that responses such as these are sentimental and empty. For the Marxist, an imaginary resolution is being projected, of social contradictions that can only be resolved by a forward march to proletarian revolution. For another kind of critic, this response to art is a sentimental turning away from a real modern life that needs to be confronted and understood.

Both kinds of critic are missing something important however. The needs I have listed – space, clean air and water and so forth and good fresh food – though they can be supplied only by a society, are in no sense socially constructed needs. They are, rather, the underlying biological needs on the basis of which the social construction of sophisticated needs takes place. Any social construction of human needs which leads human beings to renounce their own biological needs is oppression. A society which attempts to construct its workers in such a way that they do not even consider the possibility of having adequate food, or sleep, or accommodation, or leisure is a hideously oppressive society; in some ways, not unlike the society that the mill-owners described by Engels and Marx seemed to be trying to construct.

The sentimental image of the countryside is precisely an image of an alternative, healthy, unalienated society. So long as this image is alive, the actual society of industry and commerce does not seem to be the only human condition possible. To the realist critic of sentimental and escapist art, there is a devastating reply (it comes from C.S. Lewis). 'What sort of people think all the time about escape? Prisoners, and jailers.' To an extent, the urban industrial and commercial workers are prisoners dreaming of escape. Landscape articulates their dream, which is necessarily sentimental, because ill-informed. The realist critic is the jailer trying to keep them in an inhuman world. The Marxist is the agitator who tells them that everything will be all right if they shoot the prison warders and organise the prison themselves. But what they want to do is escape.

1.3.3 *Criticism and the market-place* The third answer to our question is that these works may take on some kind of external significance which has no necessary connection with their meaning. One obvious example of this is the value of paintings as commodities in the art market. Works of art are commodities of which the supply is extremely restricted, and the exchange value can therefore be very high. Modern economics can handle questions of this kind straightforwardly enough, though it would be quite hard to deal with them in terms of the labour theory of value.

A more interesting case is that of the place of works of art in the metaphorical market of critical opinion: or to put it another way, in the history of taste and judgement. There are long debates over this, which stretch over millennia. A change of critical opinion about art or literature is often the index of some major historical and social change. Thus the shift of opinion about classical works that we call the Renaissance is much more than an episode in cultural history. A Hegelian would see shifts of this kind as an index of the development of *Geist*; a Marxist would try to explain them as effects of the history of class struggle.

The recent school of critics that call themselves cultural materialists have concentrated on the way in which canons of literature have been constructed in the academy, so that the classist, racist and sexist ideologies which works of literature often contain become, literally, canonised as universal human values. The place of Shakespeare in our culture is often taken as the supreme example of this: in the old days, Shakespeare was presented as universally human; nowadays, we say that the literary study of Shakespeare is used to present a Conservative political ideology as a universally human one.

Protagonists of this view sometimes deny the possibility that art can have any value independent of its ideological uses. They argue that apparently spontaneous responses – even their own apparently spontaneous responses – to poetic or dramatic values in the plays can always be explained by ideological determinants of some kind. Critics of this school will thus give epistemological priority to their theories about ideology rather than to their responses to art and literature. This point is taken up later in this book.

1.4 Technique

It is a glaring weakness of the argument so far that I have said little about technique. Many critics in all periods, and most critics in recent periods, have regarded subject matter as something of rather secondary importance compared with the handling of pattern and of paint (or, in the other arts, of tonality and tone colour; of structure and of language; and so forth). In Marxist and cultural materialist terms, however, almost nothing of importance seems to be sayable about these issues. There is, it is true, what might be called a technological dialectic in the arts. The progress of technology makes possible new paints, new musical instruments, new artistic media like film. Artists in turn make new demands on the technology they have available. But one doesn't need to be a cultural or historical materialist to recognise this; and some standard accounts of historical materialism – e.g. Bukharin 1921 – have been pretty crude about it. A subtler point is that progress in technique makes older forms of art impossible; they sink into the condition of minor crafts, useful in restoration.

Of course there is no particular difficulty in making individual critical judgements in which artistic technique is connected, sometimes in an interesting way, with the class war. Critical interpretation is a very under-determined and open-ended activity. Nothing easier, or more arbitrary, than to connect the large-scale orchestras of the late nineteenth century with the large-scale industrial organisations then emerging, and say that one expresses the other. (Of course, it doesn't work for chamber music, but one can forget about that while writing about orchestras.)

And if your main interest is in revolutions, it must be said that there is probably nothing easier to find in any period whatever of the arts, than revolutions in technique. Those who find James Joyce significant because he offers a revolution of the word might consider the colour work of Constable and then Turner. A subtler point might be to compare the rough vigour of Constable's sketches in oils, which were done (often at the same size as the final picture) to please himself; and the refined smoothness of the final versions, prepared for a cultivated public at the Royal Academy. A whole social order can be read off here, provided you know about it already.

It has to be said, however (though it is close to being an analytical truth), that no critical interpretation is of importance to theory unless it is entailed by some general theory. And the only important general claim I can think of about the relationship between artistic technique and social dynamics is that no certain relationships are known.

1.5   The particular case: Constable

How does an interpretation of the kind I have just sketched out stand up to the consideration of some particular case? Let us take Constable as our example. On the face of it, the interpretation immediately collapses. Constable was a bourgeois painter. He was the son of a mill-owner. He never repudiated his class position: the mill is a frequent subject in his paintings, and a country house rather a rare one. For subject matter he quite favoured a species of productive machinery: water-mills, canalised rivers, locks. The people in his landscapes are usually at work: in agricultural labour, or opening a lock, or taking a cart and a team of horses to water at a stream in the rain. There are no vacant lords contemplating their acres. Why is this not a celebration of human labour?

122

We have to recognise that what has been presented so far as a stereotypical cultural form – 'English landscape' – is in fact a historically developing form; and adjust our interpretation to fit each particular case. In *The Dark Side of the Landscape*, Barrell points out 'the *distance* between Constable the observer of human landscapes and the figures in those landscapes'. He ends '. . . Constable reduces all labourers to serfs . . . but in the very same act he presents them as involved in an enviable, and almost a relaxed relationship with the natural world, which allowed his nineteenth century admirers . . . to ignore the fact that the basis of his social harmony is social division.'

To this, modern admirers will reply: this is a characteristic socialist missing of the point. Constable is precisely one of the painters who recovered the universal meaning of landscape: who offered it not as an image of possession and class stability but as an image of nature: that is, presumably, of a pantheistic God, or of the unalienated life. This is defensible; certainly, he spent plenty of his life painting and sketching directly from nature, and plenty more working up ideal images of nature from his own sketch-books. A Marxist might however want to say that just such a pantheistic God – Nature – is the ideal guardian of a class rule that it naturalises and makes invisible.

And a quite unpantheistic, quite orthodox God sometimes emerges, with a great house of his own. The background to that vigorous sketch of cart and team of horses in the rain, under a fierce sky, is Salisbury cathedral. And in case one does not quite get the point, the final, famous version exists, with identical composition: but the sun has come out, and there is a rainbow arching across to wrap the cathedral in: the picture might as well have a caption: **Salvation!** The explicit meanings of Victorian art loom ahead.[9] Constable is now using the most ancient and powerful of ideological forms – religion – to make the exploitative order of the countryside into a direct expression of eternal justice. The ruling class does not need to be present in the picture, with such an august Viceroy.

2   BUNYAN AND MILTON

2.1   *Bunyan: the Marxists, Dr Leavis, and the meaning of death*

I have suggested that Marxist critics discover the political unconscious of works of art; the assumption here is that political elements like class war are there to be discovered. An alternative view would be that such critics turn non-political works into embodiments of the class war by a process of deliberate and violent reinterpretation, on the basis of a claim to possess a privileged theory of history and of ideology. Both the strength and weakness of this view are brought out in Dr Leavis's critique of the 1930s' Marxist, Jack Lindsay, in Leavis's article, 'Bunyan Through Modern Eyes'.[10] This article has become perhaps the best-known example of the great war in the 1930s, between *Scrutiny* and the Marxists: a war which *Scrutiny* is usually supposed to have won with ease. I am not so sure.

In the late seventeenth-century allegory, *The Pilgrim's Progress*, John Bunyan finds a profound image for the life of a Christian. It is like finding one has a burden on one's back, and must set out, forsaking family and friends, to make one's way to the Cross where alone that burden can be removed, and embark on a long pilgrimage to the Celestial City. The meaning of this is clear enough: the burden is sin; the Celestial City is heaven; the journey is the Christian life.

On the way lie encounters with monsters and men, who represent temptations; and Bunyan, who was a radical and reformer in his own time and took his own sectarianism seriously, includes among these the (Anglican) hypocrite 'By-Ends'. Dr Leavis, in line with his usual principles, takes Bunyan's writing seriously but not his religious and political thought. So he abstracts away the political meaning of the episode, but comments favourably on the racy colloquial language Bunyan uses: this, he says, testifies to 'an art of social living . . . a positive culture which has disappeared and for which modern revolutionaries, social reformers, and Utopists do not commonly project any social equivalent'. By this astonishing manoeuvre Bunyan's religious and political criticism of his own society is turned into profound support for it; and Bunyan the radical is recruited as yet another literary witness to F.R. Leavis's theory of history – history as a steady spiritual and social decline from the high plateau of the seventeenth century. It is clear that the violence Leavis inflicts on actual history is every bit as great as that which the Marxists inflict.

But, of course, the Marxists also have problems. Jack Lindsay is a Marxist, and therefore a materialist: he cannot accept in its own terms an essentially unworldly system like Christianity, in which life is lived, not in terms of material wealth or human fellowship on this earth, but of individual salvation or damnation in the world to come. For a materialist, to account for the potency of the religious vision in a work like *The Pilgrim's Progress*, it is necessary to treat concepts like Heaven as metaphors for something equally potent in ordinary social life. For Lindsay, in his book, *John Bunyan, Maker of Myths*, Heaven is a metaphor for the harmonious relationships and social unity impossible in a society divided by class conflict; since these are unattainable in life, they are projected after death. As we have seen, positions like these – reductive materialist analyses of Christianity – played an important part in the development of Marxism; they are discussed in Chapter 4.

As Leavis acknowledges, Lindsay's use of this analysis is not intended as reductive. It is intended to show why even a non-believer can respond to Bunyan's heaven-symbol. Bunyan, says Lindsay, 'wanted to get outside the cramping, distorting social discord of his day into the fuller life of fellowship'. And 'The tale tells of the passage from privation and obstruction to light and joy and plenty. The heaven-symbol is brought down from beyond-death; it becomes a symbol of what the earth could be made by fellowship. Thus the allegory, which superficially is a story of how to die, is a stimulus to further living.' Thus Lindsay appropriates the religious allegory for a Marxist system that offers salvation only on earth, after the revolution. He even suggests that there is a detail of the allegory – Christiana wading over the river of death and leaving her children behind – which suggests Bunyan had a sense that something was wrong with the idea of death as the goal of life.

Leavis has a field day with this. 'Though Mr Lindsay talks of "fuller life" he proffers emptiness . . . who with any wisdom to offer, worth listening to, could have published that as his reaction to the incomparable end of part two of *The Pilgrim's Progress*?' One can see Leavis's point: that the children should be left behind is obviously right; nothing else would give an insightful metaphor for death. But the savage rejection of Lindsay's approach is puzzling: for Leavis is no more a believer in Christianity than Lindsay is, or I am; and he has the same problem as we do in explaining the immediate power and significance of Bunyan's imagery. 'It would be useless arguing with anyone who contended that the inspiration here was essentially a Utopian vision of what "the earth might be made by fellowship" ', says Leavis.

This is a fairly characteristic Leavisite rejection of the bare possibility of discussion with anyone whose critical insights are significantly different from his own. It certainly does not bode well for fellowship. But Leavis immediately makes a partial retraction: 'Whatever of that element there may be in it' (so there is, perhaps, something in it, despite the uselessness of arguing with those who think there is something in it), 'the whole effect is something far more complex and mature.' At this point one is tempted to say, well the secret is out at last: what is wrong with revolution as a goal is that it is immature. Or, perhaps what we need is a conception of human fellowship that is complex and mature (and is, no doubt, the fruit of a ripe civilisation with a complex class structure). Such ironies would be a way of suggesting that Leavis is merely providing a reactionary mystification.

But we can't, and Leavis doesn't, leave it there. There is, after all, a real human problem with which Bunyan is concerned, and which Marxism is notoriously poor at handling. It is the problem of how the individual human being is to face up to his own death. The Marxist classics – and later Marxist critics – have nothing to say on that issue at all, though it is central to religious thinking. What Bunyan offers, Leavis points out, is something that could not be reproduced today. But he wonders 'whether, without an equivalently sanctioned attitude to death that is at the same time "a stimulus to further living" (the contradiction that Mr Lindsay sees), there can be such a thing as cultural health'. Leavis's article ends here; and one can't help feeling that it is a profoundly unsatisfactory point for it to end at. For Leavis has **nothing** to offer: not even the Heideggerian concept of being-towards-death. But he points to a large hole in Marxist theory.

We might also ask, what happens to interpretations which rest ultimately on a wholesale substitution of Marx's secular eschatology for Christian eschatology, when the revolution is indefinitely postponed or, worse, goes hideously wrong?

2.2   Milton: the contradictions of revolution

The case of Milton is more difficult still for the Marxist. Milton was, in Marxist terms, a bourgeois revolutionary, and a high official in the revolutionary government, whose job, enthusiastically performed, was to defend its most extreme policy: regicide. *Paradise Lost* is a poem about a revolution in which someone who looks very like a parliamentary leader unsuccessfully rebels against someone who looks very like a Stuart monarch. But the poem is on the wrong side (officially at any rate). Satan is supposed to be in the wrong; God in the right; though there are powerful poetic energies pushing the other way, and the two revolutionary poets, Blake and Shelley, never doubted that Satan was the true hero. The fundamental official reversal of values in the poem no doubt corresponds to the fact that the political revolution failed. But that is not to say that Milton ever changed his politics.

No Marxist can doubt that *Paradise Lost* is a response to a bourgeois revolution. But it is not exactly a representation of one. What it represents is, rather, the profound contradictions in society that both produced the revolution and dictated that it should fail. The contradictory artistic intentions of the poem communicate with and express the contradictions in the Puritan ethic that sustains it; these in turn embody the social contradictions of the period. The poem that was intended to justify the ways of God to Man ends up by putting God in the dock; and it goes some way to explain the subsequent decline of the fundamentalist Christianity on which it is built. The poem is in fact seamed through with such contradictions, and it is very easy to show that it is, like *Hamlet*, an artistic failure.[11] But the demonstrations are always unconvincing. They rest on the view that art is Apollonian and serene: that is, that it lays out its conflicts consciously, and leaves them resolved. But this poem has Dionysiac energies – that is, energies based on unconscious conflicts that are left unresolved. The power of the poem is very like the power of the unfinished revolution that gave birth to it.

Leavis, in *Revaluation*, characteristically ignores the political meaning of the poem, and pretends to condemn only its way of using language. On examination, his claims for the superiority of the 'line of wit' (or Caroline courtier-poets – Chapter 1) over Milton (Chapter 2) look merely like a preference for the language of the court over that of the pulpit and the House of Commons. Leavis's unpolitical stance is simply an unconsciousness of his own politics. Once again Leavis, like Eliot, ends up effectively as a supporter of Charles I; and most literary criticism follows him.

3   CHRISTOPHER CAUDWELL

3.1   The neglect of Caudwell

The 1930s were a Marxising decade, according to Dr Leavis and the common legend of the English departments; for him, Marxism was perhaps the principal theoretical discourse against which the critic had to fight. Yet very little serious Marxist literary theory remains from that period. One major figure stands out, though he is still not properly appreciated. In terms of the depth of the philosophical problems that he was prepared to tackle (including those questions about the formation of the human subject which our contemporary theorists studied in Althusser), and in terms of the range of empirical theory that he brought to bear on literature (from the hardest areas of the natural sciences through to a speculative quasi-psychoanalysis), and in terms of his ability to integrate these into a single coherent theoretical structure within the framework of a modified dialectical materialism, far the greatest British literary theorist was Christopher Caudwell.

He is not properly appreciated, because he had two major virtues: one was anathema to orthodox literary critics, and the other anathema to the New Left. The quality that was disliked by orthodox literary critics was the vast range of theory that he employed, and his lack of interest in close critical reading. Orthodox literary critics had spent most of their professional lives establishing the independence of literary criticism as a discipline, based on the skill of close reading; the negative side of this was a tendency to reject all theoretical speculation not narrowly focused on enforcing a particular literary judgement. Leavis is almost a caricatural example of this tendency; but even Raymond Williams was so deeply marked by it that he dismissed Caudwell as having little to say, about actual literature, that was even interesting.[12]

The quality that was disliked by the New Left is that Caudwell was a dialectical materialist and understood natural science. Not only did he understand it, but he tried to bring it into an integrated Marxist world view alongside poetry. The New Left, on the other hand, is heir to the tradition of Western Marxism,[13] beginning with figures like the young Lukács, and Gramsci, and stretching even to figures like Sartre. It is a philosophically sophisticated tradition, which regards dialectical materialism as frankly vulgar; it tends to make a sharp distinction between the natural and the social sciences, and abhors scientism.

It also, quite properly, is very concerned to distance itself from Stalinism; and this, I am afraid, has included accusing dialectical materialists like Caudwell, who admired Stalin, of adopting simple mechanistic Stalinist models in which cultural forms are directly determined by the economic base. An example of such a treatment is to be found in the introduction by Sol Yurick to the 1971 edition of *Studies and Further Studies in a Dying Culture*. Raymond Williams accuses Caudwell of believing in 'capitalist poetry'; Anthony Easthope, of connecting the heroic couplet directly to mercantilism.[14]

It is, of course, quite unfair; and it has led to a peculiar aftermath. The later New Left learnt its criticism, and something of its polemical intransigence, in the school of Leavis; but it learnt its literary theories in the school of Althusser.[15] It is in that context, tricked out with French philosophical and structuralist jargon and strange idealist importations directly from Lacan, and ultimately from Hegel, that it considered its central problem: the problem of the social formation of the individual human subject, and its implications for supposedly spontaneous critical judgement. In fact, however, everything of philosophical importance in Althusser was already present in dialectical materialism. Althusser was doing very little more than serving dialectical materialism with structuralist sauce, and his work has dated far more rapidly than Caudwell's.

Caudwell's life seems to have had something of the structure of a heroic myth. He is as near to being the archetypal Communist intellectual as, in their different way, Lukács or Gramsci. Unlike them, he was largely self-educated. He was born Christopher St John Sprigg in Putney in 1907; educated at Ealing Benedictine School till sixteen and a half. He had three years as a reporter on the *Yorkshire Observer*, was editor, and then director of a firm of aeronautical publishers; invented an infinitely variable gear for automobiles; published five textbooks on aeronautics, seven detective novels and some poems and short stories before he was twenty-five. Several of his short stories are rather good;[16] I haven't read the textbooks on aeronautics or the detective stories.

He became a Communist in 1935; he seems to have mastered the classic literature with frightening rapidity. He wrote *Illusion and Reality*, a study in the sources of poetry; *Studies in a Dying Culture* and *Further Studies in a Dying Culture*; *Realism and Romance* (all of these both philosophy and literary criticism); and *The Crisis in Modern Physics*. All were published posthumously. Caudwell's entire reputation is a posthumous one. Had he lived he might have been one of the very greatest of Marxist philosophers; or he might have been a dreary party hack. But he died in action in 1937, very gallantly, in the Spanish Civil War.

Caudwell's books all tend to be about the whole known universe. This is a consequence of the Marxist synoptic vision; but it makes it difficult to know where to start abstracting. I shall begin by making one or two general remarks on the features of Caudwell's thought which modern commentators seem to dislike, but which on the whole attract me. Then I shall give an account of his most important contribution to criticism: his account of the relation between economics and literary form and content, in the history of English poetry. Finally I shall abstract some of the more general and philosophical claims from *Further Studies in a Dying Culture*. (The culture that was dying was, of course, that of the West; Caudwell confidently expected a revolution in a very short time.)

In his writing Caudwell is an impressive combination of polemical journalist and amateur philosopher on the grand scale. What licenses his universal philosophy is Marxism; what makes it possible, for a young man of twenty-nine who still had a good many intellectual gaps to fill, is journalism. The habit of journalism allows him to substitute a kind of high-level polemical rhetoric for thinking, when he needs to think his way through certain difficult problems like the relation of subject and object, mind and matter, or freedom and determinism.[17] But at least he is aware of these problems, sees that they are central to work in literary and cultural theory, and tackles them head on; and this makes his work exhilarating. One feels after reading it that there is a whole world of ideas which literary criticism was not merely not exploring but actively repressing; and in fact these ideas did not get back into focus in the Anglo-American academic world until the rise of literary theory in the 1970s.

It is Caudwell's journalistic skill which makes it possible for him to cover so much ground, without being brought to a stand by ignorance of detail. It leaves his philosophy often polemical, shallow and full of holes. He is, like many other Marxists, fond of asserting that there is some simple formula which bourgeois thinkers 'cannot see'; though the better ones have often seen through it, and seen all round it. But I think he is sometimes profound and insightful; though his insights are into general ideas, and into the relation between literary forms and history, rather than into particular works of literature.

Caudwell's thought is therefore difficult to assess, unless, of course, you are a Marxist yourself, and simply test his party line against your own. In the 1940s, it was common to dismiss him for deviating from true Communism, by incorporating bourgeois philosophy of science, and so forth. Nowadays, he is more likely to be dismissed as a Stalinist.

Stalinism is a misfortune of Caudwell's period, like Maoism in the early 1970s but with more excuse; it was hardly possible to be in the British Communist Party then and not be a Stalinist. At that time, it could reasonably look as if the only serious choices were between an obviously bankrupt capitalist system which starved millions; and a newly developing Soviet system with some local difficulties, which was yet the one hope for the world's future. It was not then clear that Stalin's local difficulties amounted to a genocidal war against his own peoples, especially peasants and national minorities. Hostility to the Soviet Union seemed then to be objective support for capitalism, imperialism and, above all, Fascism. Caudwell died fighting against the Fascists and for the legal republican government of Spain at a time when it was still just possible to believe that Stalin was, on balance, a good thing, or at least a historical necessity.

Nowadays, of course, when we hear the name Stalin, we think of concentration camps; and of the liquidation of all intellectual dissent; and we recognise that the purpose of these things was not to fight against a counter-revolution and preserve the proletariat, but to hide the fact that Stalin was engaging in genocide. So every time Caudwell jeers at the anxieties of poets like Spender and others about intellectual freedom, we think of a long line of distinguished Russian thinkers and artists harassed or destroyed for unorthodoxy; we note that quite often their unorthodoxy consisted in noticing some minor aspect of the monstrous evils that were going on; and we feel a frisson of horror. And every time Caudwell insists: 'Freedom is the consciousness of necessity' a still small voice wonders: 'Even in a cell?'

But it would be an awful thing if one were prevented from assenting to the truth of some theoretical proposition merely by the memory that Stalin once agreed with it. Sol Yurick attempts this kind of intimidation in his introduction to *Studies and Further Studies in a Dying Culture*, citing a perfectly sensible passage from one of Stalin's most reasonable pronouncements – the one on linguistics – for us to jeer at. This is of course the exact equivalent of an orthodox Marxist of some persuasion citing a passage from Lenin, Stalin, or Mao in order to close an argument and establish his own orthodoxy. Caudwell was a dialectical materialist; this is nowadays an endangered species, and is well worth studying in its native colours. But he was also a highly unorthodox one in many ways, who did his own thinking.

3.2   The economic sources of English poetry

The best-known part of Caudwell's work is his history of English poetry, based upon stages of national economic development, which forms the major section of *Illusion and Reality* (1937). This is also the part that seems to give most support to a simple and mechanistic view of culture, in which the structure of the economy is more or less mechanically reproduced at the superstructural level of art. Caudwell gives some support for this view by actually printing a chart, **THE MOVEMENT OF BOURGEOIS POETRY**, in three columns in parallel.

On the left is the label of some economic era, like **Primitive Accumulation, 1550–1600.**

In the middle is a column of **General Characteristics:**

The Elizabethan Age – Marlowe, Shakespeare. The dynamic force of individuality, realising itself by smashing all outward forms, is expressed in poetry. Its characteristic hero is the absolute prince, with his splendid public life, which is collective and through which other individualities can therefore realise themselves without negating his.

On the right is a column of **Technical Characteristics:**

(a) The iambic rhythm, expressing the heroic nature of the bourgeois illusion in terms of the ancient world, is allowed to flower luxuriantly and naturally; it indicates the free and boundless development of the personal will. It is collective – adapted for declamation; noble – suitable to princely diction;

flexible – because the whole life of the prince, even to its intimacies, is lived in easy openness. (b) The lyrics are suitable for group singing (simple metres) but courtly (ornamental stanzas) and polished (bright conceits).

(Caudwell 1937, p. 117)

The chart continues through every stage of English economic development, with its corresponding poetic accompaniment. After primitive accumulation comes **The Transition 1600–25**, in which the absolute monarch becomes a force producing corruption and poets like Donne, Herrick, Vaughan, Herbert and Crashaw withdraw from the brilliant public life of the court to their private studies. Then comes **The Bourgeois Revolt 1625–50**, in which the bourgeoisie feels itself strong enough to revolt against the monarchy. With the help of 'the people' it overthrows the Stuarts. 'But this realisation of bourgeois freedom proves dangerous; the people demand it too, and there is a dictatorship which isolates the bourgeoisie, followed by a reaction. The noble simplicity of the self-idealised revolutionary (Satan, Samson Agonistes, Christ in the desert) then vanishes in an atmosphere of defeat.'

So it goes on. **The Counter-Puritan Reaction 1650–88** produces Dryden, Suckling and Lovelace; **The Era of Mercantilism and Manufacture** produces Pope; **The Industrial Revolution** and **The 'Anti-Jacobin' Reaction** produce the Romantic movement. **The Decline of British Capitalism 1825–1900** produces the Victorians; **The Epoch of Imperialism 1900–30** produces art for art's sake, the Parnassians, Futurism and Surrealism. The Wagnerian conclusion of the whole thing is of course **The Final Capitalist Crisis 1930–?** This mountain travails and produces – Auden, Spender and Day Lewis.

It is very easy indeed to make fun of this famous chart. Indeed, if one summarises it as briefly as I have done it is impossible to do anything but make fun of it. It looks as if crude and arbitrary historical categories are being used quite mechanically to generate and explain the styles of whole schools of poets – the poets in question often being quite arbitrarily thrown together and sometimes (but these are mistakes) assigned to the wrong period. Surely Stalin would have been subtler than this? But this impression is an artefact of the summarising procedure. Wagner's *Ring* is a hilarious farce in a five-minute summary. And the chart itself is only a summary of three chapters of exposition.

What we need to recognise further is that those chapters themselves are no more than a programmatic summary of a gigantic enterprise: the reinterpretation, on an economic basis, of all the English poets. The scale of this enterprise can be seen when one considers that we honour Leavis chiefly for his ability, in a whole critical lifetime, to present a convincing reorganisation of the history of English poetry and the English novel. And

Leavis here is working with a team of collaborators, and building on the work of Eliot. What he provides is an idealist rethinking of the history of English literature, on the basis of the experience of modernism. What Caudwell provides is a materialist rethinking of the history of English literature on the basis of the theory of historical materialism.

Most critics would agree that to interpret a work of literature, or the whole *oeuvre* of a writer, in terms of the economic background is of itself a sensible and interesting undertaking; it does not need to be reductive or mechanical. The accusation made about Caudwell is that he merely offers a mechanical relationship between the two. But this is quite false, and results from ignoring most of the theory in a very complex book. *Illusion and Reality* is a study of the sources of poetry: it borrows Freudian notions like the dreamwork and deals with the psyche and phantasy. And it applies all this theory to make a theoretical connection between the state of the economy and the nature of the accompanying art.

The major intervening variable connecting economic history with art is to be found in a particular aspect of the class consciousness of the dominant or rising class in society. Specifically it is to be found in a particular aspect of false consciousness, which Caudwell calls **'the bourgeois illusion'**. Caudwell argues that there is a central illusion which persists, because it arises directly from the defining class position of the bourgeoisie, and can never be lost while that position remains; but that illusion takes on different forms in different historical periods, and it is these forms which are projected into the works of art. The artist's technique is a way of elaborating and realising these forms.

The central illusion of the bourgeois is about the nature of freedom, which is his supreme value. Because the bourgeoisie was formed, in the course of a long history, by the breaking down of the historical rights and controls which the feudal nobility had over its serfs, the bourgeois has come to see human freedom as the absence of social ties. The central task of the bourgeoisie is to break all restrictions on economic freedom of action; and at first, when there is an oppressive nobility to emancipate itself from, or to overthrow, this is a genuinely heroic enterprise. Later on, however, when capitalism has arrived, though all external bonds have been broken, the bourgeois finds himself not free, but enslaved to the blind laws of the market. He knows no way of breaking with these but to seek more freedom, more competition; this enslaves him more.

At every stage in the development of the economy, therefore, comes a new form of the consciousness of unfreedom, and a new form of the aspiration for freedom. In art, this aspiration is worked out in phantasied form. It is thus that we have, in the passage already quoted, the Elizabethan projection of the idea of freedom onto the figure of the

Renaissance prince. Thus also that we have 'the noble simplicity of the self-idealised revolutionary (Satan, Samson Agonistes, Christ in the desert)' vanishing 'in an atmosphere of defeat' with the collapse of the bourgeois revolution. The varying phantasies of this bourgeois false consciousness around the time of the French Revolution provide also the key to the vagaries of the romantic poets up to their final withdrawal into their private world of romance.

I must stress that, once again, Caudwell suffers greatly from being summarised. What is clear however is that he has given, not a simple mechanical account of the relationship of culture to society, but a complex, nuanced, dialectical one of the whole development of social consciousness, as expressed in the characteristic social phantasies underlying the development of an art form. There is here the programme for a whole school of research workers; and though it was never carried through, this programme has never ceased to exert an influence on socialist critics, even at the height of their French infatuation.

Had such a research programme ever been carried through it would of course have been necessary to answer a number of awkward questions. All Marxist criticism depends upon the materialist interpretation of history, and this gives us a certain amount of privileged information about what is happening in history at any given time. For example, we know that you can always look beneath the surface of historical events, however peaceful they may happen to be, and find a class war going on. ('All history is the history of class struggle' – *The Communist Manifesto*.) All Marxist criticism is, similarly, an interpretation of literature in terms of class struggle.

History since early feudal times has seen a steady, and finally spectacular, rise of the bourgeoisie; and certain famous historical events – the English Civil War, the French Revolution, the first Russian revolution of 1917 – qualify as decisive bourgeois revolutions, that permanently shifted the balance of power, and made the bourgeoisie into the ruling class. Then, if ever, one would expect to see class struggle reflected overtly in history; though of course idealist bourgeois historians could not be expected to see it. Starting with Marx and Engels, a series of brilliant Marxist historians put a great deal of flesh on these historical bones; by 1970 no one would have doubted the existence of bourgeois revolutions – or even that the second revolution of 1917, Lenin's revolution, was a genuine Marxist proletarian revolution that installed a new class and blew the bourgeoisie away.[18]

The last twenty years of empirical research have not dealt well with these interpretations. A new generation of historians has been making detailed analyses of the actual class composition of the two sides in the English Civil War, to find out whether one was more bourgeois than the other. Apparently it was not. It appears that the prototype of all class wars was not actually a war between classes. Under the withering stare of the revisionists, the great bourgeois revolutions seem to have disappeared from history.[19] Of course, one can keep them in a more metaphysical sense. One can say that society was certainly feudal in the thirteenth century and capitalist in the nineteenth; there was a long transition between the two, and the moment when a parliament (or even the tiniest rump of it) cut off the head of a king was clearly an important political stage in that transition.

It is clear, however, that being a Marxist critic, school of Caudwell, was never going to be an easy option. A historical materialist is committed to the interpretation of literature in accordance with a detailed theory of history. Unlike Leavis or Eliot, he doesn't derive this theory simply from a reading of the literature concerned. It is meant to be a true economic history of the society in which the literature was produced, not a projection from literary texts. It must therefore be compatible with the historical evidence. The Marxist critic is necessarily a Marxist historian, and does double scholarly duty.

There is another, slighter historical problem which we can illustrate from Caudwell's second phase of history: **The Transition 1600–25**. It is historically true that the court of James I was sexually corrupt, by comparison both with that of Elizabeth and of his son Charles I. But was James's personal character, or that of the Howard family, a historical necessity of the development of the bourgeoisie? More generally, how does Caudwell distinguish historical accidents from the inevitable march of history? The point is even more important in the next reign: it is quite possible that the very outbreak of the English Civil War depended, in a crucial way, on the personal characteristics of Charles I. If he had had even a few of the personal characteristics of Elizabeth I – such as political intelligence, a sense of the value of money, and the habit of backing able ministers rather than incompetent personal favourites – what reason is there to suppose that an equivalent to the French *ancien régime* could not have been constructed in Britain?

Neither of these problems is fatal for Caudwell's account of the history of English poetry, though they make it much more difficult to verify. It is still possible to believe in an underlying conflict over control of productive resources, worked out over centuries, and defining as it is worked out a class aspect to every historical conflict. It is still possible to regard this conflict as something that comes to consciousness in the form of projected phantasies of the kind Caudwell describes, and is then worked into art. And such an underlying causal theory still has a role to play, even if one makes no claims of complete economic determinism;

even if one makes full allowance for the element of contingency and accident in history, and for the personal role of historical agents like kings – or indeed for the personal role of authors.

3.3   Science, art and metaphysics

Caudwell's work represents also a remarkably ambitious and (I think) successful attempt to think through a consistent view of both art and science; again, the comparison with Althusser is an obvious one. He sees science and art as opposite extremes of the normal unitary relation of the self and the world that is found in human practices. The ego and the world, that is, are merely abstractions from the concrete world of human practice; and science and art take this process of abstraction a stage farther. Science creates a mock-ego (presumably an abstract 'observer') in order to explore the possibilities of the world. Art creates a mock world in order to explore the possibilities of the self.

Of course both of these, the self and the world, are conceived of as social; and discoveries in both realms return into and are tested in practice. It is not, however, the case that we can put them together and get back to concrete living again:

> science and art do not when fitted together make a complete concrete world; they make a complete hollow world – an abstract world only made solid and living by the inclusion of the concrete living of concrete men, from which they are generated.
>
> (Caudwell 1937, p. 154)

This position (I hope I am fairly representing it) has the advantage of taking both art and science seriously, and recognising the difference between them. Caudwell argues that it is practically necessary for there to be a world of phantasy in order to embody the emotional and intellectual sources of collective action. What once was done in a unitary way by religion is now done by science and art.

The whole world as described by science is as it were the world as it exists for this abstract observer, the mock-ego. (A rough parallel to Husserl's 'transcendental subject'.) Science makes available for the individual a deeper, more complex insight into outer reality, and into human beings considered objectively. But this world is opened up by the work of men in association – it is a social reality – and its enlargement permits the development of associated men to a higher plane at the same time as it extends the freedom of the individual (freedom, that is, from the constraints imposed by the external world). Science is the consciousness of the necessity of outer reality.

The world of any one work of art exists to construct some possible self in the individual auditor, or the collective audience. 'It changes the emotional content of his consciousness so that he can react more subtly and deeply to the world. . . . It makes possible new levels of conscious sympathy, understanding, and affection between men, matching the new levels of material organisation achieved by material production.' (It will be seen that this theory covers the same ground as modern theories of 'subject positioning' (Chapter 9); but it has an immense optimism about the social role of art and the value of material production which modern Marxists cannot match.)

We have even yet not explored anything like the full depth of Caudwell's theory. It is a characteristic of his work that the theoretical concepts at play in history find their ultimate place in a metaphysical account of the universe. This comes out in the *Studies* and *Further Studies in a Dying Culture*. Caudwell begins by writing (perhaps rather too dismissively) of some modern artists, including Shaw, Wells and D.H. Lawrence; they tend to appear as symptoms of bourgeois decay. He makes some interesting points; perhaps he does not quite recognise what a superb achievement it is to be a good symptom. He then works up through pacifism, love, Freud and liberty, to religion, beauty, men and nature, consciousness and finally reality. It is a mark of Caudwell's distinction that none of these papers is banal. Indeed he gets better as he works upwards; he is not very good on D.H. Lawrence or H.G. Wells, but challenging on consciousness and reality. It is at these high levels that the fundamental categories are established; you have to consider the nature of reality, of knowledge, and of consciousness in order to grasp the nature of freedom; and to grasp the nature of freedom to understand the bourgeois illusion.

Caudwell proceeds from a dialectical materialist account of reality. The universe is a material reality; and it is a becoming. This is established by thought in unity with practice. The universe is deterministic only as a whole; no part of it is self-determining. But it may be divided into parts which are mutually determining. From the mutually determining parts A and B, a new unity C emerges; this incorporates A and B but is not exhausted by them. Time is an abstraction from such emergence; space an abstraction from what remains as A and B transform into C. I am not sure whether this is Hegelian wordspinning, or a possible framework for modern relativity physics.

Mind, says Caudwell, is the body as subject and the universe as object. Body is the body as object and the universe as subject. This claim is the kind of thing Eagleton probably had in mind when he accused Caudwell of hair-raising theoretical vulgarities.[20]

So we arrive at Freedom, which is the key concept of Caudwell's ethics.

> In such a universe thought is real; it plays a real role; but matter is real. Thought is a relation of matter; but the relation is real; it is not only real but determining. It is real because it is determining. Mind is a determining set of relations between the matter in my body and the rest of the Universe. It is not all the set, for not all the necessities whereby my body and the rest of the universe mutually determine each other is known to me, not all my being is conscious being. Insofar as these relations are conscious, I am free, for to be free is to have one's conscious volition determine the relations between the Universe and oneself. The more these relations between my body and the Universe are part of my conscious volition the more I am free. These relations are necessary or determining relations. Freedom is the consciousness of necessity.
>
> (Caudwell 1938, 1948, 1971, p. 231)

There is, still, an obvious objection. This account of human freedom is an interesting approach to the philosophical problem of reconciling human freewill with causal necessity. I am not sure if it works at that level. But it certainly does not work at the political level.

The paradigm case of unfreedom is that of a man in prison. Consciousness of his imprisonment, however detailed, effective and analytic, neither is nor ensures (though it may indirectly make possible) freedom. What leads directly to freedom is escape. It really looks as if the paradigm sense of freedom simply does not fit Caudwell's philosophical sense.

A natural generalisation of this paradigm case is that the illusion of freedom exists when the supposed self appears self-determining, the reality when the real self is self-determining. If the man in the cell thinks he can walk out any time, he has the illusion of freedom; if he actually can walk out, he has the reality. Obviously this doesn't help Caudwell's case at all. The concept of freedom needs much more careful analysis. I doubt if it can coexist with a completely determinist model of science. This is the point where Caudwell offers no protection from Stalinism.

The point is particularly damaging since at the ethical level – though as a Marxist he does not call it that – Caudwell takes freedom as his principal value. Of course it is not bourgeois freedom. It is in the first instance freedom from the pressures of survival, and this is achieved by human association for production of the necessities of life. It entails a recognition of what is socially necessary. The bourgeois illusion is that you can have an individualist freedom from society; but this merely leads to subjection to impersonal and unknown economic processes. Freedom is freedom in association. He takes his *summa* from Engels, who found the idea originally in Hegel: 'Freedom is the recognition of necessity.'

One can respect this position; and the bourgeois illusion can indeed be traced in much poetry. But the implication of this argument is frightening. As we have seen, a man is free, even if the party puts him in prison, provided that he recognises the necessity that it should! (This position is dramatised in Koestler's *Darkness at Noon* and satirised in Orwell's *1984*.) Caudwell himself argued that those who protested about the lack of artistic or scientific freedom in the Soviet Union were trying to protect their own little bit of bourgeois culture; seeking such freedom was a symptom of the disintegration of bourgeois culture into many separated parts and what was needed was a unified proletarian culture.

I have said that modern Marxists have tended to reject Caudwell, as a Stalinist, scientific socialist, and dialectical materialist – categories that are very blown upon these days, though they were then Marxist orthodoxy in the West as well as in Russia. To the modern Western taste, Caudwell does raise rather a chill by listing Marx, Lenin and Stalin as three great men of, apparently, similar stature, and Trotsky, Zinoviev and Kamenev as examples of 'complete treachery'; and by demanding that both art and science should be proletarian. (One has a vision of Shostakovitch being told to write affirmative music, and of the Lysenko affair in biology, when an entirely false theory of genetics was backed by Stalin, became state orthodoxy, and helped ruin Russian agriculture.)

Nevertheless, Caudwell seems to me a serious thinker, far more convincing in his theory of literature than, say, I.A. Richards. The project of a materialist history of literature, built on the underground connections between economic conflict, unconscious class phantasy, and literary form and content, still seems much more interesting than the Eliot–Leavis notion of projecting an imaginary historical tradition from their own literary judgements, and using it for contemporary social criticism. It also seems more interesting than the notion of some modern 'cultural materialists', that the category of literature itself is a bourgeois invention.

NOTES

1. The word here has a sense slightly different form, and less sophisticated than, that in Fredric Jameson's fine book of that title (Jameson 1981).
2. Or cultural historians like Barrell who draw on Thompson rather than Althusser.

3.   *The Communist Manifesto* 1848, p. 1.
4.   Francis Hutcheson 1725, *Enquiry into the Original of our ideas of Beauty and Virtue*; Edmund Burke 1757, *Enquiry into the Origin of our Ideas of the Sublime and Beautiful*; Alexander Cozens 1759, *Essay to Facilitate the Inventing of Landskip Compositions*; 1785–86, *New Method of Assisting the Invention in Drawing Original Compositions of Landscape;* Andrew Wilton and Anne Lyles 1993, *The Great Age of British Watercolours*, Royal Academy.
5.   John Barrell 1972, *The Idea of Landscape and the Sense of Place 1730–1840*.
6.   John Barrell 1986, *The Political Theory of Painting from Reynolds to Hazlitt: the Body of the Public*.
7.   Cf. Edward Thompson 1975, *Whigs and Hunters*.
8.   For example, many contributors to Dollimore and Sinfield (eds) 1985, *Political Shakespeare*.
9.   Parris and Fleming-Williams 1991, *Constable* (London: Tate Gallery), No. 209 Sketch from 'Salisbury Cathedral from the Meadows'; No. 210 'Salisbury Cathedral from the Meadows'.
10. Leavis 1952, *The Common Pursuit*.
11. T.S. Eliot 1919, 'Hamlet', reprinted in *Selected Essays*.
12. *Culture and Society*, 1958. Williams confirms this account of his attitude in *Politics and Letters*, 1979, p. 127.
13. Cf. Anderson 1976; Merquior 1986.
14. Williams 1979, p. 144; Easthope 1991, p. 116.
15. Cf. Eagleton 1976, *Criticism and Ideology*, pp. 21–4.
16. Caudwell 1986, *Scenes and Actions*.
17. A psychoanalyst like Lacan, and trained philosophers like Althusser and Foucault, fudge these issues quite as much; but they can use a much more sophisticated vocabulary, and fool a higher class of reader. See treatment of Althusser later in this volume.
18. Some historians: Christopher Hill, E.P. Thompson, Isaac Deutscher, Eric Hobsbawm. Cf. Kaye 1984, *The British Marxist Historians*.
19. The literature on this point is too vast to quote. A good starting point is Conrad Russell 1973, *The Origins of the English Civil War*. Russell argues (p. 5) that both Marxism and nineteenth-century Whiggery grew out of the same intellectual climate, when the notion of progress was fashionable; both see the Parliamentarians, because they won, as in come sense more 'progressive'. In fact, in parliament at least, the Royalists were younger than the Parliamentarians, and it was the Parliamentarians who saw themselves as conservative defenders of traditional rights. We must question this notion of 'progress'.

     I must admit that my own response to this is to feel that historians like Russell look carefully at a leaf through a microscope and say we need to question the notion of a 'forest'. However, I am glad to say there are still Marxists with microscopes; e.g. Brian Manning 1992, *1649: The Crisis of the English Revolution*.
20. Eagleton 1976, *Criticism and Ideology*.

BOOKS

John Barrell 1972 *The Idea of Landscape and the Sense of Place 1730–1840.*
  1980 *The Dark Side of the Landscape: the Rural Poor in English Painting 1730–1840.*
Raymond Williams 1975 *The Country and the City.*
Christopher Caudwell 1937 *Illusion and Reality.*
  1938a, 1948, 1971 *Studies and Further Studies in a Dying Culture.*
F.R. Leavis 1936 *Revaluation.*
  1952 *The Common Pursuit.*
E.P. Thompson 1975 *Whigs and Hunters.*
  1977 'Caudwell' in *The Socialist Register.*

CHAPTER SEVEN

Class-Consciousness and Ideology

Western Marxists Return to Hegel

SUMMARY

The dematerialisation of Marxism begins in earnest with Georg Lukács. Lenin in 1920 denounced infantile leftism. *History and Class Consciousness*, in 1923, gave it a classic philosophical justification. When Stalinism – calling itself Marxism–Leninism – paralysed orthodox dialectical materialist thought, Western Marxism[1] – a movement of little political importance but of great significance for marginal intellectuals[2] – reverted to the idealist route to revolution. It turned Marxism into an activist theory of praxis, produced an exuberant growth in theories of the superstructure, and often restored a great deal of the underlying Hegelian problematic, as if ideas rather than economic conflicts are what lead to revolutionary change. This was a product of political failure: concepts like 'class consciousness', 'false consciousness' and 'ideology' have a political function: to explain when revolutions happen, and to explain away the fact that, in most advanced countries, they did not happen.

But these concepts, in the hands of Lukács, Goldmann and others, are also the main Marxist armament for dealing with the complexities of human culture, forming a link between economic and historical analysis and formal cultural or literary analysis. Non-Marxists think them insufficient for this purpose, and tendentious in their effect. In Western Marxism they have been emphasised to such an extent that economic materialism – determination by the economy in the last instance – has been neglected or rejected.

In recent endeavours to make cultural theory sound more 'materialist' attempts have been made to treat ideology itself as something 'material'.

These go back at least to Vološinov and the Bakhtin circle; they here involve identifying ideology with language, and changing the Saussurean model of language to a 'dialogic' one. The whole enterprise misses the point of what Marx meant by 'materialist'. But Bakhtin and his circle have been taken up by modern literary theorists as post-structuralists before their time.

1   THE CONCEPTS OF CLASS-CONSCIOUSNESS AND IDEOLOGY

The central concerns of classical Marxism are with the forces and relations of production. The central concerns of literary and cultural theory are with linguistic and cultural representations. If the Marxist tradition is to be applied to human culture, we need mediating concepts to map one on to the other – like Caudwell's concept of a characteristic 'bourgeois illusion' which is generated by the class position of the bourgeois and in turn affects the kind of art that he produces and responds to. Such concepts include **class consciousness**, **false consciousness** and **ideology**. They are ambiguous and complex; but viewed from within the Marxist tradition, they offer materialist alternatives to idealist (that is, non-Marxist) theories of culture; though there is no agreement on which of the alternatives is right.

Viewed from outside the Marxist tradition, all of them are unsatisfactory. That is not to reject Marxism as a contribution to cultural theory. Even for the non-Marxist, to say that class conflict is one conflict among others which works itself out, in disguised ways, in works of literature, is to enrich our understanding of literature. And there is no objection to saying that the functions of revealing, embodying or even concealing class conflict are 'ideological functions' of literature. The problem arises when we try to reduce literature to its ideological functions alone, or try to subsume the whole sphere of human culture under a concept such as ideology or class consciousness.

For non-Marxists, to reduce works of literature to functions of the imputed consciousness of a class, or to exponents of an ideology, seems to be exactly the wrong type of reductiveness. Concepts like that of the **'relative autonomy'** of literature go some way to mitigate the problem, but not far enough. Non-Marxists want to say, not indeed that literature is absolutely independent of politics; but that literature has many functions which are independent of each other; and only some of these are political functions.

Much of the development of Western Marxism has come from thinkers caught in this tension, who accepted Marxism, but found it too crude in its handling of human culture; and therefore tried to expand the Marxist concepts in more or less sophisticated ways. The problem is to do this without abandoning materialism.

2   THE BEGINNINGS OF WESTERN MARXISM

2.0   *Western Marxism and the orthodox Communist tradition*

Western Marxism has a curious relationship with orthodox Communism. The orthodox Communist tradition runs from the mature Marx and Engels, conceived more or less as a single theoretician, to figures like Plekhanov and Kautsky. Lenin belongs firmly to this tradition; and was perfectly capable of handling it critically – changing his mind, for example, on the importance of Hegel in it. But it was his special contribution to develop and theorise a party capable of making the first successful Marxist revolution, contrary to Marxist predictions, in an industrially backward country. Some would argue that this was a defeat not a victory: a disciplined revolutionary party became a despotic and bureaucratic ruling party, and, under the nightmare rule of Stalin, Marxism–Leninism became the theology of an inquisitorial church.

The most obvious theoretical opposition to Stalin came from Trotsky.[3] Stalin said that, for the time being, socialism had to be developed in one country or it would disappear from the world; and Communist principles everywhere else had to be subordinated to the interests of the one socialist state: the Soviet Union. Trotsky argued that, since capitalism was a global system, no genuine revolution was possible that was not a world revolution. Socialism in one country was not a real option. Later on – when Trotsky was dead – some Trotskyists argued that what the Soviet Union offered was neither socialism nor communism, but a form of state capitalism with the workers exploited just as they are under capitalism. Other socialists have argued against this: that the Soviet Union and its satellites were not state capitalist; they were workers' states, but degenerate ones. These arguments now seem rather arcane; but they probably hold the key to the interpretation of one of the two most important political developments of the twentieth century: the collapse of world Communism.[4]

Western Marxism offered an opposition of a different kind from that of

Trotsky. It was a Marxism derived from the early Lukács, from Gramsci, from Sartre, from Benjamin, from Adorno, from Marcuse, from Althusser. Of course, these thinkers did not agree with each other. Some were members of Communist parties, some not; they wrote in Vienna or Moscow, France, Germany, America or (for Gramsci) in a Fascist prison in Italy; and each of these places imposed its own conditions on their work. In that sense, there is no one Western Marxism. But they were all intellectuals, writing in a state of creative tension with their local Communist parties and the international Communist movement. They all posed, therefore, as a fundamental condition of their work, the problem of the relationship between the creative intellectual and the party: between philosophical truth and party truth. Naturally, they all appealed to intellectuals – in particular to professional philosophers, sociologists, and literary critics.

The content of Western Marxism – again on the whole – matched its conditions of production. It was a Marxism of grand metaphysical theory and of fundamental cultural critique, written from an intellectually élitist point of view. It showed little interest in detailed historiography or analytical economics. It was if anything suspicious of science and technology, and rather contemptuous of the notion that one might have a science of history. Historical materialism therefore declined, and so did the concept of scientific socialism. Socialism was not a science to be applied in building a new society: it was a critique of capitalism. And this critique was hardly ever, like *Capital*, a critique of the gross economic tendencies of capitalism. It was a critique of capitalist culture. That is why Western Marxism so easily became part of the foundation of modern literary and cultural theory, and why it failed to affect economics. It was largely a matter of the kinds of question it could answer. After an early failure by Lukács, Western Marxism got quite good at explaining the significance of Schoenberg or Joyce. But it never explained why the Communist countries could not feed themselves, and the capitalist ones had a food surplus.

Philosophically, the development of Western Marxism can be described in very complex terms or in very simple ones. A complex account would point out how Marxism had been reinterpreted in terms of every fashionable philosophical and intellectual movement of the twentieth century, so that there were positivist, humanist, existentialist, psychoanalytic and structuralist Marxisms; furthermore, earlier philosophical progenitors were found almost without limit: Kant, Rousseau, Spinoza, Descartes, Aristotle. A simple account could be encapsulated in a phrase used in the title of a book by George Lichtheim in 1963: *From Marx to Hegel*. Directly or indirectly (in the case of the anti-

Hegelian Althusser it happened through the crazy route of indebtedness to a 'wild' Freudian analyst) the 'Western Marxists' became the modern equivalent of Left-Hegelians. They became obsessed by such philosophical questions as the dialectic of subject and object. They concentrated on cultural, rather than economic transformation; and came to see the first as a precondition of the second. In short they found Marx standing on his feet, and turned him upside down to stand on his head again. But to do that is to transform Marx into Hegel.

There is no possibility in a book of this scale of giving an account of the whole of Western Marxism; it would be truer to say that I am mentioning a few people who raise theoretical issues relevant to my argument. I don't attempt to cover such figures as Brecht, Sartre or Adorno, for example, each of whom is a movement in his own right. I confine myself to a paragraph or two about Gramsci, rather more on Lukács and something on Goldmann; an interlude on the unorthodox circle of Bakhtin in the Soviet Union; and a chapter on Althusser.

It has often been pointed out that one of the main problems that Western Marxists had to theorise was the experience of political defeat.[5] The Marxist classics are in a sense very optimistic works: they paint a picture of inevitable revolution in the most developed capitalist countries. In fact it didn't happen; advanced capitalist democracies became almost immune to such revolutions, and this needed to be explained. The question was, why didn't the working-class majorities, when they had the ultimate power, choose to institute workers' states? It really looked as if capitalism was ruling by consent, not force; and the engineering of this consent needed to be explained.

It is for this purpose that Antonio Gramsci – himself for many years part of a strong working-class movement – came in the 1920s to employ the concept of **hegemony**. Capitalism maintains consent through its control of a network of cultural institutions like schools, churches, newspapers, etc. Gramsci's concept gives an enormously important role both to traditional intellectuals like priests, lawyers and scholars, who claim falsely to be detached from any particular class (and are a main support of religion and idealist philosophies), and to the new intellectuals organically created by new social groups coming into existence – the industrial technicians and economists of capitalism, and, it would seem, the party workers for the proletariat – who articulate the interests of a new class.[6]

One can see the attraction of this theory to later Marxising intellectuals; it gives a role and a meaning to an otherwise entirely marginalised group. It was not an accident that Gramsci was writing in priest-ridden Italy; his revolutionary intellectuals seem to be conceived as an alternative priesthood and would need all the priest's vocation. However, in Italy, it was the Fascists who formed an alternative, brutal priesthood and, under the leadership of the former socialist leader Mussolini, conducted a violent revolution. Gramsci had to theorise this phenomenon, fragmentarily and against tremendous odds, in gaol. His suffering has given him a powerful romantic appeal to later generations.

Other theorists further developed older Marxist concepts like false consciousness and ideology; or like Marcuse, adapted Freudian concepts like repression – even, in this case, the paradoxical concept of **repressive tolerance!**[7] – to account for the absence of working-class enthusiasm for a revolutionary transformation of society. For most Marxists, such a transformation seems liberating; they aim at a society in which the vast majority have ended class oppression and taken control of their own lives. If workers find the prospect of such liberation unattractive, it must be that they are wearing mental chains. Western Marxists came to see their main job as that of dismantling the structures of thought that sustain class oppression; and the modern left has extended this to cover gender and racial oppression as well, or even, instead. Many theorists of the past thirty years have actually seen this as the main purpose of cultural theory: the analysis of the way films and works of literature work is only a means to this political end.

There is a kind of analytical blindness that is a specific consequence of using concepts like these. It became a fundamental condition of Western Marxism that it never considered the possibility that the working classes rejected Marxism on rational grounds: because they thought they would be worse off and have less control of their lives under a government of Marxist intellectuals and bureaucrats falsely claiming to speak for the proletariat than under one of bourgeois politicians falsely claiming to speak for society as a whole. One cannot say that such apprehensions as these are ideological illusions: in the USSR, Eastern Europe and China they turned out to be true. But Western Marxists never admitted that they might be true.

2.2 Messianic sectarianism and Stalinist guerrilla wars

Georg Lukács is the archetype of all Communist literary intellectuals: the three phases of his career show a familiar pattern, which is essentially one of religious conversion. This is turned, by his great philosophical powers, into a mighty intellectual drama that has enthralled Western Marxists ever since. First comes deep sensitivity, alienation and despair: a grasp of the essential modernist dilemma of man lost in a thoroughly mechanised and quantified world. To theorise this, Lukács can call on the traditions of German idealist philosophy, romantic anti-capitalism, and the new sociological insights of the circle of Weber, which in turn lead back to Marx; though writers like Dostoevsky and Tolstoy were as important to him as Fichte and Hegel in this period; and no philosophical position was satisfactory. Then, in the aftermath of the October Revolution, came the grasp at a belief, the conversion to Communism, and the flight into a world of passionate commitment and wild but redeeming 'Marxist' dialectic. In philosophy this is really a left-Hegelian phase. Then discipline is accepted; abject self-criticism made; he moves to a characteristically nuanced Marxism–Leninism that nevertheless permits him to survive in Moscow under Stalin; and there comes the final maturation into the most erudite and original of Stalinist hacks. It will be seen that Lukács's purely philosophical history recapitulates that of Marxism itself, with modern additions.

To understand what drove Lukács on this strange journey you have to go deep back into his childhood in the nineteenth century: to consider his revulsion against his admirable and rather sympathetic father's successful banking career, and the way he set against this the image of the synagogue. I mean this last point quite literally: the boy kept a photograph of Szeged synagogue, where his uncle was Talmudist, upon his desk. It brings out the point that, although Lukács was always a secular, philosophical thinker, his lifelong hatred of the bourgeois life was fundamentally religious in nature, though the actual religion changed from time to time. His rejection of the world was always absolute and beyond reason. When the religion became Communism, it was natural for Lukács to hold that the very worst forms of Communism were better than the best forms of capitalism; a view which would be incomprehensible to a materialist.

Lucien Goldmann describes his first important book, *The Soul and the Forms* (1911), as the first public manifestation of existentialism in Western Europe.[8] It had chapters on Kierkegaard and on the metaphysics of tragedy; also, in an article on Theodor Storm, on the bourgeois way of life as 'the whip that drives the life-denying man to work without cease . . . a mask that hides the bitter, useless pain of a failed and ruined life, the life-pain of a romantic born too late'.[9] Thomas Mann called this book beautiful and profound, and, recognising his own influence in it, compared himself with a father learning from his educated son. *Theory of the Novel*, written 1914–15, is Hegelian and despairing; the classical epic, as the embodiment of an absurdly idealised harmonious ancient Greece, is counterposed to the novel as the embodiment of an age of absolute sinfulness. Some of its themes have an uncanny correspondence with problems in the modernist writers who Lukács did not then know and was later to condemn.

The philistine question is: whence comes all this despair in such a fortunate young man? Lukács came from the high bourgeoisie; his father, a rich banker and a fully assimilated liberal Jew, was intensely supportive of his literary and philosophical ambitions. Lukács in his thirties was intellectual leader of a brilliant group of young Hungarian intellectuals;[10] was already well known in the German academic world; was admired by Thomas Mann. Why this alienation, this existential despair? Why, with marriage to the young artist Irma Seidler perfectly possible, recapitulate Kierkegaard's gesture to Regine Olsen, and send her away? (Later, after a brief bad marriage to someone else, Irma committed suicide.) Why, in *Theory of the Novel*, project this vision of a world of absolute sinfulness?

The philistine answer is a sociological one. Lukács was a 'marginal intellectual', detached from the productive activities and the beliefs of his own class, and projecting the subjective experience of that role into a property of the world. Lukács was indeed the prototype of all marginal intellectuals; it was a younger friend, Karl Mannheim, from the same group, who later invented this particular sociological category, which fits so many twentieth-century thinkers. But it does not follow that the judgements of such men are false. The First World War began in 1914. The judgement that this is a world of absolute sinfulness can seldom have been more accurate. The marginal intellectual may be privileged to see the truth without the ideological blinkers of a person still sunk in the values of nation or class.

Yet there is still an ambiguity about this judgement. For the non-Marxist intellectual, and for the modernist artist, alienation is now the human condition; and there is no way out except to record it. That is an approach that has produced great twentieth-century art. Alternatively there is the Marxist view that what we are faced with is not the necessary condition of humanity, but the breakdown of a class, the bourgeoisie: while another class, the proletariat, is rising. A radical shift of consciousness is possible, on condition of identifying with the proletariat; but how crude, how elementary the new sensibility seems after the subtlety of Middle-European high culture! Lukács remained poised between a dead culture and one unborn until the October Revolution made a proletarian victory seem possible, and a new redeemed world.

The religious language is appropriate here, despite the political conclusion. Alienation is a religious experience. The archetype of the alienated life is separation from God; the archetype of the non-alienated life is living every moment in obedience to God's will. The Hegelian theorisation of God is as the absolute: the identical subject–object which exists through its own self-knowledge; and of which the Prussian bureaucracy with its state professors is a poor earthly vehicle. The move from religion to politics, from religious consciousness to class-consciousness, begins there. Marx replaced that bureaucracy by the proletariat; Lukács now gives the proletariat its full Hegelian dignity by claiming that it alone can realise the social totality, beyond which there is nothing, and a partial view of which is false consciousness. This achievement will mean the end of the sense of powerlessness with which the proletariat has viewed its fate, the end of reification, and the end of the difference between subject and object. This class consciousness, when achieved or realised, will then annihilate or transcend itself in a classless society. This is a mystical vision!

It is only the industrial proletariat whose objective situation makes it possible to impute to it a consciousness of itself as the true identical subject–object of history, which understands history in the very process of transforming it; there is no other locus of such consciousness, since there is no other class that can transform history. Meanwhile, this active consciousness will naturally be concentrated and realised in the party. Alienation will thus be overcome through the unity of theory and political practice. This was always something for which Lukács himself had to strive. But there was at least one party saint for whom this unity came naturally: Lenin. Hence the devastating effect of Lenin's criticism of the infantile leftism of which Lukács had become a prophet.

From about 1917, Lukács had moved doubtfully towards Marxism – debating characteristically whether it could be right to do evil that good might follow. Then conversion struck. He became one of Marxism's St Pauls, rapt in his vision of what the proletarian consciousness might be, and from 1919 was very ready to write it down, without needing to consult any actual proletarians (who would not have understood his philosophical prose anyway). This was in many ways a new sort of Marxism, far more revisionist than Bernstein or the neo-Kantians.[11] The dialectic of nature was dropped, and so were the inevitable laws of historical development. The privileged place of the economy was taken by the social totality. Marxist orthodoxy, said Lukács, lay not in any particular content the theory might have, but in a privileged method: that method was dialectical: and that dialectic was the self-awareness of the revolutionary struggle of the proletariat, the only class that could grasp totality. The class consciousness imputed to the proletariat by Lukács and other party intellectuals thus became the central issue of both philosophy and politics; and the politics became wildly voluntarist, impractical and extreme.

As Lukács later put it: 'Our magazine [*Kommunismus*] sought to propagate a messianic sectarianism by working out the most radical methods on every issue, and by proclaiming a total break with every institution and mode of life stemming from the bourgeois world . . . criticism at the hands of Lenin – enabled me to take the first step away from sectarianism.'[12] To a practical leader like Lenin this revolutionary phrasemongering must have been familiar. He had already had to savage the Bukharin group of the Russian party in his article 'Left-Wing Childishness and Petty Bourgeois Mentality' (1918; *Selected Works*, VII, 1935d). 'Every page of the *Kommunist* shows that our "Lefts" have no conception of iron proletarian discipline and how it is achieved; that they are thoroughly imbued with the mentality of the declassed petty-bourgeois intellectual. . . . The flaunting of high-sounding phrases is characteristic of the declassed petty-bourgeois intelligentsia. The organised proletarian Communists will certainly punish this habit with nothing less than derision and expulsion from all responsible posts.' Now, in 1920, the same line was needed for the criticism of a world-wide left-radical tendency. In *Left-Wing Communism: an Infantile Disorder* (*Selected Works*, X; *Collected Works*, 31) Lenin gave the classic rebuke to those who would abandon the practical lessons of Bolshevism and make Marxism into a politics of gesture and no-compromise with bourgeois institutions.

One can sympathise with Lenin here. Epistemologically oriented radical leftism is a complaint built into the germ-plasm of Marxism, and has recurred in every generation from the original Left-Hegelians to the British Althusserians of the 1970s. It always fails and discredits socialism. Marxism–Leninism, on the other hand, is about power: about making a revolution and preserving it in a hostile and unforgiving world. But the very radicalism and impractical messianic fervour which appalled Lenin is what has made Lukács attractive to whole generations of leftists, some of whom, like Arato and Breines (1979), want nothing better than that Marxism should become a state of 'permanent rupture' – that is, of permanent gesture.[13]

Some of the general arguments about Lukács's interpretation of Marxism have been discussed already in Chapter 4, sections 2.2 and 3.3.[14] It is on the basis of this work – contained, in particular, in the series of papers published as *History and Class Consciousness* in 1923, three years after Lenin's pamphlet – that Lukács has often been hailed as the greatest of Marxist philosophers, apart from Marx himself. On one version of philosophical greatness one can accept that description without necessarily believing a word that he ever said. On that version one finds a philosopher great not because what he says is true, or even plausible, but because he has made a classic statement of an extreme position, and thereby influenced generations of later thinkers. Heidegger and Wittgenstein are surely great in this sense. On that view Lukács reached philosophical greatness only in this, his second period, from 1919 to 1923, a period when he was no longer young but had been born again, as a new Marxist convert, a member of government in the short-lived Hungarian Soviet Republic, a secret agent of the party under the reactionary Horthy regime which followed it, and a passionate exile in Vienna. It was in this period that he laid the foundations of the Western Marxist, Hegelian, humanist and anti-scientific interpretations of Marxism; while at the same time offering a philosophical basis for the infallibility of the party which provides a better foundation for Leninism than anything Lenin himself produced; and which Lenin himself firmly repudiated.

The mature Lukács of the third period came to terms, however, not merely with Lenin, but with Stalin; and he managed to survive the period of the Moscow purges. He had now totally abandoned the position of *History and Class Consciousness*. In philosophy he firmly committed himself to the objectivity – that is, the existence independently of consciousness – of the external world; consciousness is a reflection of that world; and art also is a reflection of reality.[15] His criticism operates within this epistemological framework; but employs a very sophisticated notion of 'reflect' which may mean something like 'represent the underlying historical truth of '. For Lukács now the supreme term of critical praise is **realism**; to be good is to be realist and a new term must be found for dull realism that merely reflects surfaces: thus the 'realism' of Balzac is preferred to the mere 'naturalism' of Zola. Lukács also wages a kind of guerrilla war on behalf of **critical realism** (that is to say, of the work of writers like Balzac and Tolstoy) against the propagandist soap-operas misleadingly given the great name **socialist realism**. He agreed, naturally, that socialist realism must be the true end of art; but thought it was more nearly to be found in good writers like Gorky and Solzhenitsyn.

This looks like a word-game; but István Meszáros, a pupil of Lukács, points to a deeper meaning, which he attributes to Marx himself, and which runs roughly as follows. Values arise out of the needs of man considered dialectically as a self-mediating and historically self-constituting natural being. The world of the fact–value distinction is an alienated world of a humanly meaningless nature. Realism aims at the comprehension of the dialectical totality of man; naturalism takes it for granted that the human meaning of reality is given in the immediacy of the appearances. Naturalism, it seems, is the realism of an alienated world.[16] The naturalism/realism opposition, far from being a narrow technical distinction between the form of nineteenth-century French novels, becomes a fundamental dialectical one applying to all art.

A principal function of realism is to uncover the underlying forces of history. British critics of this period would have dismissed Scott as a very minor novelist; a nostalgic romantic and a creator of stock types. In *The Historical Novel* (1937), Lukács makes him 'the poet of historical necessity.' Lukács finds valid grounds for praise (in the presentation of complex underlying historical contradictions) that a non-Marxist critic cannot even see. This approach also illuminates the finely differentiated treatments of Balzac, Zola and Tolstoy published in *Studies in European Realism* (1950).

Perhaps none of these has the depth of *The Young Hegel: Studies in the Relations between Dialectics and Economics*, written 1938, and withheld for ten years because it rejected Stalin's view that Hegel was a feudal apologist. In this the young Hegel is seen as a left-Hegelian, very conscious of economic matters; in effect, the mature Lukács moves Hegel as far towards Marx as the younger Lukács had moved Marx towards Hegel. The Hegel book and the studies in *Goethe and his Age* (1947), must make Lukács one of the finest historians of ideas. One learns to look at German intellectual history in a different way; to have a great respect for a German enlightenment to which not only Kant, but Schiller, Goethe and Hegel belonged; and much less respect for German Romanticism. One learns also that Goethe was a great realist; something which it is easy not to notice when one is reading the second part of *Faust*.

Not till 1957, in *The Meaning of Contemporary Realism*, was Lukács free to take modernism with the seriousness it deserves; his own insights of 1911 and 1915 had shown him fully qualified to respond to it. But the form he chose – a comparison between Thomas Mann and Kafka, sandwiched between a chapter on the ideology of modernism and one on critical and socialist realism – shows the limitations of his later perspective. That first chapter ends, in the tone of a colonel or a commissar: 'modernism is not the enrichment, but the negation of art'; and though Lukács responds strongly to the power of Kafka's art, he has no adequate concepts to accommodate that power. It is I think fair to describe Lukács as a great critic, cut off by his ideology from contact with the most significant art of his time. One of the achievements of other Western Marxists – particularly Adorno – was that they did come to terms with modernism, though it is not at all clear that their Marxism survived the encounter, and their materialism never did.

When one of the greatest philosophers ever to be a Marxist starts his career in aesthetics, continues it with literary criticism, and ends it in aesthetics,[17] one can expect him to dominate subsequent Marxist thinking about art. It has not happened; the surprising thing about recent Marxist criticism is that it seems to have rejected almost all Lukács's positions. With hindsight, the intellectual reason is obvious. Lukács was a philosophical realist; he thought that all modes of reflection – science, philosophy, history, art and literature – reflect the same objective reality.[18] Recent Marxists, like those described in the next two chapters, have been heavily influenced by post-structuralism; from his point of view they would count as idealists, irrationalists[19] or even bourgeois subjectivists, and they don't believe there is an objective reality to reflect.

Lukács believed in the existence of art, prior to our theories of it; the philosophical problem was to explain how it could exist and how it functions. Recent Marxists believe that the category of art is a constructed one; we have to ask what class interests that category serves. He believed in an intrinsic hierarchy of value among works of art; they think such hierarchies are ideological constructs supporting social hierarchies. He believed that a work of art is a totality, creating a unified world; they claim to be interested in fragmentation and discontinuity. He believed works of art – really great ones – have a profound cognitive value, and are man's self-awareness, just as science is man's awareness of the external world. They believe works of art are texts, like other texts (e.g. advertisements, popular fiction); if they give access to anything, it is to ideology. He believed that art is the memory of mankind. Its significance can only be understood in the context of concrete history, and of course he thought that Marxism tells us that history. They see history as a present-day narrative that constructs the past and can construct all sorts of alternative traditions of art. He favoured realism above all literary modes, and thought modernism was the negation of art. They have tailored their whole theory to accommodate modernism, and think realism bourgeois, reassuring and non-revolutionary.[20]

Post-structuralist post-Marxists have the same relation to the mature Lukács as the infantile leftists had to Lenin. Their slogan is 'No cooperation with bourgeois artistic values', and their method is messianic sectarianism.

The difference between modern critics and Lukács extends even into highly technical questions of representation: indeed, it may be rooted there. No modern critic can discuss these issues without calling on signifier theory: the mythical Saussure who is supposed to have argued that reality is something signified rather than existing of itself, and the all too real Derrida who actually did argue that there can be no transcendental signified, beyond the play of signifiers.[21] What this problematic has replaced, and what modern critics do not seem to use, is the dialectic. The fall of the dialectic in the last thirty years is almost as startling an event in the intellectual world as the fall of the Soviet Union in the political world. Lukács naturally knows nothing of this. He has his own theory of a primary (non-linguistic) signalising system, a secondary signalising system (language) and a 'primary plus' system which includes the languages of art. But he still uses the Marxist dialectic for his theory of knowledge, with a very Hegelian dialectic hovering not too far in the background.

The central category of art is *besonderheit*, or 'speciality'. This is actually a general cognitive category belonging to the dialectic of knowledge. One knows something, not by unmediated immediate experience of individuals, and not by abstract general concepts, but by moving between the two to produce a rich field of concrete determinations (presumably direct experiences that are articulated by general concepts). 'Speciality' is a field of mediating ideas that fall between the individual and the abstract concept. In art we start and end with speciality: in art we are not interested in details for their own sake, nor merely for the abstract generalisations they illustrate. We have, rather, details in which important generalisations **inhere**; starting from artistic images, it seems that we move up to generalisations and down to details of reality, but return to the images. This seems a reasonable description of the critical process and a fair account of art; Aristotle might agree.[22]

This account of art is not purely formal: Lukács gets an evaluative criterion out of it. Art that is too close to the individual detail – the novels of Zola, for example – he censures as naturalistic; that which is too close to the universal, like Kafka, he censures as allegorical; that which moves between the two, like Balzac, Dickens or Thomas Mann, merits the praise of realism. What realism finds for us is (in the language of Lukács's earlier criticism) the **type**; in the type, the significance of history is as it were embodied. So, presumably, Merdle the financier in *Little Dorrit* would not be an allegory of capitalism, a mere embodied generalisation about it; but nor would he be a mere individual with some interesting personal idiosyncrasies, such as being a fraud with thousands of financial victims; rather, he is a type, and general truths about capitalism inhere in him, much as they do in the real live Robert Maxwell of our own period.

The merit of Lukács's mature theory, compared with some current forms of post-Marxist criticism, should be clear enough. He accepts the cognitive value of literature – that some works of literature give an independent insight into the world – without reducing literature to a set of generalisations. By a process of interpretation, he reconciles the values of Marxism with apparently quite different values within works of literature themselves. The defects in his appreciation of modernist literature seem to be much more matters of taste and general ideology than of literary theory; though it is certainly a defect of theory to stretch the term 'realism' to quite the extent that he does. I would like to admire the later Lukács as critic rather more than I do; but the new positions have neither the existential sensitivity of the early work nor the philosophical madness of the second period. They are sometimes just a little philistine; and this is natural, since they were developed under the shadow of the greatest philistine in history.

2.3   The genetic structuralism of Goldmann

After the early work of Lukács, the idealisation of Western Marxism seems to have proceeded without serious check. The reductionist economism of Marxism, which is its one distinctive and interesting feature among the major philosophies of the world, was conscientiously forgotten, or overlaid with progressively more sophisticated cultural constructions. By the time French structuralism came along the process was nearly complete; Western Marxism was almost perfectly adapted to the concerns of intellectuals – that is, to reformulating a hundred times over the subject–object relationship, explaining the different forms of subjectivity, including really 'revolutionary' concepts like the decentred subject, justifying various kinds of infantile leftism in politics, and providing brilliant interpretations of cultural phenomena. Its most important function, however, continued to be this: to hide from socialist intellectuals the rational economic reasons why the majority of people refused to turn socialist.

It is useful to look at some of the concepts which could be employed for these purposes. Lucien Goldmann's **genetic structuralism** is a genuinely important descendant of the Marxism of Lukács. Goldmann was productive from the 1940s to the 1960s – a very scientistic period; he was assistant to a genuine scientist, the psychologist Piaget; and he tries to talk like a scientist. But for him the central object of sociological enquiry is the **significant structure**. Goldmann could never say precisely what this was a structure of – except that it was something mental. In *The Hidden God* he gives 'tragic vision' as an example of a 'significant global structure'. It is clearly an ideal and arbitrary construction by the scholar; it has at best the same kind of reality as Raymond Williams's 'structure of feeling' – which may well be quite enough reality to do important critical work with: in Goldmann's case, to establish a structural homology between the tragedies of Racine, Jansenist theology, and the world-view of the French *noblesse de la robe*. This was a great critical achievement, none the worse for being as much in the spirit of Lukács's *Soul and Form* as of his later work; it draws on Marxist economism without being bound by it.

Goldmann is hostile to the static structures of most French structuralists, which seem to hang in the air somewhere between subject and object, and define both.[23] For him a significant structure is one produced historically by a **transindividual subject**. (This is meant to be a philosophically superior replacement for Kant's transcendental subject or Hegel's *Geist*). A transindividual subject is a class like the proletariat or the bourgeoisie, or even a more restricted group like (for Goldmann) the *noblesse de la robe* who played an administrative role under the French kings in the sixteenth and seventeenth centuries. Under Louis XIV they began to be replaced by a more centralised bureaucratic structure, and the foundations of their world slipped away; yet they had nothing but the monarchy to rely on. As Goldmann argues in *The Hidden God*, the Jansenist theology, of a duty which is absolute, to a God who is inaccessible, is an expression of their profoundest social experience.

It is transindividual subjects like these, rather than ordinary empirical human individuals, that are, according to Goldmann, the true subjects of history. The situation of a transindividual subject will contain certain **objective possibilities**, which may not be apparent to the individuals belonging to it. We have to distinguish between the actual consciousness of these individuals and the **possible consciousness** (Lukács's imputed consciousness – a consciousness made up by the researcher and attributed to the people he is studying). One of the things a great writer like Racine can do is to articulate the possible consciousness of such a transindividual subject. Like Lukács, Goldmann has the distinct merit of indicating why great writers are felt to be great; they help us grasp the meaning of the fundamental social conditions of our lives. But the theoretical cost of doing this is considerable; history and sociology alike have to be studies of the adventures of transindividual subjects. One can see why Althusser turned away from this line, to claim that history is a process without a subject.

I must confess that I myself have adopted a version of Goldmann's position in this very book. I continually speak of 'literary intellectuals' as holding this, that or the other more or less preposterous and interested view – perhaps thereby offending the reader, who I am sure does not hold that view. Such claims should always be taken in Goldmann's sense, as an imputation of possible consciousness to a modern *noblesse de la robe*.

2.4   Idealism and the power complex of the intellectuals

There is nothing whatever wrong with approaches like this, so long as literary criticism is the end in view. At the political level, however, the whole tradition of Lukács – like the traditions of Gramsci, of Adorno and Marcuse, and of the other strands of Western Marxism – is élitist, idealist, and voluntarist. Intellectuals can always claim, not unreasonably, to know what the objective possibilities are for some transindividual subject whose conditions they have studied. It is then fatally easy to use notions of imputed consciousness, possible consciousness, and so forth as the basis for a claim to know the true consciousness of some group better than the group itself. It is easy to see the actual consciousness of a group as something imposed on them by society as a means of control; and changing that consciousness as the obvious means of liberation. Consciousness thus becomes the true site of revolutionary struggle; and the intellectual, whose business is with consciousness, becomes the person who can win that struggle.

Actual working people in a real capitalist society often have no higher ambition than to survive. Sometimes they want to maintain their differentials over other working people; or to climb into the petty bourgeoisie. Often they are nationalist and patriotic, or sincerely, even fanatically religious. The revolutionary has the hard task of convincing them that these are false or inadequate goals; and that they should aim at a revolutionary transformation of society which will give them power over their own lives. In those circumstances the working man's view of the revolutionary may be that he is simply missing the point. It may well be, for example, that 'power over one's own life' means continuous participation in complex political structures. One might write a little sub-Brechtian dialogue here. 'I want bread, national freedom, and the faith', says the working man, 'and you offer me a committee perpetually in session.' 'What is more', he says, 'it is the likes of you who will run that committee.' The dismal political and economic record of both Western and mainstream Marxism, and the astonishing survival of nationalism and religion suggest that there are elements of truth in this reconstruction.

3 MARXIST CONCEPTS OF IDEOLOGY

The most important single concept of Marxist theory, for the general theory of culture and literature, is the concept of **ideology**. Indeed, one might put that point rather differently: if Marxism has anything to offer to the general theory of culture and literature, it must fall somewhere under the concept of ideology. But this concept is a very tricky one, and has had some extraordinary adventures in the twentieth century – which still continue, now that it is one of the key concepts of feminism.

It is in fact multiply ambiguous. Eagleton (1990a) lists sixteen definitions. Later he says there are six; but if you put in all the useful qualifications I am sure it would come to sixty. But I would suggest that the important clusters of meanings are just two: **ideology as a partial system of explicit ideas** – a system like Nazism or Marxism, for example – which may or may not be true, but which function for hidden or open political purposes; and **ideology as the total system of taken-for-granted ideas and normal experiences** within a society; a system that constitutes a life-world that appears to be natural and unquestionable, but in fact has a hidden source in the class structure, and a hidden function in reinforcing and supporting that structure. Ideology in the second sense is of course much more sinister and all-encompassing than it is in the first; but it is not clear that the second sense is a coherent one; it may be merely an Althusserian nightmare.

3.1 Ideologies as politically functional systems of ideas

The first sense of ideology is close to the ordinary, non-Marxist sense of the word. An ideology is a system of ideas like those of Marx himself which, though quite general in character, are intended to provide support for some political position. Marxism is intended to promote a revolution and get the proletariat into power. Nazism was intended to produce a new world order of racially pure nations, dominated by the Aryan race with Germany at its head. But for Marxists the ordinary bourgeois – which more and more has come to mean the ordinary person in modern developed societies – was just as ideological as the Marxist or the Nazi. His 'legal, political, religious, aesthetic and philosophical' ideas (to adapt Marx's 1859 *Preface*) all together formed a bourgeois ideology, whose fundamental purpose was to perpetuate bourgeois rule.

A fully worked out and systematic bourgeois ideology in this sense is available in the system of Hegel, which is the source of Marx's list of topics. But one doesn't have to be a Hegelian to have a bourgeois ideology. Under that capacious heading come the legal principles of our judges, the political principles of Conservatives, Liberals and most of the British Labour Party; both Protestant and Catholic Christianity; the philosophies of Husserl, of Heidegger, of Wittgenstein and of Russell's non-technical work; and one should probably add nowadays most social science and much popular natural science. Should one add also a taste for Virginia Woolf and a taste for James Bond?

To call an intellectual system an ideology in this sense is to cast a peculiar kind of doubt on the grounds for holding it. It is to suggest that the system is upheld, not because of the grounds stated for it, but because it is functional in supporting the rule of a particular class. Some social scientists, including revisionary Marxists like Elster,[24] have argued that functional arguments like this are unsound, on the grounds that you don't explain why someone should hold a belief simply by showing it upholds the fortunes of his class. But that is untrue. It is easy to see that there will be a kind of Darwinian selection process among theories, whereby those that threaten the interest of the ruling class meet with discouragement from members of that class who feel their individual interests threatened, while those that support the interests of the ruling class get ready patronage.

There is thus no difficulty of the kind Elster suggests in seeing how a class ideology can arise and be maintained. However, not everything in intellectual life can be part of ideology in this sense. In particular, natural science cannot be part of ideology; engineering theory cannot be part of ideology; these things are needed to maintain the economic base of society in being, and they do this not by being attractive to the ruling classes, but by making machines work. Moreover, though bourgeois economics is certainly part, and even the central part, of bourgeois ideology, Marxist economics cannot be. It must have a truth value and an autonomy of its own, or Marxism as the basis of scientific socialism is not possible. A complete intellectual relativism is as incompatible with belief in Marxism as it is with belief in anything else.

Once we have acknowledged that not every intellectual system can be pure ideology, we have to ask for any particular system we are considering, just how much is ideology, and how much is autonomous and self-sustaining. We can't (except in the crassest of party polemics) simply dismiss the whole of bourgeois economics as ideology. We have to ask what particular arguments on economic matters are intellectually sound, independently of their political implications; and what arguments are in fact based on covert ideological assumptions. And what goes for economics goes in all other areas of enquiry, including of course literary theory. Perhaps the most interesting question we have to ask of literature and literary theory is to what extent are they purely ideological and to what extent have they a degree of formal or intellectual autonomy, as art and thought?

We cannot answer this question if we confine ourselves to the arts alone. Essentially the same questions are to be asked about all the other intellectual areas named; and we need to compare these with putatively non-ideological subjects like mathematics and science which may turn out to contain all sorts of ideological elements mixed with the non-ideological ones. In the course of its history, Marxism has directed a great deal of intellectual activity towards a critique of all the bourgeois disciplines, with the intention of building up a Marxist point of view on virtually every topic. Engels began this, with treatises on anthropology and on natural science[25] in which he managed to find exemplifications of the Marxist dialectic even in chemistry and physics. From the beginning, of course, Marxism had a definite, anti-idealist philosophical position of its own (which Lenin took time to defend even in the twentieth century).[26] And in itself Marxism is a definite theory of history which requires the entire history of the world to be rewritten in detail to show the influence of economic factors and of the class struggle.

Marxism at most stages of its career – under the intellectual leadership of Engels in the late nineteenth century, in the 1920s and 1930s when it was a political orthodoxy in Russia, and among the young revolutionaries of the West in the 1960s and 1970s, gained much of its power from being a total world view with positions taken in every branch of human knowledge; a view which you adopted sometimes by a process of total conversion, and which made the whole world make revolutionary sense. For intellectuals there are of course serious dangers in this: one of them being that the intoxication of revolutionary ideas should become a substitute for revolutionary activity, or even serious thought about whether revolution is, in actually existing conditions, possible or desirable. When this happens, the Marxist reverts to the status of the Left-Hegelians who Marx so bitterly rejected: he is making revolutions in his head and expecting the world to conform. (As I have said, it is my thesis that most of the literary left in the last thirty years reverted to left-Hegelianism in this way and are correctly described as left-Hegelians even if their actual intellectual instrument was the 'Critical Theory' of Adorno and others, or some post-structuralist technique like deconstruction. This, as I said earlier, is to assign them an 'imputed consciousness' in the sense of Lukács or Goldmann.)

3.2   Ideology in social consciousness

The second sense of ideology used within the Marxist tradition is very different from the first, and causes a great deal of confusion. It arises from the fact that, for a Marxist, society is defined in material terms: first in terms of its forces of production, which 'we can describe with the precision of natural science';[27] then in terms of its relations of production; these form the economic foundation on which a superstructure of social institutions is built. Ideologies in the sense which we have been discussing seem, as I have suggested, to fit in somewhere above these social institutions, acting as a kind of intellectual roof – in the case of the arts, a roof garden – to hold the walls together. But what of the people who live in the society? They have a conscious experience of it, which is certainly partly moulded by their ideologies in the first sense discussed; but it would be amazing if it were wholly determined by these. Nevertheless, there is a strong tendency in the Marxist tradition to extend the concept of ideology to cover virtually the whole of conscious experience. 'Ideology' covers not just the world of systematic ideas; it covers all ideas, and emotional responses and personal loyalties too. Ideology produces the world in which we actually live.

Just as to call an intellectual system an ideology is to cast a peculiar doubt on the grounds for believing it, so to call our world-experience ideology is to cast a peculiar doubt on our grounds for believing in it. It is to suggest that a set of unconscious ideas have been inculcated in us, probably as an unconscious effect of the class conflicts in our society, and that these ideas are shaping our experiences. Of course, we can't doubt that we have the experiences. But we are able to doubt whether they mean quite what we think they mean. Let me give a benign example of such a doubt. The experience of hating foreigners or blacks or Jews or women may be a perfectly authentic experience. But the hatred will be given in experience in the form of a perception that members of these groups are deceitful, dirty, degraded, or dangerous. To come to feel that our perception is something that is ideologically implanted in us is the first step towards losing it; and of course in this case we are better off without it.

3.2.1 *Ideology, social consciousness and literary theory* This broader sense of ideology is obviously of great importance for literary theory. The whole body of literary criticism is built upon perceived responses to works of literature. The literary critic is trained to scrutinise these responses and check them for personal authenticity; and to check them against the text. But you can have perfectly authentic responses which are very close to the text, but are nonetheless partly controlled by an implanted and uncriticised ideology. Once one has become aware of this, one can at least start to reflect upon it.

The problem with this concept of ideology is that it goes a great deal too far to be useful. On this account, it is not merely a matter of a few selected experiences that are shaped by ideology, leaving the rest of our perceptions of the world veridical. On the contrary, the whole of our experience is so shaped. There is not a particle of our experience that is not shaped by the ideology behind it, and therefore, in a sense, unreliable as a guide to reality. That is why literary critics have reacted so angrily to theorists of ideology. Unless some principled basis is found for limiting the influence of unconscious ideology, one will conclude that one has no access to the text as it really is at all. Radical theorists have been very happy to draw this conclusion. But I don't think they have ever thought it through.

There is an interesting formal parallel between the radical theorist in his relation to the text, and the Kantian in his relation to the thing-in-itself. Both of them are receiving information processed by pre-existing unconscious categories of thought. Neither of them has access to the thing (or text) as it really is. And the parallel extends farther. Just as the Kantians were led on to take the next step, and deny the very existence of a thing-in-itself that can be known, so the radical theorist is led to deny the very existence of the text-in-itself. But what this means (since the subjective perception of the text is not in doubt) is that the critic is actually producing the text. Or we might argue (since the critic's subjectivity is actually formed in ideology) that the ideology is actually producing the text. It will be seen that these two critical positions are merely two familiar forms of idealism. In the first, the individual subject is credited with producing the text; in the second, *Geist* is credited with producing the text.

In fact the parallels with philosophical idealism are much more than formal ones. Since ideology in this extended sense governs all perceptions, it works exactly like the Kantian categories; since ideology develops historically, it resembles *Geist*. Once given this much power, the theory of ideology does not merely resemble Hegel's theory. It actually is Hegel's theory. Really radical theorists of ideology, who refuse to recognise that we have any access to a reality independent of ideology (to a 'transcendental signified' in Derrida's dismissive terms) are Hegelians whether they recognise it or not. They may of course be Hegelians with a deprecating ironic twist, who no longer believe in sovereign reason either.

As I pointed out in *The Poverty of Structuralism*, Roland Barthes, by the end of his career, had come to talk about **text** in terms appropriate to *Geist*. Only text, he said, could know itself: just as if text were absolute mind. In this book I shall discuss this extended view of ideology as it is formulated by people like Vološinov in 1929, or Althusser in the 1960s. It remains a widespread view, and is crucially important in cultural theory to this day.

Although my concern in this book is with literature, it should be pointed out that there are some very bad political consequences of this extended concept of ideology. The same arguments that permit an individual critic to dismiss his own authentic perceptions if he thinks they are ideologically induced, permit the politician to dismiss the authentic desires of his people if he thinks they are ideologically induced. This means that it is very easy to explain why the working class, at some particular time, don't seem to want socialism – or, if they are under a government which calls itself socialist, why they want elections or private farms or whatever. And it is very easy to dismiss such wants. Moreover, there is a strong temptation, if you think that unconscious ideology is as powerful as this, when you get into power to have a go at manufacturing it. This is the route to the totalitarian society of Stalin and others. But it is a way of strong temptation for any intellectual interested in cultural theory, and impressed by the notion that most human needs are actually manufactured ones.

3.2.2 *Ideology as material practice: the wrong way to avoid idealism* Many Marxists are I think uneasily conscious of the fact that if you give the theory of ideology too much power, Marxism collapses back into idealism again. One common solution over at least the last seventy years, has been to find a way of making ideology itself count as a material factor. One way of doing this is to call ideology a set of material practices. (It would be idealist to think of ideology as something in my mind, altering my perception of the world; but it is OK if it is something in a newspaper, altering my perception of the world.) This position sits best within a general view of Marxism as a 'philosophy of praxis'. Some sense can be made of it, perhaps, if you view Marxism from the general position of – dare I suggest it – a Gramsci; or of course of a Raymond Williams.

But these were not Marx's positions. The idealism that Marx rejected was that of the Left-Hegelians. It would not have changed his view of them in the least if you had redescribed their work, not as a revolution in the head, but as a revolution on paper, or as a set of material practices aimed at changing the prevailing ideology. Marx's central point is that you don't change the world by changing intellectual descriptions of it, but only by labour or political action. However materialist cultural practices may be in themselves, they still maintain an essentially ideal, or referential relation to practical politics and the economy. That is to say, they are practices the main point of which is to be **about** other practices; they don't directly change the other practices, but only change our understanding of those practices. Cultural politics only affects the material world if it leads to real politics or real labour.

4   THE BAKHTIN CIRCLE

4.1   Vološinov's model of ideology as language

Marx himself saw no problem for his materialism in recognising that human beings think. Why should anyone else feel that materialism is somehow compromised by this recognition, and must be shored up by translating 'thinking' into something more materialist? A useful example here is the philosopher and linguist V.N. Vološinov, one of the group of thinkers associated in the 1920s with the literary critic M.M. Bakhtin (and claimed by some to be actually identical with Bakhtin).

In his book *Marxism and the Philosophy of Language* (1929), Vološinov identifies the study of ideology with the study of social consciousness in general. He recognises that this is not the same as the more limited model of ideologies as intellectual systems with political functions, and suggests the name **'behavioral ideology'** for his more extended version. 'Behavioral ideology' so extended becomes virtually equivalent to the entire lived world (to use a phrase of Husserl). It becomes equivalent to 'human experience'. What Vološinov is looking for is a general theory of subjective human experience: and the theory he finds is that human experience is **linguistic**.

From the point of view of a Vološinov there are two things wrong with the notion of subjective experience: it is individualist, and it is idealist. The first point is a genuine Marxist one. It is that what we think of as individual subjective experiences are, when we look more closely at them, social constructions. I think, I respond, with the concepts, attitudes, responses I have got from society in the course of socialisation. The more clear and developed my individual response, the more it is actually a social one. This point is still accepted by the mature Marx; and it goes right the way back to his sixth and seventh theses on Feuerbach. The second point is, however, in Marx's terms, false. Marx does not think it idealist to refer to states of mind; he thinks the presence of conscious intentions, for example, is what marks off human labour from that of insects.[28] The trouble with idealism is not that it recognises the existence of subjective experiences, or mental events. Any rational philosophy must do this. But idealism supposes that the world is constructed in these subjective experiences, in our minds, rather than our minds and our subjective experiences being constructed in a physical encounter with the world.

Vološinov has thus in some ways adopted a false problematic. He feels that the study of ideology will remain idealist so long as ideology is recognised as mental. He therefore tries to reduce it to something that is not mental, or at least that is less mental; and what he chooses is language.

165

But language, in the Saussurean sense, won't altogether do for this purpose. (A Saussurean or Chomskyan language system is every bit as mentalistic as the subjective experiences Vološinov is trying to escape from.) So Vološinov develops an alternative view of language not as a static system of grammar, but as a flowing and continuous stream of speech, something essentially dialogic. It is language in this sense that embodies ideology in the sense of social consciousness. By this linguistic turn we have supposedly made our theory of ideology materialist.

There are three things to say of this. First, that the theory of language is an interesting one – my summary doesn't in the least do it justice – and the book is worth reading as a whole. Vološinov had considerable influence on Jakobson and, through him, the Prague school; rediscovered by the West in the 1970s, he offered a conceptual alternative to Chomsky as he had before offered a conceptual alternative to Saussure. It is not, I think, a very real alternative. As I argued in *The Poverty of Structuralism*, any account of language use must rest on one of language structure. You can't get rid of the Saussurean distinctions between concepts like *langue* and *parole*, or, within the concept of *langue*, between the synchronic and the diachronic (between contemporary grammar and historical linguistics, that is). On the contrary, you need to build any theory of language use on more sophisticated forms of these concepts.

Second, the notion that language is somehow an embodiment of social consciousness and human culture is not a particularly Marxist one; it is, rather, part of the 'linguistic turn' that has dominated twentieth-century thought. (Vološinov recognises this.) A very high proportion of twentieth-century philosophers have seen the central business of philosophy as the reform, or the reconstruction, or the analysis of language. To this day, many philosophers are prepared to reduce conceptual problems to problems in the use of language, simply as a routine manoeuvre requiring no special justification. It required special originality to hold, like Karl Popper, that **no** important philosophical issues are questions of language. But the linguistic turn is not confined to philosophers. A psychoanalyst like Lacan identifies human culture with language. And, interestingly, a literary critic like Dr Leavis who would detest the barbarous terminology of Vološinov holds a very similar view about the relationship of language to culture.

I feel rather nervous in arguing that all these distinguished people (except Popper) are wrong at every point. But the reduction of culture to language seems to me an extraordinary oversimplification. Nobody actually knows the form in which language is stored in the brain. Nobody knows the form in which our knowledge of our culture is stored in the brain. We seem to be explaining unknowns by unknowns. There are layers and layers of complexity in culture which certainly can't be reduced to questions of grammar and basic semantics, and nobody has any clear conception of language that goes beyond phonology, grammar, and basic semantics. (By modern standards, Vološinov's conception of language is very unclear, though it is much clearer than Lacan's or Leavis's.)

What people usually seem to do when they try to define some bit of culture in terms of language, is to project the qualities of the bit of culture onto the language used to express it, and then claim that the language is the key to what it has just expressed. You find the right words to express noble sentiments, and then claim they are noble words. You might as well argue that a copper wire carrying a high voltage is made of high voltage copper. (As for philosophical problems, I would argue that every philosophical problem that looks like a linguistic confusion is actually a deep philosophical problem with linguistic confusions loosely attached to it by philosophers who can't solve it. But I won't argue this here.)

Third (to make the essential point again): even if reducing ideology (here covering the whole of social consciousness) to language (here rethought as the flow of speech rather than abstract grammar and phonology) were practically possible, which it isn't, and were materialist, which it is only very doubtfully by counting language-use as a material practice, it would still not make the basic ideological relationship any less idealist in the only damaging sense of the word idealist. However material ideology itself is – as language, as a semiotic system, as a set of practices, or whatever – its relationship to the economy is referential and not causal. At least, it is directly referential, and only indirectly causal. When I speak of the economy I neither bring it into existence nor change it in any immediate way. The claim that ideology changes the world directly is always an idealist claim. All that ideology can ever do to change the material world is to affect some human practices; these practices can then sometimes change the world.

You cannot make the world different by changing the structure of your narratives about it. (Changing consciousness or ideology.) You can only change the world by doing something to it. (By revolution or by labour.) The main drive of Western Marxism during the twentieth century seems to have been a drive to forget, or deconstruct, these simple Marxist axioms, in order to get on with the really exciting business of making a revolution in culture.

4.2   Bakhtin, Vološinov and Medvedev: familiar ghosts

There is a scholarly dispute about the work of the Bakhtin–
Vološinov–Medvedev circle which I can hardly pass over, though I have
no qualifications for resolving it; and it does not affect my general point
about the belated contribution of this circle to the dematerialisation of
Marxism. Bakhtin's biographers have claimed that he is the real author not
only of the literary-critical works he himself signed – such as *Rabelais and
his World, Problems of Dostoevsky's Aesthetics*, and the four essays translated
in *The Dialogic Imagination* (1981) – but of the major work of the critic
P.M. Medvedev, *The Formal Method in Literary Scholarship*; and the two
major works of V.N. Vološinov, *Freudianism: a Marxist Critique*, and
Marxism and the Philosophy of Language; along with other writings of
Medvedev and Vološinov translated in Shukman 1983. Bakhtin thus
emerges as a universal genius at least comparable to Roman Jakobson,
while Vološinov and Medvedev dwindle to ghost-writers. The circle, in
fact, becomes a single radiant point.

What makes it all the more remarkable is that the second set of
writings is quite different in nature from the first, being explicitly Marxist
and much more theoretical in character, and it has been suggested that
Bakhtin deliberately adopted a different style and approach when he
passed himself off as one of the others, and often changed his mind on
points of substance. It all sounds very odd, even under the terrible
political conditions of intellectual life in the Soviet Union, and the
non-Slavist can form no useful opinion about it. In dealing with
theoretical positions, however, it seems best to keep the works apart.
They read rather more like the products of three different members of the
same school than the works of one man.[29]

The Bakhtin circle seems to have had more success in Western literary
criticism in the 1970s and 1980s than it did in Russia in the 1920s and
1930s. The reason is that its works were translated in the heyday of
post-structuralism; and they seemed to provide a quite unexpected Marxist
precedent for some post-structuralist positions. Since the main concern of
Western literary intellectuals at the start of this period was how to
reconcile the diametrically opposite approaches of Marxism and
post-structuralism, this was very welcome; and Bakhtin on Rabelais
offered the added bonus of a celebration of carnival and the overturning
of order, which must have recalled the atmosphere of the student
revolutions of 1968. One result of this is that there is in effect, in addition
to Derrida, de Man, etc., a composite post-structuralist called Bakhtin,
active in Western literary theory from 1968 to 1988 and highly critical of
formalism, structuralism and Chomsky. His doctrines are summarised by

(for example) Susan Stewart in Morson (ed.) 1986: she draws freely on the works of Bakhtin, Vološinov and Medvedev to produce them.[30]

Common to all the circle was a critique of Russian formalism – with its notion of the autonomy of literature, formally considered – and a critique of the Saussurean structuralist model of language – with its notion of the autonomy of *langue* as an object of study – and a celebration of the notion of language as ever-unfinished dialogue. This last notion is perhaps the profoundest that the circle had to offer. For them, dialogue took on a metaphysical significance: the individual human psyche became essentially an internalisation of social dialogues, or even at times a mere abstraction from social dialogues. (There is of course an affinity with other thinkers here – e.g. with Vygotsky – and the same approach was extensively developed later in Western social psychology – e.g. by followers of G.H. Mead. But it also has a genuinely post-structuralist sound to it.) From this standpoint, Vološinov mounted his critique of psychoanalysis – many years before the Lacanian attempt to refound psychoanalysis on a sub-Saussurean view of language, and Althusser's attempt to appropriate Lacan's theory for Marxism.

Bakhtin offers brilliant insights rather than theory – to see the novel as an essentially dialogic form (where, say, the epic is not) is not so much to produce a testable theory of genres as to propose a tendentious but interesting way of reading novels. Bakhtin, according to Stewart, offers an aesthetics that is diametrically opposed to that of Marx. Marx, in *The German Ideology*, sets out not from men narrated, thought of, or imagined, but from real active men. . . . Bakhtin, says Stewart, would say that it is precisely within narrative, and within ideological structures, that the concept of the individual subject, the 'real' man is born. In defence of Bakhtin one might point out that he is talking about the novels of Dostoevsky; and nobody doubts that characters are constructed in narrative within novels. It was left to the post-structuralists to argue that human individuality is a narrative construct in life as well as art; nothing less Marxist could well be imagined.

Medvedev is both more of a theorist and more of a party man, laying down a theoretical line in the appropriate technical language. He saw the study of literature as 'one of the branches of the science of ideologies'. Literature is an independent part of ideological reality, and literary works have a specific structure proper to them alone, which like any other ideological structure refracts socio-economic reality. But in their content, works of literature also reflect and refract other spheres of ideology – ethics, cognition, political doctrines, religion, etc. This seems a very defensible position, and it is totally compatible with the spirit and letter of Marx's economic materialism.[31]

169

Despite this feature of Medvedev's work, however, there can be no doubt that the main influence of the circle in recent times has been to facilitate moves away from economic materialism; it was the appeal of Bakhtin to post-structuralists that secured his recent popularity, not any hope of producing a satisfactory general theory of ideology, which is not something any current literary critic would want.

NOTES

1. By 'Western Marxism' I mean roughly the traditions described in the two books: Perry Anderson 1976; J.G. Merquior 1986. It is, however, a tradition formed retrospectively by modern thinkers. For my purposes it includes Lukács, Goldmann and the Bakhtin circle.
2. This is not a random insult, but a standard sociological category, developed by Karl Mannheim in *Ideology and Utopia*, to apply to intellectuals like Georg Lukács and himself. Mannheim suggested that such characters have epistemological advantages; I am suggesting that they suffer from a characteristic false consciousness. See Gluck 1985, *Georg Lukács and his Generation 1900–1918*.
3. Trotsky is also the author of one of the best-known works of Marxist criticism – *Literature and Revolution* – though presumably one wouldn't describe this as literary theory. It contains a savage attack on formalism.
4. The other I take to be the mid-century defeat of Fascism. The defeat of these two movements, Fascism and Communism, more or less determines the kind of economic and political systems which will have to tackle the economic problems of the twenty-first century, when, on all the best computer predictions, world population will overtake resources.
    My view that world Communism has collapsed is based on the assumption that China is now committed to its capitalist development policies, and that its régime will vanish when the gerontocracy dies.
5. George Lichtheim 1971; Perry Anderson 1976.
6. Antonio Gramsci 1891–1937, 'The Intellectuals' in Gramsci 1971, pp. 55ff.
7. H. Marcuse 1965, 'Repressive Tolerance' in Marcuse, Moore and Wolfe 1969, *A Critique of Pure Tolerance*.
8. Goldmann 1980, *Method in the Sociology of Literature*, p. 37; Goldmann 1977, *Lukács and Heidegger: Towards a New Philosophy*.
9. Georg Lukács 1911, p. 56.
10. Mary Gluck 1985, *Georg Lukács and his Generation 1900–1918*. The group included the poet Béla Balasz, who once brought the young Béla Bartók along to a Sunday circle, where he played his ballet score, *The Wooden Prince*. Later Balasz wrote, and Bartók composed, one of the great modernist works of the century: *Bluebeard's Castle*. No work further from Lukács's critical principles can well be imagined.

11. Eduard Bernstein 1850–1932. Cf. Kolakowski 1978, vol. II, pp. 98–114; neo-Kantians, pp. 243–54.
12. Lukács 1923, 1967, Preface to the new edition of *History and Class Consciousness.* Lenin wrote a short piece on *Kommunismus,* which he praised; picked out its infantile leftism for censure; and dismissed Lukács's article 'The Question of Parliamentarianism' as 'very poor'. Georg Lukács 1919–29, *Political Writings 1919–1929;* V.I. Lenin 1966, *Collected Works,* vol. 31.
13. Arato and Breines 1979, *The Young Lukács and the Origins of Western Marxism,* p. 226.
14. The best short account I know of Lukács's thought is Kolakowski 1978, *Main Currents of Marxism,* vol. 3. Kolakowski is good on every aspect of Marxism, but he has a special affinity for the Lukács of *History and Class Consciousness.*
15. 'Art and Objective Truth', reprinted in *Writer and Critic,* 1965.
16. István Meszáros 1970, *Marx's Theory of Alienation,* pp. 190–214.
17. The last work was actually an *Ontology* – it was completed in extreme old age, and even his own pupils found it quite unsatisfactory. The penultimate works on aesthetics are taken more seriously. See Agnes Heller (ed.) 1983, *Lukács Revalued.*
18. Királyfalvi 1975, p. 35.
19. Nothing would be easier than to extend the principles of his vast polemic against irrationalism, *The Destruction of Reason* (1962), which reaches from Schelling to Heidegger, up to Lacan and Derrida. Few modern philosophers admire his work – perhaps because the rational ones don't read Lukács?
20. Barthes 1970, *S/Z;* Bennett 1979, *Formalsim and Marxism;* Belsey 1980, *Critical Practice;* Eagleton 1983, *Literary Theory;* Dollimore and Sinfield 1985, *Political Shakespeare.* This is a tiny sample of critics holding some or all the views cited; but the list is endless.
21. See Jackson 1991, *The Poverty of Structuralism,* for extended discussion of this.
22. Some analyses of Lukács's aesthetics in English: G.H.R. Parkinson (ed.) 1970, Chapter 4; G.H.R. Parkinson 1977, Chapter 7; Béla Királyfalvi 1975.
23. Jackson 1991, *The Poverty of Structuralism.*
24. Jon Elster 1985, *Making Sense of Marx.*
25. Friedrich Engels 1884, *The Origin of the Family, Private Property and the State;* 1940, *Dialectics of Nature.*
26. V.I. Lenin 1908, *Materialism and Empirio-Criticism.*
27. Karl Marx 1859, *Preface.*
28. Karl Marx 1867a, *Capital,* Chapter 7, section 1.
29. See Vološinov 1929 (trans. 1973, 2nd edn 1986 translator's introduction); Shukman (ed.) 1983 (editor's introduction); Holquist and Clark, 1984 *Mikhail Bakhtin,* Boston: Harvard UP (biography of Bakhtin).
30. Susan Stewart 1986, 'Shout on the Street: Bakhtin's Anti-Linguistics'. In G.S. Morson 1986, *Bakhtin: Essays and Dialogues on his Work.*
31. P.N. Medvedev 1983, 'The Immediate Tasks facing Literary Critical Science', in Shukman (ed.) 1983, *Bakhtin School Papers.*

BOOKS

V.I. Lenin 1920a *'Left-Wing' Communism – An Infantile Disorder*, 1920b *'Kommunismus'*;
both in Lenin 1920 *Collected Works, vol. 31.*
Antonio Gramsci 1919–37 *The Modern Prince and Other Writings.*
1971 *Selections from the Prison Notebooks.*
1985 *Selections from Cultural Writings.*
Georg Lukács 1911 *Soul and Form.*
1920 *The Theory of the Novel.*
1919–29 *Political Writings, 1919–29: The Question of Parliamentarianism and Other Essays.*
1923 *History and Class Consciousness.*
1937 *The Historical Novel.*
1938 *The Young Hegel: Studies in the Relations between Dialectics and Economics.*
1947 *Goethe and his Age.*
1950 *Studies in European Realism.*
1957 *The Meaning of Contemporary Realism.*
V.N. Vološinov 1929 *Marxism and the Philosophy of Language.*
George Lichtheim 1971 *From Marx to Hegel.*
Lucien Goldmann 1964 *The Hidden God.*
István Meszáros 1970 *Marx's Theory of Alienation.*
1972 *Lukács' Concept of the Dialectic.*
Perry Anderson 1976 *Considerations on Western Marxism.*
J.G. Merquior 1986 *Western Marxism.*

CHAPTER EIGHT

Structural Marxism and Power Fantasy

Althusser and Foucault

SUMMARY

Louis Althusser has had more influence on recent literary theory than any other Marxist philosopher, including Lukács and Sartre; but he wrote little on the subject himself. Althusser was in fact a philosopher of science, though not of a kind to appeal to Popperians. His life's project was to provide a philosophical justification and reworking of the science of Historical Materialism; and to provide or reconstruct Dialectical Materialism as the philosophy of that science. His chosen method of working was to make a close rereading of Marx's works, in particular, *Capital*, in order to find the hidden philosophical assumptions that make them scientific. This is rather a literary way of doing philosophy of science; and some critics have applied Althusser's method of 'symptomatic reading' to literature as well. But the true source of his influence on literary theorists is different.

Althusser flourished in the age of French structuralism; his theories became known as structural Marxism. After the 1968 failed revolution in France (which he missed), he produced a theory of ideology and ideological state apparatuses which virtually relocated the class struggle in the production lines of subjectivity: the schools and colleges. This was the basis of his influence in Britain in the 1970s. He was never a genuine structuralist; but he coquetted with structuralist terminology, and his theory was briefly seen as the central feature of a revolutionary synthesis of structuralist, Freudian and Marxist ideas, which had considerable vogue. It is this synthesis which influenced Pécheux, Macherey, Eagleton, Bennett, etc. for a time.

Althusserian theory lost influence in the 1980s and was replaced by that of Foucault: a very personal post-Marxist historiography of ideas that seemed to offer fewer dogmatic hostages than Marxism and was adaptable to radical concerns other than class. In effect, Foucault offered a royal road for radicals, and it was the road out of Marxism, and towards the Rainbow Alliance of every victim group. Foucault's early work suggests a conception of governing patterns of thought for each era – '*epistemes*' – that recalls Hegel; later work moves to a philosophy of knowledge constructed in relations of power, which is influenced by Nietzsche; this is a poor theory of truth, though rather a good one of ideology.

1 THE LINEAGE OF ALTHUSSER

1.0 The renaissance of Marxism

Probably the most important figure in the great renaissance of Marxist theory in the 1970s was Louis Althusser. I am talking here from a rather specialised point of view. I mean the renaissance of Marxist theory among British literary critics and film critics in the 1970s. Briefly it seemed as if a synthesis of Marx, of Freud, and of Saussurean linguistics under the aegis of Althusser could provide a framework for the analysis of culture.[1] A historian of Marxism like Kolakowski barely notices Althusser. But for a short time he seemed like the most significant importation the new New Left had made; and E.P. Thompson of the old New Left devoted half a book to refuting him.[2]

1.1 Althusser and theory

Louis Althusser was a French philosopher and a member of the French Communist Party at a time – the 1950s and early 1960s – when it was very difficult to be both. The official philosophy of the party was a Stalinist version of dialectical materialism; few philosophers of any stamp could take this seriously, but public disagreement with it could have led to expulsion from the Party, and put him in the fellow-travelling position of Sartre. As he put it in the introduction to his collection of articles, *For Marx*:

There was no way out for a philosopher. If he spoke and wrote the philosophy the Party wanted he was restricted to commentary and slight idiosyncrasies in his own way of using the Famous Quotations.

Alternative Marxist philosophies – for example a left-wing humanism based on Feuerbachian concepts of the alienation of man's essential nature – could be derived from Marx's early works, and were growing increasingly popular.

> To force their best opponents to pay them some attention, some Marxists were reduced, and by a natural movement which did not disguise a conscious tactic, to **disguising themselves** – disguising Marx as Husserl, Marx as Hegel, Marx as the ethical and humanist young Marx – at the risk one day of taking the masks for the reality.[3]

Althusser rejected both of these approaches. He constructed a new Marxist philosophy on the basis of a new reading of *Capital* and other late works. This was openly hostile to humanist Marxism, which he believed to be based on Kantian, Hegelian and Feuerbachian views that the mature Marx had rejected. Where his philosophy differed from orthodox Communist positions it was partly protected from the ideologues of the Party by the fact that much of it – including almost the whole of his influential book *Reading Capital* – was too difficult for them to understand.

Althusser's view was that Marx had founded a new science: the science of history, the history of social formations, which in effect superseded all the existing (bourgeois) human sciences. He had done this by rejecting the old Hegelian and humanist problematics within which the human sciences had been placed. He had presented history as 'a process without a subject', a process affecting the relations of production and other, political or ideological relations.

For the ordinary bourgeois historian this is likely to seem a less than stunning discovery; most of them think of historical processes as impersonal. But if you look at the origins of the Marxist tradition it is different. According to the Hegelian view of history, the historical process is seen teleologically – that is, in terms of its ultimate goal – as the progressive manifestation of spirit, or mind. It is a process with a 'subject', at least at the end of history: Absolute Mind. Marx apparently derived the notion of a process without a subject from the Hegelian progress towards Mind, by removing the teleology.

According to a Feuerbachian humanist or to the early Marx, merely inverting Hegel, the subject of history would be Man. Again it is a process with a 'subject'. And – to give the most obvious example of a Hegelianising Marxist philosopher of the twentieth century – according to Lukács, in *History and Class Consciousness* (1923), the subject of history would be the proletariat, whose consciousness was embodied in the Party. Again, history is a process with a 'subject'. It is against this new left–Hegelian background that the notion of history as a process without a subject looks novel.

Althusser makes enormous claims for the importance of Marx's new science. According to him, only three sciences of this scale – scientific continents, as it were – had been founded in the history of the world: Mathematics, in the time of the Greeks, Physics, in the time of Galileo, and this new Marxist **historical materialism**. Just how large a claim this is for Marxism can be seen by the fact that the continent of Physics would include everything from physics to biology – everything we ordinarily call natural science, in fact. Althusser did not claim that these three continents cover the whole of mathematical, natural and social scientific knowledge; in addition to the continents, there are a few little islands like psychoanalysis. But it is clear that he expected the whole of social science to be connected to Marxism; as we shall see, he himself built a causeway between historical materialism and Lacan's version of psychoanalysis.

The significance of Marxism for philosophy is as great as its significance for social science. Every new continent of science, says Althusser, induces a great transformation in philosophy. Mathematics brought about the birth of philosophy (Plato); physics a profound transformation (Descartes); Marxism brought the end of classical philosophy, which was in future to be no longer an interpretation of the world, but a transformation of the world.

Marxist theory was also of enormous practical importance:

> **The union, or fusion of the Workers' Movement and Marxist theory** is the greatest event in the history of class societies, i.e. practically in all human history. Beside it, the celebrated great scientific–technical 'mutation' constantly resounding in our ears (the atomic, electronic, computer era, the space-age, etc.) is, despite its great importance, no more than a scientific and technical fact: these events are not of the same order of magnitude, they only bear in their effects on certain aspects of the productive forces, and not on what is decisive, **the relations of production**.
>
> ('Marx's Relation to Hegel', Althusser 1970).

I quote this because it helps to explain the great enthusiasm Althusserian Marxists felt for 'theory', however dry or obscure it might appear. Enthusiasm is less nowadays as it becomes less possible to conceive a union of Althusserian theory and the workers' movement – except for some workers in literary theory of course. Even they are now growing old. But this passage remains as a reminder of the days when Theory seemed more important than the atom bomb.

1.2 *Althusser's theory of social structure*

Althusser was writing at the height of the French vogue for structuralism. He used the word 'structure' quite a bit, and claimed that Marx's greatest intellectual discovery was something called 'structural causality'. Later, he utilised the notion of 'the subject' while rejecting that of 'ideas'. So he was inevitably regarded, for a time, as a 'structuralist'. But this was never true: he had no interest in the linguistic model as applied by Lévi-Strauss or Barthes, rejected 'the structuralist ideology', and did not even offer an explicit combinatorial theory of the structure of society. What he did offer was a new and looser theory of the relationship of base and superstructure.

Stalinists were supposed to hold a rather mechanistic position according to which the economy fairly directly controlled political and ideological structures; and the state of the economy – the contradictions between forces and relations of production – determined when, for example, it was possible to make a revolution. Althusser held that a revolution was 'overdetermined' – a phrase borrowed from Freud – with contradictions of many different kinds. There isn't a simple causal chain stretching from the economy to the ideological sphere, but rather a 'structural causality' of the whole structure. In some states of society, the political or ideological levels might be the decisive ones; and these levels have a history of their own, not simply determined by the economy. It is the role of the economy to determine what level is decisive in a particular society: e.g. that, in some feudal society politics rather than economics might be dominant. Only in this sense is the economy decisive in the last instance; all it decides is what sector is the decisive one. Althusser spoke of this type of social structuration as 'structure in dominance'.

It will be no recommendation to the Althusserian to say this, but this view appeals quite strongly to bourgeois common sense. It seems obvious that, for example, religious differences can lead to a war, and a war can wreck an economy; in which case it is the ideological sphere that is influencing the economic sphere. It seems obvious also that the kind of war that is possible will be determined by the economy, since you can't fight with weapons that you can neither make nor get supplied. And there are analogous economic limitations on religious and other views: Egyptian God-Kings exist because controlling the irrigation system requires a powerful priesthood. So the needs of the economy fundamentally determine what are the possible outcomes of struggles in the other spheres.

It is also obvious that in a complicated society there will be a currently dominant mode of production, along with others left over from the past, or newly developing; and a similarly complicated picture will obtain for political institutions and systems of thought. In such a society, everything is likely to interact with everything else with quite unpredictable results; but unless the economy is maintained in being so that people can eat and reproduce, the whole society will collapse. Althusser accommodates all these facts in his system.

I don't think myself that the Althusserian concepts of structure in dominance, dominant mode of production, ideology and politics as levels or instances of the social formation, etc. mean anything more precise, when located in Althusser's theory, than I have suggested in the informal paragraphs above. What the theory does is to give much more theoretical scope to the superstructure than the Stalinist theory it superseded – almost as much as the humanist European Marxisms with which it was competing – and to encourage the development of a much more elaborate theory of the superstructure itself. This later flowered into an influential theory of ideology.

Althusser however claimed much more for his formulations than this, and a new generation of Marxist theoretical historians grew up who attached fanatical importance to using them correctly. Marx had founded the new science of human history, and rendered all non-Marxist historiography obsolete. But Althusser had gone beyond this by stating the correct concepts for Marxist historiography; in doing so, he had rendered most Marxist history-writing obsolete as well (including pretty well all the work of British Marxist historians like E.P. Thompson). The way was therefore clear to rewrite the whole of human history from a correct theoretical standpoint; especially clear, since Althusser wrote no history of his own, and probably knew none. Of course this very highly structured theoretical vacuum was especially attractive to bright radical scholars trying to make their way. For a time after 1968 there was a kind of theoretical terrorism in academia, as wandering bands of young Marxist sociologists ambushed and destroyed the older generation of Marxist historians.[4]

Althusser claimed that the concept of structural causality was Marx's greatest theoretical discovery. It is hard to agree with this. The concept is supposed to be present in Marx in a practical state, but only spelt out theoretically by Althusser himself, and it makes very little sense in him. It is of course true that a structure like, say, a bridge has load-bearing properties that are not possessed by the heap of girders and rivets from which it is made; and there is no doubt societies have structural properties of this kind. As the example of the bridge shows, structural causality of this kind can be explained by ordinary mechanical causality, operating in some structured object. But Althusser's 'structural causality' is more paradoxical than this. It is a causality exerted by the structure on its elements; and it is a structure present only in its effects! Yet it is to be distinguished not only from mechanical causality but from the Hegelian notion of an expressive totality. The concept of a structure present only in its effects and yet causing those effects is so paradoxical that it suggests we are moving into the post-structuralist phase of theory, where logical aporias were welcomed; this approach has no connection with science, though it rather brings to mind the layman's conception of some of the paradoxes of quantum mechanics.

1.3   Ideology and 'the subject'

Althusser missed the 1968 events – the largest general strike in history among the French workers, and a powerful protest movement in the French universities, with sit-ins and demonstrations and a rich growth of home-made revolutionary ideology which led some people to comment that at last imagination had taken power. Structural Marxism was not a major player in this game; there was an unkind slogan: 'Structures don't take to the streets!' Althusser meanwhile was in hospital in a depressive phase of the manic-depressive illness that led him, years later, to kill his wife. Not till he came out could he start to theorise the new kind of revolutionary situation, in which critical struggles seemed to be taking place in educational institutions.

The result, in 1969, was the enormously influential paper 'Ideology and Ideological State Apparatuses'. This set out the theory that was used by many on the left to bind together Marxism, structuralism and Lacanian psychoanalysis into a comprehensive theory of society, subjectivity, culture and social revolution. Its main feature was a hypertrophy of the traditional Marxist notion of 'ideology' in which it came to stand in for what the anthropologist would call 'culture', and began to offer an account of the nature of the self. (Or, as Althusser would have it, of 'the subject'.)

The fundamental idea here (and I shall begin with fundamental ideas and postpone to the next section some of the more dubious of Althusser's metaphorical technical terms like 'interpellation') is one that is fairly familiar in Western sociology, and has no necessary political implications. It is that the human animal becomes a human being by being socialised into a set of roles in society. We become human by internalising the surrounding culture. Thereafter, whenever we speak, decide how to act, or even think anything, it is substantially our culture which is speaking, deciding, thinking through us. In Anglo-American sociology this view had never been combined either with Marxism or psychoanalysis. Althusser, taking his own original reading of Marxism, and Lacan's highly personal reading of Freud, managed to combine it with both.

Althusser was quite strongly influenced by Lacan. Indeed, his whole project, of rereading Marx's texts in the light of contemporary French philosophy, is a copy of Lacan's project of rereading Freud's texts. (He repaid the debt by helping to find Lacan a venue for his later seminars.) Althusser wrote an article 'Freud and Lacan' (1964) which had considerable influence; in this, Lacan is presented as a Freudian who has reinterpreted the master in terms of Saussurean linguistics. This is not an unreasonable interpretation, and can be supported by many of Lacan's remarks in the 'Discourse of Rome' (1953) and other *Ecrits*. But it is not in fact true; Lacan took from Saussure only one or two technical terms and formulae, and changed the significance of everything he did take.[5] But Althusser probably had too little interest in linguistics to see this. However, Althusser's use of Lacan sustained the myth that Althusser himself was a structuralist, and that some kind of synthesis was possible between Marx, Freud and Saussure – or Saussureans like Barthes – in which Lacan would play a crucial part.

This synthesis was to have a Marxist part and a Freudian part. The Marxist part is an extension of the notion of false consciousness to cover our whole consciousness of ourselves as individuals. Our ordinary experience of the world is as free individuals who can make our own decisions about what we do. But this is an illusion. We experience the world through ideology; so experience is not to be trusted. Our very selves are constructed, as we grow up, through internalising this ideology. The Freudian part is an explanation of how this false ego is constructed in childhood. It draws upon Lacan's claim that the ego is an early product of misrecognition.

A very brief account of what the Althusserian left has made of Lacan is Easthope, 'Reply to Rée' (*Radical Philosophy* 25, 1980).

> That the ego is in and for itself ('I think therefore I am'), owing nothing to anyone, dependent upon nothing but itself and thus freely owning commodities, freely exchanging labour power for wages, acting freely according to or against the law, freely choosing its political representatives – all this is the central support in bourgeois ideology, as Althusser (under the influence of Lacan) tries to argue. . . . Lacan offers to explain how the ego comes to conceive itself in an autonomy, to think itself as a source of meaning. . . . For Lacan the consciousness of the subject depends upon its being (in language) and cannot exist apart from this. This is, at the least, not incompatible with historical materialism. . . .

I will translate this into simpler terms. Althusser thinks that the ordinary experience of choosing freely what to do is a bourgeois illusion; the very self that seems to experience such freedom (usually, in this philosophy, miscalled 'the subject') is a product of ideology; it comes into existence when the child first learns to speak a language – or to put it in more Lévi-Straussian or Lacanian terms, enters the symbolic order of language. These views were naturally an inspiration to literary critics, and other intellectuals, not only because they seemed to explain the nature of our experience – the way in which we experience the world within an ideology – but because of the amount of theoretical autonomy they give to the ideological sphere; for literary critics are much better at making a revolution at the ideological level – making us see things as new – than at affecting the economy.

There is however an obvious danger of idealism here; Marx, it will be remembered, was very caustic about intellectuals who made great revolutions 'in their heads'. Althusser makes it clear that the ideological level has a material existence, as a set of practices like teaching, preaching, etc. In 'Ideology and Ideological State Apparatuses' he speaks of the state as containing both 'repressive state apparatuses' like armies and police forces, which hold down the people by force, and 'ideological state apparatuses' like churches and schools, which engineer consent. So intellectuals can make material revolutions in the latter. As Jonathan Miller's socially committed vicar put it thirty years ago:[6] 'What we need is to get violence off the streets and into the churches, where it belongs.' Or, of course, into the colleges; or at least, into the syllabuses.

1.4   Althusser's philosophical problem

There is one practice from which it is very difficult to expel idealism. This is Althusser's own philosophy. The problem with the position just described is that it is completely relativist: everything is ideology, including the claims that Althusser himself is making. No philosopher before the post-structuralists could be satisfied with such a position; least of all Althusser, since he was on intellectual grounds a committed anti-Hegelian, and on political grounds was committed to a materialism as solid as that of Lenin in 1908 (*Materialism and Empirio-Criticism*).[7] Althusser repeatedly affirmed the anti-idealist formula of the priority of being over knowledge; and he spent as much effort as Karl Popper in trying to distinguish between science and ideology.

Already in *For Marx* and *Reading Capital* Althusser had gone to some trouble to distinguish between ideology and scientific knowledge, and to explain how you get from one to the other. This is the famous theory of the 'epistemological break' between ideology and science (between alchemy and chemistry, for example, or between Ricardian and Marxist economics); and the equally famous theory that the raw material of science is in part ideology; that the methods of science operate on that; that science is what these methods produce. These belong to the most philosophical, the most questionable, and potentially most idealist parts of Althusser's work.

Their central purpose is to show that Marxism is a science, and not just another bit of ideology. A science is another practice, and indeed, a productive practice. What you do is to take a set of generalities – Generalities 1 – which happen to be present in your ideology, as your theoretical raw material. Marx, for example, took Ricardo and French socialism. You take another set of generalities – Generalities 2 – which are instruments of theoretical production. Marx used methods based originally on Hegel, though he made decisive alterations in them. And you produce a third set of generalities – Generalities 3 – which are your theoretical product. Marx produced *Capital*.

What this process produces is objects of knowledge. These are not to be confused with real objects; they are objects in thought, which have the property of appropriating real objects for thought. However material the practice of science is, what science produces is a thought-object. The electron, or the class-system, of science is not to be identified with the real electron, or the real class-system. Althusser warns us sternly that if we confuse thought and the real, by reducing the real to thought, or conceiving the real as a result of thought (as if, in my illustration, science had actually produced electrons by thinking about them), then like Hegel we shall fall into speculative idealism. If we confuse thought with the real by reducing thought about the real to the real itself (as if in my illustration the concept of the electron were an abstraction from the experience of one) we shall fall into empiricist idealism.

Althusser's philosophy still has to explain how such an ideal object can appropriate a real one for knowledge; and how we can know when it has. And Althusser does not make things easy for himself. He rejects the notion that the ideal object is a 'model' of the real one. He rejects all forms of empiricism – i.e. he doesn't think there is any simple way, outside the science itself, in which you can compare the ideal object of science with the real one. The only way you can know that you have succeeded in building the right ideal object is to make sure you have done your science correctly. If you have done your physics correctly your ideal electron will be scientifically correct; if you have done your Marxism properly, your ideal class-system will be scientifically correct.

But, as Ted Benton points out in *The Rise and Fall of Structural Marxism* (1984), this leaves one only the choice of dogmatism or idealism. Any self-consistent discourse can produce ideal objects of its own and claim that they correspond to reality. But that is pure dogmatism. On the other hand, it is always possible to drop one's interest in real objects – things in themselves – and concentrate only on the ideal ones. That is classical idealism; and it remains idealism however material are the production processes – the discursive processes – by which the ideal objects are produced. In fact it seems to me that Althusser, like most sophisticated modern Marxists, has put his materialism in the wrong place. He has been careful to categorise science as a material production process of immaterial objects. But what he needed to do was to describe a plausible ideal process for investigating material objects.

Althusser himself is saved from idealism because he is able to take the dogmatic road. He **knows** Marxism is true; and that *Capital* is a correct formulation of it. He knows therefore that the theoretical constructs in *Capital* – like classes, or value – correspond to real objects. He is therefore able to deduce the correct Marxist philosophy by a process of **symptomatic reading**. This is a process that he took from Freud, by way of Lacan. When a psychoanalyst listens to what a patient says, he looks at gaps and failures of association and sees these as symptoms of underlying complexes. With astonishing chutzpah, Althusser applied the technique of symptomatic reading to Marx's *Capital*, looking for gaps in the argument where there are unstated philosophical assumptions, so that he could deduce Marx's philosophy!

This is a perfectly valid line of argument, given Althusser's dogmatic assumptions, though it seems queer to regard Marx's philosophy as the unconscious of *Capital*. Of course, it wouldn't be a basis for examining Marx critically, if that were the objective, since it must rest on the assumption that all his arguments are valid once you supply his philosophy. Just how dogmatic it is can be seen by the fact that what Althusser chooses to examine in *Reading Capital* are Marx's theories of value, which few economists, even among those most sympathetic to Marx, would defend. For that reason, of course, it was a good demonstration of orthodoxy as a Marxist.

Many literary critics since then have employed the technique of 'symptomatic reading', looking at the 'gaps and silences' in various texts, in order to supply either a psychological or a political unconscious. It is a very powerful technique, illuminating when used by a scrupulous critic, and capable of proving anything at all when used by a critic who is unscrupulous or merely silly. Of course both Marxists and psychoanalysts have comprehensive bodies of theory available, which produce some control over what it is reasonable to read into gaps in a text. Literary critics usually rely on intuition or prejudice, and sometimes on versions of post-structuralist arguments which seem to imply that anything goes; in which case, of course, anything does.

1.5   The concept of scientific knowledge in Althusser

Althusser in his first phase has the strange habit of denying that he is writing philosophy, on the grounds that Marxists don't. Marxism is concerned with practice; Marxist theory – e.g. *Capital* – is theoretical practice; Marxist philosophy is the theory of theoretical practice. This irritating terminology is later dropped, except by some of Althusser's followers; it had a vogue in the English work of Hindess and Hirst before they dropped Marxism altogether (cf. 'The Odyssey of Paul Hirst' – *NLR* 159, September 1986). But it had a hangover. It is still not uncommon for literary critics and theorists to indicate their intellectual allegiances by talking about '*Critical Practice*' – as in the title of a book by Catherine Belsey.

The danger of this terminology is that it suggests a crude anti-intellectualism which is quite uncharacteristic of Althusser (or indeed Belsey); as if one were claiming that practice took place without being guided by a theory, or as if there were no philosophical claims underlying the theories. In fact this is not true: Althusser is primarily a philosopher – to be precise, an epistemologist – and has to be discussed as such; the entire lineage of theorists and critics influenced by him are basing their work on very controversial philosophical positions which have to be examined as such. Althusser's idealism – if idealism it is – arises directly out of his theory of knowledge as a theory of knowledge-objects constructed in thought or discourse. This is inherited by the post-Althusserians, and in particular by the literary theorists among them, along with all its problems.

Althusser's theory of scientific knowledge is central to his earlier philosophy; and it is a very odd theory. It is dominated by a rejection of empiricism so strong that it seems to leave no room for empirical checks upon theory at all, and has been interpreted – e.g. by Hindess and Hirst 1975 – as licensing the utmost contempt for evidence. As I have said, according to this theory, a science proceeds by constructing an object of knowledge. This knowledge-object is absolutely different from the corresponding real object, and cannot be compared with it by any direct method. It is constructed and validated by the procedures of that science, and by those alone. No independent check is possible. Already, some

Marxist theorists like Lukács had drawn a line between the natural and the social sciences, and postulated different methods for each. Althusser rejected this view and went beyond it. What he did was to postulate a whole series of sciences, each with its own methods and its own object of knowledge, and each established by its own 'epistemological break' with earlier ideology in that area. These sciences were listed as Mathematics, Natural Science, Marxism (the only genuine social science) and possibly Psychoanalysis (the only genuine psychological science). But it is not suggested that this list is a final one, or that new sciences (even a science of literature) are not possible. Pierre Macherey (1966) and Terry Eagleton (1976) found it possible to propose such a science.

It is a common feature of all these sciences that they offer exclusive access to their own respective objects of knowledge. You can't appeal to any higher criterion – direct experience, or common sense, for example – to overthrow their claims. Faced with a mathematical theorem, the only way we can check it is by following the procedures of mathematics. Faced with an unlikely scientific claim – for example, the claim that matter is mostly empty space – we can only check it by following the procedures of natural science, including experiments. Faced with an unlikely Marxist claim – for example, the claim above that the autonomy of the self is an illusion, a mere support for bourgeois ideology – we can only check it by following the procedures of scientific Marxism. Similarly for Lacanian psychoanalysis: Lacanian theory will settle what evidence is relevant to its own truth. Literary theory will determine what counts as literature.

The view that we can settle such questions as these by just looking at the evidence is stigmatised as 'empiricism', and said to be a disguised form of idealism. For Macherey and, later, Eagleton, the standard methods of literary criticism are an obvious example of empiricism: just looking at a poem, and supposing we can extract knowledge of it directly from it by naive reading. Without a theory to define an object of knowledge we can have no firm scientific knowledge of literature.

Empiricism is given a very strange description by Althusser: he thinks of it as the theory that the object of knowledge is a part of the real object, which merely has to be abstracted from the real object. I don't know of any avowed empiricist who believes this. So far as this is Althusser's notion of empiricism, he is probably justified in thinking that empiricism is idealist; more to the point, it is obvious nonsense. Traditionally, empiricism is simply the thesis that all knowledge is derived from experience. There are problems with this thesis – like Hume's problem – which empiricists have tried to meet. But they are not the problems Althusser describes.

A true empiricist would say that what renders a discourse scientific is precisely that it provides clear specifications for the ways in which its own constructs can be checked against experience – that is, experiment or observation. In a natural science, we expect it to be possible to deduce from the theories of that science what sorts of experiment or observation will count for or against those theories. We may have to wait for a long time to develop the appropriate empirical test, but we must be able to see our way to making it in principle. The question of whether we accept Newton's theory or Einstein's turns, in the end, on a minute difference in the orbit of a planet, or a proportionately larger one in the trajectory of a fundamental particle.

I myself think the same thing should be true in social science. Few Marxists would agree. Most Marxists would probably say that the test of a theory in Marxist social science is revolutionary practice; but this needs closer specification; to make a whole revolution is rather a large-scale test for any small part of the theory. Althusser is fertile in denunciations of empiricism, and of empiricist misunderstandings of Marxist theoretical concepts. He is quite barren of suggestions on how one might test any of these concepts empirically.

The practical effect of this approach is to render Althusserian theories of society pretty well invulnerable to contrary evidence. This is a feature that greatly annoyed some distinguished English Marxist historians, at the height of the Althusserian vogue, and provoked E.P. Thompson's furious polemic *The Poverty of Theory*. The effect on literary theory is more complicated. I discuss it below, and in the next chapter on British Marxist theory of the 1970s.

1.6   The strange status of 'knowledge-objects'

Althusser himself has a fairly conventional, and I think perfectly defensible view of the status of art and literature. These are not science, and Althusser does not think they give scientific knowledge. But he does not think they are simply to be categorised as ideology, either. Ideology, for Althusser, includes our whole lived experience of the social world. Art and literature offer a certain distance from this experience, which makes it possible to become conscious of it. They enable us to see ideology, and perhaps to see the contradictions in it. This is a plausible view; I suppose most people who teach Shakespeare or Dickens will agree that they make us conscious of the ideology of their societies and of the contradictions within it. A theory of this kind also leads naturally to a scale of values for art; we would admire more those works which make us conscious of the deeper contradictions in our ideology . . . and so on.

However defensible this theory is, it has had little influence on Althusserian literary theorists. They have been more impressed by Althussser's theories of symptomatic reading, by his theories of the construction or the positioning of the subject, and above all by his account of the objects of scientific knowledge. Bizarrely, Althusser's theory of science has been far more influential than his theory of literature on theorists of literature.

If you think of a science not in Althusserian terms as a specially privileged type of discourse, but as one among many specialised types of discourse, you can extend the theory of science discussed above to a discipline like literary criticism. On this view, the 'knowledge-object' of the literary critic is constructed by the procedures of the literary critic, and by those alone. The object of knowledge here – the work for study – is absolutely different from the work in itself, which is quite inaccessible. The implications of this view for the study of literature in universities are of course very profound. There is no way of appealing from what the critics and theorists say to the works themselves, directly experienced. English – so far as it is available for study at all – is something constructed in discourse, according to the rules of a particular discourse.

Before we resign ourselves to this conclusion, it will be as well to examine Althusser's point of view in its original context, as a theory of scientific knowledge. Is it reasonable to describe the work of physicists, for example, as the production of knowledge-objects? I don't think there is any particular problem here about the notion of 'production': there is a clear sense in which scientists produce knowledge just as assembly-line workers produce industrial products. If you ask concretely what, in the course of his working life, a scientist actually does produce, the answer will be: thousands of observations, and a few more or less fruitful hypotheses, which are both the intellectual point of the enterprise and a guide to setting up the experimental conditions under which the observations are made. The scientist's 'knowledge', in fact – what he has produced and what he will put in a paper or a book – is a set of propositions.

If the propositions in a scientific paper or textbook are what Althusser means by a knowledge-object, then he is absolutely right to say there is a difference between knowledge-objects and real objects; it is a difference of logical kind; one is a statement and the other a material object. And there is no difficulty in explicating the notion that the knowledge-object appropriates the real object; it simply means that scientific statements are statements about the real world. But in this case the use of the term 'knowledge-object' is mystificatory. It is a kind of pseudo-materialism in which we pretend that the statements we make are objects that we produce. Marx never fell into pseudo-materialism of this kind.

But Althusser might mean something different from this. When we read a textbook in physics (or for that matter, economics or linguistics) we often find ourselves in a simplified, idealised world of frictionless planes, planets with their whole mass concentrated at the centre, cannon firing balls that meet with no air resistance (or, one might add, markets in which the perfect knowledge of all participants makes it possible instantaneously to fix a price which balances supply and demand, and sentences whose grammaticality is in no way affected by their meaning or the context they are placed in). Couldn't we describe this as a world of ideal objects, 'knowledge-objects', which are quite distinct from real roads, real planets, real guns, real markets and real remarks?

We can indeed; with two important reservations. First, it seems odd to say that scientists 'produce' these ideal objects; a scientist doesn't produce a frictionless plane in the same sense that he produces a scientific textbook that mentions one. There are no frictionless planes in the lab. Second, scientists are never satisfied to stay with ideal objects that don't correspond to reality. They don't leave things there. Having worked out the principles for calculating the trajectory of a cannon-ball fired in a vacuum, the scientist will go on to work out the effects of air friction; and in the end, he will supply principles which apply to real guns fired on earth at real targets. Althusser would presumably have to think of this as the dialectical process by which the ideal object appropriated the real one for knowledge, and as the mechanism which produces a knowledge-effect. But it is hard to see the Althusserian terminology here as anything but an obstacle to understanding what is actually going on.

There is, for example, a subtle kind of misunderstanding to which the Althusserian position leads directly. For Althusser, the ideal objects exist in thought; they are structurally combined only in thought; only then do they appropriate the real object for knowledge. So the trajectory of real cannon-balls is only appropriated when we have combined the idealised frictionless trajectory with idealised air resistance. However, that is not quite right. The scientist would say that air resistance is a real effect in the physical world, detectable by other means than its influence on trajectories. The structure which includes the initial force exerted on the cannon-ball, and the force of gravity, and air resistance, is a structure in material reality not just in the head. I suspect Althusser would accept this, as Engels or Lenin would; but his terminology pushes in the opposite direction.

A more plausible view might be that the real distinction between science and everyday, ideological thinking is that science involves theoretical constructs like 'electrons', 'protons', and 'neutrons', or 'classes', 'social formations' and 'modes of production'. It is these which are the relevant 'thought-objects' that must not be confused with real objects. But this is a wholly idealist view of the nature of science. A corresponding realist view would be that science forms hypotheses that electrons, protons, neutrons, classes, social formations and modes of production really exist, and tries to explain the behaviour of real objects, and real history, in terms of them. This is the traditional Marxist view, common to Marx himself and to Lenin (1908); sophisticated contemporary defences are available from Timpanaro 1970, Bhaskar 1978 and 1986, and others.

On the idealist interpretation of the nature of science, we distinguish sharply between my knowledge of everyday objects and my knowledge of scientific constructs. My knowledge that the table is solid wood is knowledge of the real object. But my knowledge that it contains electrons is knowledge of some quite different knowledge-object-table, not to be confused with the real table, and made out of knowledge-object-electrons. Surely this is absurd: a science of this kind simply won't behave as science does behave. In particular it won't be usable for practical purposes. Consider a television set. This is a device in which a beam of electrons draws a picture on a phosphorescent screen. It will be no use if these electrons are only knowledge-objects, and draw a picture only in the theoretical knowledge of the viewer. We need real electrons to draw a real picture.[8] And the same is true of social science. It will be no use if the proletariat is only a knowledge-object, and makes a revolution only in the theoretical knowledge of a Marxist theorist. We need a real proletariat to make a real revolution.

We have seen that the claim that there is an absolute difference between the real object and a set of true propositions about it is obviously true (and entirely trivial). We are now in a position to ask what is the nature of a claim that the object of knowledge, in the sense either of the object I am acquainted with (in Althusser's terms, the object which is given in ideology), or the object my propositions are about (in Althusser's terms, the knowledge-object of science), is absolutely different from the real object. It is of course, a familiar claim; it is Kant's claim about the difference between phenomena in experience, and things in themselves. We cannot know things as they are in themselves. We can only know them as they are constituted by the categories of the mind, acting upon intuitions (sensations). If Althusser takes this view he is either a neo-Kantian or some other form of idealist.[9] But this is quite inconsistent with his Marxism.

1.7   Althusser and cultural theories

Althusserian theory – in particular the theory of 'Ideology and Ideological State Apparatuses' – has influenced cultural and literary theories in four major ways. The first is by providing a theory of the self, or individual personality, in which individual experience and action, and indeed the very feeling of being an individual and being capable of such experience, are seen as effects, rather than causes, of ideological practices. This theory is misleadingly described, for reasons which have to do with the history of continental philosophy and French psychoanalysis, and the influence of Husserl and Lacan in particular, as a theory of the '**subject**'. The word 'subject' here denotes much more than its normal philosophical sense of 'the abstract subjective pole of experience when experience is analysed into subject–object relations'. It means something more like 'personality'.

The word 'subject' is confusing in itself; it is usually made even more confusing by the habit of thinkers in this field, from Lacan and Althusser themselves down to the humblest popularisers, of continually making puns on four other senses of the word: (a) the grammatical subject of a sentence; (b) the subject of a discussion or an academic subject like English; (c) the subject of a monarch, and a hypothetical process of subjection that has produced him; (d) a universal Subject with a capital letter representing society at large and having some of the properties of Hegel's Absolute Mind. The claim that there is some connection between any or all of these is of course not to be ruled out *a priori*: but any such claim needs to be carefully explained and justified. Althusser has no actual arguments, but offers a brief lyrical essay on Christian ideology.[10] Usually, the connection is merely implied by a clever pun. This is mystification. An example of the 'theory of the subject' in its fully mystified form is to be found in Coward and Ellis 1977. (For analysis, see Jackson 1991.)

One particular disadvantage in this treatment is that it hides the fact that the basic theory of individuality as a bourgeois illusion has a very long history in Marxist theory, going back to Marx himself. There is, as we have seen, an excellent treatment of it by Caudwell dating from the 1930s.

The second contribution, however, is new. It is a part Marxist, part psychoanalytic theory of 'discourse'. Discourses are the semiological practices – mostly, but not exclusively, practices in using language – which, among other things, call the self into being as a choosing, experiencing, individual self. To use Althusser's half-technical, half-metaphorical phrase, discourse 'interpellates the individual as a subject'. The word 'interpellate' means roughly 'call upon', in the sense in which a cabinet minister is called upon in the House to take responsibility for his actions. The idea is that the individual human organism becomes a human individual: (a) by being talked about as an individual; (b) by being talked to as an individual; (c) by recognising or in Lacanian terms misrecognising himself by imaginary identification as that individual; (d) thenceforth by acting, thinking and feeling as that individual.

The great attraction of this theory is the range of things it purports to explain. It explains how the animal becomes a person – because discourse calls him to be one. It explains how the female animal becomes a 'gendered subject' – because discourse calls her to be one. (It thus provides the underpinning for theories of patriarchal ideology employed by feminists to this day.) It explains how ideology is incorporated into the most private and fundamental parts of the self. The ideology was in the discourse that called up those parts of the self. It even explains how, when we are reading a work of literature, we can take up a subjective position induced by that work, and different from the normal self. The work of literature is a discourse; and it calls up a new 'subject' to receive it. Discourse, in fact, can always call spirits from the vasty deep; and they do come when it interpellates them.

This theory is of enormous importance to modern literary and cultural theorists; it provides the essential structure of their claims about the effectivity of discourse, and that structure often remains when Althusser and Marxism have been abandoned. Unfortunately, the theory won't work. It is very obviously a piece of hand-waving, towards a whole family of theories of learning and socialisation, the details of which are largely, though not entirely, unknown. It is logically impossible that the theory should work at its lowest level. The self cannot be called up in discourse until enough of the self exists to understand language. There has to be an early learning phase which can, at most, only partly be described in Lacanian terms – for Lacan offers no serious account of, say, language acquisition, in the sense in which it is studied by psycholinguistics. At the other end of the scale, adult uses of language involve a complex interplay of semantic and pragmatic considerations – it would be premature to talk of 'rules' – which have hardly yet been clarified. How these interact with the construction of the self is something which child psychologists would be very glad to know, but which they don't yet know; and the word 'interpellate' doesn't tell them.

The theory is in fact most satisfactory at its upper levels, in relation to reading literature, when one can supply some content to the notion of 'interpellation' by introspection into what it feels like to be button-holed by a narrative. Even here, however, there are major disadvantages in labelling novels, conversations, telephone directories, the behaviour (or perhaps the criteria) of working scientists, the code of manners of some sub-society, etc. with the all-purpose word 'discourses'. Chief among them is the fact that we do not have any extensive theories of discourse; attempts to construct them – like, for instance, Michel Pécheux's *Language, Semantics and Ideology* – have to rely very heavily on borrowings from existing bourgeois fields like grammar, logic, and so forth, sometimes to interesting effect. When this is not done, the word 'discourse' is a label for a theoretical vacuum dressed up as a political position.

The third contribution of Althusser to literary theory is the new theory of ideology, and particularly of the production of ideology in material apparatuses, which can lead to new theories of literary production – they came too late for Macherey, but affected Eagleton. It has been pointed out that there are, in Althusser's essay, 'Ideology and Ideological State Apparatuses' and in other works, two approaches to ideology of very different political significance. The concept that ideology is constructed in schools and colleges leads directly to an examination of what is taught there, or even to a political struggle about what should be taught there. The concept of ideology being a general medium in which we live, and will always live, even after a putative revolution, leads away from a political struggle. You can struggle to purify the air, or to poison it, but not to stop breathing it altogether.

The ideology of a society which had completed its revolution, abolished capitalism, and had no state, would presumably be quite different from any present-day one. It would therefore interpellate its subjects in quite different ways. But is it possible to believe that these new subjects would be qualitatively different from the old ones? Would they have no conception of self-identity? Of making individual choices as opposed to accepting social ones? Would they be unable to see any meaning in the pronoun 'I', or to grasp what it is to eat a piece of chocolate oneself as opposed to seeing someone else eat it; or what it is to be in pain oneself as opposed to seeing someone else in pain? These things can't be the case; our new subjects will still have individual bodies and separate brains. These considerations point to something that has been left out of the ideology–interpellation theory; a sense in which it isn't materialist enough, and ignores the vast common physical basis of all possible human societies and personalities.

The fourth Althusserian contribution to literary theory is easily the most malign. It is the idealist aspect of Althusserian methodology: the theory that science works by the production of 'knowledge-objects' that are not to be confused with real objects. The trouble is, this has been taken as a model for a theory that goes well beyond the defensible, if rather subjectivist view that works of literature are constructed in the process of reading by readers, to the much more radical position that 'literature' is something produced as an object of study by critics. (Bennett 1979; Eagleton 1983; Widdowson 1982, etc.) The argument here is constructed in the usual fashion for idealist arguments. We are told that the object − literature − exists not in itself, but only in virtue of the analytic category applied by the observer. It follows that literature cannot have existed before this analytic category came into being − i.e. roughly at the beginning of the nineteenth century; and it will not exist if we decide, as Marxists, that the category of literature has no place in our theoretical scheme. This claim is taken up in the next chapter.

This argument is in fact a very general one, and of rather embarrassing power. If it is valid for literature, it will apply to any object of theoretical enquiry whatever. It will be true for psychoanalysis − the ego and the id did not exist before Freud invented them − and for Marxism − the class war becomes Marx's invention, not his discovery. Indeed, we can go further. No doubt, before the time of Isaac Newton, people fell downhill. But they did not do so under the influence of gravity; for that concept had not then been invented. It might surprise us to learn that Newtonian theory can be used to calculate the dates of events before Newton's time: for example, eclipses in some ancient empire. But it should not surprise us. On this view, these eclipses are no more than knowledge-objects, knowledge-eclipses taking place in our knowledge of the ancient empire and not at all to be confused with the real eclipses which may have occurred in the real empire, in which no doubt the sun was eaten by a wolf.

Incidentally, the joke about gravity comes from Marx and Engels 1965, *The German Ideology* (p. 24). The serious point of the whole paragraph is that Althusser has argued himself into precisely the left-Hegelian position which Marx and Engels began their work by attacking; and the 1970s' Althusserians all dutifully trooped into the idealist lobby after him.

2   FOUCAULT AND THE DISCOURSE THEORISTS

The dematerialisation of Karl Marx was completed by Michel Foucault and the discourse theorists who have drawn both on Althusser and Foucault. Michel Foucault was a man of the Left − at least in so far as a passionate identification with the victim makes one a man of the Left − a historian of ideas and a philosopher. In a healthy Marxist culture, no one would have had a greater power to build a satisfactory materialist history of ideas. Yet in fact no one has done more damage to materialist Marxism, in the sense of leading left-wing cultural theorists away from it.

As a historian, what Foucault produced was a series of histories of ideas and practices, about certain special areas the choice of which throws a revealing light on his own personal interests: in particular, madness, illness, crime and sexuality. He began with a history of ideas about madness, and practices in dealing with the mad. Next came ideas about illness and the birth of clinical medicine. Then he wrote a parallel study of ideas about life, political economy and language, purporting to show certain epistemic regularities beneath them all, in a certain period. Then – after a methodological book, defending his position and modifying his terminology – he wrote a study of ideas about crime and practices of punishment and social discipline. Finally – up until his death from Aids – a study of ideas about sexuality and practices of dealing with it. All these work by bracketing, or setting aside, questions about the reality or actual nature of madness, illness, crime, or whatever, and concentrating on the history of our ideas about it and the institutions we have evolved for dealing with it.

These histories are immensely erudite, with vast bibliographies which themselves represent only a part of Foucault's reading. They recover much little-known material, often of an exciting and disturbing kind, and presented in vivid anecdotes. Balance and fairness are not part of Foucault's stock in trade. It has been said that it is his tactic to use the past to make us uneasy about the present, without ever making us admire the past. Thus he gives an account of a public execution that makes the modern reader physically sick; only to go on and persuade us that modern humane prisons are in a subtle way worse. In his first book, he made no excuses for the chaining up of madmen: but he presented the freeing of them from their chains as only the condition of a deeper moral imprisonment.

In many ways Foucault is more of an imaginative writer than a historian. Sheridan, his translator and commentator, speaks of his 'sumptuous prose'. But there is more than that. Like an imaginative writer, he tends to impose his personal obsessions onto history, often in the form of some dominant image. Jeremy Bentham's panopticon – the never-built circular building with a central tower, from which one warder could watch every inhabitant, ideal for prison, barracks, hospital, school – becomes an image of the power of the objectifying gaze in producing at once knowledge and control. This is like Dickens in *Little Dorrit*, making the debtor's prison the image for the whole of commercial society. The basis of these images is the feeling of being an outsider, a victim, a deviant, rejected, excluded. For Foucault, those with power (and responsibility) can never do anything right. He has a 'hermeneutics of suspicion'; he can give a bad account of any practice. It is this which has appealed to the left.

There is a sense in which the work of Foucault is a necessary supplement to that of a wholly abstract Marxist theorist like Althusser. Althusser offers a broad theory of the institutional production of ideology, to provide the world of lived experience in which we seem to live. But the theory operates with gigantic abstract categories, which provide little insight into the detailed processes of ideology production. Foucault offers a detailed analysis at the micro-level of the way in which power relationships are transformed into apparent truths about the world. He has no abstract, general theory of society. If these two can be put together, they provide a composite theory that is incomparably stronger than either separately. Cultural theory since the 1960s has in fact drawn freely upon both, with devout Marxists like Eagleton acknowledging Foucault's influence.

Yet Foucault is not a Marxist, but a passionate and effective opponent of Marxism. Far from supplementing Marxist theory, and thereby strengthening it, he has done more than anyone else to provide a route for theorists on the left to fellow-travel out of Marxism; and not only out of that, but out of materialism, out of science, and out of rationality at the same time. The main motive for this is doubtless political. If you go by its political effects in the twentieth century, then Marxism (it has been said) looks very like a machine for designing concentration camps. If you consider the confidence with which Communist parties, in France and elsewhere, have asserted their control over legitimate theory, then Communism looks like an intellectual concentration camp; and Theory looks like a by-product of political power, whose main function is to legitimate political power, and finally to provide an ideological justification of the concentration camps.

Foucault's work is in large part a libertarian reaction against this nightmare vision; but one that remains trapped within the nightmare. He never adopted the notion of a free market in ideas, in which truth wins out because it is a more reliable product, with lower human costs in the long run. Indeed, this concept seems to be largely unintelligible within the intellectual tradition we are considering. Instead, we might say, in a kind of shorthand, that Foucault began by moving backward in intellectual history from Marx to Hegel. He developed – in books like *The Order of Things* and *The Archaeology of Knowledge* – the notion of an **episteme**, as it were a positive unconscious of knowledge, for a given period and a particular group of disciplines (like, say, linguistics, economics and biology). The episteme in some sense controls the statements that can be made, on any side of a question, in the relevant disciplines. It is this insight that led to Foucault being labelled, for a time, as a structuralist. He appeared to be uncovering the necessary underlying structures in historical systems of ideas. And he was distinctly not reducing those systems of ideas to their supposed material determinants, as a good Marxist should.

Foucault's next move, as an epistemologist, was forward to Nietzsche. All his work, in a sense, had been given to tracing the genealogy of ideas; but now he found that there had always been in the stories he had told a subtle essence underlying both ideas and practices: something that was responsible for producing them both. That essence was power. But it was not a unitary power that could be reduced to better access to material resources, or to the hegemony of a dominant class. It was rather, a subtle being, a differentiated régime of power and knowledge in inextricable combination, present in all human and institutional affairs. And there are no independent truths to be found, outside this régime. Power-knowledge is what actually produces truth.

The point has not been noticed very widely; but this position is a transparently theological one. What is it that is omnipresent, and is so by being immanent in every human and institutional relationship; that is at once knowledge and power and that produces the only truths we can have? Why, Omnipotence, of course: the older name for which is God. There is possibly a personal nightmare here: perhaps of Foucault exposed forever to the pitiless vision of God, knowing and judging him. But to say this is not to evaluate Foucault's position as epistemology.

As epistemology it is very paradoxical. In normal usage, truth is a property of statements: namely the property of corresponding semantically with the fact they assert. The standard example is:

> The statement 'Snow is white' is true if and only if snow is white.

In principle, the truth of a statement does not depend on the person who makes it, or the occasion on which it is made; though of course there are indexical properties of utterances which affect the statements they are deemed to make. If I say 'It is raining.' I tacitly sign the statement and issue a date-stamp: I convey that it is raining here and now; and it is this statement which is true or false. But it is paradoxical to suggest that anybody short of God can have any power to make the statement true or untrue. The suggestion that it is my knowledge that it is raining that makes it rain is a very pure sort of idealism. The suggestion that it is 'power' that makes it rain is, literally, a belief in magic. So also (though the point is less obvious) is the suggestion that it is the power of the doctor that makes me ill, or the power of the statistician that creates population pressures.

It is however very easy to take Foucauldian theory, make two minor changes to it, and reinsert it into the hardest and most materialist form of Marxism. At the bottom end of the scale we can rescue the concept of 'power' from its status as a theological phantom, and give it its normal meaning of ability to do something oneself or to make someone else do it. We can then recognise – not as a matter of metaphysics but as a matter of fact – that power in this sense flows from control over material resources (including the resources of one's own body) or stored labour. Marxism is then restored as a causal theory (something that pleases me but that most Foucauldians definitely don't want).

We can then ask ourselves what it is, at the level of ideas, that is produced as an effect of power. Traditional Marxism says it is ideology; and distinguishes this from scientific truth. We can now see (perhaps with some bewilderment) that all Foucault has done is to make a terminological change. He has replaced the word 'ideology' with the word 'truth'. So long as this remains a purely terminological change, it is harmless enough; but as soon as we try to integrate it with the usual sense of 'truth' we produce the magical paradoxes described above. It is these paradoxes that produce the characteristic post-structuralist aporia, the sense of the ground disappearing beneath our feet, for which so many literary people these days have a strong taste. But traditional Marxism, retaining the distinction between ideology and truth, offers a far better, and far subtler, theory.

This terminological change is in fact a rhetorical device, adopted in order to give the concept of truth all the dependency, and all the relativism-to-power of the usual concept of ideology. No doubt this has a political purpose, and a very personal meaning for Foucault himself. It removes from him the nightmare whereby he might be judged, and those victims with whom he has identified might be judged, against the standard of an objective impersonal truth, and judged to be insane, or ill, or criminal, or sexually deviant.

But it also removes from us the possibility of appealing to a standard of truth against oppression under a false ideology. We can no longer, for example, claim that we are objectively not insane, or criminal, or ill, even if we are locked up under some such pretext because we are engaging in political resistance. If power makes truth, then we aren't engaging in political resistance if power says otherwise.

Foucault's actual politics were those of the Rainbow alliance: back the victim of power wherever he or she appears. It is a curious feature of Foucault's epistemology that the political and ethical position it goes best with is an utterly un-Foucauldian one: power-worship.

In 1982, in one of his last statements,[11] Foucault announced a second major change in his problematic. Right from the beginning, it appeared, he had been concerned not with the phenomena of power, but with the different modes by which human beings are made subjects. They are made subjects, it appears, by objectivising them. There are three ways of doing this: the way of the sciences, linguistics, economics, biology; the way of 'dividing practices': dividing the mad from the sane, the sick from the healthy, the criminals from the 'good boys'; and the ways in which we objectify ourselves: as for example, when we come to see ourselves as 'the subjects of sexuality'.

I think this statement should lead us to supplement rather than significantly change our analysis of the earlier work. It is not the first time Foucault had revalued the whole of his earlier work in the light of a new idea. 'What could I have been talking about but power', he wrote, on an earlier occasion, when it was perfectly clear he had been talking about classification. Power is now found to be something exercised by one subject over another; it is still not power to do something by oneself, nor power over things. Basically Foucault is still exploring the paranoid nightmares of subjectification/objectification: the fear of being classified as sexually deviant, or criminal, or sick, or mad, or indeed of being classified at all. (As a lifelong promiscuous homosexual he had rational grounds for this fear.) And he is still warding them off by the same method: of speaking exclusively about discourses and institutions, and bracketing the question of the reality of those phenomena which the discourses are supposed to be about, and to which the institutions are supposed to be an organised response. Behind this is the paranoid fear of discovering oneself to be an object; which is always the fundamental reason why people object to the sciences.

3   IS THERE A THEORY OF DISCOURSE?

The combined work of Althusser and Foucault has flowed into a very ill-defined object called discourse theory. I am not sure that discourse theory exists at all, even in the rather limited institutional sense in which semiotics exists.[12] In my terms, I am not sure it makes any coherent claims. In Althusser's terms, I am not sure it has an object of its own.

The concept of discourse theory is at least three ways ambiguous. It might be meant as a theory of the use of language – i.e. it might correspond, in Saussurean terms, to a theory of *parole*, or in Chomsky's terms, to a theory of linguistic performance; or even, if we allow the field to broaden a bit to cover signs as well as language, to a theory of semiotic performance. Alternatively, on Foucauldian lines, it might mean something much narrower than that – a study of the practices, and the rules governing acceptable statements, in various specialised disciplines at particular periods. Finally it might mean something far broader, deeper and more important than either of these – a study of the common assumptions which define whole cultures, and which are presumably stored in some verbal form; assumptions which actually constitute subjectivity itself. In this sense it would occupy the same logical space as an anthropologist's theory of culture; or Lacan's theory of the symbolic; or Althusser's concept of ideology.

Cutting across this three-way ambiguity is a distinction of a different kind, which is related to Marxist politics. The above accounts are, after all, neutral between political positions; but the whole point of discourse theory, for some who practise it, is to wage class war. They want, like Barthes, only much more aggressively, to examine selected discourses in order to dismantle bourgeois assumptions about the world and install their own. They see the state ideological apparatuses not as explanatory hypotheses but as sites for class conflict. On this view, to install discourse theory in the English syllabus is a step – one doesn't need to think it more than a small step – towards changing the economic structure of society. There is a strange continuity-in-difference here, that joins the Marxist with his old closest opponent. People used to taunt the Leavisite with thinking that civilisation could be saved by close reading. With no less fairness, one could charge the discourse theorist with thinking that capitalism can be smashed by a commentary.

Of course, that is a philistine way of putting it. Here is Michel Pêcheux, explaining what is really involved:

> This aspect of the 'political' practice of a new type constituted by
> Marxism–Leninism aims to transform the configuration of the 'complex of
> ideological state apparatuses' such that in the contradictory relationship of the
> reproduction/transformation of the relations of production, transformation
> predominates over reproduction, by a 'reversal-rearrangement' of the
> relationships of unevenness-subordination which characterise the 'complex
> whole in dominance' of the ideological state apparatuses and ideological
> formations inherent in capitalist relations of production. (For example, the
> transformation of the relationship between education and politics evoked
> above, a transformation that involves both the relationships of subordination
> between different ISAs – the school, the family, trades union organisations,
> political parties – and the relationships which these apparatuses have with
> forms of practice and organisation not inscribed in the state apparatus.)[13]

I am not going to discuss discourse theory in detail; though perhaps it is unfair to use a passage like this as a tombstone under which to bury it.

Pécheux has read widely and doesn't always write like this. But it is useful to have an example of the kind of thing which I have earlier described as Althusserian 'intellectual terrorism'. A highly tendentious theory of the functioning of educational institutions is defended by employing language so complex that all one's intellectual energy is employed in decoding it; nothing is left over for criticising points of substance. A great deal of Althusserian writing – for example, most of the articles published in *Screen* in its most creative period – was like this, and, as we shall see in the next chapter, some elementary points went unquestioned as a result.

Discourse theory may not exist as a coherent explanatory theory of an ordinary materialist kind; but it has been very influential in post-structuralist contexts in at least two important ways. It is characteristic of the work of Foucault, and of the later Althusserians, to discuss discursive effects while bracketing, or setting to one side, the question of reference to an independently real world; to talk as if, in Derrida's terms 'there is no outside-text' or no 'transcendental signified', and as if human knowledge is a purely discursive effect. It is a characteristic feature of the work of Lacan, and those influenced by him, to talk of the ego not as in Freud, as an aspect of the self specialised to deal with outer reality, but as something misrecognised as the self; and to talk of subjectivity as an effect, rather than a cause of discourse. For those who take both these lines, the result is a world actually composed of discourse, in which the objects we talk about, and the subjects who talk, are both the more or less illusory effects of discourse.

On the face of it this is simply a rather pedantic reversal of a commonplace, to achieve an interesting paradox. The standard view is that discourses have the features they have, because they are produced by subjects (minds) and are about objects (things). The new view is that subjects and objects alike are the effects of discourse. Why should anyone believe this? Why, in particular, should literary intellectuals believe this? (Very few other people do.) There is one situation in which we are presented with discourses that are not produced by the subjects to whom they are ascribed, and do not refer to the objects to which they purport to make reference. This is the case of fiction. In this case, as in life, we infer the character of a speaker from the dialogue (s)he is given, and of objects from the narrative that describes them; but here the character and the object alike have no existence save in our inference. All the post-structuralist is doing is to extend to life what is a commonplace property of fiction. In effect, the post-structuralist is treating reality as a fiction. There is a certain psychological truth in this – we do construct our picture of the world as a story that will make sense of our perceptions in the light of our beliefs. But the post-structuralist wants to make a psychological theory into an ontological one, and say that the world and the self are discursively constructed. I call this position **discursive idealism**.[14]

4   THE COMING OF THEORY AND STRUCTURALISM

It is useful at this point to place Althusser and Foucault within the larger intellectual movements of the period. Continental literary theory began to be imported into Britain at the end of the 1960s; it went largely under the rather confusing name 'structuralism'.[15] Structuralism, properly speaking, is the name of a theoretical model in the science of linguistics, derived from the work of Saussure and several others. This model dominated linguistics from roughly the 1920s to the 1960s, when it was superseded by more sophisticated theories: in particular, by Chomsky's generative grammar. It was adapted as a theoretical model in literary studies in Prague in the late 1920s and flourished throughout the 1930s; Prague School structuralism was the true successor to Russian Formalism which had been crushed in its own country.

Claude Lévi-Strauss heard about structural linguistics from Roman Jakobson in New York in 1942; and adapted it as a model for anthropology in the mid-1940s. So structuralism, far from being a French invention, reached France rather late, and was slow to develop. Jacques Lacan, influenced by Lévi-Strauss, started borrowing some terminology from Saussure in 1953. But by the 1960s, just as the model had been superseded in linguistics (!), structuralism had become a Parisian craze; there were varieties of it in everything from mathematics to Piagetian developmental psychology to Barthesian semiology, and Althusser and Foucault were also tagged structuralists. It had, in the popular eye, superseded phenomenology and existentialism as a putative general framework for the human sciences: indeed, as the beginnings of an era of precise scientific theory in the human sciences.

This did not last. Already in the mid-1960s a powerful philosophical reaction was occurring. The plain truth was that very few people wanted a precise scientific theory in the humanities. Graduate students in particular, who lived through the period in 1968 when imagination took power, and lost, were highly unsympathetic both to scientific Marxism (which seemed to be the theory behind the Gulag) and bourgeois social science (which seemed to be the theory behind the Vietnam war). They were therefore very ready to be receptive to what seemed like powerful philosophical arguments that showed no such scientific theories of human culture to be possible. This is the situation in which the ambiguous rhetorics of Lacan, of Foucault, of Derrida, of the later Barthes, of Kristeva, of Deleuze and Guattari, of Baudrillard, and of Lyotard swept the intellectual field.

The popular name for this movement was post-structuralism. But it might just as well have been post-phenomenology, post-existentialism, post-Freudianism, or of course post-Marxism. The common feature of 'post-structuralist' writings, whichever of these disciplines they were founded upon, was to try to extend that discipline – often by looking for just those points which had been systematically excluded when the discipline was set up – to the point where the discipline seemed to undermine itself and reverse itself. Thus the usual post-structuralist idea that the subject is an effect of discourse is a reversal of an older common-sense notion in phenomenology and existentialism that the subject is the source and origin of discourse. Jean Baudrillard performs a similar reversal on Marxist materialism. Setting out in 1968 to supplement Marxist theories of production by a theory of consumption – of consumer objects that act as signs structuring the world – he develops by 1973 a theory that replaces Marxism, in which all political economy rests upon the sign.[16] Allowing for the fact that 'the sign' is the term this school of philosophers employs when it wants to talk about what German idealism would call the idea or the concept, it will be seen that Baudrillard has actually reversed the founding gesture of Marxist materialism, and reinstalled a slightly pre-Feuerbachian variety of left-Hegelianism.

There was some justification for the various post-structuralist critiques. Structuralism, when it was the Parisian vogue, had produced numerous 'scientific programmes' in the human sciences where the science was entirely metaphorical. Indeed I would say myself that there has never been any genuine scientific structuralism except in linguistics from 1916 till 1953, when the model was mathematically refuted.[17] But post-structuralism was much more than a movement of healthy scepticism and a critique of pseudo-sciences. It had a profoundly anti-rational side, which comes out at times in a dazzlingly paradoxical rhetoric; and sometimes, as Pêcheux acknowledged, as a kind of constitutive facetiousness. It must never be forgotten that the great works of post-structuralism – *S/Z*, *Of Grammatology*, *Anti-Oedipus* – are constituted around jokes. And although the objects of those jokes – structuralism, semiology and Lacanian theory – certainly deserved the implicit criticism, there was, always, associated with post-structuralism the deep desire that science – certainly, the kind of science that operates in the area of the humanities, like anthropology or linguistics – should not be possible.

Hence writers like Foucault and Baudrillard draw on Nietzsche – the greatest of all philosophical opponents of science and of the idea of 'truth' – and deny the validity of standard philosophical distinctions such as that between sign and referent.[18] And by 1979, Jean-François Lyotard, a philosopher who was a considerable Kantian, had reached the startling conclusion that the enlightenment project was over: there may be reasons (different ethical and political projects, different sciences) that we can think about, but there is no such thing as Reason to unify them all.[19]. Lyotard cannot be dismissed as a left-Hegelian: his work is a quite explicit return to a critical analysis of Kant.

What was imported into Anglo-America, under the name 'structuralism', was thus an ambiguous mixture of total opposites, of structuralism and post-structuralism, of an attempt to put literary criticism on a strictly scientific, linguistic basis, and of an attempt to show that no such basis is possible; that any such attempt leads to insoluble aporias and paradoxes. In the first instance, the constructive tendency dominated. English and American books gave their accounts of Saussure, of Propp's morphology of the folk tale, of Russian Formalism, of Structuralism. One of the best of these was Fredric Jameson 1972, *The Prison House of Language*: Jameson is aware of the doubleness of his heritage. Another fine book, Jonathan Culler 1975, *Structuralist Poetics*, actually adopted an up-to-date model of language, and proposed the notion of **literary competence** (analogous to Chomsky's **linguistic competence**).

But in due time the negative, and at times anti-rational, current took over. The over-bold structuralist project died (though I am glad to say that something very like it in spirit persists outside literary theory in modern linguistics, cognitive psychology and artificial intelligence studies). In the United States Derridean and DeManian textual mysticism overtook New Criticism as an orthodoxy and Jonathan Culler abandoned his own theory and joined the deconstructive party. The British response was much more political. For a long time there was an attempt to harness the wild rhetorical energies of post-structuralism to political revolution – specifically, to creating a revolutionary consciousness. The empiricist and culturalist New Left of Raymond Williams gave way to the Althusserian and theoreticist new left of *New Left Review* after Perry Anderson took it over; and to the Althusserian and Lacanian new left of *Screen*. Between them, these took what took itself to be Marxist theory to unheard of levels of idealist sophistication. In Paris, however, the party was over; and the exhausted French were beginning to tidy Marxism away.

NOTES

1. Jackson 1991, *The Poverty of Structuralism*, Chapter 3, section 2; Coward and Ellis 1977, *Language and Materialism*; Easthope 1988, *British Post-Structuralism since 1968*.
2. Kolakowki 1978, vol. III; Thompson 1978, *The Poverty of Theory*.
3. Althusser 1965, pp. 27–8.
4. Thompson 1978, *The Poverty of Theory*; Anderson 1980, *Arguments within English Marxism*.
5. Althusser 1964 in Althusser 1970, *Lenin and Philosophy*, and 1984, *Essays on Ideology*; Lacan 1953, in Lacan 1977, *Ecrits*; Jackson 1991, *The Poverty of Structuralism*, Chapter 3; Jackson, forthcoming, *Making Freud Unscientific*.
6. In *Beyond the Fringe*. A satirical review by a brilliant group of Cambridge graduates in the early 1960s (London: Methuen 1983).
7. Althusser 1970, *Lenin and Philosophy*.
8. It is of course true that the illusion of smooth movement depends on persistence of vision in the observer. But the picture is real enough; you can photograph it.
9. Many would describe him as a Leibnizian rationalist; I don't feel competent to comment on this. See also Norris 1991 *Spinoza and the Origins of Modern Critical Theory*, for a relation to Spinoza.
10. Althusser 1984, p. 51.
11. Michel Foucault 1982, 'Afterword: the Subject and Power', in Dreyfus and Rabinow 1982, *Michel Foucault: Beyond Structuralism and Hermeneutics*.
12. For the question of whether semiotics exists, see Jackson 1991, *The Poverty of Structuralism*, pp. 245–8.
13. Michel Pécheux 1975, *Language, Semantics and Ideology: Stating the Obvious*. This is a strange combination of genuine learning, pretentiousness, and a facetiousness which is no doubt derived from the post-structuralist environment in which it was written. For a serious defence of discourse theory, see Diane Macdonell 1986, *Theories of Discourse*. Macdonell is, however, unreliable on linguistics; cf. Jackson 1991, *The Poverty of Structuralism*, pp. 57–8. This weakens her arguments.
14. See Jackson 1991, *The Poverty of Structuralism*, Chapter 6 for discussion.
15. The account of structuralism I give here is sketchy in the extreme. I have told the proper story in my previous book, Jackson 1991, *The Poverty of Structuralism*.
16. Jean Baudrillard 1968, *The System of Objects*; 1970, *Consumer Society*; 1972, *For a Critique of the Political Economy of the Sign*; 1973, *The Mirror of Production*. Selections from these in Baudrillard 1988, ed. Mark Poster.
17. See Jackson 1991, *The Poverty of Structuralism*, for extensive discussion.
18. Baudrillard 1979, *On Seduction*.
19. Lyotard 1988, Interview with Reijen and Veerman, in Featherstone (ed.) 1988.

BOOKS

Louis Althusser 1965 *For Marx.*
  1970 *Lenin and Philosophy.*
  1978 'The Crisis of Marxism' in *Marxism Today.*
  1984 *Essays on Ideology.*
  1990 *Philosophy and the Spontaneous Philosophy of the Scientists.*
Louis Althusser and **Etienne Balibar** 1968 *Reading Capital.*
Michel Foucault 1961 *Madness and Civilisation.*
  1963 *The Birth of the Clinic.*
  1966 *The Order of Things.*
  1969 *The Archaeology of Knowledge.*
  1975 *Discipline and Punish.*
  1980 *Power/Knowledge* (Interviews).
  1984 *The Foucault Reader.*
  1989 *Foucault Live* (Interviews).
M. Pécheux 1975 *Language, Semantics and Ideology: Stating the Obvious.*
Trevor Pateman 1983 'Review of Pécheux 1975', *Journal of Linguistics*, XIX, 2.
Rosalind Coward and **John Ellis** 1977 *Language and Materialism.*
Vincent Descombes 1979 *Modern French Philosophy.*
Kate Soper 1986 *Humanism and Anti-Humanism.*
Peter Dews 1987 *Logics of Disintegration.*
Alex Callinicos 1982 *Is There a Future for Marxism?*
Ted Benton 1984 *The Rise and Fall of Structural Marxism.*
Gregory Elliott 1987 *Althusser: the Detour of Theory.*
Mark Cousins and **Athar Hussain** 1984 *Michel Foucault.*
Mike Gane (ed.) 1986 *Towards a Critique of Foucault.*
David Hoy (ed.) 1986 *Foucault: A Critical Reader.*
Alan Sheridan 1980 *Foucault: The Will to Truth.*
Diane Macdonell 1986 *Theories of Discourse.*
Michele Barrett 1991 *The Politics of Truth: from Marx to Foucault.*
Leonard Jackson 1991 *The Poverty of Structuralism.*

CHAPTER NINE

The Rejection of Literature

From Raymond Williams to the English Althusserians

SUMMARY

Radical theory in the last thirty years in Britain can be seen from two different points of view. From one point of view it has provided the most sophisticated development of Marxist cultural theory that the world has ever seen, casting doubt on the very existence of literature as a Marxist category of analysis, drawing upon an extraordinary variety of philosophies to extend the Marxist model, and in the end transcending the limitations of Marxism itself.[1] From another point of view one would say that the last thirty years have seen the final apotheosis and evaporation of Marxism, as it cut loose completely from its economic and even its historical base: literary and cultural theory have offered a fine vantage point to watch this process of phosphorescent decay,[2] and post-structuralist and post-modernist philosophy have provided a rationale for accepting it.

It is in these years that there has been the most thoroughgoing replacement of economic politics by cultural politics, and of a materialist notion – that the world has a brute material existence and can be changed only by physical labour – by an idealist notion – that the world is constructed by discursive, meaning-giving processes which form human subjectivity, and can be changed by changing these processes, and therefore changing human subjectivity. It is in these years that it has been explicitly denied that the actual content of history has either theoretical or political importance; that we have had a movement called 'cultural materialism' where the chief theoretical concern has been to get away from 'the base-superstructure metaphor' (i.e. from materialism); and that a theory of the subject-positions offered by texts has attracted more interest than studies of class-relations and economic forces. It is in this period that we have had a replacement of the politics of class by that of ethnicity, gender, etc.; a replacement of putative working-class mass movements by the micro-politics of local opposition-to-power in various forms, and by a putative rainbow alliance of disparate oppositional groups.

It is natural that such a politics should culminate in bold proposals to seize the commanding heights of the English Departments and to make a revolutionary change in the syllabuses. In the new departments of cultural studies or political rhetoric both classical (economistic) Marxism and classic literature will disappear; probably finding their true Hegelian sublation in courses in media studies without significant political content.

1   THE LAST THIRTY YEARS ON THE LEFT

When the great revival in Marxist theories of literature began, in the late 1960s, nobody could have guessed its paradoxical outcome: that in the 1970s Marxists would have ceased to believe in the existence of Literature; and in the 1980s they would have ceased to believe in Marxism. Nobody would have guessed that, in the 1990s, there would be no Marxist theory of literature; that the whole problematic would be displaced. What we have now is a post-Marxist account of texts, or discourse, or ideological institutions, and the formation of the subject. This chapter traces some of the steps – in the work of Raymond Williams and the English Althusserians – towards this consummation.

These developments in cultural theory can be mapped onto the development of what was once called the New Left. The first phase of the New Left began about 1956, at the time when the Soviet invasion of Hungary made the British Communist Party intolerable even to some who had been in it in the worst days of Stalin. It was an attempt to open up a space for radical thought that was neither orthodox Communist nor parliamentary Labour. It was associated with the journals *New Reasoner* and *Universities and Left Review*, later amalgamated as *New Left Review*. Its concerns are set out very clearly in a book E.P. Thompson edited in 1960: *Out of Apathy*.[3] It looked for a democratic socialist revolution that was very different from the Russian one. It rejected affluence as a goal for society, almost as strongly as it rejected NATO and the bomb.[4] It attacked the conservatism and pseudo-objectivity of contemporary human sciences, and called for a new radicalism of the intelligentsia, based on Hegel's conception of the role of the intellectual.[5] This left-Hegelian or

Polytechnic intelligentsia was shortly to emerge. Culturally the first New Left looked back to the radical elements in the English tradition: to William Morris's, for example.[6] Its great enterprise was to rescue English culture and English history from their age-old appropriation by the upper classes. Its classic achievements were to be Raymond Williams's *Culture and Society* and *The Long Revolution*, and E.P. Thompson's *The Making of the English Working Class*. It showed little grasp of economics.

The New Left no sooner got going, than it had a palace revolution. The young Perry Anderson took over *New Left Review* in 1962 and started draconian doctrinal reforms. The second New Left had little time for the English left-wing tradition. It contemptuously rejected 'English empiricism' and much of the cultural baggage (Lawrence, Orwell . . .) which the first had been ambivalent about. It hated 'Englishness'. It set itself to import sophisticated theories of all kinds from the Continent.[7] An endless, unsaturatable market developed for these, as the new universities and the polytechnics produced the new left-wing intelligentsia that had been looked for. Vast numbers of academic books were produced for the new or expanded sociology departments. In the area of culture, most of these were on the sophisticated left. Already by 1968, a culture of the academy had developed that was ready to welcome the French revolution; this seemed like a practical culmination of the excitement of French theory. A whole generation was radicalised by the short bright promise of Paris, 1968. After it failed, for years (till hope died), there were academics who thought of themselves as trying to develop a revolutionary consciousness, that might prepare for the social revolution that would surely come.

For many literary theorists now living, the high point of British Marxism came between 1968 and 1974.[8] Partly this is a question of political hopes. At the beginning of this period in France, a vast general strike and a student rebellion nearly toppled de Gaulle's government; the British had their heady moments too, in the London School of Economics and (who now remembers it?) the Hornsey College of Art; and Raymond Williams, Stuart Hall and a little group of associates, brought out the *May Day Manifesto*.[9] At the end of this period, a British Conservative government was brought down, through its failure to handle a miners' strike. In between, a rush of French theory was imported, some of it newly developed in the aftermath of the 1968 revolutions; and this theory included what seemed to be the most sophisticated version of Marxism ever known. Althusserian Marxism was thought for a time to provide a kind of binding cement for many structuralist and post-structuralist positions, making them part of a new and comprehensive Marxism.[10] Though Althusserianism has gone, and seems ludicrous now,[11] its mark on British literary theory was permanent. These were the years in which British Empiricism was banished for ever and replaced by Theory. And these were the years when that change seemed to matter, because the promise of Althusser seemed almost plausible: the junction between Theory and the Workers' Movement was to be the greatest event in class society – in all human history to date. Theory then was the propaedeutic to social revolution.

Looking back on it now, that hope seems naive, or worse. The men of 1968 have very often been successful in their personal careers. But none of their political hopes have been achieved. It is clear now that we ought to have taken seriously the way that the young Marx and Engels, at the beginning of *The German Ideology*, denounced the Left-Hegelians, and their revolutions-in-the-head. All the achievements of the cultural left in the last twenty years have been left-Hegelian revolutions in the head. The left has achieved total victory in cultural studies. The traditional concerns of the right – patriotism, Christianity, moral value, tradition, and literary standards – exist now only as objects of commentary, never as serious positions from which to speak. The traditional position of the centre – liberal humanism (which I suppose I myself occupy) – comes to be seen as a far right position (!), designed to occlude the realities of class, race and gender, and something to expose, not to speak from. There simply is no sophisticated account of cultural studies that is not left-wing.

It is an astonishing triumph for the intellectual left; and if one holds that the development of a revolutionary consciousness is a step towards revolution, then it is hard to see why we seem to be so much less near social revolution than we were in 1968, or, indeed, 1945. What has happened in the non-academic world, while we have all been talking?

For two decades it has seemed as if every ideological advance by the left either accompanied, or by some process of reaction brought about, permanent material and political gains for the right. The miners' strike brought the fall of the Conservative government of Edward Heath; and this led to a mildly reformist Labour government, first under Wilson, then Callaghan, which ended by making a fairly successful attempt to lower inflation by way of an incomes policy. That 'success' was intolerable to the left in the Labour Party and the trade union movement; and so that government too was 'brought down by a workers' movement'; that is to say, Callaghan lost the election of 1979 because there had been a winter of industrial discontent which the Conservative leader, Margaret Thatcher, could exploit. But all that happened was the election of a Conservative government which is still in power to this day (1993). Indeed, Mrs Thatcher herself would still be in power, if she had not lost the confidence of her own party. Out of power, the Labour Party was taken over by its left, and split. The partial and temporary ideological victory that the left had won led to the extinction of the Labour Party as a political force.

In the broader world, NATO and affluence[12] won. The conservative politicians Ronald Reagan and Margaret Thatcher, working, as Marx would perhaps have recommended, by economic means, won the Cold War without fighting, and the Soviet Union disintegrated, regretted by few of its citizens. The relevance of this to our concerns is not that any significant part of the New Left has ever supported the Soviet Union, or thought it socialist. The point is, rather, that the political consensus of the world in general and of the United Kingdom in particular has moved towards the right. If this is so, then thirty years of cultural politics, almost all of it relentlessly left-wing, from the early work of Raymond Williams through the Althusserian rigour of the 1970s to the current publications of Verso, must be accounted a complete failure. We would all have been much better off developing the Leavisite critique of technologico-Benthamism and voting Liberal – or possibly Social Democrat.

The conjunction of Marxist theory and the Workers' Movement never came about. What did happen was the conjunction of Marxist theory and post-structuralism, in which Marxism was decisively changed into an idealist system of thought. Anthony Easthope puts it succinctly: Marxism 'is the parent culture onto which post-structuralism became grafted'.[13] Looking back on that moment, from the heights of left post-structuralism in 1988, this historian of British post-structuralism concedes that the Althusserian texts were 'contaminated with idealism'. But he gives an extraordinary account of idealism. Althusser is an idealist because he still sees mode of production as real, and ideology and politics as appearance; and because he thinks the reality of mode of production is given 'prior to its discursive construction'.[14] What is interesting about this is that these two features are very close to Marx's position in the 1859 *Preface*; and their 'idealism' is very much what Marx thought of as defining his own materialism!

It looks then as if the influence of post-structuralism has brought about a major philosophical change in the bases of 'Marxism'. Roughly speaking, materialism and idealism have changed places. What once made Marxism count as materialist – namely, the causal priority of the economic level over the political, legal and ideological levels, and the reality of production, labour, etc., independently of any ideological theories about them – now counts as idealist. And what would once have been idealism – even specifically Hegelian idealism – namely, the idea that the entities with which Marxists are concerned are constructed in discourse – now counts as materialism. I don't think Easthope is unrepresentative here. Indeed, in this chapter I shall avoid quoting anybody who I think is unrepresentative. I think he represents a majority movement. It is indeed that movement – to reject the traditional materialist bases of Marxism and to reformulate it on a post-structuralist and idealist basis – which I have christened 'the dematerialisation of Karl Marx'; and which gives the title to this book.

It is no doubt coincidence that the dematerialisation of Karl Marx in this specific technical sense should coincide with his dematerialisation in a larger sense – namely the disappearance of most of the régimes that called themselves Marxist throughout the world, and the collapse of many Communist parties elsewhere. Certainly I had no thought when I chose my title that it would take on so extended a meaning!

2   TRADITION, MARXISM AND CULTURAL MATERIALISM IN THE WORK OF RAYMOND WILLIAMS

It was an outburst of genuine sentiment at the death of Raymond Williams in 1988 that informed us that we had had a great socialist theorist and critic living in our midst. What the Francophile left had said of him in his lifetime would often have suggested otherwise. In the radical 1970s he had been a museum specimen of British empiricism and reformist compromise; at best one of the old New Left, the author of a muddled heresy sometimes called culturalism; and justifiably superseded by the rigorously theoretical new New Left in its Althusserian phase. But Williams outlasted the vogue for Althusser. He stands now (1993) as the man who offered a socialist alternative within literary studies both to the élitist culturalism of Eliot and Leavis, and to the economistic Marxism of a Christopher Caudwell.

He has left behind him three distinct legacies: an alternative reading to that of Leavis of the high cultural tradition; a significant school of Marxist or post-Marxist critics who call themselves **cultural materialists**;[15] and a new academic subject called **cultural studies**. In his life, and in the account which follows, these three strands are necessarily interwoven.

211

2.1   The working-class boy and the high cultural tradition

Williams was a working-class scholarship boy, born in 1921, who came up to Cambridge from the Welsh border country; he interrupted his first degree studies by commanding tanks in the war – an experience which gave him considerable moral authority when he refused to fight in Korea. He went out of Cambridge again to teach in adult education for fifteen years; then came back to be a Cambridge don. This background was crucial to his personal vision and development. All his work shows a deep loyalty to his working-class origins, and his Welsh border origins; a desire to educate the working class, combined with a real respect for the culture it already has; and a conscientiously bloody-minded refusal to accept the superiority of middle-class Cambridge English social standards. Although he was a Communist Party member as an undergraduate, his socialism is actually rooted in this complex of experience, and has nothing to do with theoretical Marxism. He finally accepted Marxism only towards the end of his life, and then only in a diluted, non-economistic form.

He is in this, as in other ways, the very opposite of Georg Lukács, with whom (because they both approved of a kind of realist writing?) he has been compared. Lukács hated and despised the upper bourgeoisie from which he came, the class of his father the banker; and he built astonishing epistemological fantasies about a proletariat which he hardly knew. Williams admired his own class, and loved and admired his father the railway signalman. His life's work was to rescue the notion of culture from its appropriation by a small segment of the upper middle classes: to do justice to, and understand, the real culture of the people under the economic pressures that were upon them.[16] Williams never substituted theoretical diagrams for human reality; sometimes this was a theoretical weakness, and it certainly seemed so during the Althusserian terror.

Williams's first love was drama. Among his earliest works of criticism was *Drama from Ibsen to Eliot* (1952). This was later revised to *Drama from Ibsen to Brecht* (1968). The change is significant for Williams's political development. Behind both stands a passionate undergraduate love affair with Ibsen. Williams is here an example of something quite common which makes modern cultural materialists a little uncomfortable: that the most transformative experience of a working-class intellectual's life is often the encounter with one of the great bourgeois writers (or sometimes with a whole bourgeois genre); one probably needs to have some theory of intrinsic literary value to account for this.

But his greatest achievement must be to have provided a serious left-wing alternative to the Leavisite tradition in literary criticism.

Williams was never actually a student of Dr Leavis; nevertheless he became, as a graduate student directly after the Second World War, a left-wing Leavisite. His Workers' Educational Association teaching continued and developed the approach of Leavis and Denys Thompson's *Culture and Environment*, and this eventually produced his most famous books: *Culture and Society, 1780–1950* (1958), *The Long Revolution* (1961) and one that stands slightly by itself: the Penguin Special of 1962, *Communications*, with its analysis of the content of newspapers and even comics. These can be described in part as an attempt to prise the concept of culture out of the grasp of a class-based élite; and this can be seen either as a completion of a programme implicit in early Leavisite work or as opposition to Eliotic and late Leavisite orthodoxy. This work is not, however, literary criticism. It is the product of a decision to reject the framework of literary criticism as such, along with the primarily evaluative approach to high literature that is characteristic of literary criticism. The best classification is **cultural history and analysis**.

In *The English Novel from Dickens to Lawrence* (1970; delivered first as a course of lectures in Cambridge in the last days of Leavis there) he offered a counterblast to Leavis's *The Great Tradition* – which did not stop Williams being the nearest to an ally Leavis could find, in a university committee upon the novel syllabus. *The Country and the City* (1975) is equally a counterblast to the Leavisite conception of a lost organic society against which the modern world is to be judged. (His personal reaction to Leavis is given in the articles 'My Cambridge' and 'Seeing a Man Running' in the collection of essays and reviews, *What I Came to Say* (1988). It is a moderately admiring one.)

The Country and the City demolished the Leavisite idealisation of agriculture as the basis of healthy civilisation. The notion of an organic society of the past, now decayed, is shown to be a perpetually recurrent myth, that we can take back and back through the centuries with no ultimate time horizon. The organic society has always gone. But Williams goes beyond this: he reinserts the myth, represented in literature, into the actual social history from which it came, including in its last phases the remembered border society from which he, Williams, came. This is probably his best book. It doesn't give the same reasons as materialist anthropology for rejecting the myth of the agricultural golden age,[17] but it gives equally important ones.

2.2   *Raymond Williams and traditional scholarship*

Raymond Williams's books were histories of cultural conditions, key ideas and cultural forms, based on literary and other sources. Because of the developments that came out of them, it is tempting to see them as something formally original within the tradition of English studies as a whole; but this would be a mistake. The main thing original about Williams's approach was the left-wing point of view: though this was something particularly valuable when criticism was dominated by the reactionary positions of T.S. Eliot. It is tempting also to see the origins of his mix of critical and cultural analysis only within the *Scrutiny* group, in the work on education of Denys Thompson and more particularly in Q.D. Leavis's *Fiction and the Reading Public*; and this is reasonable. But there is another less revolutionary model.

Far from being a radical and forward-looking break from literary criticism, Williams's approach could be seen as a reversion to the accepted tradition of historical and cultural scholarship that had flourished before the critical revolution of the 1930s, and in fact quietly and massively continued throughout the noisy career of Leavis. Cultural and historical background studies were frequent in Victorian literature either as part of full-scale histories, or in essays (Macaulay, Carlyle, Froude, Morley, etc.) They are commonplace in twentieth-century academic study of English; e.g. C.S. Lewis: *The Allegory of Love, The Discarded Image*. The most famous of all, which is still in regular use nation-wide, is by Leavis's enemy, E.M.W. Tillyard: *The Elizabethan World Picture*. Tillyard was Williams's tutor in English before Williams was called up in the Second World War.

But the closest parallel is in the work of Basil Willey, who became lecturer in the English School at Cambridge in 1923, and Professor in 1946. His lecture courses were published in 1934, 1939 and 1949: *The Seventeenth-Century Background, The Eighteenth-Century Background*, and *Nineteenth Century Studies: Coleridge to Matthew Arnold*. In the extended interviews in *Politics and Letters*, Williams casually acknowledges the existence of Willey's work; of course he knew it; everybody did. But he doesn't treat it as an important source or influence. There is no suggestion here of any lack of originality in Williams; his grasp of the whole material side of culture is far greater. But in writers studied there is about 50 per cent overlap between Willey's work and *Culture and Society*; and any Cambridge man would have recognised Williams's work as similar in kind to Willey's.

We have to note then that Williams's left-Leavisite phase did not begin till he came back from the war; but his model of literary scholarship was available to him long before, and it came from the right, not the left. It is not an accident that Williams was appointed at Cambridge; he was doing a very Cambridge thing, and was in some ways a more typical Cambridge scholar than Leavis was. (He was also much better on syllabus committees.)

Another type of scholarship was, political stance apart, equally original and equally traditional. This was the historical study of word meanings. In *Culture and Society* Williams begins by listing a group of keywords: industry, democracy, class, art and culture, which encapsulate the ideas he is concerned with, and which he intends to clarify. These words are, however, only the tip of an iceberg; scores of keywords were accumulating in Williams's notebook, which the publishers would not let him put in. Eventually they made a book on their own: *Keywords* (1976), more than 100 words with their meanings as they changed over time, elucidated with all Williams's historical scholarship and with some aid from *The New English Dictionary on Historical Principles (The Oxford English Dictionary)*. This is in the tradition of William Empson's *The Meaning of Complex Words* (1952), and C.S. Lewis's *Studies in Words* (1960), though the politics is different from either.[18] The three entries under **B** give the flavour: Behaviour, Bourgeois and Bureaucracy. The conceptual roots of the whole modern world lie there. Significant for the future of our subject is the lengthy entry on **literature**.

These verbal studies are interesting and valuable, but there is a methodological worry about them. Words and word-meanings treated in this way are like dead butterflies: essentially specimens for a collection. They give an interesting insight into ideas of the past, or the present; but they are no substitute either for original literary texts, or for comprehensive scientific or philosophical theories. Words in a poem are living: they take on their full meaning from a context of imagined utterance, in an imagined society. Raymond Williams is a competent critic, and knows about that. But words in a theory are, in intention, precise and technical; they too take on their meaning from something wider, but it is the logical and empirical articulation of the theory as a whole. There is no evidence that Williams had any understanding whatever of natural science or abstract philosophy, or the least sympathy with this technical way of using language. Indeed, his fundamental understanding of the way language works seemed to be close to that of Dr Leavis. His own technical terms – 'structure of feeling' for example, or 'knowable community' – were always context bound, transparent and natural in their own place, but difficult to fix and make permanent sense of in an abstract theory.

2.3 Raymond Williams and Marxist theory

This weakness led to disaster in his next book, *Marxism and Literature* (1977). The book is historically important, because it exhibits the moment when Williams became reconciled with Marxism, and says why; and from this book the Williams version of **cultural materialism** descends. Williams had rejected the Marxism of the 1930s, because of its mechanistic reductionism: that is, because it was viewed as a scientific theory in which superficial phenomena like human cultural activities were to be explained by deeper ones like the state of the forces and relations of production. Williams seems to have rejected this approach in much the same spirit as one would find in any Leavisite or indeed in any right-wing *littérateur*: not so much thinking the science wrong as reacting with total incomprehension to the very possibility of scientific explanation in this area. His comments in *Culture and Society* on Christopher Caudwell are the most blinkered and intellectually snobbish dismissal which that distinguished speculative thinker ever received ('. . . for the most part his discussion is not even specific enough to be wrong . . .').

Williams was, then, and always remained, utterly opposed to (though probably quite ignorant of) the important school in anthropology also known as **cultural materialism** which is discussed in the next chapter (Harris 1968, 1975, etc.). This school is based very precisely on the mature Marx–Engels view that political, legal and ideological phenomena are based upon, and are historically to be explained with reference to, the economic basis of society. The reason that he was able to accept Marxism in the seventies was that it was a different Marxism: it was what Perry Anderson and J.G. Merquior call Western Marxism (Anderson: *Considerations on Western Marxism*, 1976; Merquior: *Western Marxism*, 1986; see Chapter 7 above).

This Marxism, as we have seen, descends from the work of the early Marx of, for example, the *Economic and Philosophical Manuscripts of 1844*, a Marx still emerging from a left-wing version of Hegelian philosophy; the Marx whose *Theses on Feuerbach* laid the foundation for a philosophy of praxis. In this Marx the real foundation of society is not an arid conjunction of the forces of production and the relations of production, but the sensuous activities of living men. It is this Marx that Williams found easy to accept – the Hegelian Marx of the early Lukács, or the Marx of Gramsci – who had now been recovered or invented and at any rate imported (with his only serious opponent the unbelievably arid Marx of Althusser). This permitted Williams to take his own culturalism and rechristen it cultural materialism: what was materialist about it was of course that it was a study of material practices and cultural institutions. Not, heaven forfend, a study of the way all these – cultural forms and the practices that embody them – can be explained in economic terms. For Williams, the base-superstructure distinction was an illuminating metaphor, not a theory; and a metaphor that it was time to get away from.

But that is not the reason *Marxism and Literature* is a bad book. Very good theoretical works have been written about Western Marxism, which has been, from the beginning, a Marxism by academics – mostly professional philosophers – and for academics – often literary critics. The standard of exposition in Western Marxism is often unbelievably high. Williams's book is bad because of its method. As Dr Johnson pointed out, all things sink to questions of grammar when a grammarian addresses them. In Williams, Marxism sinks to a system of keywords. These words are present in all their ambiguity and variation; Williams's semantic scholarship does not flag. But of the varying theoretical systems that gave these words their senses there isn't a trace. It is as if a textbook on chemistry had been written by a lexicographer who had never managed to grasp the periodic table or understand the controversy over molecular orbital theory.

It is a symptom of the intellectual debility of the far left that, once the infatuation with Althusser was over, they accepted *Marxism and Literature* as a serious contribution to socialist theory.

Williams came to see it as his own essential method to reverse the procedures of formalism and put literature back into the social totality – which in his case was always a historically conceived social totality – in which it was formed. It is in the spirit of Western Marxism to see this procedure, rather than economic reductionism, as the essentially Marxist one, and it is only in this spirit that Williams can be seen as a Marxist, or indeed as a materialist. Whether this tolerant spirit was available to him at any particular point of his career depended very much on which form of Marxism was then in fashion. Possibly the most savage criticism Raymond Williams encountered during his lifetime came from a student and long-time admirer of his, Terry Eagleton, in *Criticism and Ideology* (pp. 21–42). There was much more to this savagery than a mere Oedipal attempt to overthrow an admired intellectual father, acknowledged as such within that very book. Eagleton was at that moment a passionate Althusserian, and arguing from the point of view of a rigorously theoretical Marxism. His rebuke of Williams was more than personal, it was generational, and representative. It had the whole weight of the second New Left, which had taken continental Theory on board, dismissing the first New Left, which had to make do with British empiricism (p. 34).

217

In an ironic twist, it was Williams who survived, and whose ideas are perhaps most fruitful now. Althusser's ideas had pretty well collapsed by the early 1980s; and I doubt if anybody now defends them – though, as I tried to demonstrate in the previous chapter, they have an enormous and malign effect in the epistemological underpinnings of literary theory. But the position they are tacitly used to support – that literature is a bourgeois category with which a Marxist need not be concerned – is not an Althusserian one. Half of it – as we shall see later in this chapter – comes from Williams.

2.4   The rise of cultural studies

Culture and Society, *The Long Revolution* and *Communications* turned out to be books of enormous academic importance: between them they helped open up a new academic discipline, **cultural studies**, which became and to some extent remains a competitor to academic English degrees, based as they are on evaluative literary criticism. Williams traced the origin of these works to his fifteen years in adult education; and in turn they provided the academic discipline needed to underpin the new liberal studies courses in technical colleges all over the country, as they developed at the beginning of the 1960s. Later on, in the 1970s, anyone involved in setting up one of the new communication and cultural studies courses in what became the Polytechnic system would find Williams presiding over half his concerns and Chomsky over the other half, with the Birmingham Centre for Contemporary Cultural Studies in the background. (These courses tended to be a mix of work on the media and work on linguistics, psychology, etc.)

Cultural studies is, and always has been, a difficult discipline to pin down. Although consistently left-wing, and often more or less Marxist, it from the beginning rejected the materialist notion that culture could be seen as a mere reflection or consequence of the economy. On the contrary, its initial impulse was to recover, even to celebrate, the creative culture of the working classes, in opposition to the élite culture that has been co-opted for Conservatism. Its first classics were Thompson's *The Making of the English Working Class*, the Williams books and Hoggart's *The Uses of Literacy*. Its first important institutional realisation was the Centre for Contemporary Cultural Studies, founded at Birmingham in 1964, and directed first by Hoggart, then, for the decade after 1969, by Stuart Hall, a former editor of *New Left Review*. It is tempting to see this change as another example of the replacement of the empiricist English New Left by the theoreticist Continentalising New New variety; but that would not be quite correct. *The Popular Arts* (1964), by Stuart Hall and Paddy Whannel, is quite untheoretical: an educational book in the left–Leavisite tradition. As time went by, Hall proved to be never less than a sceptical and rational Marxist, who wrestled with the new theory and would go only so far. As he put it in 1983,[19] 'Gramsci is where I stopped in the headlong rush into structuralism and theoreticism. At a certain point I stumbled over Gramsci, and I said: "Here and no further!"' Hall remains a central figure in cultural studies, and cannot be seen simply as a footnote to Williams.

Cultural studies progressed through Althusserian and Gramscian theoretical models, which are discussed later. Hall 1992 provides an account of its progress. Like most disciplines in this field, it has expanded enormously in recent years. A vast international conference – *Cultural Studies, Now and in the Future* – was held at Illinois in 1990, and the papers of this conference, collected as Grossberg, Nelson and Treichler 1992, are the best attempt I know to give an account of the subject. If I had to venture a characterisation I would say that cultural studies is a kind of popular left-wing anthropology, concentrating on the more superficial aspects of society, like the popular arts, rather than what is fundamental, like economic arrangements. But that would be to make a traditional Marxist judgement about what is superficial which the cultural studies specialist, like Williams before him, would repudiate. There is a whole dimension of this subject which is concerned with sophisticated theories of representation, and with the 'construction' of cultural identities. Many practitioners see the reality of society here, rather than in economics.[20] Some have moved philosophically to a nominally post-modernist position, in which the **theories** of Marx and Freud are seen as **narratives** – grand narratives whose time is now over, and perhaps part of a whole intellectual project whose time is now over.[21]

It is still possible that there will be a gradual transformation of literature degrees from the literary critical model to some cultural studies model. Easthope 1991 argues for this transformation. But something else strange (besides post-modernist idealism) is liable to happen in the development of these new courses. Williams's vision was essentially historical; his purpose was to take the whole tradition of English culture and appropriate it for socialism. Other scholars like Hall are fully historically aware, even if history is not their central inspiration. But the new courses are often quite unhistorical;[22] they lack a whole dimension. A student educated in them would unconsciously assume that the society of the present is the only one that has ever existed, and that the only alternative to present society would be a socialist transformation of present society. This makes socialism utopian. And these courses are not necessarily even socialist. They can become – and in the long term there is a strong economic pressure on them to become – a purely commercial preparation for work in the media. A traditional Leavisite English degree has far more ·radical bite than that, as well as far more historical depth.

3   A MARXIST 'SCIENCE' OF THE TEXT

Anyone active in Eng. Lit. in the late 1960s and 1970s would encounter the brilliant New Left critics who had taken on the job of importing foreign theory into provincial Britain. After a decade they had developed a characteristic double mannerism which combined an extreme, slavish humility toward the French, with a sadistic self-confident bullying of their elder British colleagues. Here is an example of the first characteristic:

> Any English Marxist who tries now to construct a materialist aesthetics must be painfully conscious of his inadequacies. It is not only that so many issues in this field are fraught and inconclusive, but that to intervene from England is almost automatically to disenfranchise oneself from debate. It is to feel acutely bereft of a tradition, as a tolerated house-guest of Europe, a precocious but parasitic alien.
>
> (Eagleton 1976, *Criticism and Ideology,* p. 7)

It is hard to believe that this is by a student, a colleague, and an admirer of the sturdily independent Raymond Williams. Indeed it is hard to believe that a passage like this is not ironical, since these are exactly the words one would like to have written, in order to be sarcastic about the French. But at this stage Althusser's Marxism was really seen as almost the final word in a majestic debate across the centuries, to which British Labourism had contributed much less than nothing.

There is a continuity-in-difference in this passage which reminds one of a much earlier theorist. It sounds uncommonly like T.S. Eliot when he was being supercilious about the lack of tradition in Blake.

> We have the same respect for Blake's philosophy (and perhaps for that of Samuel Butler) that we have for an ingenious piece of home-made furniture; we admire the man who has put it together out of the odds and ends about the house. England has produced a fair number of these resourceful Robinson Crusoes; but we are not really so remote from the Continent, or from our own past, as to be deprived of the advantages of culture if we wish them.
>
> (Eliot 1932, *Selected Essays*, p. 321)

It is amazing how this ancient voice from the far right captures the general tone of the new New Left in its dealings with the sturdy English Leavisites, or the homely English philosophers of language, or with a peasant like Raymond Williams. It is, in fact, though easily acquired by scholars of working-class origin, the tone of highly educated upper-class condescension. It says: 'Don't think for yourself; culture is already there; and culture is German or French.'[23] To this the literary left added a desperate desire for political orthodoxy, and a belief that their own orthodoxy was a new social science.

Thus in *Criticism and Ideology*, Williams was continually rebuked for his provincialism. Williams's worst offence was to keep on discovering for himself concepts that there either was, or was going to be, a proper Marxist word for: thus the proper word for 'structure of feeling' is ideology (p. 33). And to be uninterested, as Williams was aggressively uninterested, in Marxist doctrinal correctness came perilously close to anti-intellectualism (p. 33). One is glad to see that the left later came again to admire Williams as much as, once, Althusser: and to junk Althusser.

Nonetheless, they had, as we have seen, a perfectly good reason for rejecting Williams. Williams had, effectively, no theory of literature; indeed, he had a lifelong record of resistance to theory. He had tried to develop the existing traditions of literary and cultural analysis in a socialist sense. But he had made no epistemological break with them. What was needed (we were told in 1976) was to move to a new terrain altogether: the terrain of scientific theory. This seems ridiculous now, but did not then. There were significant parallels in other areas that had nothing to do with Marxism. In linguistics in the 1970s people felt, with some justification, that if you weren't doing the subject with the algebraic methods introduced by Chomsky, you weren't seriously doing it at all.[24] Some economists felt much the same about their mathematical methods. This was a period when empiricism was under justified attack in most academic fields, and abstract theory was at a premium. So it was a period when it was very easy to damn the literary critic's requirement of faithfulness to the actual experience of reading, as a form of 'empiricism'; and to offer to replace it by the most abstract and arid forms of Marxist 'science'.

Where the literary left were perhaps unfortunate was in the particular model of theory that they had. By post-structuralist standards, Althusser is a clear, consistent and modest writer; by any others, he is extraordinarily empty, paradoxical, and pretentious. If they had had any interest in any natural science whatever, they could hardly have accepted Althusser's model for a scientific theory: a Hegelian dance of abstract categories which magically produces a knowledge of its own object. They were by no means uncritical of Althusser himself; but it is on this basis that they tried to establish a science of criticism. As Eagleton put it, in *Criticism and Ideology* (perhaps the most ambitious of these attempts)[25]: 'The guarantor of a scientific criticism is the science of ideological formations' (p. 97).

The main claims of his version of scientific criticism were that we can distinguish a general mode of production and a literary mode of production; a general ideology, an aesthetic ideology, and an authorial ideology; and that these interact in immensely complex ways changing through time. In these theories, individual authors are seen as merely agents or bearers of such categories. It is possible to describe the history of literature in terms of this interaction, and Eagleton has, by the standards of Althusserian science, a good deal of empirical information to offer, in particular in his Chapter 4, which is a Marxist critical history of English literature from Arnold to Lawrence. His analysis is interesting and not always reductive. But of course he has no predictive theories to offer, and therefore no empirical science in the ordinary sense. This is not science but dogmatic political interpretation pretending to be science.

What makes this account sound like 'science' in Chapter 2 is a presentational feature. With his usual sharpness, and presumably inspired by the practice of referring to Althusser's 'ideological state apparatuses' as ISAs, Eagleton grasped the essential principle of constructing a scientific theory on Althusserian lines: abbreviation. So he abbreviates his main technical terms and speaks of the GMP and the LMP, of GI, AI, and AuI; and links his abbreviations together with Althusserian terms like overdetermination.

The result is one of the most densely initialled pieces of prose in English criticism:

> An LMP which is itself an amalgam of historically disparate elements may thus combine in contradictory unity disparate ideological elements of both GI and AI. A double-articulation GMP/GI–GI/AI/LMP is, for example, possible, whereby a GI category, when transformed by AI into an ideological component of an LMP, may then enter into conflict with the GMP social relations it exists to reproduce.[26]

This last sentence is, I gather, the scientific version of the claim that, while the general ideology of a society exists to support and reproduce the general mode of production, categories from it may be turned against that mode by the aesthetic ideology associated with the literary mode of production. This explains how romantic poets protest against an individualistic commercial society in the name of individualism.

Translated so, this is not actually a nonsensical or even paradoxical theory; and it is compatible with a much more orthodox economistic Marxism than one would think from the terminology. I had better make it clear that I have a great respect for the substantive things Eagleton has to say about the way these various modes of production and types of ideology have interacted in the course of literary history, and think his contribution to this history equal in interest to that of, say, Caudwell. But it is clear that this kind of writing is a parody of science; though it is surprisingly efficient as a form of labelling indicating political allegiance. It resembles science only in the way that Egyptian scarabs made for the tourist trade and covered with meaningless hieroglyphics resemble original scarabs. This did not matter to the new New Left, who knew no better. It resembled the prose style of a paper about DNA, rather than the prose style of Dr Leavis. This is what mattered.

It is easy to make fun here. But there is a serious issue about the place of formalism within literary theory which goes beyond the practice of any particular theorist. What **is** the difference between Chomsky's 'NP's and 'VP's, abbreviations which everybody would agree form part of a real formalisation of grammar with considerable empirical content, and Althusser's 'ISA's, or Eagleton's 'LMP's, which don't have that status? Unfortunately many sophisticated theorists at the very highest levels – including the great continental theorists whom we are being asked to admire, Lacan and Althusser – simply did not know enough science or mathematics to know what counts as a formalisation.

In Chomsky's work on language, or in physics or chemistry, or in any branch of applied mathematics, formal rules of combination are defined over the symbols used, which at one and the same time make empirical claims about the domain being described, and are capable of being manipulated by some well-defined algebraic rules to produce testable predictions. No such rules or predictions are provided in Eagleton or Althusser, and their formulations are accordingly empty. It must be said, however, that this is one stage better than the algebraic formulations in Lacan's *Ecrits*. Some of these look exactly like algebraic formulae but obey no known algebraic rules. It turns out that they have to be interpreted as rebuses – pictorial riddles! And this is presented as an important part of Lacan's theory, not as an example of the playfulness of the unconscious. It is this kind of sheer silliness that we must bear in mind when we are evaluating the extravagant claims for French theory made above.

The third chapter in *Criticism and Ideology* is called 'Towards a Science of the Text'; but in fact the empirical content disappears: this is French philosophy, with a radically metaphysical, and a radically metaphorical approach to epistemology. It begins by describing the text as a production of ideology, but the sense is now shifted from the ordinary sense, and ordinary Marxist sense, of production (the P in GMP) and becomes the 'production' of a play! This produces a characteristically post-structuralist reversal of causality, and pun. It is not that ideology causally produces texts, but that texts are a theatrical production of pre-existing ideology.

There are then five pages of metaphysical analysis of the production of plays. 'The production is not in this sense the soul of the text's corpse, nor is the converse relation true, that the text is the informing essence of the production. . . .' The rest of the chapter explores the relationship between the text, ideology, and history. It appears that ideology is a 'production' of history. The literary work is thus a 'production' to the second power, and partly cancels itself, to invert back into an analogue of knowledge, at least if it can be assisted with some judicious Marxist criticism (p. 85).

This seems to me a highly mystified version of a familiar position (see my Chapter 6 above): that to make a work of literature tell us about the class war, you have to perform two acts of interpretation using Marxist theory: one on the work itself, and one on the history within which it was produced. But of course that view rests on Marx's own materialist metaphysics – including the assumption that history is real – and reflectionist epistemology. It won't speak French.

It would be unfair to depart from this particular phase of British Althusserianism without giving an example of the criticism it could produce. This often managed to combine non-reductive complexity with crass provocation of humanists. Thus in Chapter 4 Eagleton argues that we should **not** reduce George Eliot's art to its ideology; the ideology is actually something signified by an amalgam of literary forms – pastoral, historical realism, fable, mythopoeic and didactic discourse. . . . Few humanists would disagree. But before this he says:

> The phrase 'George Eliot' signifies nothing more than the insertion of certain specific ideological determinations – Evangelical Christianity, rural organicism, incipient feminism, petty-bourgeois moralism – into a hegemonic ideological formation which is partly supported, partly embarrassed by their presence.

Humanists – from E.P. Thompson to the far right – feel indignant at the implication that (for scientific purposes) George Eliot is not a person. But the materialist objection to this claim is that it is in spirit entirely left-Hegelian, and is the type of discourse that was demolished by Marx and Engels at the beginning of *The German Ideology*.

4   ALTHUSSER, FILM THEORY AND THE THEORY OF THE SUBJECT

A far more exciting body of theory was being developed, in the early 1970s, by the group of Althusserians and semioticians who had managed to capture the commanding heights of *Screen*.[27] This was nothing less than a new theory of human subjectivity: a large project, one might think, for a film magazine. These critics were formalists, in so far as they were interested in the formal aspects of both film and literature; for this they used the new vocabulary of semiotics.[28] But they were also Marxists; so they wanted to show that these formal aspects had an ideological significance. Following Althusser's version of Lacan's psychoanalysis, they could find this ideological significance in the theory of the subject: an extraordinary place for a Marxist to find it.

The ordinary humanist believes that human discourses are produced by human subjects. The post-structuralist anti-humanist reverses this, and says that the human subject is called into existence – interpellated – by the practices that we call discourses. Such practices include films and novels; so the literary intellectual can study in these nothing less than the process of subject formation, or at least subject positioning; and perhaps can even work out ways in which we can advance the revolution by constructing revolutionary subjects.[29]

There can be no question here of bringing out the intricacies of an argument that went on for years, employed some of the most difficult of post-structuralist concepts, and was intensely difficult to follow at the time. I shall try both to simplify the argument and bring out a deep flaw in it, by dividing it into two questions: the question of the type of subjectivity implied for the ideal reader or viewer by the formal structures of a literary text or a film; and the question of the type of subjectivity present in actual people on more ordinary occasions.

In literary and film studies the notion of a **subject** which is **an effect of the text** can arise by the following simple argument. It is obvious that the dialogue in a play implies characters to speak it, and each of these has a different subjective view of the world, according to his position in it. It would be stupid to mistake each or any of these characters for the author. It is hardly less obvious that the narrator in a novel is also a kind of character, with his own implied subjectivity; and this is so whether that narrator is given a personal name or left anonymous. Formally and logically, the character of the narrator should never be identified with that of the author. The author is a real person; the narrator is like the characters in a drama – someone known only by inference from the text ascribed to him, and in that sense an effect of the text.

If we turn to film, we can make a further generalisation. There may well be no narrator, but there is a point of view, imposed by the use of the cameras. Once one considers the question, it is obvious that what both literary texts and films are doing, is to imply a certain point of view from which the story (say) is to be seen. They are, one might say, putting the viewer or reader or radio listener in a certain **subject position**. One might almost say they are creating a kind of artificial subject. So much, I think, is uncontroversial and not in the least post-structuralist; it is very much what any competent critic would have said in the 1950s; and something very like it was said by the Marxist critic Christopher Caudwell in the 1930s.

The controversial part comes when we move to real subjectivities – the real personal consciousnesses of actual people – and apply to them the principles developed by Lacan and Althusser. Common sense and most philosophers hold that the conscious mind produces discourses – i.e. in the ordinary causal sense, the subject is the cause of discourse. But we only know other minds – and perhaps we only know our own minds! – by the discourses they produce. Post-structuralists therefore reverse this and claim that the subject is an effect of discourse. Some Marxists are attracted by this reversed form because they feel it is more materialist; discourses are material, and minds ideal. (See Chapter 7 above for criticism of this position in the work of Vološinov.)

Non-post-structuralists of course would say that the subject is not an 'effect of discourse' but a hypothesis intended to account for discourse. They would say that it is precisely because, in the real world, subjects cause discourses, that, in the real world, when we hear a discourse we infer a subject behind it; and therefore, in fiction, one way of counterfeiting the existence of a subject is to construct a discourse. The post-structuralist position, on this analysis, is simply a standard idealist confusion between the causes that make something exist in reality, and the grounds for our knowledge that it exists.

Such a confusion could never have got off the ground without the aid of the psychoanalyst Jacques Lacan and the Marxist philosopher Louis Althusser. They approach these issues slightly differently. Lacan held (to oversimplify slightly) that the true subject is the subject of the unconscious; the ego is something constructed by that subject in what Lacan calls 'the imaginary', or phantasy, and is almost like a neurotic symptom. It is far from being, as Freud thought it, an essential structure for dealing with reality: it is a product of misrecognition and itself misrecognises the world. Lacan also said – this is the crucial point – that the unconscious is structured like a language because it is an effect of language. (The only real basis of this claim seems to be that the analyst infers the unconscious from what the patient says!)[30]

Althusser held that the subject is constructed in ideology by a process of interpellation – that is, by being called upon to answer in certain roles. Althusser's 'subject' seems to correspond roughly to Lacan's 'ego', and ideological misrecognition to Lacanian misrecognition; though they don't correspond exactly, and provide endless opportunities for learned confusion. What is common to all these 'subjects' and 'egos' is that they are not substantial entities: they are all inferred from the practices they engage in – in particular linguistic practices – and the discourses which interpellate them. In that sense those real-life 'subjects' who are our friends and neighbours are as much the effects of a text as are the characters or the narrator of a book. Joe Bloggs is the effect of all the numerous texts that have interpellated him in the course of his life. It is not merely that we infer him from those texts, as if he were a character in a book; he infers himself from those texts! Or more precisely, his existence as a subject arises from the way these texts write him.

Althusserian post-structuralism often adopted a kind of revolutionary left-Hegelian triumphalism over the human subject, which it claimed to have **decentred** and removed from the position of philosophical dominance it had had in Sartre or Husserl. One needs therefore to point out something very obvious. There is a great deal of difference between the subjectivity – that is, the total personality – of a real person, which is something that survives and develops throughout life, which is capable of responding, at the age of sixty, to some discourse it met at the age of ten, which is so incredibly tough and enduring that you can normally dissipate it only by physically destroying the body in which it operates; and the temporary illusion of partial consciousnesses which lasts while you read a book. To put it bluntly, a person who didn't remember who he was, and supposed herself to be the narrator of the last book they read, would be rapidly admitted for clinical observation.

If we are going to adopt this kind of terminology a great deal of work will have to be done to keep arguments about real subjectivities apart from arguments about fictional ones. Unfortunately the ambience of post-structuralist argument (with its predilection for puns, and for pretending to break down logical barriers) doesn't favour clarity. Again and again, arguments about the subjectivity implied by texts are treated as if they applied to the subjectivities of actual readers, or even of human beings in general.

Thus consider the most famous of all modernist texts, *Ulysses*. The wide range of styles and approaches in this text might be said to imply a multiple and complex subjectivity in the narrator/reader. If we may compare such a subjectivity with the boring unified bourgeois subject, we may well feel it is a revolutionary one. The modernist form of *Ulysses* thus becomes a revolutionary gesture because it tends to produce a revolutionary subjectivity.[31] By arguments of very much the same kind, the **expressive realism** of a nineteenth-century novelist like George Eliot can be made into a recuperative and indeed conservative gesture, independently of the content of her novels.[32]

The reservations I am implying here are not directed at the critical practice, in the strictly limited professional sense of the word, of a Colin MacCabe or a Catherine Belsey, or to their successors. Often these critics provide acute insights into the way the text manipulates its implicit reader, thrusting him/her into the most extraordinary subject positions. When the feminists happened along, they had no difficulty in finding characteristic ways in which a film may manipulate the spectator into the subjectivity of a man gazing from a position of dominance at a woman who is submitted to that gaze – a position of **dominant specularity** – even if the actual spectator is a woman, and she objects to such dominance/submission. (The James Bond films, with the active and lethal agent surrounded by a harem of pin-ups, are an obvious but unsubtle example of this.) Such approaches offer cultural analysis of great power.

One's reservations only arise when the post-structuralist foundations of this type of criticism encourage us to deny the difference between two types of subject, and three levels of reality, which we are concerned with here. The film, after all, is fiction; and the subject constructed by it in the mind of the viewer is also a fiction, which exists only as long as the master fiction which is creating it has to run.

(a) I view my James Bond film from my position of dominant specularity; but the 'subject' that is viewing is no more than a fiction that entered the mind of the real person who entered the cinema.

(b) If I go on, after the film is over, viewing real women in that way, that is the action of the real subject, which is unlikely to be performed if the real subject is a woman; and is unlikely to be a successful mating strategy if the real subject is a man.

(c) And if I think about the film, as a cultural object external to myself, I shall get an insight into another reality: the ideology of my own society. The work of art will act to give a distanced view of ideology, just as Althusser said it would.

To sum up, 'creating human subjects' is quite beyond the powers of a literary or filmic text, though no doubt it can make major temporary modifications to subjectivity, while the illusion lasts, and minor permanent ones.

5   THE ABOLITION OF LITERATURE AND MARXISM

One of the most frequent complaints of conventional critics in the 1970s was that the Althusserians seemed to want to abolish literature. This was not at first entirely true. As we have seen, the first impulse of the Althusscrians was not to abolish literature, but to formulate a 'scientific' theory of its relationship with the current mode of production. The second was not to abolish it, but to formulate a post-structuralist theory of its relationship with 'the subject'. But in due course the arguments for abolishing it prevailed. These arguments are set out most clearly, perhaps, in the short book by Tony Bennett called *Formalism and Marxism* (1979): a book whose odd treatment of Saussure I have already had occasion to criticise in *The Poverty of Structuralism*. Bennett drew his arguments from a wide range of theorists: from Saussure; from Raymond Williams; from Althusser; from the Russian Formalists and the early structuralism that developed out of their work; from Bakhtin and Vološinov; from Macherey.

What we mean by 'abolishing literature' is of course 'abolishing literature as a category of analysis'. Bennett and company were not intending to burn the works of Shakespeare. But they were intending to deny that the works of Homer, Virgil, Dante, Shakespeare, Milton, Wordsworth, Dickens and Joyce share any intrinsic quality of 'literariness' that justify grouping them together as literature and separating them from other non-literary writings of their own periods.[33] Of course if they have no intrinsic common defining qualities, then collecting them all together as 'literature' has been the work of the critics – in our own period, of bourgeois literary critics, who have created an imaginary set of universal human values which 'literature' from every period is supposed to exemplify.

Arguing against 'literature' thus becomes part of a larger, and very savage, 'Marxist' campaign against 'humanism' – a philosophy that was held to rest upon the assumption that there are universal and transhistorical human values, and a philosophy that was attributed to every opponent of Althusserian Marxism from reformist socialists to Christian anti-humanists like T.S. Eliot. The argument that 'literature' is a historically relative category is a literary counterpart to the argument of traditional Marxism that 'human nature' is a historically relative category, being, as Marx called it, the ensemble of the social relations (*Theses on Feuerbach*, VI). As Norman Geras was to show in 1983,[34] it is untrue that historical materialism is incompatible with the concept of human nature, or that Marx had no concept of human nature. But the very need for Geras's book showed how widespread the opposite position was in the 1970s.

There are two lines of argument against having a universal category of literature. The first is to show that the category of 'literature' in its customary modern meaning is a recent (nineteenth-century) historical invention. Hence anything written before that time can't be literature. Homer, Chaucer, Shakespeare and Milton were something else, and the bourgeoisie have reinterpreted them as literature. The second is to show that we don't even now have a clear category of literature – none of the obvious definitions will work. We can show this by trying each of them out in turn and providing snappy counter-examples – Eagleton does this, with incomparable brio, in *Literary Theory* (1983).

What sort of evidence will show that the category of 'literature' is a recent historical invention? What Bennett offers in 1979 is evidence of a change in the meaning of the word. He got this evidence from Raymond Williams 1977, *Marxism and Literature*. But Williams's main source was a document that was unrevolutionary in the extreme: it was the *Oxford English Dictionary*. Here are the relevant parts of the NED definition:

> 1. Acquaintance with letters or books; polite or human learning; literary culture.

This is given as an obsolescent sense. It goes back to 1375 (!) but is still the normal dictionary meaning in 1818. The last entry for it is 1880.

> 3. Literary production as a whole; the body of writings produced in a particular country or period, or in the world in general. Now also in a more restricted sense, applied to writing which has claim to consideration on the ground of beauty of form or emotional effect. . . .
> *This sense is of very recent emergence both in Eng. and Fr.*

The first example of this sense is given as 1812; astonishingly late. It is still our normal sense of the word, until the Althusserians get their way.

There is thus hard evidence of a shift in the meaning of the word 'literature' at the beginning of the nineteenth century. In *Keywords* Williams offers a discussion of a whole complex of semantic shifts around words associated with literature; in *Marxism and Literature* he argues that the categories of 'literature' and 'the aesthetic', so 'deeply implanted in modern culture', are 'historically specific: a formulation of bourgeois culture at a definite point of its development'. Bennett takes this position and runs with it. He is going to reserve the term 'literature'

> for the dominant forms of bourgeois writing as a historically limited category referring to a particular type of cultural practice. (Bennett 1979, p.16)

It follows immediately, as far as I can see, that the Homeric epics and classical Greek tragedies are not literature, despite having been falsely assimilated to the category of literature by critics in the bourgeois period. The Marxists of the 1980s will not make this mistake; they will view this work as a different type of cultural practice, specific to its own period. The same will presumably apply to the work of Dante, Shakespeare and

Milton. Strictly speaking nothing will count as literature until about the time of Shelley. This is a great deal to infer from a change in the meaning of words.

Our second line of argument is to show that none of the existing definitions of literature will work. Bennett does this for Russian formalism: I look at his argument later on. Eagleton rapidly disposes of the notion that literature is fiction, or specially heightened language, or self-referential language, by finding obvious counter-examples to each – cases which we would agree to be literature that don't satisfy the definition, or cases that we would deny to be literature that do.

These lines of argument seem to suffer from the Raymond Williams disease – they are purely verbal. They argue from the existence or non-existence of words to that of things. Bennett and other writers of this period are not unaware of this methodological problem; they constantly discuss it; they are conscious, and even proud, of the surprising positions on truth and representation that they have been pushed into by the influence of post-structuralism. They offer sophisticated arguments for these positions drawn from Ferdinand de Saussure (as reinvented in Paris in the 1950s) and Louis Althusser.

Saussure is treated as a linguistic philosopher, who argues that language produces the system of meaning through which we appropriate real objects; so the question of whether literature exists is really a question about language or signification.[35] This is the normal account of Saussure given to this day in most English departments; but it is not what he actually said. The real Saussure was a scientific realist who said of his own theoretical terms *langue* and *parole*:

> Note that we have defined things and not words; the definitions are not endangered by certain ambiguous words that do not keep their meaning from one language to another . . . it is a bad method to start from words when defining things.[36]

Saussure did think that the oppositions in our language forced distinctions into the confused mass of thought; but he would have been astonished at the notion that the oppositions in our language determine the structure of social or physical reality. I do not in the least know why our English departments still believe in this unhistorical Saussure, invented perhaps by Lacan in the 1950s.

The same problem of misinterpretation doesn't arise for Althusser. Bennett, Eagleton and others of this period not only understand Althusser's problematic; they virtually live inside it; and they are conscious of producing a significant advance in Althusserianism by turning Althusser's problematic against Althusser's literary theory. Here, as elsewhere, far the greatest significance of Althusserianism is in epistemology. Literary theorists, and even more, film theorists, of the 1970s took to heart the proposition that England was a country sunk in empiricism, and what it needed was theory. Translating this into literary study, they identified the standard methods of literary critics – close reading, impressionistic judgement, tentative generalisations on an *ad hoc* basis – as empiricism. This empiricism, they claimed, rested on the notion that the work of literature was something that transparently revealed its meaning to the gaze, without any theoretical work being done.

To this they counterposed the Althusserian notion that the object of knowledge is created by the theory that describes it. A poem is thus a theoretical construction: it is something produced by theoretical work, and the illusion that the poem is out there, and the critic is doing no more than closely observe it, results from repressing the consciousness of the work done to produce it. The same point applies to canons; the canon of literature isn't something given, by the accident that some books happen to be better than others. It is something produced by critical practice. And that practice takes place in the Ideological State Apparatuses (colleges and universities). But if books and canons alike are the product of critical practice, a different practice could well produce a quite different canon, and a different set of books. The revolutionary gesture that now emerges is that one should seize the Ideological State Apparatuses, fire the canon, and construct a new set of readings. This is the sole item in the programme of the New Left that has ever been even partially implemented. Its élitist nature, of course, needs no arguing.

Althusserian thinking in Britain, in the social sciences and then in literary and film theory, went far beyond anything Althusser himself would have tolerated. The work of Hindess and Hirst[37] rapidly out-Althussered the master. He had left little space for empirical testing of theories. They left none. For them theories about society could not possibly be overthrown by facts; there could be no facts outside of theory. Empirical history had no bearing whatever on Marxism; it was not only theoretically but even politically irrelevant. (I suppose the past, by definition, does not exist; only its remains do, in the present, to be interpreted by theory in relation to the theory and politics of the present.) Having followed Althusser in reducing Marxism to a dogmatic epistemology, Hindess and Hirst proceeded to question the status of epistemology. Marxism then disappeared altogether.

The collapse of the Althusserian synthesis of Marxism and post-structuralism left British Marxist critics in a rather curious position. Some, like Easthope, have persisted with this model, and have attempted to use it as the theoretical basis for a transformation of English into

Cultural Studies.[38] Others moved on to Foucauldianism and the microphysics of power, or back to Raymond Williams's style of culturalism, now rechristened cultural materialism, here to rejoin some rational Marxists like Stuart Hall, who had never really left. Others, like Eagleton, stayed with Marxism and are still to be heard referring to the working class or theorising about ideology. But at the same time, by astonishing intellectual gymnastics, they have kept in touch with the most idealist critiques from modern post-structuralism; and they are deeply influenced by the relativism which the collapse of Althusserian dogmatism left behind it.

6   THEORY AND THE ABOLITION OF THE LITERATURE DEPARTMENTS

In 1983 Eagleton squared a circle by producing a best-selling popular textbook of abstruse literary theories; a brilliantly clear summary of phenomenology, hermeneutics, reception theory, structuralism and semiotics, post-structuralism, and psychoanalysis which manages to read like a single connected statement of one coherent view: the state of the art in literary theory in 1983. As if that wasn't enough, he also managed to structure the book as a coherent argument for an educational programme, which took the development of leftist literary theory to its logical conclusion. The argument can be summarised as follows: there is no such thing as literature; it has neither a specific subject-matter nor specific methods of its own. Departments of English literature should therefore be abolished; they should be closed down and replaced with departments of political rhetoric.

The cost of such masterly compression, as we shall see, was a good deal of philosophical fudging. where serious intellectual problems are turned into political slogans. In his preface, Eagleton sees this as a feature rather than a bug; he denies that there can be any neutral way of presenting theory, and hopes that the fact he is arguing a particular case will add to the interest. In some ways it does; and it certainly added to the influence the book had on the mass of Marxist students in the early 1980s. This is Eagleton's most influential Marxist book, though it contains no exposition of specifically Marxist literary theory at all. Marxism here is a set of fundamental assumptions rather than an object of exposition. It is the unexamined truth against which every other theory is tested, and by the light of which every phenomenon is seen.

Perhaps this was simply the best way of hiding the fact that the most sophisticated and up-to-date form of Marxist theory yet known had just collapsed. But it might show what a high degree of confidence it was possible to have, both in sophisticated Marxism and in sophisticated literary theory, and in their mutual compatibility, if you were writing around 1982. Such confidence becomes at times an arrogance as great as anything shown by Leavis. The Preface offers Eagleton's opponents a choice of two simple positions: either they are aware of modern theory, or they are hostile to theory altogether. It doesn't consider the possibility that they might be strongly interested in theory but think this particular package didn't make sense.

Eagleton opens with the arguments intended to show that literature doesn't exist – and the fudging begins here. The main argument for the non-existence of literature that Eagleton offers is the Socratic one referred to earlier: he provides a series of possible definitions of literature, and a counter-example to knock each one down. But the most that this can show about the real world is that works of literature form a fuzzy class, like the Wittgensteinian category of games, where it is not possible to provide a single criterion covering solitaire, association football and ludo. Eagleton mentions the analogy to games but misrepresents its significance; it is as if he thought that Wittgenstein had demonstrated the non-existence of games, whereas he was actually arguing that conceptual categories usually are fuzzy in this way. One implication of this argument is that the existence of literature is about as well established as the existence of games. Most of us would settle for that!

It would have been easy to show that the works of literature which have become established as great – the works of Shakespeare, Milton, Wordsworth, etc. – are not 'objectively' so: they have been actively chosen, over the centuries, often on highly ideological criteria; on a different ideology, one might choose different ones. This would commit Eagleton to a post-Leavisite re-reading of the literary tradition, from a Marxist point of view, but not to the abolition of literature as a category. But the arguments he presents point to a stronger claim: that literature doesn't exist at all, independent of our theories, as an object to be studied, 'in the way that insects exist'. The anti-empiricist Althusserian heritage is clear enough here: literature, as an object of study, is a theoretical construct.

The obvious answer to that is that insects also are a theoretical construct. In many idiolects, spiders and ants alike are insects: for entomologists, spiders are not insects and ants are. That, however, doesn't stop the differences between arachnids and insects being real and physical, and existing independently of human discourse; nor does it stop entomology being an empirical science, as applicable to the Pliocene, when there were no entomologists about, as it is to the present. Similarly, the fact that 'literature' is a theoretical construct doesn't prevent there being a great deal of actual literature that pre-exists that construct and to account for which that construct was constructed. I return to this point in the next section and the next chapter.

Eagleton's goal is to show that literature is constituted by value-judgements (not merely selected by them) and that the value-judgements by which it is constituted are historically variable; and that these value-judgements themselves are a by-product of changing social ideologies. As value-judgements change so literature might change: we might find a society in which there was general human enrichment and Shakespeare had ceased to be literature (says Eagleton, with an unconscious reminiscence of *Brave New World*, in which that very thing happened). The ancient Greek dramatists may not be eternal: suppose we did some archaeological research and found out more about their original meaning – they might cease to speak significantly to us. (Surely one of the oddest arguments in the history of literary theory!)

There is a double problem here of which Eagleton is considering only half. It is indeed a problem for proponents of universal human values that tastes in literature often change; but it is equally a problem for social relativists that they often do not. Eagleton here is taking for granted the variability of all literary values, and simply ignoring the difficulties posed for that assumption by the relative permanence of some works of literature. He even suggests, desperately, that perhaps we keep changing the way we read them, so they aren't really the same works. What makes this fudge particularly striking is that the philosopher who raised this particular difficulty, in connection with the 'eternal charm' of Greek tragedy, was Karl Marx.[39] Marx's solution – that Greek tragedy has the charm of 'normal childhood' – is notoriously unsatisfactory; but Eagleton's solution is simply to run away from the problem.

Eagleton's purpose is, of course, to be able to come up firmly with the judgement in the next chapter, which tells what has become the standard New Left story of the Rise of English, that literature, in the sense in which we have inherited the word, is an ideology. This sounds crudely reductive, not merely by ordinary philosophical standards but by those of all educated Marxists from Marx and Engels downward. Eagleton supports it by a violently tendentious (though often rather admiring) account of the rise of English Literature **as an academic subject**, which reads its function wholly in terms of class values and their propagation and preservation. The essential argument runs: why make the study of English literature available to the people? – because if you give them a share of spiritual wealth, they won't ask for material wealth. 'If the masses are not thrown a few novels, they may react by throwing up a few barricades.'

Eagleton tells the story of English literature itself only as a prelude to the much more important story of English studies in the university, and he gives critics the starring role – even to the point of reversing his order of exposition, so that ideas expounded by Professor George Gordon at the beginning of the twentieth century 'find a resonance' in Victorian literature and lead on to Matthew Arnold in the nineteenth century; and a passionately worshipful account of Dr Leavis in the 1930s is followed by a mention of T.S. Eliot in the 1920s. The writers thus sink to mere illustrators of the ideology of their principal academic critics and expositors. This reversal of the logical priority between creation and criticism is common among modern academic theorists. Indeed at times the suggestion seems to be that the critics actually **produced** English literature for their ideological purpose; and that leaves critics with a different ideology all set to produce something else.

Eagleton's conclusion follows logically enough from his premises; it seems to me the weakest, but is certainly the most typical and symptomatic, part of his 1983 book; a practical proposal which is so sketchily thought out that it is not clear how seriously he himself takes it, based on arguments inherited from his first chapter, which are little more than puns; and as a practical proposal, immediately qualified out of existence on tactical grounds; yet somehow encapsulating the whole destiny of 1980s' Marxism as a guide to political or academic policy. It is a proposal, made in the third year of Mrs Thatcher's reign, for socialists to seize the commanding heights of the ideological production system.

His proposal is to replace English Literature as a subject by (political) rhetoric. Rhetoric, he says, covers both the practice of effective discourse, and the science of it; it was the received form of critical analysis all the way from ancient society to the eighteenth century. And rhetoric must have a purpose; a moral purpose is not enough; any fully moral purpose will be a political one. Other possible names for the new subject are 'discourse theory' and 'cultural studies'. The subject will cover discourses, sign-systems, and signifying practices of all kinds; any sort of text will go in it, from film and television to the languages of natural science. And any method or theory will do 'which will contribute to the strategic goal of human emancipation, the production of "better people" through the socialist transformation of society.' 'Literature' might have some place in this, but departments of literature as we presently know them in higher education would cease to exist. (In the short term, however, they must be unconditionally defended against government cuts.)

This proposal, and others like it,[40] can probably be taken as a fair sample of the final tendencies of the Marxist episode of modern literary theory. To the democratic humanist, it is a fairly startling proposal, considering that English Literature is the most popular single subject in higher education at the present time. Our present society, with all its imperfections, pays for large numbers of students to spend three years reading the best poems, plays and novels in the language, and writing analytical and appreciative essays about them, in the same language. Other students study drama, music and the older visual arts; rather fewer study film and television, arts which have not been around so long. Are they all to be replaced by discourse theory? If not, why not?

One can see that there might be a case for adding courses in political rhetoric, discourse theory, cultural studies, etc., where there is demand; and this has happened; some of us spent many interesting hours discussing and accrediting such courses,[41] years before Eagleton wrote his book. And I notice that in the *Times Literary Supplement* of 18 December 1992 Eagleton reviewed 1,582 pages of publications on Cultural Studies, and complained that the subject was well on the route to becoming institutionalised, and sometimes wasn't socialist. . . . Nobody stops students applying to these courses. But how can it conceivably be emancipatory to refuse to support students who wish to read poems, plays and novels, and to make them analyse the language of papers in chemistry and political documents instead?

Eagleton didn't see this, presumably because of the arguments he had used to persuade himself that English Literature doesn't – objectively – exist. If it doesn't exist it doesn't make sense to say that students want to study it. There is nothing **there** for them to want to study until the academics have constituted the subject. It is a bit like the priest's claim in *A Portrait of the Artist as a Young Man* that only the priest has the power to bring God down into the wafer; which Joyce presents as a fantasy of power. Academics can presumably constitute literature in any way they want; and will constitute it according to their ideology. Hence any argument about what should be taught as literature is really an argument about politics and ideology. If we want a socialist transformation of society we must construct a new 'Literature'. This is a fantasy of **taking** power.

7 'LITERARINESS' AND THE HISTORICAL NATURE OF 'LITERATURE'

One curious side-effect of modern theory is that the objective history of literature has disappeared. We – from Tillyard to Williams – used to take it for granted that literature had a chronological dimension: English literature, for example, started in about the eighth century AD and Western literature in the eighth century BC, or earlier. And we used to suppose that these chronological properties of literature at least were objective ones. But from the point of view that history is actually a construction of modern historians for political purposes, it is possible to regard every history of literature as a type of validatory myth. The myth of the old scholars was racist, imperialist and anti-aristocratic: its object was the history and literature of the English-Speaking Peoples. Naturally it started with *Beowulf,* and worked up progressively to a peak in Shakespeare and Wordsworth – with their patriotic elements very highly regarded. What it validated was patriotism and the British Empire; it received its mortal blow in the First World War.

The myth of the Leavisites and to some extent of the New Critics was that of the spiritually healthy pre-industrial society, suffering in turn from dissociation of sensibility and from the industrial revolution, and hence declining from Shakespeare, through Milton and Wordsworth into the abyss of Shelley and the bog of late romanticism; to be rescued only by the dry intelligence of a modern sensibility. That myth validates the English School as the heart of a university, and validates its great effort, not to save, but to resist modern civilisation.

Eagleton's history of 'The Rise of English' is representative of the modern school; it has become a collective possession of the left, expounded in books from Widdowson (ed.) 1982 to Easthope 1991; this saga of the academic subject is the way these professional teachers see English literature now. Seen as a history, it is a rather tendentious one; sometimes little more than a projection of the politics of the Cambridge English tripos onto the history of Western culture. But its real function is again as a validatory myth. The myth of the new theorists is that of English, constructed as a subject in the universities to replace religion and to save the capitalist state. This validates the notion of a revolutionary takeover of the syllabus committees, and the production of a social revolution from these unlikely sites. It seems ridiculous, but is actually not much more improbable than the Leavisite enterprise.

A genuinely materialist approach to the arguments of this unfortunate period would probably lead us to quite different conclusions. Thus consider Bennett's account of the approach of Russian Formalism.[42] This movement attempted to isolate and theorise a quality of 'literariness'. Bennett picks out the formalist attempt to define literariness in terms of 'defamiliarisation' – the way in which, as Jakobson put it 'the reader of a poem or the viewer of a painting has a vivid awareness of two orders: the traditional canon and the artistic novelty as a deviation from the canon.' Bennett argues – in a more complex way than I have space to follow here – that this reveals the intertextual and relational quality of literariness, the extent to which literature is not a matter of a succession of texts containing some common literary essence, but of the way one historical discourse acts on another, and hence argues the need to perceive literature in a historical and concrete fashion and not abstractly.

One may well agree with him on all these points; but the implicit conclusion that when we do this, the traditional notion of literature will disappear, does not at all follow. The reason is that Bennett has failed to take the historicisation of literary study seriously. Suppose we follow his formula exactly, and work through the whole of human history seeing how each literary form reacts against the previous ones. Suppose we are careful to look at Western literature in a historical and concrete fashion and not abstractly – i.e. to place the individual works in their own society and whatever literary institutions it had. We might well end up with the conclusion that we can establish a continuous tradition of Western literature that starts with the Homeric epics and continues with Greek lyric and Greek tragedy, proceeding through the usually recognised channels of influence and historical continuity down to *Ulysses* and beyond; and that gives us deep insights into Western social history. The argument would be that each of these discourses is an artistic novelty in relation to the ones that came before; and they retain their novelty, and their status as art, only so long as readers recognise the whole tradition. By this sophisticated argument we would re-establish a tradition that would be familiar to Engels or to Marx.

In a curious and intellectually satisfying way, this approach is compatible with the views of Roman Jakobson, T.S. Eliot, and both the Hegelian and Marxist dialectics. It incorporates both the Formalist concept of defamiliarisation and T.S. Eliot's concept of an ideal order; both Hegel's concept of the historical growth of culture by the supersession/preservation of its own past, and Marx's concept that the culture of a period represents at the ideological level the society of that period and its underlying economic conflicts. There is overwhelming literary and historical evidence for a conception something like this; and there is after all nothing whatever in the principles of historical materialism to limit the number of centuries over which we can perceive literature – or any other historical phenomenon – in a historical and concrete fashion.

We can see from this example that negative arguments against simple theories of literature are by no means certain to destroy the concept of literature – they may merely lead to more complex and satisfying theories of it. This however is not the way things were going in the early 1980s, when there was much more excitement in the thought of destroying the authority of the canon of Dr Leavis than in that of providing a philosophically plausible account of the dialectical nature of the literature of the world. What excited literary Marxists was not the thought of a new substantive theory of literature, but the thought of a new world in which literature would be, conceptually, swept away – a symbolic equivalent of the proletarian revolution, which might have to do if the real thing did not actually materialise.

NOTES

1. Cf. Easthope 1991 and Barrett 1991 as representative critics or social theorists with views like this.
2. My own position. There is of course, every shade of opinion between, from Marxists like Callinicos 1989 who write against post-modernism, to those like Eagleton 1990b *et al.* who seem to feel they can use Marxist principles to pick and choose within post-modernism.
3. E.P. Thompson (ed.) 1960, *Out of Apathy*. There is a retrospective review of the early New Left in: Oxford University Socialist Discussion Group (eds) 1989, *Out of Apathy: Voices of the New Left 30 Years On*. Old men remember.
4. E.P. Thompson, 'At the Point of Decay'; 'Outside the Whale' in Thompson (ed.) 1960.
5. Alasdair MacIntyre, 'Breaking the Chains of Reason' in Thompson (ed.) 1960.
6. E.P. Thompson 1955, *William Morris – Romantic to Revolutionary*.
7. E.P. Thompson, 'The Peculiarities of the English' in Thompson 1978, p. 35.
8. 'In 1974 British Marxism reached its peak, both in theory and practice.' Easthope 1988, *British Post-Structuralism since 1968*.
9. 'The *May Day Manifesto* was one of the culminating points of the political experience of the English New Left. Its complex analysis and political proposals were the work of Williams, E.P. Thompson, Stuart Hall and some of the contributors to *New Left Review*. It failed to arouse any keen interest in the Italian Left . . . Williams' share was approximately defined as 'cultural socialism . . . in the Morrisian tradition' (Fernando Ferrara in Eagleton (ed.) 1989). Ferrara greatly admired Williams.
10. Coward and Ellis 1977, *Language and Materialism*.

11. Thus sympathetic recent writers like Michele Barrett 1991, while acknowledging his importance, find much of Althusser impossible to take seriously. In the 1970s, however, he was not merely taken seriously; he was used terroristically. See previous chapter.
12. Affluence is relative. In the West, millions were and are out of work; this is a measure of social control. In Eastern Europe, till the very end, the Communist Parties retained despotic control. But the economies declined. At about the point where one was better off unemployed in the West than employed in the East, the revolutions against Communism broke out.
13. Easthope 1988, p. 2.
14. Ibid., p. 17.
15. Cf. Dollimore and Sinfield 1985, *Political Shakespeare: New Essays in Cultural Materialism*.
16. Cf. 'Culture is Ordinary', in Williams 1989b, *Resources of Hope*.
17. See next chapter.
18. Empson has reviews of both Lewis and Williams in *Argufying* (1987), p. 142, p. 184.
19. Nelson and Grossberg 1988, p. 69.
20. Cf. E. Laclau and C. Mouffe 1985; Barrett 1991.
21. Lyotard 1984; 1989; Featherstone 1988; Appignanesi 1989.
22. Cf. Catherine Hall, in Grossberg *et al.* 1992, p. 272.
23. What it actually says is 'Look for cultural authority to tell you what to think and feel.' This is what Eliot on the right has in common with the Marxists: the preference for authority over direct personal judgement. Cf. Eliot 1923, 'The Function of Criticism' in Eliot 1932, *Selected Essays*.
24. Cf. Jackson 1969, 'Radical Conceptual Change and the Design of Honours Degrees' – I was as enthusiastic about theory as anybody, and actually I still am.
25. Compare the earlier book by P. Macherey 1966b, *A Theory of Literary Production*.
26. It is interesting to compare this with the passage from Pécheux quoted above in the Althusser chapter; Eagleton is much clearer.
27. The Society for Education in Film and Television 1981, *Screen Reader 2: Cinema and Semiotics*. Anthony Easthope 1988, *British Post-Structuralism since 1968*.
28. See Jackson 1991, *The Poverty of Structuralism*, for comments on this.
29. 'Until Marxism can produce a revolutionary subject, revolutionary change will be impossible': Coward and Ellis 1977, p. 91.
30. For discussion of Lacan, see Jackson 1991, Chapter 3, section 2; Chapter 7, section 3; and Jackson, forthcoming, *Making Freud Unscientific*.
31. Colin MacCabe 1978, *James Joyce and the Revolution of the Word*; Coward and Ellis 1977, *Language and Materialism*.
32. Catherine Belsey 1980, *Critical Practice*.
33. All critics of this school agree in ignoring the fact that Dickens, Wordsworth, Milton, Dante and Virgil all supposed themselves to be in essentially the same business as their predecessors; they each intended to add to an existing tradition of literature even if that word was not yet in existence.
34. Norman Geras 1983, *Marx and Human Nature: Refutation of a Legend*.
35. Bennett 1979, pp. 4–5.

36. 'Il est à remarquer que nous avons défini des choses et non des mots; les distinctions établies n'ont donc rien à redouter de certains termes ambigus qui ne se recouvrent pas d'une langue à l'autre . . . c'est une mauvaise méthode que de partir des mots pour définir les choses' (Saussure 1916b, Critical Edition, p. 31). The whole passage is discussed in Jackson 1991, *The Poverty of Structuralism*, pp. 206ff. Bennett is discussed, ibid, pp. 237ff.
37. Hindess and Hirst 1975; 1977; Hirst 1977; 1986.
38. Easthope 1988; 1991.
39. Marx 1859, Unpublished Introduction to the *Critique of Political Economy*, section 4.
40. For example, Easthope 1991, *Literary into Cultural Studies*.
41. On subject panels and boards of the Council for National Academic Awards, which used to validate Polytechnic degree courses. Not everything interesting happens at Oxford or Cambridge.
42. Bennett 1979, Chapters 2–4. For further discussion of Formalism and Structuralism, see Jackson 1991, *The Poverty of Structuralism*, Chapter 2.

BOOKS

E.P. Thompson (ed.) 1960 *Out of Apathy*.

Oxford University Socialist Discussion Group (eds) 1989 *Out of Apathy: Voices of the New Left 30 Years On*.

E.P. Thompson 1968 *The Making of the English Working Class*.

Raymond Williams 1958 *Culture and Society 1780–1950*.

1961 *The Long Revolution*.

1962 *Communications*.

1970 *The English Novel from Dickens to Lawrence*.

1975 *The Country and the City*.

1976 *Keywords*.

1977 *Marxism and Literature*.

1979 *Politics and Letters*.

1988 *What I Came to Say*.

Terry Eagleton 1976 *Criticism and Ideology*.

1983 *Literary Theory*.

1990a *The Ideology of the Aesthetic*.

1990b *The Significance of Theory*.

Tony Bennett 1979 *Formalism and Marxism*.

Catherine Belsey 1980 *Critical Practice*.

The Society for Education in Film and Television 1981 *Screen Reader 2: Cinema and Semiotics.*

Peter Widdowson (ed.) 1982 *Rereading English.*

Nelson and **Grossberg** (eds) 1988 *Marxism and the Interpretation of Culture.*

Anthony Easthope 1988 *British Post-Structuralism since 1968.*

Leonard Jackson 1991 *The Poverty of Structuralism.*

CHAPTER TEN

Two Forms of Cultural Materialism

Materialism in Anthropology and in Cultural Studies

SUMMARY

Cultural materialism is a name given to two quite different, even opposing
bodies of theory in anthropology and cultural studies respectively. The
anthropological theory develops the scientific side of scientific socialism. It
is the basis of a research programme of extraordinary variety and scope
which aims to explain the whole of human prehistory, history and
ethnography in terms of economic pressures. It is visibly continuous with
the mature work of Marx, and that of Engels in *The Origins of the Family,
Private Property and the State*, but incorporates ecological variables, along
with the most up-to-date ethnographic and archaeological data. It retains
the economism of classical Marxism, and the commitment to science, but
drops the radical politics; if it has any political implication, it is that we
should have a much deeper awareness of the cultural implications of
ecology, and put ecological questions, rather than class, ethnic, or sexual
ones at the centre of global politics.

The very different literary theory of the name – which is also the
essential core of that curious variety of left-wing popular anthropology
called cultural studies – keeps the old-fashioned radical political thrust of
Marxism, and broadens it from class issues to racial and feminist ones; but
it drops the science and the economic theory, and its radical values are
therefore not grounded in any general theory of human history, as those
of Marxism were. Its interests are superstructural; its value theory is
relativist; it fits fairly happily with purely formalist types of intellectual
radicalism like post-structuralism; it concentrates on cultural rather than
economic struggle and sees artistic culture essentially as a site – perhaps

the main site – for political contests rather than something of intrinsic value for humanity in general. With the advent of cultural materialism Marxism thus splits into two rather weaker successor states.

Most readers of this book will probably be familiar with the various forms of literary cultural materialism. I am going to argue for the anthropological kind; that is, for the hardest of hard-line economic materialism; and to raise the question: what would literary theory look like if questions of literary canons, traditions, classical literatures and so forth were seen from the viewpoint of a materialist cultural anthropology?

1   CULTURAL MATERIALISM IN EARLY AND MODERN ANTHROPOLOGY

Anyone interested in developing rational theories of human culture, whether in literary study or in anthropology, must continue to wonder what contribution the legacy of Marxism can make to these. Marxism and Marxist literary theory both seem to have died in the last thirty years; but they died of different diseases. Marxism, as a body of theory at least, collapsed because large parts of it – in particular the economic doctrines, and the predictions about the nature and likelihood of revolutions – were unscientific and untrue, and had disastrous practical consequences which have devastated whole economies, and turned subcontinents into prison camps. Marxist literary and cultural theory, on the other hand, became unfashionable among intellectuals because, with the triumph of post-structuralism and post-modernism, it appeared too scientific, too mechanistic and too concerned with truth.

Marxism is, moreover, teleological; it offers meta-narratives; it is essentialist; worst of all, it is economistic. For literary theory therefore, and also for the increasingly influential form of popular anthropology called cultural studies, it is unacceptable. The closing paper of the 1990 Illinois conference on cultural studies put it clearly enough. A return to pre-postmodern Marxism 'is untenable because the terms of that return are predicated on prioritising economic relations and economic determinations over cultural and political relations by positioning these latter in a mechanical and reflectionist role'.[1] Or to put it more traditionally, Marxism is materialist rather than left-Hegelian. To make a world fit for cultural studies to function in, Marx has to be dematerialised.

My thesis is that while Marx clearly got his economics wrong, he got his materialist interpretation of history right. We can construct an adequate materialist theory of human culture (a materialist anthropology, of which cultural materialist literary theory would be a proper part) only by recognising the explanatory primacy of economic variables; though we have to add population factors and ecological factors to those which classical Marxism admitted. In my view such an extended materialist theory throws a powerful light upon literature, just as it does on all other cultural practices; though it needs to be supplemented with political, social and cultural history. But it must be added that such a theory makes sense only if we abandon the rhetoric of post-structuralism and adopt a realist philosophy in both the human and the natural sciences; and it has no special connection with the political left.

What is labelled 'cultural materialism' in modern literary theory is not a materialist theory of literature, and certainly not an attempt at a scientific research strategy into the history of literature in various human societies. It is, rather, a politically committed interpretative practice. These 'cultural materialists' hold that cultural objects – plays, poems, stories, etc. – should be studied as parts of the whole complex of cultural practices in society. Materialism in this sense is therefore a materialism of 'material practices' and institutions; it is counted idealist to attribute an intrinsic meaning or value to Shakespeare's texts, but materialist to discuss the way they are read, produced, studied, etc., especially if this has political implications. Literary cultural materialists do not see it as their first priority to explain cultural practices in economic terms; they try to distance themselves from what they see as the Marxist base-superstructure metaphor. But they retain a strongly left-wing political stance, seeing it as a priority in cultural theory to fight against social oppression, racism, sexism, etc.; and they often live happily with the cultural and discursive relativism of the post-structuralist era, drawing often on Foucault, and occasionally on Derrida. They are not in ordinary scientific terms especially materialist.

Cultural materialism in anthropology is quite different. It is an attempt at scientific explanation, and retains the philosophical realism, and the materialism, of natural science. It aims to explain the vast range of human cultural practices (which must in principle include the arts), and the historical succession of different forms of society, in terms of underlying economic variables. It descends from, and resembles, classical Marxism; but it does not employ the dialectic and it has a commitment to explaining the facts about human societies rather than to making revolutionary changes in them. It calls upon a wider range of explanatory variables than Marxism did: they include natural resources, population levels in relation to available technology, calorie and protein levels of various types of food supply, along with the energy costs of securing them, etc. This makes it the obvious scientific basis for the theorisation of ecological problems. But its practical conclusion is just as likely to be that sacred cows should be retained in India, as that social revolution should take place there. The leading exponent of cultural materialism has been Marvin Harris, and it is largely his formulations that I have discussed here.

The fundamental principle of anthropological cultural materialism is that, however coherent its internal development, no part of society or culture takes its form in independence of economic variables, and many aspects of human cultures can be explained by economic variables in ways often entirely hidden from the members of the cultures themselves. The fundamental structures of culture are not transparent or autonomous. This creates problems of ideology and false consciousness already familiar from their working out in the Marxist tradition: we can find ourselves claiming as anthropologists to know why men go to war and women commit infanticide when the men themselves would give quite different reasons for going to war and the women would deny that they committed infanticide. We then have to ask ourselves familiar questions about the status of a social science that claims to reveal to us aspects of other societies which are concealed from members of those societies, but open to the anthropologist observing them. And we have to press that point further and note that, on the same principles, there will be familiar aspects of our own society that we do not understand by introspection, but that we can explain to ourselves, by applying the principles of cultural materialism.

The anthropological principles we shall be discussing apply to the study of literature in a peculiarly direct way. All literary critics are practising cultural anthropologists, intuitively exploring the world of social meaning behind the works that they are studying. A purely abstract and formalist approach to literature is impossible. Every work of literature in the world is a part of some human culture, in the anthropologists' sense of the word, and can only be made sense of within that culture. This is as true for works of literature that are produced in one culture and appreciated in a later one as it is for purely contemporary works; for a modern critic to appreciate a nineteenth-century English novel requires an intuitive anthropological understanding both of nineteenth-century English society and of our own. To give a concrete example: no critic could succeed who was unable to give an account of the meaning of marriage and of money in both societies.

The principles of anthropological cultural materialism suggest that beneath those intuitive accounts of social meaning are levels of scientific explanation in terms of economic interests, and conflicts of economic interest. It is these which it should be the special function of cultural materialist literary theory to explore.

1.1   Materialist strategies in explaining cultural systems: sacred cows and fierce Indians

Cultural materialism is a research strategy rather than a single theory. Faced with an ethnographic account either of some whole culture like that of the Yanomami, or some special feature of several cultures like the taboo on eating pork in the Middle East, the cultural materialist will examine the material costs and benefits of the customs concerned, measuring these in terms of factors such as calorie intake and protein intake for effort expended, at various population densities and levels of natural resources. This analysis includes, but goes beyond, what a Marxist would call the forces and relations of production; it is a crippling weakness of Marxism that it has never paid adequate attention to population density or ecology.

In denying the autonomy of culture such a strategy denies one of the favourite principles of most schools of cultural anthropology; and there is a danger of pushing it (as Harris sometimes does) towards a complete economic determinism. But as we have seen when discussing Marxism itself, this does not follow. We can still maintain that human cultures are creative human responses to material conditions, and that many different responses are always possible, while accepting that the material factors have explanatory primacy. Cultural materialism sees human physical needs, and the available resources and technology of a society – whether this means virgin forests and stone axes, or coalfields and steam-engines – as the primary explanatory variables; and political structure, patterns of warfare, religious beliefs, cultural forms, etc. as the elements that are to be explained; and it sees the economy as the level that mediates between these two. In this it preserves the defensible parts of Marxism.

A simple example of this strategy in action is Harris's account of the functions of the sacred cow among the Hindus – the cow that wanders the streets of the town, steals its food, and must not be killed. This is an example of a custom which has been considered both by ordinary non-materialist cultural anthropology and by Western developmental economics. In a curious way, both of these agree: they think these cows are non-functional. Ordinary cultural anthropology offers explanations of the sacredness of the cow in terms of the internal structure of Hindu culture. In effect, it is sacred because it is sacred. Developmental economics treats the sacred cow as a burden on the economy; for development to take place, most of them have to be slaughtered.

Harris points out that the cow in question is an exceedingly tough breed of milk animal, which as a scavenger recycles energy otherwise lost (cow-dung is a standard fuel). The wholesale slaughter of sacred cows would in effect mean making society less energy-efficient and also moving wealth from poor peasants with a single cow that strays and scavenges to rich ones with whole herds kept on pasture. The cow in India is not really treated with any particular tenderness; it has a very hard life, and the last drop of milk is extracted. The cow is also a producer of draught animals: oxen. The taboo on killing it has an economic function. India has famines. The temptation to kill a cow in a famine is overwhelming, but it is killing your capital; you can't then produce oxen to work the farm. It is precisely in circumstances like these, over the centuries, that societies evolve religious taboos. People need strengthening against short-term temptations that spell long-term economic ruin. This last point needs emphasising: it is a general principle which explains the underlying long-term economic rationality often found in apparently irrational religious principles.

The materialist strategy illustrated here is not by any means limited to odd occasional customs like that of the sacred cow. Again and again, by careful attention to the specific economic circumstances of each society, the whole bewildering variety of human cultural customs can be given a rational economic explanation. In a virtuoso popular book of 1975, Harris managed to explain why in some circumstances pigs are forbidden food, while in others a whole society is built round feasting on them; why in some societies the central activity has been the economically crazy one of competitively destroying wealth (potlatch feasts); and so forth. One particularly beguiling argument explains the connection, for the band-level society of the Yanomami Indians, between protein deficiency, small-scale war, and the physical battering of women.

This last explanation is a *tour de force*, and one that should be of enormous interest to modern feminists. The Yanomami have recently been grossly sentimentalised – not least by their original ethnographer Napoleon Chagnon[2] – since capitalism began to wipe them out; but their society in the period when it was first studied seems to have been one of the most horrible on earth. The men – who were all aggressive drug addicts – fought and killed each other constantly about women (each band would raid other bands to steal their women), and when they were not doing this they battered and wounded the women. They explained their constant warfare as a consequence of a shortage of women: but this shortage was artificially created by the women practising female infanticide (though they denied that they were doing this).

Such a society, described at the level of its own consciousness, poses many insoluble questions. If women are in short supply why are they not treated better? Why do the women create an artificial shortage of women?

Why do women bring up little boys to be aggressive to little girls? Chagnon could offer no answers to these questions, which make the society seem not merely unpleasant but crazily irrational.

Harris offered an answer in terms of food supply. The Yanomami, probably forced out of their original ranges, were in areas that lacked game; and they didn't know how to fish: so they lacked protein. The custom of constant warfare between bands was an adaptive response to keep the population down. It did this only in small part through deaths in battle. The main effect of warfare was to make it necessary for each band to have doughty warriors. High prestige therefore went to men, and they were brought up to be aggressive. Women were subordinates, and of low prestige. Hence the female infanticide – which is a way of ensuring that your own band will have a high proportion of warriors, and will win women from other bands. It is also an extremely efficient way of limiting the population as a whole.

It appears that in Yanomami society – assuming the original ethnographic description but taking Harris's interpretation of it – female infanticide, far from being an unfortunate side-effect, is the main purpose of the entire social system, and the one thing that enables the society to survive. The whole system of war and wife-battery that makes up most of the daily lived experience of these poor devils is a superstructural effect. This raises the question of whether our own lived experience is equally far from the underlying economic realities of our society. No doubt it is.

1.2 Anthropology and the stages of prehistory

Anthropological cultural materialism is an up-to-date scientific version of the historical materialism of Marx and Engels, shorn of the Hegelian dialectic and the political commitment, and generalised to apply to precapitalist societies. It rejects the ludicrous Marxist dismissal of population pressure as a significant factor in economic change, and it draws upon a hundred years of empirical research in anthropology and archaeology of which Engels could know nothing. Whatever one's reservations about the idealist nature of some current anthropological theories, the standard of purely scientific knowledge both in anthropology and archaeology has been transformed since Engels's time. Even by the 1960s, Murdock was publishing an ethnographic atlas in which 600 societies were described and several dozen classificatory features given for each society.[3] Since that time, the output of descriptive anthropologists from American graduate schools has been phenomenal; though not of course sufficient to describe all the remaining primitive cultures before modern industrial society drives them into extinction. Obviously no account of these could depend simply on the Marxist classics.

Cultural materialism in anthropology is a direct descendant of Marxist anthropology, which was founded by Engels in his book *The Origins of the Family, Private Property, and the State in the Light of the Researches of Lewis H. Morgan*. This is not, in fact (how could it possibly be?) an original study in anthropology; it is a reworking, within a mature Marxist framework, of the then most recent anthropological account of the early development of human society. We can bring out the character of Morgan's work by quoting the full title of that account: *Ancient Society, or Researches in the Lines of Human Progress from Savagery through Barbarism to Civilisation*. Morgan's theory is in fact a theory of the **stages of human social development**; it is not necessarily a materialist one.[4]

Such a theory is based on the assumption that you can look at contemporary primitive societies like those of the American Indians, and get a picture of the family structure and the way of life of our early ancestors. Such an assumption could be taken for granted in the eighteenth and nineteenth centuries; it has come to seem less plausible in the twentieth. One obvious reason for denying it is that American Indians, studied in the nineteenth century, have just as much history behind them as English factory workers: in time, they are equally removed from the primitive. Many non-Marxist theorists would argue that the structure of such societies illustrates merely the great variety of possible human social arrangements. It has nothing to say about history.

To believe, as nineteenth-century and some early twentieth-century anthropologists did, that the social organisation – e.g. the clan structure – of American Indian tribes throws light on the social organisation of early Germanic or Greek peoples, you must either assume that there is some necessary order in historical development laid down by God or by the structure of the human mind, and that, for mysterious reasons, some peoples have got stuck at an early stage of this necessary sequence; or assume the Marxist principle that social structure is at least in part determined by technology or economics. The former position is difficult to defend; the latter leads to cultural materialism.

Throughout the twentieth century, many of the most influential schools of cultural anthropology have rejected both positions. Some have held that while cultures can be analysed and compared scientifically, they are not in any sense determined by their economic basis; rather, it is the culture that determines what counts as economic.[5] This view makes materialist social science impossible; some anti-Marxists will find it sympathetic. Others have held that the cultures of particular societies are unique systems of meanings not strictly comparable with each other, and probably not capable of being comprehended by another culture, like our own, at least if we insist on using our own inappropriate scientific categories instead of empathy or humanistic insight.[6] This view – cultural relativism – makes any social science impossible; post-structuralists will find it sympathetic, but I think the proper name for it is obscurantism. Its fundamental move is a refusal to believe we can have an objective science of society.

In short, there have been several varieties of what Engels would have had no difficulty in recognising as idealism. There is an excellent account of the conflict between idealism and materialism in anthropological theory up to the 1960s in Harris 1968.

It will be noted that any sophisticated account of anthropology as a study of different cultures as unique systems of meanings can be readily deconstructed by arguments of the kind given about Lévi-Strauss in Derrida 1967, 'Structure, Sign and Play in the Discourse of the Human Sciences'. The claim is that the categories of the anthropologist are just as culture bound as those of the native; anthropology conducted so becomes merely myth about myth.[7] These arguments do not bite if we follow Darwin and Marx in assuming a common material substructure to all human cultures; this gives the basis, on realist philosophical assumptions, for a scientific theory which applies to all of them.

Such a theory would not be an imposition of the materialist meaning-categories of our own culture onto the non-materialist meaning-categories of other cultures; it would be an attempt to explain the meaning-categories of our own culture and those of other cultures alike in terms of constructs which are – though never more than hypothetical – intended to be hypotheses about all possible human cultures. An example of such a concept would be the efficiency – in terms of calories expended versus calories obtained – of some such mode of production as hunting with bow and arrow. Such a concept would be meaningless in terms of the direct experience either of a hunter-gatherer or a modern cultural theorist; but has a precise meaning within a modern system of natural science.

The new anthropology, in conjunction with archaeology, linguistics, comparative anatomy, etc., gives us a rather different picture of human history and prehistory from that given by Marxism. It would deny that all history is the history of class conflict. It returns to Darwin and Malthus in recognising that the root of historical change is the tendency of population to outgrow resources, given a current mode of production. Class conflict, where it occurs, is a consequence of this. What happens when population outgrows resources for some mode of production like, say, hunting and gathering is that it is replaced by some more intensive mode of production like, in this case, agriculture, which can support larger populations on the same resource base. According to the cultural materialist, such a transition is likely to occur when the costs of hunting and gathering – measured in terms of calories expended for calories acquired – rise above those for agriculture. Cultural materialists agree with Marxists that such a transition in mode of production leads to great changes in the structure of society and the overall culture.

Consider now the culture of early humans, as it is reconstructed from anthropological studies of contemporary hunter-gatherers, archaeological studies of early hunter-gatherers, and biological studies of *homo sapiens*. Early humans were rare animals, living in small nomadic bands; this is known from archaeology. They were probably fluent speakers of languages as complex as English or Japanese. This view rests on Chomsky's linguistics – which suggests that the fundamental structures of language are innate – and comparative anatomical studies of *homo sapiens* and *homo neanderthalensis*.[8] Some of them may have known more than one language, since the small nomadic bands probably met at the limit of their ranges. At that stage of cultural evolution, they needed language; the cognitive load of their culture on them was probably as great as that of ours on us, and language is pre-eminently a cognitive encoding system. If they were anything like modern hunter-gatherers they were clever hunters of animals (women mostly taking small ones) and resourceful gatherers of plant foods (women did most of this, and produced most of the diet).

Economically they were often in easy circumstances. They could feed themselves very easily on a couple of hours' work, or less, in a day, and had time for an abundant social life. They probably had a factual knowledge of the local plants and animals that far outclassed that of a professional university naturalist; at least, this is what the University of Chicago found when they investigated the Kalahari bushmen.[9] Yet they were great talkers and in the evening told wonderful stories of talking animals at the beginning of the world. All hunter-gatherers seem to do this. They thus had available distinct discourses of natural history and literature, and were perfectly capable of distinguishing between them. (Such observations as this – also familiar from village and other pre-state level societies – are sufficient to dispose of the fantasy that literature is a 'bourgeois' phenomenon. It is a human phenomenon.)

Politically they were almost certainly egalitarian, without chiefs or 'big men'; sexual specialisation of labour was already in existence, since this is pre-human, but in many societies the position of women was as high as it has ever been, and sometimes, in some societies, a woman led the band. Personally they were rather modest: boasting was bad form. The true structure of their society was determined by kin, not by class. They had classificatory systems determining who should marry who that make the modern anthropologist gape; and it is by kinship that one band was linked to another. They loved children, but regularly practised abortion and infanticide; there were some macho societies, as among the Australian aborigines, in which, after an easy childhood, adolescent boys were obscenely tortured before they could be counted as men.

There is strong evidence for every bit of this composite picture, which is based on studies of modern hunter-gatherers: Australian aborigines, Kalahari bushmen, forest-dwelling pygmies; what it does not represent is the difference, the individuality of each culture, which is of course not known. What the cultural materialist would say is that almost every feature above depends on the primary economic adaptation, hunting and gathering. It is that which makes man rare and nomadic: a large static local population would rapidly deplete all the local natural resources. Such a band creates no surplus to support specialist craftsmen, priests, or big chiefs; if any individuals tried to tyrannise, the others could move away and form another band. Sometimes there were murders; but there was no warfare. Abortion and infanticide were often normal and essential methods of birth-control. Sub-incision and similar rites (the obscene tortures I referred to) were, literally, ways of separating out the men from the boys. (When boys are brought up by women, but need to be acculturated into a macho society, strong measures are needed.)

It is such societies as these which Morgan and Engels called **savagery**; they are also the nearest that reality has ever come to what the Marxist tradition called **primitive communism**. It is interesting to find that modern anthropology supports – with very significant qualifications – the ancient biblical and Hesiodic myth of a golden age before agriculture, in which nature was a garden whose fruits simply drop into human hands. It doesn't in the least support the Leavisite myth of a golden agricultural age, before modern industry.

1.3   Historical change and its ideological reflection

On the basis of cultural materialism it is possible to explain the most profound changes in society – namely, the changes from one mode of production to another; and it is also possible to explain much smaller episodes, like the Hundred Years' War, or the rise of the novel.[10]

Consider, for example, the most important change in the history of mankind: the change from palaeolithic hunting and gathering of the kind described above to neolithic agriculture. Why did it happen? Are we to suppose that some people made some technological discoveries – how to cultivate grain, how to breed sheep – and discovered that they liked the settled way of life thus made available? Such discoveries had to be made, of course, for agriculture to be possible. But is the change in mode of production no more than a side-effect of the discovery of some new technical ideas? The case is far otherwise. Technical discoveries are made and neglected all the time; they are only exploited when there is economic need. The hunter-gatherers of the Kalahari, investigated by the University of Chicago in the 1960s, were well aware of the possibilities of agriculture, but could see no point in it whatever, so long as there were Mongongo nuts to be gathered.[11] And they were perfectly right; primitive farming produces a poorer diet than hunting and gathering, and requires many times the hours of work; the work is uncongenial and indeed unhealthy; and a settled existence is associated with epidemic diseases from which hunter-gatherers are free. Cost-benefit analysis adequately explains why hunter-gatherers, even on marginal land, choose to stay as such.

Here is an example of a crude materialist, though not necessarily Marxist or Harrisian, account of the change from hunting-gathering to agriculture, which explains both why it happened, and why it was irreversible, without making any assumptions about the innate preferences of human beings; and then goes on to explain the ideological understanding of that change by the agriculturalists.

(a)   Agriculture is an intensive mode of production compared with hunting-and-gathering; the same territory can support more population; so agriculture is necessary at a certain point of population growth.

(b)   Agriculture and nomadic hunting-and-gathering cannot coexist on the same territory: hunters-and-gatherers, in the nature of their own way of life, don't recognise grain and sheep as agricultural products, but look upon them as natural products to be taken wherever they are found. So they simply take the grain and the sheep that the peasants have raised.

(c)   The peasants try to stop them. Since agriculture makes possible a far higher population density than hunting-and-gathering, there are always more cultivators than hunters, and they can kill off the hunters.

It will be seen that this is a completely objective historical process which occurs independently of the wishes of anybody involved. Once the techniques of farming are discovered, and provided the population goes on increasing, farming is bound to supersede hunting, even if everybody in both societies prefers hunting. (They usually do – agricultural societies always retain hunting as a leisure activity, and class societies restrict the best game to the ruling classes.) It will be seen also that there is a subjective side to this historical conflict. Agricultural peoples develop an ideology of property – not necessarily individual property, but perhaps the property of the tribe or a God – and see hunter-gatherers as lazy thieves. One can see that they need to do this, to motivate them both to work and to exterminate their more primitive neighbours.

It would of course be possible to tell the story of the conflict not objectively, as above, but subjectively, from the point of view of either of the peoples involved. One could imagine a visiting anthropologist from an entirely different culture doing this, and producing a balanced history based on first-hand accounts. The question of presentation and explanatory principles remains, however. The anthropologist might accept the subjective accounts of both sides to the conflict, and present the story as a tragic clash of irreconcilable ideologies. That would be idealist history, and halfway to an epic poem. Or he might offer the materialist account I have given above, in which the subjective experiences of the participants are not denied, but the course of history is explained in terms of variables like available technology, population pressure, etc. That is materialist history.

Similar transitions have occurred many times over in later history. My own guess is that any mode of production which for any reason – in terms of population, or organisation, or technology – confers long-term military superiority will supersede a mode that does not. And with the new mode of production will come a whole set of ideas organised around it. Between the peoples organised around each mode of production there will be great ideological differences, and they will see the world in different ways.

1.4   The materialist history of mankind

Accounts of major economic transitions of the kind I have just illustrated can be employed on a very grand scale to organise a materialist view of the entire history of mankind. Harris[12] argues that the main motor of historical change is population increase up to the carrying level of the existing mode of production. The nomads run out of game; the agriculturalists run out of land; the factories run out of resources; and it becomes necessary to switch (sometimes in the midst of violence and war) to new, more intensive modes of production. These in turn involve a new organisation of society, which produces new ideas – even new kinds of personality – to sustain it. I would argue that it is in this way that all 'progress' has taken place; and this incidentally is why so much progress has not improved the lot of the average person at all – only increased the global population. On this view the ecological crisis is not new; it is the permanent, though ever-changing condition of human history.

It is in my view one of the richest possibilities in cultural studies to analyse the whole history of human culture as a complex reflection or representation of this material history. It would be a disaster for cultural studies if the demise of Marxism led to the abandonment of attempts to interpret cultural phenomena in terms of an underlying economic reality; this remains perhaps the profoundest insight into the social basis of culture that we have. What is missing from this approach, however, is the dogmatic Marxist claim for the pre-eminence of class struggle. This viewpoint is an ecological rather than a class one. When resources are scarce, of course, class or ethnic struggle will arise and will be of historical importance. But the class war is no longer the prime explanatory variable.

1.5   Anthropology and the literary critic

One of the gross disadvantages of the dominance of French theory in the last thirty years is the almost complete disappearance of the influence not merely of Marxist anthropology but of any serious anthropology from literary criticism and theory. In the first half of the twentieth century, both literature and criticism were heavily influenced by the anthropology of Fraser and his followers: classical studies, in particular, were transformed by this, and the work of Gilbert Murray and Jane Harrison, for example, is still of value. The reason for this is that despite the rather literary, library-orientated nature of the anthropology of the period, it did attempt to explain features of early literature in terms of such concepts as tribal structure and ritual. This approach is not entirely dead even yet; consider the superb *Homo Necans: the anthropology of ancient Greek sacrificial ritual and myth* (Walter Burkert 1983). Significantly, this is not only a work in classics, but by a German scholar.

An example of the way in which Marxist theory in conjunction with anthropology could once be used to suggest solutions for a difficult problem in the history of culture – a problem which indeed could hardly be stated without some such historical theory – is to be found in the work of the English classical scholar George Thomson, in his masterpiece of 1941, *Aeschylus and Athens*. Thomson's general problem is that of the origin of drama – a field very well worked over by classical scholars in this century, since the irruption of anthropology transformed it, and persuaded scholars to look for the origin of mythology and drama in primitive ritual. His strength is in having an extraordinarily well-worked-out framework of materialist anthropological history to draw upon, which goes back to Engels, and before that to Morgan.[13] This strength of course becomes something of a weakness when the anthropology goes out of date – no one now would adopt Thomson's view of totemism, for example.

The more scientific approaches to anthropology of the mid-twentieth century have been less important for literature, but the central concept of idealist cultural anthropology which I referred to earlier – that the culture of each society offers a unique set of meanings in terms of which that society systematically interprets the world – has been enormously influential. It is this concept which is at the basis of whatever is valid in modern cultural relativism. There is very little to be said for the kind of cultural relativism which is based on emotional hostility to science or to American policy in Vietnam, or on post-modernist claims that the enlightenment project (of engaging in rational analysis of the world) is now over.[14] There is a good deal to be said for the basic anthropological stance that every human culture, however crazy and disoriented it may seem in the perspective of our culture, makes sense in its own terms, and must be understood in those terms before there is any attempt either to judge it or to explain it materialistically; though that would not be a good reason for refraining from materialist explanations altogether.

Given the richness of the Anglo-American tradition of empirical descriptive anthropology, it is a great pity that literary theorists of the last thirty years have come to identify anthropology with the late, unscientific mythological structuralism of Claude Lévi-Strauss. Every literary theorist in the English-speaking world has read some at least of Lévi-Strauss and has read Derrida's critique of him, 'Structure, Sign and Play in the Discourse of the Human Sciences', with its ultimate, anti-metaphysical relativism. In the early 1970s, for example, I suppose that everybody who had not already read it in the original French, read the Weightmans's translation of *Introduction to a Science of Mythology*, or at least looked at the title-pages of the four massive, fanciful volumes: *The Raw and the Cooked*, *From Honey to Ashes*, *The Origin of Table Manners*, and *The Naked Man*. No literary critic or theorist that I know of read Marshall Sahlins's book, published in English at that time: *Stone Age Economics,* or the materialist attack on Sahlins in Marvin Harris's theoretical work, *Cultural Materialism.*

This applies as much to professed Marxist theorists as to eclectic ones. It is a kind of scandal, though it is not particularly surprising. It is a scandal because Sahlins's book represents a serious study of the economics of primitive societies, which ought to have provoked a careful revaluation of the distinguished Marxist tradition in anthropological theory. Lévi-Strauss's book, on the other hand, is a rambling folly which Lévi-Strauss himself described as mythology about mythology. It is not surprising, because the Althusserian Marxism, popular among literary theorists in that horrible decade, is a philosophical construction that has little interest in any kind of fact; on the other hand, it owes a great deal to the methods and speculations of Jacques Lacan, and he owed a great deal to the original conceptions of Lévi-Strauss.[15]

One reason why the Marxist tradition in anthropology has been neglected is that it descends from Engels. A peculiar feature of Western Marxism in the last thirty years has been that Engels has often come to stand for everything in the Marxist tradition that led to Stalinist orthodoxy. In fact, the true offence of Engels, in the eyes of Western Marxists, was his heroic attempt to present a version of Marxism in which philosophical speculation was largely superseded by detailed scientific understanding of the world. It is true that this attempt failed. But one gets the impression that some of the most important Western Marxists would have hated it to succeed. For a Gramsci, a Lukács, or even, in most of his works, an Adorno, there was no question of looking for a better sort of objective social science. That was not what Marxism was about; and it would have seriously limited the political voluntarism of the first two and the philosophical purity of all three. These anti-scientific and anti-materialist attitudes remain on the left nowadays, even when Marxism has gone.

2   CULTURAL IMMATERIALISM

From the point of view I have been elaborating, the chief defects of the 'cultural materialisms' found in literary and cultural studies are that they are not materialist; and they are not scientific. They are deliberately non-economistic; they are consciously trying to get away from the 'base-superstructure metaphor' whereas they ought to be consciously trying to explain as much as possible in terms of it – or, more precisely, in terms of a theory (not a metaphor) of economic causation. The same criticisms apply to other types of post-Marxist theory: for example to the neo-Gramscian framework of analysis of popular culture and to Foucauldian forms of the history of ideas, institutions and types of subjectivity.

I don't want to do literary 'cultural materialism' an injustice, so I shall follow the description given by two of its recent practitioners: Jonathan Dollimore and Alan Sinfield in their book *Political Shakespeare* (1985). It draws on what they call the analytic, rather than the evaluative sense of culture, which is used in the social sciences and especially anthropology, and 'seeks to describe the whole system of significations by which a society or a section of it understands itself and its relations with the world'. This suggests the idealist anthropological sense of culture; but that would not be quite fair. They go on to say: ' "Materialism" is opposed to "idealism": it insists that culture does not (cannot) transcend the material forces and relations of production. Culture is not simply a reflection of the economic and political system, but nor can it be independent of it. Cultural materialism therefore studies the implication of literary texts in history.'

Nothing is said here about scientific explanation, and Dollimore and Sinfield have no theoretical contribution to make to a general, but politically neutral, science of human culture. They have other fish to fry. Cultural materialism, for them, includes work on the cultures of subordinate and marginalised groups like schoolchildren and skinheads; and work on the economic and political system of Elizabethan and Jacobean England and the particular institutions of cultural production like court, patronage and theatre; and all stations in between. And this work is intensely political. 'It registers its commitment to the transformation of a social order which exploits people on grounds of race, gender, and class' (all quotes, pp. vii-viii).

How is this commitment to be realised? Consider Sinfield's most recent work on Shakespeare and his contemporaries: *Faultlines: Cultural Materialism and the Politics of Dissident Readings* (1992). He is attacking the usual enemies: the Christian essentialist-humanists who have determined the canon; the ideological legitimation of oppressive social orders. His attack on the canon is one of almost unbelievable modesty. We don't have to endorse reactionary values as the insights of genius, transcending historical contexts. 'Canonical texts may then be respected as serious attempts to comprehend and intervene in the world, and we may quarrel with them as questionable constructions made by other people in other circumstances. This is a rough program for cultural materialism, and it is the dominant method of this book' (p. 22). What an excellent method; what a modest programme!

'Faultlines' are the cracks in ideological structures where dissidence pokes out; and substantial literary texts tend to be written across them (p. 235). This is a version of a standard Marxist position clearly present in Caudwell or Lukács: the point for classic Marxists would be that such contradictions in the texts represent underlying economic contradictions; a determinate Marxist reading leads out of the text into real (material, economic) history. The point for Sinfield seems to be that such works are not susceptible to any decisive reading; strategies of intellectual containment do not quite contain. But when everything is said and done, the whole conflict is still only about readings; the class enemy is clearly the man in the next room in college, who is using literature to defend humanism, the canon and literary determinacy; his name is Bradley, Tillyard, Kermode, James Wood (with whom Sinfield has regular spats in *The London Review of Books*) or, and specially, some New Historicist critic (probably not Stephen Greenblatt but an ideal-type derived from him) who in his model of dissident discourses entrapped in dominant ones sounds, in a sophisticated way, like Tillyard reborn. But whichever enemy we are considering, the class struggle has been replaced by the classroom struggle.

Anthropological cultural materialism also has views on race, gender, and class, which are worth comparing with these; I will take my example from gender. The modern capitalist demand for labour, cash crops, and raw materials has upset the demographic balance throughout the world. Population continues to grow in the third world because of the favourable cost-benefit ratio (to a family in a society with no welfare state) of children as child labour and as social security for the parents in their old age. Population falls in the first world as the cost of raising children increases and the economic return from them approaches zero. As capital flows overseas, inflation in the first world produces a requirement for two wage-earners per small family. 'From this we get quite plausibly the generation gap, the flamboyant redefinition of sex roles, delayed marriages, "shacking up", communes, homosexual couples, and one-person families.'[16]

It will be seen that anthropological cultural materialism here offers a materialist explanation of the appearance of certain political causes such as gender politics; literary cultural materialism offers a political commitment to those causes but no explanation for them. And the two may well be mutually destructive. If Harris is right, left-wing gender politics in the first world is merely a superstructural adaptation to the global scale of modern capitalist industry, and is wholly complicit with it. Perhaps to support feminism in the first world is to support capitalism; to oppose capitalism might be to try to return first-world women to traditional family roles, in a generally poorer world. This may not be true; what is impressive is the sheer weight of hidden economic determination that is possible and that we need to explore.

It would be a mistake here to separate out literary cultural materialism from other movements of the post-Marxist, or Marxist-revisionist left

(Sinfield for example draws heavily on both Althusser and Foucault as well as Williams) or treatments of popular culture from treatments of classic literature. All show the same fundamental drive towards dematerialising socialism; moving away from economic reductionism; grounding cultural judgements in a politics which is itself ungrounded in anything but hyper-active liberal conscience. We can usefully illustrate this in the field of cultural studies, which was once seen as the most obvious area for Marxist analysis.

Consider the neo-Gramscian theoretical framework adopted in the anthology *Popular Culture and Social Relations*, edited in 1986 by Tony Bennett, Colin Mercer and Janet Woollacott, with articles by Stuart Hall and others. The authors are impressed by the immense sophistication of modern theory; depressed by the marginalisation of socialist discourse about culture – by the manifest fact that nobody cares what socialist intellectuals think. Looking back, they want to supersede the two great schools of socialist cultural theory: the (Althusserian) structuralist and the post-Williams culturalist. They want also to supersede the two standard left-wing attitudes: on the one hand a traditional intellectual contempt for popular culture when compared with high culture, and on the other an attempt to recover and celebrate an authentic working-class culture of the past. Both of these, they think, lead to unthinking contempt for the popular culture of the present.

Their solution is found in Gramsci: in the concept of hegemony, and in the view of popular culture neither as the domain of a set of values imposed by the dominant classes who own and control the media, nor as a spontaneous uprush of authentic proletarian culture, but as an always renegotiable compromise between the two – as a site of negotiation. In the absence of classical Marxist theory, however, it is not clear who are negotiating, or for what. It seems less the working-class organic intellectuals negotiating with the bourgeois ones about who should seize control of the television companies than the contributors to Open University Course U203 negotiating with each other about what critical language to employ when writing about television programmes.

By 1992, we can see cultural studies moving back from even this much socialism. Eagleton, in the review already mentioned at the end of the last chapter, could write that the neo-Gramscian paradigm seemed 'so eminently accurate and judicious a case that it is hard to see how it could be effectively challenged'; and, for the record, I would entirely agree with him. But we are fuddy-duddies. Gramsci, for more modern minds, is 'the last bulwark of totalising theory'. Tony Bennett, now relying on the work of Laclau and Mouffe, argues that the Gramscian moment is over; the assumptions underlying Gramsci – in particular about class – can no longer be sustained theoretically nor be of much service politically.[17]

The papers in Grossberg, Nelson and Treichler are still left-wing, if rarely Marxist and never materialist; here, it seems to me, we have a large collection of academics looking for a personal identity in oppositional politics, and using whatever theories come to hand for the purpose. Consider the feminist who explained how much she enjoyed the pornographic fanzines written by a group of working-class American women around the (male) leading characters in *Star Trek*.[18] This upsets every possible stereotype, and I love it. Elsewhere in cultural studies – particularly in some North American work – Eagleton found rampant capitalism: the rejection of value-judgements within 'a style of discourse at once clamorously "anti-élitist" and politically vacuous . . . the most craven capitulation to the logic of the market place'.[19]

This of course is very much what an old-fashioned economic materialist would have predicted. What seems clear is that there is simply no logical connection between cultural studies and socialism, though for historical reasons many cultural analysts are more or less socialists. There is no reason why in the long term cultural studies courses should not become wholly integrated in capitalist economies, serving as media training, and there are strong economic pressures for this to happen. Moreover, the one major defining feature of cultural studies – its concentration on the recent and the popular – is in itself a way of presenting advanced capitalism as the unchallengeable horizon of historical possibility. It is not simply that, as a principled basis for opposition to capitalism, the Leavisite canon is a much better bet; **any** historically based study which gave access to alternative social possibilities (Homer, the Chinese classics, Red Indian folklore) would be a better bet.

These modern approaches are aspects both of socialist cultural theory and of a cultural campaign for a socialist transformation of society. They fail because they neither are nor contain a reductive economistic science, nor any practical method to organise the workers. A really old-fashioned Marxist might complain that they are an attempt to bring about the revolution by means of literary commentary. I have some sympathy with that objection. Once you have grasped the weight of material determination of cultures, all forms of cultural politics look rather silly. I suggest that literary cultural materialism is a way in which traditional literary discourse, far from being transformed into something quite different by economic materialism, has managed to tame and subordinate that approach for the purpose of left-wing literary commentary, and will probably have no political effect at all.

3   THE ANTHROPOLOGY OF THE LITERARY CANON

I have argued that cultural materialism in anthropology is the legitimate heir to scientific socialism, and preserves whatever is intellectually defensible in it. It preserves, that is, the regulative principle that the study of human culture should be a scientific investigation into underlying causes rather than a purely empathetic or humanistic affair. And it adopts the empirical hypothesis that the history of human cultural development can be explained in large part by the history of human economic conflict. It maps out both of these onto concrete, if very large-scale, histories that historians can test, rather than Hegelian or Althusserian schemata, or Foucauldian fantasies. It rejects the dialectic, and the details of Marxist economics. Radicals won't like it, because it offers little support to radical politics, which is so often a politics of gesture, self-fulfilment, and world-renewal-myths. It is free from fantasies about revolution, and offers little to ethnic or gender politics save explanatory hypotheses. It suggests a politics which is ecological, but rational.

It is natural to ask whether there is or could be at least a candidate literary theory on these lines which preserves everything that is defensible in Marxist cultural and literary theory. I think there is, or can be; but it will run counter to almost all the received ideas of the last thirty years. Philosophers and critics have expended great intellectual labour over that period, largely to exclude the possibility of such a theory. Insofar as post-structuralism has a single theme, it is that a formal theory of culture always subverts itself. We need to meet some of these criticisms.

My general position is that the study of literature is at one and the same time essentially historical, and a proper part of cultural anthropology. The literary institutions in society are subject to the same kind of material – that is, economic – determination as any other institutions; they evolve, like other institutions, to satisfy economic needs. At the same time, literature is essentially historical, in two distinct ways. First, the cultural conventions in which literature is written and understood have a history of their own, which interacts with general history: people of a particular time understand themselves partly in terms of these historically constructed cultural conventions. Second, there is an irreducibly specific history of literature in which particular works like *The Bible* or *The Iliad* influence particular writers who may well live thousands of years later. Hence literature has a dimension in literary-historical time as well as one in social space.

3.1   The 'radical' critique of anthropology

But anthropology itself has not escaped the attentions of the epistemological radicals. It has been seen, with some justification, as an intellectual arm of Western colonialism, designed to produce knowledge that colonial rulers can use; it has also been seen as a way of neutralising the challenge of alien ethical standards; or of 'creating' alien cultures as a form of European self-image. A recent book by Anthony Pagden – *European Encounters with the New World* – explores these troubling issues. Pagden is scholarly and balanced; but a more radical reviewer, Ziauddin Sardar,[20] sticks his neck out for him. 'Anthropology ensures . . . that the more things change, the more Western perceptions of non-Western cultures remain the same. . . . The West still thinks in terms of good and bad savages.'

I suggest that this view is absurd. All cultures are ethnocentric; but it is a specific discovery of Western cultural anthropology, correcting the pre-existing prejudices in Western culture, that 'savage' cultures are as sophisticated in their own way as Western ones. Just as the first big thing comparative linguistics tells us is that there are no primitive, cognitively inferior languages, so the first big thing cultural anthropology tells us is that there are no primitive, cognitively inferior peoples. Radical epistemology, of course, wants to see the very objectivity that makes possible that discovery as a characteristic of Western culture, and to relativise it. But, as usual, epistemological radicalism is less politically radical than solid scientific research based on realist assumptions about the object of research. The objective, comparative study of cultures has corrosive effects on traditional ethnocentric assumptions both in the East and in the West. The conflictual, relativising perspective in which the West's assumptions about the East are seen as no better or worse than the East's assumptions about the West leaves both sets of assumptions unchastened.

For a scientific approach to the world's literature to be possible, within a scientific anthropology, we need radically different philosophical assumptions. I would identify my own position as one deriving from a general philosophical realism, with a conjecturalist epistemology, and a Tarskian theory of truth.[21] This is not the place for a full-scale defence of such a position, though the footnotes will give some indication of it; it is enough to say that this is intended as a philosophical alternative to post-structuralist and relativist positions, which I reject in every area from philosophy of science to aesthetics.

3.2 The five realist principles of a literary anthropology

The first philosophical principle necessary for an objective cultural anthropology is philosophical realism; and I suggest that this is necessary for an anthropology of literature too. Human cultures, in their almost limitless variety and difference, are described by anthropologists, not invented by them. They exist independently of the observer and are open to scientific study. So do, so are, literatures. To invert Eagleton, we can say that just as insects exist and have existed, in the present and the past of the natural world, independently of the entomologists who produce theories about them, so works of literature – poems, plays and stories – exist and have existed, in the social world, in innumerable human cultures present and past, independently of later critics and literary historians who have studied them.

The concept of literature is constructed, or reconstructed from a pre-existing 'common-sense' notion, by the literary theorist, just as the concept of insects is constructed, or reconstructed from a common-sense notion, by the entomologist. But literary theorists don't (in that capacity) construct works of literature any more than entomologists construct insects. In both cases there is something there with a structure of its own to have a concept of; and it will still be there, or have been there, even if nobody ever forms a classificatory concept of it. Natural biological processes produce insects; cultural processes produce literature; both types of process go on working even when (as in most periods of human or natural history) there are no French-trained philosophers around to observe them.

The second principle that we need to adopt is an epistemological one which is crucial for the philosophy of any empirical science. It is that what we call 'knowledge' is at once conjectural and empirical; it is conjectural because it is empirical; and this applies as much to the cultural sciences and to the study of literatures as to the natural sciences. That knowledge has this essentially uncertain character is a consequence of our first, realist assumption, not a denial of it. If the world exists independently of any propositions we believe about it, then it is possible for those propositions to be true or false; and the only way we can check whether they are true or false is by making the experiment of acting upon them. I thus find myself, by way of a realist ontology and a conjecturalist epistemology, in agreement with the young Marx that the sole test of our knowledge is in practice. But that is not to say that knowledge can ever be identified with practice, nor that practice can make knowledge certain.

The whole idealist tradition of arguing that we construct the world in our heads, or in discourse, is a mystified recognition of a truth about human ideas of the world: that we construct ideas in our heads, or in discourse, **before checking them against reality by acting on them**. The Derridan principle, that there is no 'transcendental signified', nothing that escapes the play of signifiers, is actually true if we take it to mean that there is no idea about the world that is innately given as true, and no idea that is not constructed in discourse. It would be quite false if we took it to mean that there were no objects, independent of our ideas about them, which can make our actions succeed or fail. That principle would return us directly to idealism. I am afraid Derrida's work is usually used to defend rather than to attack idealism; what his own purpose is I do not know.

The advantage of philosophical realism and epistemological conjecturalism for literary theory is that they make available for us several types of discourse that it is not easy to do without. We can, for example, talk of truth, and explicate it as '**correspondence with reality**'. We can talk of **science** as making **hypotheses** about the world. We can say that **fiction** makes assertions which do not correspond with reality, and are not meant as truth-claims. We can thus distinguish in principle between truths, scientific hypotheses and fictions. On the basis of such distinctions as these, we can discuss the way in which literature throws light upon a social world that exists independently of literature. These are all things which, on the face of it, literary theory needs to be able to do. Of course, the rough definitions above need refinement; and we shall need to supplement notions like literal correspondence with reality with notions like metaphorical correspondence. But these are straightforward developments along well-mapped paths.

The contrast with many contemporary relativist positions could hardly be more marked. The modern theorist often prides himself on undercutting the distinction betweeen the literal and the metaphorical, between the original and the supplement, between truth, hypothesis and fiction; and this is seen, not as an invitation to muddleheadedness but as a mark of superior sophistication. The fact is that these distinctions **do** collapse if you **do not** adopt a realist position in philosophy. The closer you get to the view that there is no non-textual reality, the harder it is to make a distinction in principle between truth and fiction. It is a mark of post-structuralist debility that most modern critics don't mind this at all. An intelligent response to Derrida would be to accept practically every argument that could be extracted from his work, and to treat them all as *reductio ad absurdum* arguments directed against the premises of post-structuralist critics.[22]

267

The third principle that we should take, this time from the materialist version of anthropology rather than cultural anthropology in general, is that it is the business of science to explain the world, and not merely observe it. The purpose of science is not merely to record observations, nor even to establish law-like relationships between those observations, but to offer explanatory hypotheses. For this purpose, some research strategy is needed. Materialist anthropology assumes that, because of the nature of human beings as social animals exploiting a limited physical resource base, one fundamental type of explanation for cultural forms will be economic.

In order to test such a research strategy, it is not sufficient to find one or two cultural forms for which economic explanations are plausible. One needs in principle to look at the whole range of human cultures, throughout the whole of human history. Only so can we hope to distinguish between, say, the phenomena which are genetically programmed for all human beings (like the capacity to speak a language) and those which require explanation in terms of a particular economic and political situation (like the rise of the novel). I don't myself believe that it is appropriate to give an economic explanation for the bare existence of the arts – human beings seem to be genetically programmed to tell stories, sing and dance, play games, etc., as they are to use language. But it is my conviction that every particular cultural and artistic development in human history can be given an intellectually interesting economic explanation, though the explanation will never explain everything.

The argument that the economic has explanatory priority is not the same as a philosophical claim that the economic is an essence, and the cultural merely an appearance. The experience of reading a short story is as real as the experience of eating a potato. And the potato is in no sense the essence of the short story. But the cultural materialist would expect the complex cultural institution of which short story reading is part to be partially determined by struggles over potatoes – or more generally, over control of material resources, and would be interested in finding out exactly how it was determined. (A non-trivial question – what is the connection between one of the most famous collections of short stories – 'Dubliners' – and a powerful collective experience, half a century before, of there being no potatoes to eat in Ireland?)

The fourth principle that we derive from materialist anthropology is that human culture is historical. It is indeed to the credit of the materialist stream within anthropology that it has retained a historical perspective, where non-materialist cultural anthropology has been so concerned with celebrating the uniqueness of each culture, that it has forgotten that every culture must be historically formed. It is at this point that the traditional standpoint of the humanities can offer a massive correction to pure anthropology. It is clear that to a very great extent the elements of human culture – religions, philosophies, sciences, etc. – develop autonomously in accordance with a logic of their own, each new development building upon earlier ones, sometimes in the immediate and sometimes in the very remote past. Hegel, here, got it right, as did T.S. Eliot and Harold Bloom.[23] Human culture is historically constructed. We inherit everything from the past, either in the form of an unconsciously accepted set of rules in the culture, or in the form of a consciousness of past history, to which we refer.[24] Originality takes the form, not of jumping out of our culture – we literally can't do that – nor of severing our connection with the past – we can't do that either, only become unconscious of it – but of encapsulating the past as a part of the meaning of the new thing that we do.

The case is made specially clear when we consider literature. *Paradise Lost* is a Christian epic articulating a political and ideological conflict of the seventeenth century. But its new articulation of that conflict is literally unintelligible if we do not already have in our minds the pre-existing articulation of such conflicts provided by Graeco-Roman mythology and the Christian religion. And it is partially unintelligible if we do not have in our minds the actual texts of the Bible, of Homer, of Virgil, and of others. A materialist would, I hope, want to explain the whole historical development in terms of economic conflict; would want to see the whole history of literature as at once a revelation and a concealment of a deeper economic history that partly causes it, and that gives it much of its meaning and general human significance. But the route to such an understanding is through the actual history of literature proceeding with its own relative autonomy, within which Homer and the Bible directly influence Milton, jumping across the centuries to do so. It is not by way of an easy economic allegorisation, in which each work is seen as an automatic outgrowth of the economically determined culture of its own time.

What is the implication of these philosophical principles for the study of literature? It is possible to argue that what is wrong with modern literary cultural materialists is that they are not theoretical enough, they are not anthropological enough, they are not materialist enough, and they are not historical enough. They may play with the analytic, rather than the evaluative sense of culture, but they are not really committed to it. Literary cultural materialists, like anthropological ones, ought to be interested in uncovering the systematic relationships between the material determinants of human life and their embodiments in art and literature throughout the whole of human history. But one has no sense that they are just as interested in stone-age societies as in our own, and as ready to recognise literature in one as in the other; nor that they are interested in fully generalisable theoretical explanations covering all human history.

3.3 The anthropological status of classics and canons

Looked at from an anthropological point of view, modern literary theory is extraordinarily parochial, both in the literature which it is concerned with, and the politics. Consider, for example, the Williams/Bennett suggestion (see p. 230) that the category 'literature' should be restricted to: 'the dominant forms of bourgeois writing as a historically limited category referring to a particular type of cultural practice'. This is not really a theoretical proposition, but a move in a war against a specific type of high culture, embodied in certain literary canons and certain ways of regarding them. One can see this by asking what theoretical category Bennett is going to use to cover the forms of writing that his definition has left out. The answer is that he hasn't thought about it. He has no category.

Suppose instead we ask empirical anthropological questions that can't be settled from the *Oxford English Dictionary*. How old is literature? How many different kinds of society do we find it in? What other types of human activity does it naturally group with? What social functions does it have, and are they always the same? For questions of this sort, it is clear that we must think of 'literature' as a fuzzy class of objects including, but not necessarily limited to, poems, plays and stories, and, since most human societies have been illiterate, we must abandon the prejudice that these are necessarily written down. With this refinement of the common-sense notion of 'literature' to guide us, we can see that all types of human society from hunter-gatherer band level societies to advanced industrial ones have produced poems, plays and stories, though the forms have varied. This is not quite Dr Leavis's concept of literature. But it looks as if, whether or not 'literature' in this sense is a category of our own society, it is a reasonable non-evaluative theoretical category for a general anthropology to use. It then becomes a matter of scientific and theoretical argument – of very much the same kind as an entomologist engages in over the category of 'insects' – how useful this category is.

One might further argue that poems, plays and stories group naturally, as fuzzy classes do, through a whole series of interconnections, with music, painting, sculpture, mime, dance, and, nowadays, film. (For example, most poems are lyrics of songs; music goes with dance; plays go with mime; etc.) A further anthropologically possible category – not made any less possible for scientific use by the fact that we happen to use it in our own society – is 'the arts'. Then the obvious anthropological generalisation is that the arts are cultural universals like the institution of marriage, say; though their particular forms are culture specific, just as the forms marriages take and the varieties of kinship terminology are culture specific. The arts almost certainly go back to the palaeolithic (there is physical evidence for this in the case of painting and sculpture, and possibly music).

What is the relationship of 'the arts' to other social institutions? One obvious way of putting it, which is not the less theoretically satisfactory for being obvious, is that they have served many different functions: religious functions, state celebrations, paid entertainment, even private relaxation; but there is no special reason to identify them with any one of these functions. (Even in our own society, the same poem might fulfil any one of these functions. On this view there is no sense whatever in the kind of argument that runs: 'the ancient Egyptians didn't have poems, in our sense; it was all religion then'. What might be sensible would be to say that they had religious poetry but no other kind – if indeed those are the facts of the case.) I have suggested that we do not need to offer any cultural materialist explanation for the existence of the arts; they are probably part of the species-specific behaviour of *homo sapiens*, like language. But there is a rich enough field for cultural materialism in explaining the specific forms the arts assume in each society, and the social functions they fulfil.

Some of the most committed cultural radicals will have no objection to anything said so far. Their commitment is not against the existence of literature, in the sense of poems, plays and stories, but against that of literature, in the sense of a privileged group of such works, which define the higher values of a culture. What they are really against is literary **canons**, literary **classics**, **classical literatures**, **traditions** and **great traditions** in the sense of Eliot and Leavis.[25] They are fighting for liberty – the liberty to put contemporary literature or popular television series on the syllabus. Their use of the anthropological sense of culture is a strategic one, with a rather small end in view. For this reason they talk about privileged classes of literature as if the nineteenth-century bourgeoisie were the first to recognise them, despite the evidence glaring at them from the pages of Ben Jonson, Shakespeare, Dante, Virgil, Aristotle and, of course, the Bible to show that the phenomenon is as old as civilisation. A Marxist might say that it is as old as class society, is an aspect of class society, and serves the social purpose of class domination. But this question too needs anthropological examination, since non-state societies have their classics.

The first priority of a cultural materialist approach to literary canons, etc., seen as social institutions, would be to provide an accurate ethnographic and historical account of them. The second would be to provide a materialist explanation of their features, and their history. The claim that literature (plays, poems, etc.) is a bourgeois phenomenon is simply bad ethnography and bad history; it is factually incorrect. The claim that literature (the privileging of certain plays, poems, etc. over others for certain cultural purposes) is a bourgeois phenomenon is also bad ethnography; it has occurred in numerous pre-capitalist societies. The claim that such privileging always serves the purposes of class domination, however, is a possible claim and an interesting one. It is worth exploring this by considering the range of ways in which, in different cultures, particular works have been picked out; and seeing what explanations suggest themselves for this practice.

Perhaps the most obvious purpose for which writings are specially selected – and for which they may or may not be specially written – is religious. Numerous religions from times well before Judaism have had **sacred books**, which for believers may have great indwelling power. Blasphemy against such sacred books may be punished by death – even in the twentieth century, if the book concerned is the Koran! For the sceptical anthropologist, on the other hand – and I hope all anthropologists will be sceptical on such a point – being a sacred book is an ascribed, rather than an intrinsic quality. It hasn't necessarily anything to do with the content. The London Telephone Directory could be sacred if some religion decided it was – though it would have to be a very silly religion. The anthropology of sacred books is a proper part of the anthropology of religion, and our materialist explanations will be largely those which we give for religion.

It is clear that class conflict plays some part here – often being the force that underlies conflict between two religions, or two sects of the same religion. It is doubtful if class can be the whole story. Ethnic rivalries and nationalism are also important, and interact with class issues – consider the circumstances in which the Jews 'found' their sacred book in the temple, on their return from Babylonian exile. As radicals have painfully discovered in the last thirty years, it seems impossible to reduce ethnic rivalries to class conflict; though one can certainly use competition for material resources to explain some of the history of both these conflicts.

But it is doubtful if all these together can completely account for religion. There are general human needs to be addressed – such as the need for consolation in the face of death. As we saw in considering Jack Lindsay's interpretation of Bunyan, there are certain aspects of the concept of heaven which are not captured by the image of life after the revolution. Few religions could be more transparently hierarchical than that of Egypt, which extended the social hierarchy of the kingdom forever beyond the grave. But even that early and powerful sacred book, *The Book of the Dead*, is addressing some needs that are not class-bound.

Another major function of literature throughout the history of the world has been education. There is a tendency in the modern left to tell the story of 'The Rise of English' as if the early twentieth century was the first moment in which education was based on literary study. Ethnographically, however, one would have to recognise education by the study of **literary classics** as a standard institution in most large-scale societies for thousands of years now. Examinations on the classics were the main means of selecting Mandarins in the ancient Chinese empire. Western civilisations have based higher education on them ever since classical Greece, sometimes reading classics in their own language, and sometimes those in a foreign language. The classical Greeks studied Homer; the Romans studied archaic and classical Greek; Medieval Europe studied Latin books; Renaissance Europe kept these and added Greek ones. The twentieth-century innovation was not to base higher education on literature; it had always been based on literature. It was to reduce the importance of ancient, as opposed to modern, languages and to bring in a great deal more higher education not based on literature at all, but on the natural and the social sciences.

As in the case of sacred books, true believers like, say, Dr Leavis have tried to work out what intrinsic qualities confer classic status on particular books. Our sceptical anthropologist is more likely to argue that being a classic is an ascribed quality: classics are, and have been for thousands of years now, simply books chosen as texts by the educational institutions of the day. But that doesn't mean they have no properties of their own, or that the judgements that have been made of them by so many serious readers in the past are merely a projection of what the teachers taught; to think that (as some cultural materialists appear to do) would be to show an ethnocentric contempt for most ancient readers. There is overwhelming (though never unanimous) testimony that the books chosen as classics in every culture are mostly experienced as very good; one can spend one's whole life enjoyably in rereading them. How that can be requires an explanation, presumably in terms of the interaction of formal literary structures with cultural norms.

Literary education of this kind has always been tied in to class systems; indeed education always is, since élites always act to secure the education of their own children. But to suppose that the only reason for prescribing the classics of another culture is to secure the ascendancy of a particular class in one's own would be a mistake. For an English writer in the time of Sidney, Greek and Latin literature were incomparably richer than English; they provided the essential formal models for any future literature. By the time of Swift, this was not obviously so; by that of Macaulay, it was obviously not so. Greek and Latin literature, however, went on being the basis of ruling-class education till the twentieth century; and there were elements of symbolic class war in their supersession by English classics. To tell the whole story in class terms is to miss the point that Sidney, Swift and Macaulay agreed upon; that there were qualities in the writing of these works, distinct from any political implication they might have, that readers valued and a writer could learn from. It is not conceivable that they were all unconsciously talking about class all the time; partly because they were all consciously talking about class for some of the time; and partly because the nature of the class war changed, and they were not all on the same side of it.

Much of the excitement in recent literary debate has been generated by attacks upon 'the literary canon'. What is a canon that it should be so important? It arises first for sacred books. There are often considerable uncertainties about what books actually are sacred; from this rises the problem of forming a canon. In some cultures – Tibetan, Orthodox Judaic? – religious and educational institutions are difficult to distinguish; and the sacred books are the same as the classics. In Western culture this has never been so; indeed the sharp opposition between canonical scriptures and humanist classics has been a source of great intellectual energy and important theoretical developments, in the time of Augustine, of Aquinas, and the Renaissance, for example.

The habit of modern critics, of calling the English classics 'the canon', reads rather like a comic supplement to this great history – as if they collectively made up a modern bible. It suggests that the English classics are sacred; but nobody seriously believes this; it is indeed a hangover from the nineteenth-century notion that we needed a successor to Christianity and English Literature could provide it. The term obscures the fact that there can be good rational reasons for studying classic literature. One of these is that it provides an incomparable insight into human cultural history, including the processes which have constructed the critics themselves.

There is a foolish tendency among those who favour, say, cultural studies courses based largely on recent texts from the entertainment industry, but interpreted by the most sophisticated and up-to-date Marxist and post-Marxist theory, to claim that they are enlarging the scope of literary study. Mostly they are narrowing it enormously, by contracting the historical dimension to a point. Courses limited in this way are incapable of illuminating large-scale historical change; and they are ethnocentric in the extreme. And they are likely to be left behind by very small-scale historical change. A course on these lines, set up in the revolutionary excitement of the 1970s, might be a conscious attempt to construct, or to position, a new revolutionary class, on the eve of taking over.[26] It would be pointless to reproach such a course for lack of cultural continuity. But what is the use of it when the revolution does not come, and does not come, and will never come? When even the weaker students cease to believe in the revolution; and the white-haired staff are forced to turn to new radicalisms – to the third world, to feminism – which cannot be theorised within the old Marxist paradigm? (Aeschylus would have retained his relevance.)[27]

I am not, incidentally, attacking cultural studies courses as such, or even mistaking my caricature for the often impressive real thing; merely returning with interest a foolish stereotypical attack that is often made on those who favour extended historical study.

The real problem in the design of English literature courses was never that of respecting a sacred canon. It was to some extent that of providing a new or old class with an adequate self-understanding, which must include an adequate understanding of its own historical evolution and continuity. The traditional literature degree has as a tacit assumption that the class concerned is a ruling class, whose internal tradition goes back centuries, or even millennia. Many of the young lieutenants in the trenches in the First World War had read Homer in the original at school: Sarpedon's speech about the responsibility of aristocrats to defend the community which gives them their privileges spoke directly to them. We, now, in a modern literature degree, can read Homer in such a way as to understand something of what formed them. And though 'Homer's'[28] direct personal influence must have applied mainly to an educated minority, the 3,000-year literary tradition that he founded provided a space in which education was pursued and value-judgements were made. This is worth anthropological study.

It is the business of the rational study of literature to investigate these massive cultural continuities, and to try to explain them, preferably on materialist lines, in which literary continuities are seen as symptoms of more fundamental historical continuities, and the literary importance of works is tied in closely with their significance in revealing the workings of history. Only in this way can the structure of human culture be even partially understood. And only on this basis is a limited amount of conscious historical freedom possible. You cannot escape from history, only take off from your own present position within it; and you can only do that effectively if you understand what that position is. A study of the classics that disguise and reveal the fundamental development of one's own culture can be the most relevant and immediate present education, even when those classics are 300 or 3,000 years old, even when those classics are opposed to one's most fundamental convictions, and particularly when one's framework of analysis is a cultural materialist one.

NOTES

1. Angela McRobbie 'Post-Marxism and Cultural Studies: a Postscript', in Grossberg *et al.* (eds) 1992, *Cultural Studies.*
2. N. Chagnon 1968a, *Yanomamo: The Fierce People*; 1992, *Yanomamö: The Last Days of Eden.* I gather that between these two books infanticide retrospectively disappeared!
3. G.P. Murdock 1967, *Ethnographic Atlas*; Harris 1969, *The Rise of Anthropological Theory*, Chapter 21.
4. Harris 1968, pp. 180–215.
5. Marshall Sahlins 1974, *Stone Age Economics*, is far the most rational argument for this.
6. Consider such a classic work as Ruth Benedict 1935, *Patterns of Culture.*
7. For discussion see Jackson 1991, *The Poverty of Structuralism*, pp. 91–3.
8. Lieberman 1984.
9. Lee and DeVore 1976.
10. Cf. Ian Watt 1957.
11. Lee and DeVore 1976.
12. Harris 1969, *The Rise of Anthropological Theory*; 1978, *Cannibals and Kings*; 1980, *Cultural Materialism.*
13. Lewis H. Morgan 1877, *Ancient Society*; Friedrich Engels 1884, *The Origins of the Family, Private Property, and the State in the Light of the Researches of Lewis H. Morgan.*
14. Cf. Baudrillard 1988; Lyotard 1989.
15. Lévi-Strauss moved from a strictly scientific view of anthropology in the mid 1940s to a total denial of scientific intentions in the late 1960s and 1970s. For full discussion see Jackson 1991, *The Poverty of Structuralism.* For Althusser see Chapter 7, this volume.
16. Harris 1980, pp. 112–13. (Harris doesn't mention immigration restrictions and consequent racism in his list, but the point is obvious.)
17. Tony Bennett 1992, 'Putting Policy into Cultural Studies' in Grossberg *et al.* 1992.
18. Constance Penley 1992, 'Feminism, Psychoanalysis, Popular Culture'.
19. Eagleton 1992, 'Proust, punk, or both: How ought we to value popular culture?' *The Times Literary Supplement* (18 December 1992). This is a review of Grossberg *et al.* 1992, along with Connor 1992, McGuigan 1992 and Agger 1992.
20. *The Independent*, 6 January 1993.
21. Jackson 1991; Bhaskar 1978; 1986; Popper 1959; 1963; 1972; Feigl and Sellars 1949; Linsky 1952: articles by Frege, Russell, Tarski, Carnap, Quine.
22. For further argument, see Jackson 1991, *The Poverty of Structuralism*, Chapter 5: 'Textual Metaphysics and the Anti-Foundation Myths of Derrida'. I will state here, without elaboration, that in my view Derrida has discovered a very powerful technique for uncovering metaphysical assumptions in texts. His method is, however, helpless against explicit metaphysical claims. All you can deconstruct are the illustrative examples which may or may not accompany the claims.

23. T.S. Eliot 1919, 'Tradition and the Individual Talent', in Eliot 1932; Harold Bloom 1975, *A Map of Misreading*.
24. Jackson 1991, p. 67.
25. T.S. Eliot 1919, 'Tradition and the Individual Talent', in Eliot 1932, *Selected Essays*; F.R. Leavis 1936, *Revaluation*; 1948, *The Great Tradition*.
26. This is a hypothetical or ideal-type course intended to make an analytical point, not a claim about actual cultural studies courses.
27. *The Oresteia* (fifth century BC) – probably the key text in Western literature on the subjection of women.
28. There was probably no such person. 'Homer' was a tradition of bardic writing going back to the Mycenaean Age. Our classical tradition, like our sacred book, takes us back to the Bronze Age.

BOOKS

Lewis H. Morgan 1877 *Ancient Society, or Researches in the Lines of Human Progress from Savagery through Barbarism to Civilisation*.

Friedrich Engels 1884 *The Origins of the Family, Private Property, and the State in the Light of the Researches of Lewis H. Morgan*.

Marvin Harris 1969 *The Rise of Anthropological Theory*.

1975 *Cows, Pigs, Wars and Witches*.

1978 *Cannibals and Kings: the Origins of Cultures*.

1980 *Cultural Materialism*.

1990 *Our Kind: Who we are, where we came from, and where we are going: the evolution of human life and culture*.

Marshall Sahlins 1974 *Stone Age Economics*.

Philip Lieberman 1984 *The Biology and Evolution of Language*.

Jonathan Dollimore and **Alan Sinfield** (eds) 1985 *Political Shakespeare*.

Tony Bennett, **Colin Mercer** and **Janet Woollacott** (eds) 1986 *Popular Culture and Social Relations*.

Lawrence Grossberg, **Cary Nelson** and **Paula Treichler** (eds) 1992 *Cultural Studies*.

Bibliography

Ackroyd, Peter 1984 *T.S. Eliot* London: Hamish Hamilton.

Adorno, Theodor 1956 *Against Epistemology: a Metacritique: Studies in Husserl and the Phenomenological Antinomies* Oxford: Basil Blackwell.

Adorno, Theodor 1966 *Negative Dialectics* London: Routledge.

Adorno, Theodor 1967 *Prisms* London: Neville Spearman.

Agger, Ben 1992 *Cultural Studies as Critical Theory* Falmer.

Agulhon, Maurice 1973 *The Republican Experiment: 1848–52* Cambridge: CUP.

Alexander, Arch B.D. 1907 *A Short History of Philosophy* Glasgow: James Maclehose Glasgow University Press.

Althusser, Louis 1965 *For Marx* London: Verso.

Althusser, Louis 1970 *Lenin and Philosophy* London: Verso.

Althusser, Louis 1984 *Essays on Ideology* London: Verso.

Althusser, Louis 1990 *Philosophy and the Spontaneous Philosophy of the Scientists* London: Verso.

Althusser, Louis 1978 'The Crisis of Marxism' in *Marxism Today* (ed. Martin Jacques) London: The Communist Party.

Althusser, Louis and **Balibar, Etienne** 1968 *Reading Capital* London: Verso.

Anderson, Perry 1969 'Components of the National Culture' in Cockburn and Blackburn 1969 London: Penguin.

Anderson, Perry 1974 *Lineages of the Absolutist State* London: NLB.

Anderson, Perry 1976 *Considerations on Western Marxism* London: Verso.

Anderson, Perry 1980 *Arguments within English Marxism* London: Verso.

Anderson, Perry 1983 *In the Tracks of Historical Materialism* London: Verso.

Appignanesi, Lisa (ed.) 1989 *Postmodernism: ICA Documents* London: Free Association Books.

Arato, Andrew and **Breines, Paul** 1979 *The Young Lukács and the Origins of Western Marxism* London: Pluto Press.

Arvon, Henri 1970 (trans. Helen Lane 1973) *Marxist Aesthetics* Ithaca and London: Cornell University Press.

Ashton, Robert 1978 *The English Civil War: Conservatism and Revolution 1603–49* London: Weidenfeld and Nicolson.

Avineri, Shlomo 1968 *The Social and Political Thoughts of Karl Marx* Cambridge: CUP.

Ayer, A. J. 1956 *The Problem of Knowledge* London: Penguin.

Bachelard, Gaston 1934 (trans. Arthur Goldhammer 1984) *The New Scientific Spirit* Boston: Beacon Press.

Barker, F., Hulme, P., Iverson, M. and **Loxley, D.** (eds) 1983 *The Politics of Theory* Colchester: University of Essex Press.

Barker, F., Hulme, P., Iverson, M. and **Loxley, D.** (eds) 1986 *Literature, Politics and Theory: Papers from the Essex Conference 1976–84* London: Methuen.

Barrell, John 1972 *The Idea of Landscape and the Sense of Place 1730–1840: an Approach to the Poetry of John Clare* Cambridge: CUP.

Barrell, John 1980 *The Dark Side of the Landscape: the Rural Poor in English Painting 1730–1840* Cambridge: CUP.

Barrell, John 1986 *The Political Theory of Painting from Reynolds to Hazlitt: the Body of the Public* New Haven and London: Yale UP.

Barrett, Michele 1991 *The Politics of Truth: from Marx to Foucault* Cambridge: Polity Press.

Barthes, Roland 1966 *Criticism and Truth* London: The Athlone Press.

Baudrillard, Jean (ed. Mark Poster) 1988 *Jean Baudrillard: Selected Writings* Stanford: Polity Press.

Beardsley, Monroe C. 1966 *Aesthetics from Classical Greece to the Present* New York: Macmillan.

Beer, M. 1921 *A History of British Socialism* The National Labour Press, Ltd (George Bell and Sons London).

Bell, Michael 1988 *F. R. Leavis* London: Routledge.

Belsey, Catherine 1980 *Critical Practice* London: Methuen (New Accents).

Bennett, Jonathan 1966 *Kant's Analytic* Cambridge: CUP.

Bennett, Jonathan 1974 *Kant's Dialectic* Cambridge: CUP.

Bennett, Tony 1979 *Formalism and Marxism* London: Methuen (New Accents).

Bennett, Tony 1986 'Popular Culture and "the turn to Gramsci" ' in Bennett *et al.* 1986.

Bennett, Tony, Mercer, Colin and **Woollacott, Janet** (eds) 1986 *Popular Culture and Social Relations* Milton Keynes: Open University Press.

Benton, Ted 1984 *The Rise and Fall of Structural Marxism* London: Macmillan.

Berkeley 1878 *The Principles of Human Knowledge* London: Routledge.

Berlin, Isaiah 1939 *Karl Marx: His Life and Environment* Oxford: OUP.

Bhaskar, Roy 1978 *A Realist Theory of Science* Sussex: Harvester Press.

Bhaskar, Roy 1986 *Scientific Realism and Human Emancipation* London: Verso (NLB).

Blackburn, Robin 1969 'A Brief Guide to Bourgeois Ideology' in Cockburn and Blackburn 1969.

Blackburn, Robin (ed.) 1986 *New Left Review 159: Alternatives to Capitalism* London: NLR.

Blaug, Mark 1958 *Ricardian Economics: a Historical Study* Connecticut: Greenwood Press.

Bloom, Harold 1973 *The Anxiety of Influence: a Theory of Poetry* Oxford: OUP.

Bloom, Harold 1975 *A Map of Misreading* Oxford: OUP.

Bloom, Harold 1979 'The Breaking of Form' in Hartman 1979 *Deconstruction and Criticism* London: Routledge.

Brecht, Bertholt 1957 (trans. 1964 John Willett) *Brecht on Theatre: The Development of an Aesthetic* London: Methuen.

Bukharin, Nikolai 1921 *Historical Materialism: a System of Sociology* Michigan: University of Michigan.

Burgess, Tyrrell (ed.) 1969–74 *Higher Education Review* London: Cornmarket/Tyrrell Burgess Associates.

Burgess, Tyrrell 1972 *The Shape of Higher Education* London: Cornmarket Press.

Burkert, Walter 1983 *Homo Necans: the Anthropology of Ancient Greek Sacrificial Ritual and Myth* Berkeley and London: University of California Press.

Byatt, A.S. 1978 *The Virgin in the Garden* London: Chatto and Windus.

Callinicos, Alex 1982 *Is There a Future for Marxism?* London: Macmillan.

Callinicos, Alex 1983 *Marxism and Philosophy* Oxford: OUP.

Callinicos, Alex 1989 *Against Postmodernism: a Marxist Critique* Cambridge: Polity Press.

Callinicos, Alex 1991 *The Revenge of History: Marxism and the East European Revolutions* Cambridge: Polity Press.

Carver, Terrell 1981 *Engels* Oxford: OUP.

Cassirer, Ernst 1945 *Rousseau Kant Goethe: Two essays* New Jersey: Princeton University Press.

Caudwell, Christopher 1937 *Illusion and Reality* London: Lawrence and Wishart.

Caudwell, Christopher 1938 *Studies in a Dying Culture* London: John Lane, The Bodley Head.

Caudwell, Christopher 1938a, 1948, 1939 *The Concept of Freedom* London: Lawrence and Wishart.

Caudwell, Christopher 1938, 1948, 1971 *Studies and Further Studies in a Dying Culture* New York and London: Monthly Review Press.

Caudwell, Christopher 1939 *The Crisis in Modern Physics* London: John Lane, The Bodley Head.

Caudwell, Christopher 1986 *Scenes and Actions* London: Routledge and Kegan Paul.

Caws, Peter, 1979 *Sartre* London: Routledge.

Chagnon, Napoleon A. 1968a *Yanomamo: The Fierce People* New York: Holt, Rhinehart and Winston.

Chagnon, Napoleon A. 1968b 'Yanomamo Social Organisation and Warfare' in Fried, Harris and Murphy (eds) *War: the Anthropology of Armed Conflict and Aggression* (pp. 109–59).

Chagnon, Napoleon 1974 *Studying the Yanomamo* New York: Holt, Rhinehart and Winston.

Chagnon, Napoleon 1992 *Yanomamö: the Last Days of Eden* New York: Harcourt Brace Jovanovich.

Chomsky, Noam 1966 *Cartesian Linguistics* Harper and Row.

Chomsky, Noam 1979 *The Washington Connection (The Political Economy of Human Rights I)* Nottingham: Spokesman.

Chomsky, Noam 1979 *Language and Responsibility* Brighton: Harvester Press.

Chomsky, Noam 1988 *Language and Politics* Montreal and New York: Black Rose Books.

Chomsky, Noam 1989 'Noam Chomsky: An Interview' *Radical Philosophy 53* London: Radical Philosophy Group.

Chomsky, Noam and **Herman Edward S.** 1979 *After the Cataclysm (The Political Economy of Human Rights II)* Nottingham: Spokesman.

Clark, Ronald W. 1988 *Lenin: the Man Behind the Mask* London: Faber and Faber.

Cockburn, Alexander and **Blackburn, Robin** (eds) 1969 *Student Power: Problems, Diagnosis, Action* London: Penguin (in association with *New Left Review*).

Cohen, G.A. 1978 *Karl Marx's Theory of History: A Defence* Oxford: OUP.

Cohen, Ralph (ed.) 1989 *The Future of Literary Theory* London: Routledge.

Cohn-Bendit, Daniel 1968 *Obsolete Communism – the Left-Wing Alternative* London: Penguin.

Connor, Steven 1992 *Theory and Cultural Value* Oxford: Blackwell.

Copleston, Frederick (SJ) 1946 *A History of Philosophy: vol. 1: Greece and Rome* New York: Doubleday Image Books 1962.

Copleston, Frederick (SJ) 1963 *A History of Philosophy: vol. 7 Part II Schopenhauer to Nietzsche* New York: Doubleday Image.

Cornford, F.M. 1914 *The Origin of Attic Comedy* London.

Cornford, F.M. 1965 *Thucydides Mythistoricus* London: Routledge.

Cornforth, Maurice 1968 *The Open Philosophy and the Open Society* London: Lawrence and Wishart.

Cousins, Mark and **Hussain, Athar** 1984 *Michel Foucault* London: Macmillan.

Coward, Rosalind and **Ellis, John** 1977 *Language and Materialism* London: Routledge.

Craig, David (ed.) 1975 *Marxists on Literature: an Anthology* London: Penguin.

Crick, Bernard 1987 *Socialism* Milton Keynes: Open University Press.

Croce, Benedetto 1898–1900 *Historical Materialism and the Economics of Karl Marx* London: Frank Cass and Co. 1914, 1966.

Croce, Benedetto 1909 (rev. 1922) *Aesthetic as Science of Expression and General Linguistic* London: Peter Owen/Vision Press.

Danto, Arthur C. 1989 'Beautiful Science and the Future of Criticism' in Cohen 1989.

Derrida, Jacques 1967 *Writing and Difference* London: Routledge.

Descombes, Vincent 1979 (trans. 1980 Scott-Fox and Harding) *Modern French Philosophy* Cambridge: CUP.

Dews, Peter 1987 *Logics of Disintegration* London: Verso.

Dobb, Maurice 1973 *Theories of Value and Distribution since Adam Smith: Ideology and Economic Theory* Cambridge: CUP.

Dollimore, Jonathan and **Sinfield Alan** (eds) 1985 *Political Shakespeare: New Essays in Cultural Materialism* Manchester: Manchester University Press.

Dowling, William C. 1984 *Jameson, Althusser, Marx – an Introduction to the Political Unconscious* London: Methuen (University Paperbacks).

Doyle, William 1989 *The Oxford History of the French Revolution* Oxford: Oxford University Press.

Drakakis, John 1985 *Alternative Shakespeares* London: Methuen.

Duncan, Graham 1973 *Marx and Mill* Cambridge: CUP.

Durkheim, Emile 1895 (trans. 1938, Solovay, Sarah and Mueller, John H.) *The Rules of Sociological Method* New York: Free Press.

Eagleton, Terence (later Terry) 1966 *The New Left Church* London: Sheed and Ward.

Eagleton, Terry 1976 *Criticism and Ideology* London: Verso.

Eagleton, Terry 1983 *Literary Theory: an Introduction* Oxford: Basil Blackwell.

Eagleton, Terry 1984 *The Function of Criticism* London: Verso.

Eagleton, Terry 1986a *Against the Grain* London: Verso.

Eagleton, Terry 1986b *William Shakespeare* Oxford: Basil Blackwell.

Eagleton, Terry (ed.) 1989 *Raymond Williams: Critical Perspectives* Cambridge: Polity Press.

Eagleton, Terry 1990a *The Ideology of the Aesthetic* Oxford: Basil Blackwell.

Eagleton, Terry 1990b *The Significance of Theory: the Bucknell Lectures in Literary Theory* Oxford: Basil Blackwell.

Eagleton, Terry 1991 *Ideology: an Introduction* London: Verso.

Eagleton, Terry 1992 'Proust, Punk, or Both: How ought we to value popular culture?' *The Times Literary Supplement* (18 December).

Easthope, Anthony 1980 'Reply to Rée' *Radical Philosophy 25* London: Radical Philosophy Group.

Easthope, Anthony 1983 *Poetry as Discourse* London: Methuen (New Accents).

Easthope, Anthony 1988 *British Post-Structuralism since 1968* London: Routledge.

Easthope, Anthony 1991 *Literary into Cultural Studies* London: Routledge.

Eddington, Sir Arthur 1928 *The Nature of the Physical World* London.

Eliot, T.S. 1919 'Tradition and the Individual Talent' in Eliot 1932.

Eliot, T.S. 1920 *The Sacred Wood* London: Methuen.

Eliot, T.S. 1932 *Selected Essays* London: Faber and Faber.

Eliot, T.S. 1933 *The Use of Poetry and the Use of Criticism: Studies in the Relation of Criticism to Poetry in England* London: Faber and Faber.

Eliot, T.S. 1939 *The Idea of a Christian Society* London: Faber and Faber.

Eliot, T.S. 1945 *Knowledge and Experience in the Philosophy of F. H. Bradley* London: Faber and Faber.

Eliot, T.S. 1948 *Notes Towards the Definition of Culture* London: Faber and Faber.

Eliot, T.S. 1965 *To Criticise the Critic and other Writings* London: Faber and Faber.

Eliot, T.S. 1957 *On Poetry and Poets* London: Faber and Faber.

Elliott, Gregory 1986 'The Odyssey of Paul Hirst' in Robin Blackburn (ed.) *New Left Review* 159 (September/October 1986).

Elliott, Gregory 1987 *Althusser: the Detour of Theory* London: Verso.

Elster, Jon 1985 *Making Sense of Marx* Cambridge: CUP.

Empson, William 1930 *Seven Types of Ambiguity* London: Chatto and Windus/Penguin Books.

Empson, William 1987 *Argufying* London: Chatto and Windus.

Engels, Friedrich 1845 *The Condition of the Working Class in England* Oxford: Basil Blackwell.

Engels, Friedrich 1877 *Herr Eugen Dühring's Revolution in Science (Anti-Dühring)* London: Martin Lawrence.

Engels, Friedrich 1884 *The Origins of the Family, Private Property, and the State in the Light of the Researches of Lewis H. Morgan* London: Lawrence and Wishart.

Engels, Friedrich 1888 (published 1936) *Ludwig Feuerbach and the Outcome of Classical German Philosophy* London: Lawrence and Wishart.

Engels, Friedrich 1940 *Dialectics of Nature* London: Lawrence and Wishart.

Evans, Mary 1981 *Lucien Goldmann* Sussex: Harvester Press.

Featherstone, Mike (ed.) 1988 *Theory, Culture and Society, Vol. 5, No. 2–3: special issue on Postmodernism* London: Sage Publications Ltd.

Feigl, Herbert and **Sellars, Wilfred** 1949 *Readings in Philosophical Analysis* New York: Appleton Century Crofts.

Feynman, Richard 1985 *QED: The Strange Theory of Light and Matter* London: Penguin.

Findlay, J.N. 1958 *Hegel – a Re-examination* London: Allen and Unwin.

Findlay, J.N. 1959 'The Contemporary Relevance of Hegel' in Findlay 1963.

Findlay, J.N. 1963 *Language, Mind, and Value* London: Allen and Unwin.

Foucault, Michel 1961 *Madness and Civilisation* London: Tavistock.

Foucault, Michel 1963 *The Birth of the Clinic* London: Tavistock.

Foucault, Michel 1966 *The Order of Things* (originally *Les Mots et les Choses*) London: Tavistock.

Foucault, Michel 1969 *The Archaeology of Knowledge* London: Tavistock; New York: Pantheon.

Foucault, Michel 1975 *Discipline and Punish* London: Penguin.

Foucault, Michel 1980 *Power/Knowledge (Interviews, etc. 1972–77)* Sussex: Harvester Press.

Foucault, Michel 1984 *The Foucault Reader* London: Penguin (Peregrine).

Foucault, Michel 1989 *Foucault Live (Interviews 1966–84)* New York: Semiotext(e) Foreign Agents Series.

Fourier, Charles 1972 *The Utopian Vision of Charles Fourier: Selected Texts on Work, Love, and Passionate Attraction* London: Jonathan Cape.

Fraser, J.G. 1890–1915 *The Golden Bough* London: Macmillan.

Freud, Sigmund 1929 *Civilisation and its Discontents* London: Hogarth.

Galbraith, J.G. and **Salinger, Nicole** 1981 *Almost Everyone's Guide to Economics* London: Penguin.

Gane, Mike (ed.) 1986 *Towards a Critique of Foucault* London: Routledge and Kegan Paul.

Geras, Norman 1983 *Marx and Human Nature: Refutation of a Legend* London: Verso.

Gilbert, Katherine and **Kuhn, Helmut** 1956 *A History of Aesthetics* London: Thames and Hudson.

Gleick, James 1987 *Chaos* London: Cardinal (Sphere).

Gluck, Mary 1985 *Georg Lukács and his Generation 1900–1918* London: Harvard University Press.

Goldmann, Lucien 1948 *Introduction à la philosophie de Kant* Paris: Gallimard.

Goldmann, Lucien 1964 *The Hidden God: a Study of Tragic Vision in the Pensées of Pascal and the Tragedies of Racine* London: Routledge.

Goldmann, Lucien 1970 *Lukács and Heidegger: Towards a New Philosophy* London: Routledge.

Goldmann, Lucien 1980 *Method in the Sociology of Literature* Oxford: Basil Blackwell.

Gould, Julius (ed.) 1965 *Penguin Survey of the Social Sciences 1965* London: Penguin.

Gouldner, Alvin 1971 *The Coming Crisis of Western Sociology* London: Heinemann.

Gouldner, Alvin 1980 *The Two Marxisms* London: Macmillan.

Gramsci, Antonio 1919–37 *The Modern Prince and Other Writings* New York: International Publishers.

Gramsci, Antonio 1971 *Selections from the Prison Notebooks* London: Lawrence and Wishart.

Gramsci, Antonio 1985 *Selections from Cultural Writings* London: Lawrence and Wishart.

Green, J.R. 1874 *A Short History of the English People* London: Macmillan.

Grossberg, Lawrence, Nelson, Cary and **Treichler, Paula** (eds) 1992 *Cultural Studies* London: Routledge.

Guattari, Félix and **Negri, Toni** 1985 *Communists Like Us: New Spaces of Liberty, New Lines of Alliance* New York: Semiotext(e).

Guest, David 1939, 1963 *Lectures on Marxist Philosophy* London: Lawrence and Wishart.

Hall, Stuart 1992 'Cultural Studies and its Theoretical Legacies' in Grossberg *et al.* 1992.

Hall, Stuart A. and **Whannel, Paddy** 1964 *The Popular Arts* London: Hutchinson.

Hampshire, Stuart 1941 *Spinoza* London: Penguin.

Harland, Richard 1987 *Superstructuralism* London: Methuen (New Accents).

Harrington, Michael 1976 *The Twilight of Capitalism* London: Macmillan.

Harris, Marvin 1969 *The Rise of Anthropological Theory* New York: T.Y. Crowell.

Harris, Marvin 1975 *Cows Pigs, Wars and Witches* London: Collins/Fontana.

Harris, Marvin 1978 *Cannibals and Kings: the Origins of Cultures* London: Collins.

Harris, Marvin 1980 *Cultural Materialism* New York: Random House (Vintage Books).

Harris, Marvin 1990 *Our Kind: Who we are, where we came from, and where we are going: the evolution of human life and culture* New York: Harper and Row.

Harrison, Jane 1903 *Prolegomena to the Study of Greek Religion* Cambridge: CUP.

Harrison, Jane 1912 *Themis: a Study of the Social Origins of Greek Religion* Cleveland and NY: Meridian.

Harrison, Jane 1913 *Ancient Art and Ritual* Bradford: Moonraker Press.

Hayman, Ronald 1976 *Leavis* London: Heinemann.

Hegel, G.W.F. 1807, 1831 (trans. Baillie 1910, rev. 1931) *The Phenomenology of Mind* London: Allen and Unwin.

Hegel, G.W.F. 1812 *Science of Logic* Allen and Unwin.

Hegel, G.W.F. 1953 *The Philosophy of Hegel* (selected Carl J. Friedrich) New York: Random House.

Heilbroner, Robert 1953, 1980 *The Worldly Philosophers: the Lives, Times and Ideas of the Great Economic Thinkers* London: Penguin.

Heller, Agnes (ed.) 1983 *Lukács Revalued* Oxford: Basil Blackwell.

Hindess, Barry and **Hirst, Paul Q.** 1975 *Pre-Capitalist Modes of Production* London: Routledge.

Hindess, Barry and **Hirst Paul Q.** 1977 *Mode of Production and Social Formation* London: Routledge.

Hirst, Derek 1986 *Authority and Conflict: England 1603–58* London: Edward Arnold.

Hirst, Paul Q. 1979 *Law and Ideology* London: Macmillan.

Hirst, Paul Q. 1986 *Marxism and Historical Writing* London: Routledge.

Hobsbawm, E.J. 1962 *The Age of Revolution: Europe 1789–1848* London: Weidenfeld and Nicolson.

Hobbes, Thomas 1651 *Leviathan* London: Dent.

Hoggart, Richard 1957 *The Uses of Literacy: aspects of working-class life, with special reference to publications and entertainments* London: Chatto and Windus.

Holbrook, David 1961 *English for Maturity* Cambridge: CUP.

Hook, Sidney 1936 *From Hegel to Marx* London: Gollancz.

Hovell, Mark 1918 *The Chartist Movement* Manchester: Manchester University Press.

Howard, M.C. and **King, J.E.** 1989 *A History of Marxian Economics* London: Macmillan.

Howarth, Herbert 1965 *Notes on Some Figures behind T.S. Eliot* London: Chatto and Windus.

Hoy, David (ed.) 1986 *Foucault: A Critical Reader* Oxford: Basil Blackwell.

Hunt, E.H. *British Labour History 1815–1914* London: Weidenfeld and Nicolson.

Hunter, Ian 1992 'Aesthetics and Cultural Studies' in Grossberg *et al.* 1992 *Cultural Studies* London: Routledge.

Hutcheson, Frances 1725 *An Inquiry into the Original of our Ideas of Beauty and Virtue* London.

Hutchison, T.W. 1978 *On Revolutions and Progress in Economic Knowledge* Cambridge: CUP.

Hyppolite, Jean 1955 *Studies on Marx and Hegel* London: Heinemann.

Ilyenkov, E.V. 1977 *Dialectical Logic: Essays on its History and Theory* Moscow: Progress Publishers.

Jackson, J. Hampden 1957 *Marx, Proudhon, and European Socialism* New York: Collier Books.

Jackson, Leonard 1969 'Radical Conceptual Change and the Design of Honours Degrees' *Higher Education Review* (Summer 1969).

Jackson, Leonard 1974 'The Myth of Elaborated and Restricted Code' *Higher Education Review* (Spring 1974).

Jackson, Leonard (review) 1976 'Squirrel Business' *Higher Education Review* (Autumn 1976).

Jackson, Leonard 1982 'The Freedom of the Critic and the History of the Text' in Barker *et al.* 1983.

Jackson, Leonard 1991 *The Poverty of Structuralism* London: Longman.

Jackson, Leonard forthcoming *Making Freud Unscientific* London: Longman.

James, Patricia 1979 *Population Malthus: His Life and Times* London: Routledge.

Jameson, Fredric 1972 *The Prison House of Language* Princeton: Princeton University Press.

Jameson, Fredric 1981 *The Political Unconscious: Narrative as a Socially Symbolic Act* London: Methuen.

Jeans, Sir James 1930 *The Mysterious Universe* Cambridge: CUP.

Jefferson, Ann and **Robey, David** (eds) 1982 *Modern Literary Theory: a Comparative Introduction* London: Batsford Academic and Educational.

Johnson, Hewlett 1945 *The Socialist Sixth of the World* London: Gollancz.

Jones, J.R. 1972 *The Revolution of 1688 in England* London: Weidenfeld and Nicolson.

Kamps, Ivo (ed.) 1991 *Shakespeare Left and Right* London: Routledge.

Kant, Immanuel 1781 *Critique of Pure Reason* London: Everyman.

Kant, Immanuel 1790 *Critique of Judgement* Oxford: OUP.

Kant, Immanuel 1879 *Critique of Practical Reason and other works on the Theory of Ethics* London.

Kant, Immanuel 1968 *Critique of Judgement* New York: Hafner Publishing.

Kaufman, Gerald 1966 *The Left* London: Anthony Blond.

Kaufmann, Walter 1965 *Hegel: Reinterpretation, Texts and Commentary* New York: Doubleday.

Kautsky, Karl 1899–1921 *Karl Kautsky: Selected Political Writings* London: Macmillan.

Kaye, Harvey J. 1984 *The British Marxist Historians* Cambridge: Polity Press.

Kellner, Douglas 1984 *Herbert Marcuse and the Crisis of Marxism* London: Macmillan.

Kettle, Arnold 1951 *An Introduction to the English Novel: Vol. I To George Eliot; Vol. II Henry James to 1950* London: Hutchinson.

Kettle, Arnold 1963 *Karl Marx: Founder of Modern Communism* London: Weidenfeld and Nicolson.

Királyfalvi, Béla 1975 *The Aesthetics of György Lukács* London: Princeton University Press.

Knox, Israel 1936 *The Aesthetic Theories of Kant, Hegel, and Schopenhauer* Sussex: Harvester Press.

Kolakowski, Leszek 1978 *Main Currents of Marxism: its Origins, Growth, and Dissolution* (3 Vols): *I The Founders, II The Golden Age, III The Breakdown* Oxford: OUP.

Korsch, Karl 1938 *Karl Marx* New York: Russell and Russell.

Krapivin, V. 1985 *What is Dialectical Materialism?* Moscow: Progress Publishers.

Kuhn, Thomas S. 1962 *The Structure of Scientific Revolutions* Chicago: University of Chicago Press.

Kuusinen, O. 1961 *Fundamentals of Marxism–Leninism* London: Lawrence and Wishart.

Labica, Georges 1987 *Karl Marx: Les Thèses sur Feuerbach* Paris: Presses Universitaires de France.

Laclau, Ernesto and **Mouffe, Chantal** 1985 *Hegemony and Socialist Strategy: Towards a Radical Democratic Politics* London: NLB.

Laski, H.J. 1927 *Communism* London: Home University Library.

Latimer, Dan 1989 *Contemporary Critical Theory* London: Harcourt Brace Jovanovich.

Leach, Edmund 1970 *Lévi-Strauss* London: Collins/Fontana.

Leakey, Richard and **Lewin, Roger** 1978 *People of the Lake: Man: His Origins, Nature, and Future* London: Penguin.

Leavis, F.R. 1932 *New Bearings in English Poetry* London: Chatto and Windus.

Leavis, F.R. (ed.) 1933 *Towards Standards of Criticism* London: Lawrence and Wishart.

Leavis, F.R. 1936 *Revaluation* London: Chatto and Windus.

Leavis, F.R. 1937 'Literary Criticism and Philosophy' in Leavis 1952.

Leavis, F.R. 1948 *The Great Tradition* London: Chatto and Windus.

Leavis, F.R. 1952 *The Common Pursuit* London: Chatto and Windus.

Leavis, F.R. 1955 *D.H. Lawrence: Novelist* London: Chatto and Windus.

Leavis, F.R. 1967 *Anna Karenina and other Essays* London: Chatto and Windus.

Leavis, F.R. (ed.) 1968 *A Selection from Scrutiny* (2 Vols) Cambridge: CUP.

Leavis, F.R. 1969a *English Literature in Our Time and the University* Chatto and Windus.

Leavis, F.R. 1969b *'English' – Unrest and Continuity* University of Wales at Gregynog: reprinted *TLS*.

Leavis, F.R. 1972 *Nor Shall My Sword: Discourses on Pluralism, Compassion, and Social Hope* London: Chatto and Windus.

Leavis, F.R. 1974 *Letters in Criticism* London: Chatto and Windus.

Leavis, F.R. 1975 *The Living Principle: 'English' as a Discipline of Thought* London: Chatto and Windus.

Leavis, F.R. 1982 *The Critic as Anti-Philosopher* London: Chatto and Windus.

Leavis, F.R. and **Leavis Q.D.** 1969 *Lectures in America* London: Chatto and Windus.

Leavis, F.R. et al. (eds) 1932–33; 1933–34 *Scrutiny Vol. I, Vol. II* Cambridge: CUP.

Leavis, Q.D. 1932 *Fiction and the Reading Public* London: Chatto and Windus.

Leavis, Q.D. 1983 *Collected Essays: 1. The Englishness of the English Novel* Cambridge: CUP.

Lee, Richard B. and **DeVore, Irven** 1976 *Kalahari Hunter-Gatherers: Studies of the !Kung and their Neighbours* Cambridge: Harvard University Press.

Lefebvre, Henri 1966 *The Sociology of Marx* London: Allen Lane, Penguin.

Lenin, V.I. 1904 (republished 1941) *One Step Forward, Two Steps Back* London: Lawrence and Wishart.

Lenin, V.I. 1905a *Two Tactics of Social-Democracy in the Democratic Revolution* Moscow: Foreign Languages Publishing House.

Lenin, V.I. 1905b *The Revolution of 1905* London: Martin Lawrence (1931).

Lenin, V.I. 1908 *Materialism and Empirio-Criticism* Peking (1972).

Lenin, V.I. 1911 *The Paris Commune* London: Martin Lawrence (1930).

Lenin, V.I. 1914 *The War and the Second International* London: Martin Lawrence (1931).

Lenin, V.I. 1917a *Imperialism: the Last Stage of Capitalism* London: Communist Party of Great Britain.

Lenin, V.I. 1917b *The State and Revolution* London: Martin Lawrence (1931).

Lenin, V.I. 1920a *'Left-Wing' Communism: an Infantile Disorder* Moscow: Progress Press.

Lenin, V.I. 1920b *'Kommunismus*: Journal of the Communist International for the Communist International for the Countries of South-Eastern Europe (in German), Vienna, No. 3 1–2 (1 Feb. 1920) to No. 18 (8 May 1920)' in *Collected Works vol. 31* Moscow: Progress Press.

Lenin, V.I. 1930 *The Teachings of Karl Marx* London: Martin Lawrence.

Lenin, V.I. 1934 *Lenin on the Historic Significance of the Third International* London: Martin Lawrence.

Lenin, V.I. 1935a *After the Seizure of Power 1917–18* London: Lawrence and Wishart.

Lenin, V.I. 1935b *The Period of War Communism (1918–1920)* Moscow: Cooperative Publishing Society of Foreign Workers in the USSR.

Lenin, V.I. 1935c *From the Bourgeois Revolution to the Proletarian Revolution* Moscow: Cooperative Publishing Society of Foreign Workers in the USSR.

Lenin, V.I. 1935d *Selected Works vol. VII* London: Lawrence and Wishart.

Lenin, V.I. 1939 *The Theoretical Principles of Marxism (Selected Works XI)* London: Lawrence and Wishart.

Lenin, V.I. 1961 *Collected Works 38: Philosophical Notebooks* London: Lawrence and Wishart.

Lenin, V.I. 1966 *Collected Works vol. 31: April–Dec. 1920* Moscow: Progress Publishers.

Lenin, V.I. 1967 *On Literature and Art* Moscow: Progress Publishers.

Lenneburg, Eric H. 1967 *Biological Foundations of Language* Chichester: Wiley.

Lentricchia, Frank 1983 *Criticism and Social Change* Chicago: University of Chicago Press.

Lévi-Strauss, Claude 1949 *The Elementary Structures of Kinship* London: Eyre and Spottiswoode.

Lévi-Strauss, Claude 1958 *Structural Anthropology Vol. I* London: Penguin (formerly Basic Books).

Lévi-Strauss, Claude 1968 *Introduction to a Science of Mythology 3 Origin of Table Manners* London: Jonathan Cape.

Lévi-Strauss, Claude 1976 *Structural Anthropology Vol. 2* London: Penguin.

Lewis, C.S. 1936 *The Allegory of Love: a Study in Medieval Tradition* Oxford: OUP.

Lewis, C.S. 1954 *English Literature in the Sixteenth Century, Excluding Drama* Oxford: OUP.

Lewis, C.S. 1961 *An Experiment in Criticism* Cambridge: CUP

Lichtheim, George 1961 *Marxism* London: Routledge.

Lichtheim, George 1970 *Lukács* London: Collins/Fontana.

Lichtheim, George 1963, 1971 *From Marx to Hegel* New York: Herder and Herder.

Lieberman, Philip 1975 *On the Origins of Language* New York and London: MacMillan.

Lieberman, Philip 1984 *The Biology and Evolution of Language* London: Harvard University Press.

Lifshitz, Mikhail 1933 *The Philosophy of Art of Karl Marx* London: Pluto Press 1973.

Linsky, Leonard (ed.) 1952 *Semantics and the Philosophy of Language* Urbana: University of Illinois Press.

Locke, John 1884 *Locke on Civil Government* London: Routledge.

Locke, John 1960 *Two Treatises on Government* Cambridge: CUP.

Lodge, David 1972 *Twentieth-Century Literary Criticism* London: Longman.

Lodge, David 1988 *Modern Criticism and Theory* London: Longman.

Lovelock, James 1988 *The Ages of Gaia: a Biography of our living Earth* Oxford: OUP.

Löwy, Michael 1976 *Georg Lukács: from Romanticism to Bolshevism* London: NLB.

Lukács, Georg 1911 *Soul and Form* London: Merlin Press.

Lukács, Georg 1920 *The Theory of the Novel* London: Merlin Press.

Lukács, Georg 1919–29 *Political Writings, 1919–1929: The Question of Parliamentarianism and Other Essays* London: NLB.

Lukács, Georg 1923, 1967 *History and Class Consciousness* London: Merlin Press.

Lukács, Georg 1937 *The Historical Novel* London: Merlin Press.

Lukács, Georg 1947 *Goethe and his Age* London: Merlin Press.

Lukács, Georg 1950 *Studies in European Realism: A sociological survey of the writings of Balzac, Stendhal, Zola, Tolstoy, Gorki and others* London: Merlin Press.

Lukács, Georg 1957 *The Meaning of Contemporary Realism* London: Merlin Press.

Lukács, Georg 1962 *The Destruction of Reason* London: Merlin Press.

Lukács, Georg 1965 *Writer and Critic* London: Merlin Press.

Lukács, Georg 1938, 1954, 1966 *The Young Hegel: Studies in the Relations between Dialectics and Economics* London: Merlin Press.

Lukács, Georg 1971 *Georg Lukács: Record of a Life* London: Verso.

Lukács, Georg 1978 *The Ontology of Social Being, 1. Hegel* London: Merlin Press.

Lyotard, Jean-François 1984 *The Postmodern Condition* Manchester: Manchester University Press.

Lyotard, Jean-François 1989 *The Lyotard Reader* Oxford: Basil Blackwell.

MacDonald, J. Ramsay 1911 *The Socialist Movement* London: Williams and Norgate.

Macdonell, Diane 1986 *Theories of Discourse* Oxford: Basil Blackwell.

Macherey, Pierre 1966 *A Theory of Literary Production* London: Routledge.

MacIntyre, Alasdair 1970 *Marcuse* London: Collins/Fontana.

Mahaffy, John P. and **Bernard, John H.** 1889 *Kant's Critical Philosophy for English Readers* London: Macmillan.

Mandel, Ernest and **Novack, George** 1970 *The Marxist Theory of Alienation* New York: Pathfinder Press.

Mandel, Ernest 1972 *Late Capitalism* London: Verso.
Mandel, Ernest 1979 *Revolutionary Marxism Today* London: NLB.
Mandel, Ernest 1984 *A Social History of the Detective Story* London: Pluto Press.
Mannheim, Karl 1936 *Ideology and Utopia* London: Routledge.
Mannheim, Karl 1956 *Essays on the Sociology of Culture* London: Routledge.
Marcuse, Herbert 1941 *Reason and Revolution* London: Routledge.
Marcuse, Herbert 1964 *One-Dimensional Man* London: Routledge.
Marcuse, Herbert 1965 (Cape Editions 1969 with Wolfe and Moore) 'Repressive Tolerance' in: *A Critique of Pure Tolerance* London: Jonathan Cape, Cape Editions 1969.
Marcuse, Herbert 1968 *Negations: Essays in Critical Theory* London: Allen Lane.
Marshall, Alfred 1890 *Principles of Economics* London: Macmillan.
Marx, Karl 1840s–1859 *Early Writings* London: Penguin.
Marx, Karl 1840s–90s *Essential Writings of Karl Marx* London: Panther 1967.
Marx, Karl 1840s–90s (ed. T.B. Bottomore and M. Rubel 1956) *Karl Marx Selected Writings in Sociology and Social Philosophy* London: C.A. Watts and Co.
Marx, Karl 1844 *Economic and Philosophical Manuscripts of 1844* Moscow: Progress Publishers.
Marx, Karl 1847 *The Poverty of Philosophy* New York: International Publishers.
Marx, Karl 1857–8 *Karl Marx: Pre-Capitalist Economic Formations* London: Lawrence and Wishart.
Marx, Karl 1859 *A Contribution to the Critique of Political Economy* Chicago: W.H. Kerr and Co.
Marx, Karl 1867a (trans. Moore and Aveling) *Capital: a Critical Analysis of Capitalist Production* London: George Allen and Unwin.
Marx, Karl 1867b (trans. Moore and Aveling) *Capital: a Critique of Political Economy* New York: Random House.
Marx, Karl 1867c (trans. Fowles 1976) *Capital: a Critique of Political Economy Vol. I* London: Penguin Books.
Marx, Karl 1875, 1891 *Critique of the Gotha Programme* Peking: Foreign Languages Press.
Marx, Karl 1885 (trans. Kerr 1919, 1956) *Capital Vol. II The Process of Circulation of Capital* London: Lawrence and Wishart.

Marx, Karl 1894 (trans. Kerr 1909, 1959) *Capital Vol. III The Process of Capitalist Production as a Whole* London: Lawrence and Wishart.

Marx, Karl 1936 *Letters to Kugelmann* London: Lawrence and Wishart.

Marx, Karl 1942 *Selected Works Vols I and II* London: Lawrence and Wishart.

Marx, Karl 1961 *Marx on Economics (extracts from his works on economics)* London: Penguin.

Marx, Karl 1973 *Marx in his own Words* London: Penguin.

Marx, Karl and **Engels, Friedrich** 1840s–90s, ed. Lewis S. Feuer *Marx and Engels: Basic Writings on Politics and Philosophy* London: Collins/Fontana.

Marx, Karl and **Engels, Friedrich** 1848 *The Communist Manifesto* Moscow: Progress Publishers.

Marx, Karl and **Engels, Friedrich** 1965 *The German Ideology* London: Lawrence and Wishart.

Marx, Karl and **Engels, Friedrich** 1971 *Articles on Britain* Moscow: Progress Publishers.

Marx, Karl and **Engels, Friedrich** 1974 *Karl Marx and Frederick Engels on Literature and Art* New York: International General.

Matthews, Betty (ed.) 1983 *Marx: 100 Years On* London: Lawrence and Wishart.

Matthews, T.S. 1973 *Great Tom: Notes Towards the Definition of T.S. Eliot* New York: Harper and Row.

McGuigan, Jim 1992 *Cultural Populism* London: Routledge.

McLellan, David 1975 *Marx* London: Collins/Fontana.

McTaggart, Ellis and **McTaggart, John** 1910 *A Commentary on Hegel's Logic* New York: Russell and Russell (reissue 1964).

Meek, Ronald L. 1977 *Smith, Marx, and After: Ten Essays in the Development of Economic Thought* London: Chapman and Hall.

Mepham, John and **Ruben, David-Hillel** (eds) 1979a *Issues in Marxist Philosophy, 2 Materialism* Sussex: Harvester Press.

Mepham, John and **Ruben, David-Hillel** (eds) 1979b *Issues in Marxist Philosophy, 3 Epistemology, Science, Ideology* London: Harper and Row.

Mepham, John and **Ruben, David-Hillel** (eds) 1981 *Issues in Marxist Philosophy, 4 Social and Political Philosophy* Sussex: Harvester Press.

Merleau-Ponty, Maurice 1955a *Les Aventures de la Dialectique* Paris: Gallimard.

Merleau–Ponty, Maurice 1955b *Adventures Of The Dialectic* London: Heinemann (trans. Joseph Bien 1973).

Merquior, J.G. 1986 *Western Marxism* London: Paladin (Granada).

Meszáros, István 1970 *Marx's Theory of Alienation* London: Merlin Press.

Meszáros, István 1972 *Lukács' Concept of the Dialectic* London: Merlin Press.

Meszáros, István 1989 *The Power of Ideology* Brighton: Harvester Wheatsheaf.

Miliband, Ralph and **Panitch, Leo** 1990 *Socialist Register 1990: The Retreat of the Intellectuals* London: Merlin Press.

Miliband, Ralph and **Saville, John** (eds) 1979 *The Socialist Register 1979* London: Merlin Press.

Miliband, Ralph and **Saville, John** 1981 *The Socialist Register 1981* London: Merlin Press.

Milton, John 1674 *Paradise Lost* London and New York: W.W. Norton.

Minogue, Kenneth 1985 *Alien Powers: The Pure Theory of Ideology* London: Weidenfeld and Nicolson.

Monod, Jacques 1970 *Chance and Necessity: an Essay on the Natural Philosophy of Modern Biology* London: Collins.

Morgan, Lewis H. 1877 *Ancient Society: or Researches in the Lines of Human Progress from Savagery through Barbarism to Civilisation* Chicago: Charles H. Kerr and Co.

Morley, John 1904 *Critical Miscellanies 3 Vols* London: Macmillan.

Morrill, J.S. 1976 *The Revolt of the Provinces: Conservatives and Radicals in the English Civil War, 1630–1650* London: Allen and Unwin.

Morson, Gary Saul (ed.) 1986 *Bakhtin: Essays and Dialogues on his Work* Chicago: University of Chicago Press.

Mortley, Raoul 1991 *French Philosophers in Conversation* London: Routledge.

Mulhern, Francis *The Moment of Scrutiny* London: NLB.

Murdoch, Dugald 1987 *Niels Bohr's Philosophy of Physics* Cambridge: CUP.

Murray, Gilbert 1935 *Five Stages of Greek Religion* London: Watts and Co.

Murry, J. Middleton, MacMurray, John, Holdaway N.A. and **Cole, G.D.H.** 1935 *Marxism* London: Chapman and Hall.

Napier, Lt-Gen. Sir William 1857 *The Life and Opinions of General Sir Charles James Napier* Vols I and II (of 4) London: John Murray.

Napoleoni, Claudio 1975 *Smith, Ricardo, Marx* Oxford: Basil Blackwell.

Nelson, Cary and **Grossberg, Lawrence** (eds) 1988 *Marxism and the Interpretation of Culture* London: Macmillan.

Nietzsche, Friedrich (6) 1967 *On the Genealogy of Morals and Ecce Homo* New York: Vintage Random House.

Norris, Christopher (ed.) 1984 *Inside the Myth; Orwell: Views from the Left* London: Lawrence and Wishart.

O'Brien, D.P. 1975 *The Classical Economists* Oxford: OUP.

O'Connor, Alan 1989 *Raymond Williams: Writing, Culture, Politics* Oxford: Basil Blackwell.

Open University 1971 *School and Society: a Sociological Reader* London: Routledge.

Open University 1977 *School and Society* London: Routledge.

Orwell, George 1961 *Collected Essays* London: Heinemann (Mercury Books).

Oxford University Socialist Discussion Group 1989 (eds) *Out of Apathy: Voices of the New Left 30 Years On* London: Verso.

Pagden, Anthony 1992 *European Encounters with the New World* Yale.

Palmier, Jean-Michel 1968 *Sur Marcuse* Paris: Union Générale D'Editions.

Parkinson, G.H.R. (ed.) 1970 *Georg Lukács: The Man, his Work, and his Ideas* London: Weidenfeld and Nicolson.

Parkinson, G.H.R. 1977 *Georg Lukács* London: Routledge.

Parkinson, G.H.R. (ed.) 1982 *Marx and Marxisms* Cambridge: CUP.

Parsons, Talcott and **Shils, Edward A.** (eds) 1951 *Towards a General Theory of Action* New York: Harper and Row.

Pateman, Trevor 1983 Review of Pécheux 1975, 1982 *Language, Semantics and Ideology* Cambridge: CUP: *Journal of Linguistics* XIX, 2 (September).

Pateman, Trevor 1988 Review: Newmeyer, *The Politics of Linguistics, JL* (March).

Paton, H.J. 1947 *The Categorical Imperative: a Study in Kant's Moral Philosophy* London: Hutchinson.

Pécheux, M. 1975 *Les Vérités de la Palice* (trans. Harbans Nagpal 1982 *Language, Semantics and Ideology: Stating the Obvious* London: Macmillan).

Plamenatz, John 1975 *Karl Marx's Philosophy of Man* Oxford: OUP.

Plato fourth century BC *The Republic* London: Penguin.

Plato fourth century BC (trans. Cary) *The Works of Plato Vol. I* London: George Bell and Sons.

Plato fourth century BC *Plato's Epistemology and Related Logical Problems* (selections by Gwynneth Matthews) London: Faber and Faber.

Plekhanov, G. 1908 *Fundamental Problems of Marxism* London: Lawrence and Wishart.

Popper, Karl 1945 *The Open Society and Its Enemies, Vol. I Plato; II Hegel and Marx* London: Routledge and Kegan Paul.

Popper, Karl 1957 *The Poverty of Historicism* London: Routledge.

Popper, Karl 1959 *The Logic of Scientific Discovery* London: Hutchinson.

Popper, Karl 1963 *Conjectures and Refutations: the Growth of Scientific Knowledge* London: Routledge.

Popper, Karl 1972 *Objective Knowledge: an Evolutionary Approach* Oxford: OUP.

Popper, Karl 1974 *Unended Quest* London: Collins/Fontana.

Prigogine, Ilya and **Stenders, Isabelle** 1984 *Order out of Chaos: Man's New Dialogue with Nature* London: Heinemann.

Proudhon, Pierre–Joseph 1840 *What is Property: an Inquiry into the Principle of Right and of Government* New York: Dover Publications.

Proudhon, Pierre–Joseph 1969 *Selected Writings of Pierre-Joseph Proudhon* London: Macmillan.

Rée, Jonathan 1979 'Marxist Modes' *Radical Philosophy 23* London: Radical Philosophy Group.

Ricardo, David 1817 *On the Principles of Political Economy and Taxation* (Volume I of the *Works and Correspondence*) Cambridge: CUP.

Richards, I.A. 1924 *Principles of Literary Criticism* London: Kegan Paul, Trench Trubner and Co. Ltd.

Richards, I.A. 1929 *Practical Criticism: a Study of Literary Judgement* London: Routledge Ltd.

Ritchie, David G. 1893 *Darwin and Hegel* Swan Sonnenschein and Co. London.

Rousseau, Jean Jacques 1913 *The Social Contract and Discourses* London: Dent.

Royce, Josiah 1919 *Lectures on Modern Idealism* Yale: Yale UP.

Russell, Bertrand 1946 *A History of Western Philosophy* London: Allen and Unwin.

Russell, Bertrand 1967 *Autobiography – Vol. 1 1872–1914* London: Allen and Unwin.

Russell, Conrad 1973 *The Origins of the English Civil War* London: Macmillan.

Russell, Conrad 1990 *The Causes of the English Civil War* Oxford: OUP.

Ryan, Kiernan 1989 *Shakespeare* Hemel Hempstead: Harvester Wheatsheaf.

Ryle, G. 1949 *The Concept of Mind* London: Penguin.

Sahlins, Marshall 1974 *Stone Age Economics* London: Tavistock Publications.

Sahlins, Marshall 1976 *Culture and Practical Reason* Chicago and London: University of Chicago Press.

Sardar, Ziauddin 1993 'Fearful Similarity in the Old and New Worlds' in the *Independent* (6 January).

Sartre, Jean–Paul 1945 *Existentialism and Humanism* London: Methuen.

Sartre, Jean–Paul 1948 (trans. 1950) *What is Literature?* London: Methuen.

Saussure, Ferdinand de 1916a (trans. Wade Baskin 1959) *Course in General Linguistics* Maidenhead: McGraw-Hill.

Saussure, Ferdinand de 1916b (Critical Edition, Tullin de Mauro 1972) *Cours de Linguistique Générale* Paris: Payot.

Schacht, Richard 1983 *Nietzsche* London: Routledge.

Scruton, Roger 1981 *The Politics of Culture* Manchester: Carcanet.

Scruton, Roger 1982 *Kant* Oxford: OUP Past masters.

Scruton, Roger 1985 *Thinkers of the New Left* London: Longman.

Scruton, Roger 1986 *Spinoza* Oxford: OUP.

Sheridan, Alan 1980 *Foucault: the Will to Truth* London: Tavistock.

Shukman, Anne (ed.) 1983 *Bakhtin School Papers* Oxford and Colchester: Russian Poetics in Translation 10, RPT Publications and University of Essex.

Sinfield, Alan 1992 *Faultlines: Cultural Materialism and the Politics of Dissident Readings* Oxford: OUP.

Singer, Charles 1959 *A Short History of Scientific Ideas to 1900* Oxford: OUP.

Smirnov, A.D., Golosov, V.V. and **Maximova, V.F.** 1981 *The Teaching of Political Economy* Moscow: Progress Publishers.

Smith, Adam 1776 *An Inquiry into the Nature and Causes of the Wealth of Nations* Oxford: OUP.

Smith, G. (ed.) 1989 *Benjamin: Philosophy, Aesthetics, History* Chicago: Chicago University Press.

Smith, Peter 1981 *Realism and the Progress of Science* Cambridge: CUP.

Smith, Philip M. 1985 *Language, the Sexes, and Society* Oxford: Basil Blackwell.

The Society for Education in Film and Television 1981 *Screen Reader 2: Cinema and Semiotics* London.

Soll, Ivan 1969 *An Introduction to Hegel's Metaphysics* Chicago: Chicago University Press.

Soper, Kate 1986 *Humanism and Anti-Humanism* London: Hutchinson

Soviet Communist Party 1955 *History of the Communist Party of the Soviet Union* London: Lawrence and Wishart.

Speck, W.A. 1988 *Reluctant Revolutionaries: Englishmen and the Revolution of 1688* Oxford: OUP.

Stace, W.T. 1923 *The Philosophy of Hegel* New York: Dover Publications.

Stalin, Joseph 1933 *Leninism.* Vol. II London: Modern Books.

Stalin, Joseph 1940 *Leninism* London: Lawrence and Wishart.

Stalin, Joseph 1941 *The October Revolution* Lawrence and Wishart.

Stalin, Joseph 1953 *Works Vol. V* Moscow: Foreign Languages Publishing House.

Stebbing, L. Susan 1937 *Philosophy and the Physicists* London: Methuen.

Stewart, Ian 1989 *Does God Play Dice?: the New Mathematics of Chaos* London: Penguin.

Stewart, Michael 1976 *Keynes and After* London: Penguin.

Strachey, John 1935 *The Nature of the Capitalist Crisis* New York: Covici, Friede.

Strawson, P.F. 1966 *The Bounds of Sense: an Essay on Kant's Critique of Pure Reason* London: Methuen.

Susser, Bernard 1988 *The Grammar of Modern Ideology* London: Routledge.

Tallis, Raymond 1988 *Not Saussure: a Critique of Post-Saussurean Literary Theory* London: Macmillan

Talmon, J.L. 1952 *The Origins of Totalitarian Democracy* London: Secker and Warburg.

Tarski, Alfred 1944 'The Semantic Conception of Truth' *Philosophy and Phenomenological Research* 4 (1944) and numerous collections.

Taylor, C. 1975 *Hegel* Cambridge: CUP.

Thompson, Denys (ed.) 1964, Summer; 1965 Spring *The Use of English.* Vol. XVI Chatto and Windus (journal).

Thompson, E.P. 1955 *William Morris – Romantic to Revolutionary* London: Merlin Press.

Thompson, E.P. (ed.) 1960 *Out of Apathy* London: New Left Books/Stevens and Sons.

Thompson, E.P. 1968 *The Making of the English Working Class* London: Victor Gollancz Ltd.

Thompson, E.P. 1975 *Whigs and Hunters* London: Allen Lane.

Thompson, E.P. 1977 'Caudwell' in *The Socialist Register*.

Thompson, E.P. 1978 *The Poverty of Theory and other essays* London: Merlin Press.

Thompson, E.P. 1980 *Writing by Candlelight* London: Merlin Press.

Thomson, George 1941 *Aeschylus and Athens* London: Lawrence and Wishart.

Thomson, George 1974 *The Human Essence* London: The China Policy Study Group.

Timpanaro, Sebastiano 1970 *On Materialism* London: Verso (NLB).

Todd, Emmanuel 1985 *The Explanation of Ideology: Family Structures and Social Systems* Oxford: Basil Blackwell.

Tolstoy, Leo, Crosby, Ernest H., Shaw, G. Bernard *et al.* 1900 *Tolstoy on Shakespeare* Christchurch: The Free Age Press.

Torr, Dona 1940 *Marxism, Nationality and War*, 2 Vols London: Lawrence and Wishart.

Toulmin, Stephen (ed.) 1962 *Quanta and Reality* London: Hutchinson.

Toynbee, Arnold 1934–61 *A Study of History* Oxford: OUP.

Trotsky, Leon 1924 *On Lenin* London: George Harrap.

Trotsky, Leon 1966 *Literature and Revolution* Michigan: University of Michigan Press (Ann Arbor Paperback).

van Reijen, Willem and **Veerman, Dick** 1988 'An Interview with Jean-François Lyotard' in Featherstone 1988.

Vazquez, Adolfo Sanchez 1966 (trans. 1977) *The Philosophy of Praxis* London: Merlin Press.

Veerman, Dick 1988 'Introduction to Lyotard' in Featherstone 1988.

Vernant, Jean-Pierre 1965 (trans. anon for Routledge 1983) *Myth and Thought among the Greeks* London: Routledge.

Vernon, John 1984 *Money and Fiction – Literary Realism in the Nineteenth and Early Twentieth Centuries* Ithaca and London: Cornell University Press.

Vološinov, V.N. 1929 *Marxism and the Philosophy of Language* Cambridge: Harvard University Press.

Walkerdine, Valerie (ed.) 1989 *Counting Girls Out* London: Virago.

Walsh, William 1980 *F.R. Leavis* London: Chatto and Windus.

Walton, Paul and **Gamble, Andrew** 1972 *From Alienation to Surpus Value* London: Sheed and Ward.

Watson, George 1962 *The Literary Critics* London: Penguin.

Watt, Ian 1957 *The Rise of the Novel* London: Penguin.

Wellek, René and **Warren, Austin** 1949 *Theory of Literature* London: Penguin.

Wells, Roger 1983 *Insurrection: the British Experience 1795–1803* Gloucester: Alan Sutton Ltd.

Wesson, Robert G. 1976 *Why Marxism? The continuing success of a failed theory* London: Temple Smith.

White, Hayden 1989 'Figuring the nature of the times deceased' in Cohen 1989.

Widdowson, Peter (ed.) 1982 *ReReading English* London: Methuen.

Wiener, Jon 1988, 'The War Secrets of a Literary Critic' *The Listener* Vol. 119, no. 3053 (10 March).

Willey, Basil 1934 *The Seventeenth-Century Background* London: Peregrine.

Willey, Basil 1939 *The Eighteenth-Century Background* London: Penguin (with Chatto and Windus).

Willey, Basil 1949 *Nineteenth Century Studies: Coleridge to Matthew Arnold* London: Penguin (with Chatto and Windus).

Willey, Basil 1963 *More Nineteenth Century Studies: a Group of Honest Doubters* London: Chatto and Windus.

Williams, Raymond 1952 *Drama from Ibsen to Eliot* London: Chatto and Windus.

Williams, Raymond 1958 *Culture and Society 1780–1950* London: Penguin.

Williams, Raymond 1961 *The Long Revolution* London: Chatto and Windus.

Williams, Raymond 1962 *Communications* London: Penguin (with Chatto and Windus).

Williams, Raymond 1966 *Modern Tragedy* London: Chatto and Windus.

Williams, Raymond 1968 *Drama from Ibsen to Brecht* Penguin (Chatto and Windus).

Williams, Raymond 1970 *The English Novel from Dickens to Lawrence* London: The Hogarth Press.

Williams, Raymond 1975 *The Country and the City* London: Chatto and Windus.

Williams, Raymond 1976 *Keywords* London: Fontana/Croom Helm.

Williams, Raymond 1977 *Marxism and Literature* Oxford: OUP.

Williams, Raymond 1979 *Politics and Letters: Interviews with New Left Review* London: NLB.

Williams, Raymond 1981 *Culture* London: Collins/Fontana.

Williams, Raymond 1983 *Writing in Society* London: Verso.

Williams, Raymond 1988 *What I Came to Say* London: Hutchinson.

Williams, Raymond 1989a *The Politics of Modernism* London: Verso.

Williams, Raymond 1989b *Resources of Hope* London: Verso.

Wilson, Charles 1965 *England's Apprenticeship 1603–1763* London: Longman.

Wilson, Edmund 1940 *To the Finland Station: a Study in the Writing and Acting of History* London: Macmillan.

Wimsatt, W.K. 1947 'The Concrete Universal' in *PMLA* LXII (March).

Wimsatt, W K 1954 *The Verbal Icon: Studies in the Meaning of Poetry* Kentucky: University of Kentucky.

Wimsatt, W.K. and **Beardsley, Monroe** 1946 'The Intentional Fallacy' in *The Sewanee Review* LIV (Summer).

Wimsatt, W.K. and **Beardsley, Monroe** 1949, 'The Affective Fallacy' in *The Sewanee Review* LVII (Winter).

Winch, Peter 1958 *The Idea of a Social Science and its Relation to Philosophy* London: Routledge.

Wolfson, Murray 1964 *A Reappraisal of Marxian Economics* New York: Columbia University Press.

Wright, Erik Olin, Levine, Andrew and **Sober, Elliott** 1992 *Reconstructing Marxism: Essays on Explanation and the Theory of History* London: Verso.

Wuthnow, R., Hunter, J.D., Bergeson, A. and **Kurzweil, E.** 1984 *Cultural Analysis* London: Routledge.

Zima, Pierre V. 1978 *Pour une sociologie du texte littéraire* Paris: Union Générale d'Editions.

Zinoviev, G. and **Lenin, V.I.** 1915 (1931) *Socialism and War* London: Martin Lawrence.

Zohar, Danah 1990 *The Quantum Self* London: Bloomsbury Publishing.

Indexes

Index

188–90, 193, 195, 206, 209–11,
216, 219, 224, 229, 235, 239, 244,
245, 250, 252, 266
and human nature 71–3
Marxism as theory and practice 75–7
Marxism, Hegelian 59–82
Marxism, humanism and cultural
history 109–11
Marxism, materialism and chaos
theory 77–80
Marxism, renaissance of 174
Marxism, scientific 83–106
Marxism, the three sources of 60
Marxist theories of history, society,
revolution and value 83–106
Marxist theory, foundations of 29–106
Marxist theory and literature 107–224
Medvedev 168, 169, 170
Merquior 174, 216
Milton vi, 3, 18–20, 100, 123, 126,
127, 229, 230, 231, 234, 238, 269
Morgan 251, 254, 258, 276

Nelson 219, 244, 263, 276
Newton 37–8, 186, 193
Newton 38

Orwell 139, 208

Pagden 265
Pécheux 173, 192, 199, 200, 202, 206
Plato 31, 32, 34–7, 44, 50, 176
Popper 52, 54, 166, 181
Pound 100

Ricardo 93, 96, 101, 182
Russell 46, 52–4, 159

Sahlins 258, 259, 276
Shakespeare 18, 19, 21–3, 100, 119,
121, 131, 186, 229, 230, 234, 235,
238, 246, 260, 271, 276
Shelley 17–20, 126, 231, 238
Sinfield 5, 260–2, 276
Smith 72, 93, 101
Soll 54, 58
Spenser 18, 22
Strawson 41, 44
Swift 18, 101, 102, 273, 274

Taylor 54, 58
Thompson, Denys 213–14
Thompson E.P. 104, 116, 117, 142,
174, 178, 186, 207, 208, 218, 224,
244
Thomson 112, 257, 258
Tillyard 214, 238, 261
Tolstoy 5, 103, 148, 152, 153
Treichler 219, 263, 276

Virgil 229, 269, 271
Vološinov 226, 229

Wagner 132
Whannel 219
Willey 214
Williams vi, 4, 5, 65, 104, 128, 142,
156, 164, 203, 206–8, 210–21,
229–31, 233, 238, 244, 262, 270
and cultural materialism 216–17
and cultural studies 218–19
and Marxist theory 216–18
and traditional scholarship 214–15
working class and high cultural
tradition 211–13
Wimsatt 15, 21, 29

INDEX OF TOPICS

abolition of literature 228–33
abolition of Marxism 228–33

aesthetical idea 111
alienation vi, 23, 24, 59, 64, 66–8,

306